W9-BRK-193

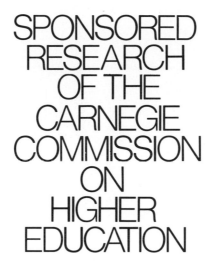

SPONSORED
RESEARCH
OF THE
CARNEGIE
COMMISSION
ON
HIGHER
EDUCATION

SPONSORED RESEARCH OF THE CARNEGIE COMMISSION ON HIGHER EDUCATION

McGRAW-HILL BOOK COMPANY
New York St. Louis San Francisco Düsseldorf
London Sydney Toronto Mexico Panama
Johannesburg Kuala Lumpur Montreal
New Delhi São Paulo Singapore

This book was set in Helvetica by Progressive Typographers, Inc.
It was printed and bound by Von Hoffmann Press, Inc.
The designer was Edward A. Butler.
The editors were Nancy Tressel, Janine Parson, and Michael Hennelly.
Audre Hanneman edited the index.
Milton J. Heiberg supervised the production.

Library of Congress Cataloging in Publication Data
Main entry under title:

Sponsored research of the Carnegie Commission on
Higher Education.

"In this book . . . independent studies and essays
prepared for the Carnegie Commission on Higher Education have been digested . . . for easy reference ——."
—Dust jacket.

Companion volumes: Priorities for action; final
report of the Carnegie Commission on Higher Education
and A digest of reports of the Carnegie Commission on
Higher Education. The three volumes comprise the Commission's Summary report, 1967–1973.

1. Education, Higher—United States. I. Carnegie
Commission on Higher Education.
LA227.3.S69   378.73   74-8975
ISBN 0-07-010073-X

1 2 3 4 5 6 7 8 9   VHVH   7 9 8 7 6 5

Reappraisals of higher education are nothing new: Britain is justly proud of the monumental report which carries Lord Robbins' name; Germany has the equally impressive series of publications from the *Wissenschaftsrat*. But the reappraisal by the Carnegie Commission goes far beyond these; the monographs being produced under the Commission's sponsorship cover an astonishing range of topics and its interim reports are setting out not just logistics, but a comprehensive philosophy for American higher education.

Lord Eric Ashby
Universities Facing the Future
1972

CONTENTS

house The academic melting pot Black elite Women and the power
to change Antibias regulation of universities Higher education and
earnings

FOREWORD

Three distinct volumes comprise the summary report of the Carnegie Commission on Higher Education at the conclusion of its endeavors from 1967 to 1973. The first volume, *Priorities for Action: Final Report of the Carnegie Commission on Higher Education,* reviewed the objectives of the Commission and presented its principal findings and recommendations. The second volume, *A Digest of Reports of the Carnegie Commission on Higher Education,* includes condensations of the 21 policy reports issued by the Commission, an index to the Commission's recommendations, and suggested assignments of responsibility for action on the recommendations that were made. This third volume of the summary report is devoted to the more than 80 research projects sponsored, in whole or in part, by the Commission.

Most of the abstracts included in this book have been taken directly from the reports after a final manuscript became available. In about a dozen instances, however, complete manuscripts for the full reports were not available to our staff as the volume went to press. In those cases, the abstracts were prepared for us by the authors themselves in advance of publication. In all instances an effort was made to preserve the ideas and approach of the authors rather than to write book reviews. In keeping with that objective, drafts of the abstracts were sent to the authors before final editing of the volume was completed. The compendium includes many ideas that are entirely those of our independent authors and are not necessarily consistent with the Commission's own policy recommendations.

One goal of this compilation is to present abstracts of our sponsored research reports in concise, clear, and comprehensible form. Another is to present, in one volume, a distillation of a substantial body of contemporary, interdisciplinary research into higher education.

The research and writings represented in this volume were accomplished by men and women in a variety of academic disciplines. To these authors and their research staffs, the congratulations of the Carnegie Commission are extended with a great sense of pride and appreciation. The authors are too numerous to name here, but they are fully identified in an appendix to this volume.

It is especially appropriate for us to express here our thanks to the McGraw-Hill Book Company, whose association with us throughout the life of the Commission has made it possible for the words and ideas of our many authors to find their way into books of widely recognized quality. This accomplishment was made despite tight schedules and complicated logistics that required almost constant communications between Berkeley and New York, and with authors in such distant places as Cambridge, Paris, Jerusalem, and Addis Ababa. For their unique publishing achievement, it is a pleasure for us to thank Dan Lacy, senior vice-president of McGraw-Hill

Book Company; Thomas H. Quinn, publisher of the Scholarly Books division; Nancy Tressel, editor of the Scholarly Books division; Marie Longyear, Janine Parson, Cheryl Love, Laura Givner, Michael Hennelly, and Audre Hanneman of Editing Services; Milton J. Heiberg, Joe Campanella, Bill Greenwood, and Alice Cohen, production supervisors; Edward Butler and Elliot Epstein, designers of the series; and Victor de Keyserling, publicity and public relations.

Finally, we wish to express our appreciation to the members of our own staff who supervised the preparation of these reports and assumed editorial responsibilities for them. In particular, we wish to thank our associate director and editor, Verne A. Stadtman; assistant editors Terry Y. Allen, Sidney Hollister, and Karen Seriguchi; secretaries Patti Kramer, Norma Rapone, and Jeanne Marengo; and orders secretaries Susan Cornell and Laura Raboff. We also wish to express our thanks to Richard Lewis, who prepared many of the abstracts contained in this volume and who assumed responsibility for organizing the compilation.

ERIC ASHBY
The Master
Clare College
Cambridge, England

RALPH M. BESSE
Partner
Squire, Sanders & Dempsey,
*   Counsellors at Law*

JOSEPH P. COSAND
Professor of Education and
*   Director*
Center for Higher Education
University of Michigan

WILLIAM FRIDAY
President
University of North Carolina

THE HONORABLE PATRICIA
    ROBERTS HARRIS
Partner
Fried, Frank, Harris, Shriver, &
*   Kampelman, Attorneys*

DAVID D. HENRY
President Emeritus
Distinguished Professor of
*   Higher Education*
University of Illinois

THEODORE M. HESBURGH,
    C.S.C.
President
University of Notre Dame

STANLEY J. HEYWOOD
President
Eastern Montana College

CARL KAYSEN
Director
Institute for Advanced Study
*   at Princeton*

KENNETH KENISTON
Chairman and Director
Carnegie Council on Children

KATHARINE McBRIDE
President Emeritus
Bryn Mawr College

SPONSORED
RESEARCH
OF THE
CARNEGIE
COMMISSION
ON
HIGHER
EDUCATION

INTRODUCTION

The ever-increasing importance of education in America has been accompanied in recent years by an increase in the number and variety of commentators who concern themselves with it. This growing attention reflects both the modern centrality of higher education to our national life and the fact that, for a long time, the subject remained relatively neglected by serious scholars.

Martin Trow has classified research as being either "predictive" (as in enrollment projections), "directive" (rationalizing specific action), or "illuminative" (clarifying particular concepts or issues). In the burgeoning field of higher education research, "predictive" or "directive" data stem mainly from what may be termed *institutional research*. This type of research focuses on studies which are largely specific to the problems of one particular institution, or to a system of higher education in one state or geographical region. Much of the *research on higher education,* however, performs Trow's third function and is "illuminative." This variety of research normally begins by identifying issues and problems across a broad front and undertakes to contribute to the comprehension and resolution of them. These two basic varieties of research in higher education frequently overlap and the dynamic which results serves to accelerate the pace at which knowledge about higher education in America is being assembled.

One reason that research into higher education has recently expanded so remarkably is that scholars in many disciplines have become intrigued with how their technical knowledge and methodology might be used to broaden understanding of the subject. *The American College,* edited by Nevitt Sanford, which was published in 1962, and is a collection of monographs by psychologists and sociologists concerned with various problem areas in higher education, was a landmark publication because it constituted the first major effort of a group of social scientists to investigate their own professional environment.

A number of economists, Seymour Harris, William G. Bowen, Theodore Schultz, and Howard Bowen, among them, have become concerned with the financing of higher education, and with the relationship of higher education's costs to benefits for both individuals and the larger society. Historians like Richard Hofstadter, who has examined anti-intellectualism in America, and Walter Metzger, who collaborated with Hofstadter on a history of academic freedom, and Laurence Veysey, who chronicled the emergence of the American university; sociologists such as Christopher Jencks and David Riesman, who studied the college and university as a social institution in *The Academic Revolution;* and other social scientists, like John Corson, who have concerned themselves with decision making and with governance, made major contributions to our knowledge of higher education.

Finance, budgeting procedures, program budgeting, and other functions of management in higher education, which were previously all but ignored, also are areas increasingly worked by authors of diverse interests and academic discipline, who seek to describe present practice or prescribe for future efficiency.

This is not to suggest that educationists have not been diligent. To the contrary, the output of research in higher education from schools of education nationwide dramatically increased during the 1960s.

Further research has been generated by special interest groups. The American Association of University Professors, for example, now undertakes annual surveys of faculty salary structures; the Educational Testing Service, the College Entrance Examination Board, and the American College Testing Program, among others, contribute continuously to our understanding of testing, admissions, curriculum and evaluation; and such entities as the American Council on Education and the American Association for Higher Education make further contributions by systematic data gathering and the commissioning of special reports for presentation to conferences.

Since World War II, the federal government has contributed to the effort by expanding its support of research in higher education. Government-financed educational research is now conducted on many campuses through research and development centers, contract programs, and other activities. Research and development centers, geared to long-term research on specific topics, operate at such diverse institutions as the University of Oregon (advanced study of educational organization), the University of Wisconsin (cognitive learning), and Stanford University (teaching).

Also financed federally is the Educational Resources Information Center (ERIC), a division of the Office of Education, whose clearinghouse on studies on higher education obtains and disseminates educational research from a wide variety of sources.

When state and regional planning surveys; institutional self-studies; computer-collected data banks, such as that operated by the American Council on Education; and such interstate compacts as the Southern Regional Education Board (SREB) and the Western Interstate Commission for Higher Education (WICHE) are added to the account, it may be said that higher education is one of the fastest growing areas of serious scholarship in America.

Much of the interest in higher education in the 1960s was stimulated by the fact that America's colleges and universities were growing rapidly. From 1870 to 1970 the number of students enrolled in full-time higher education doubled every 14 to 15 years. In 1900, 4 percent of the age group went to college; in 1970 over 40 percent were attending college. An educational operation of this magnitude requires massive financing, and some 2½ percent of the gross national product is currently expended on higher education.

Concurrently with the physical expansion of higher education in the sixties, internal turmoil shook the campuses. Because of its challenging character and dramatic proportion, this turmoil served to generate even more interest in colleges and universities.

It appeared to many observers that the American university of the middle 1960s was undergoing a transformation possibly as important, and potentially as traumatic, as that experienced in the last quarter of the nineteenth century, when the forces of German intellectualism and the land-grant movement came together to generate change and development.

This situation, and its inherent dangers, was carefully watched by the charitable foundations that had long provided support and funding to higher education. In 1967, the annual report of the Carnegie Corporation of New York warned:

. . . it is more and more apparent that American colleges and universities are strained physically and financially, and that a crisis may be approaching. While some steps are being taken to meet the immediate problems there is general agreement on the need for a long range, more thorough examination of where American higher education is now headed, where it should be headed, and how it is going to get there.

Under the auspices of the Carnegie Foundation for the Advancement of Teaching (CFAT), and with funding from the Carnegie Corporation, such an examination was made the responsibility of a newly formed Carnegie Commission on the Future of Higher Education (CCHE). The Commission's charge was to:

. . . look at the relationship of the function and structure of higher education to the changing needs of American society. It will ask: what forms should this system of incredibly diverse institutions take? What should be the roles of junior colleges, state colleges and universities, and private liberal arts colleges and universities? Having examined these questions the Commission will suggest possible patterns of development, including those that seem most likely to occur on the basis of projections from current rates of growth as well as those that seem less probable but perhaps more desirable. The Commission will, finally, estimate the costs of these various possibilities, propose how these costs can be met, and consider whether the public will be willing and able to meet them.

From its creation, the Commission consciously endeavored to encourage and add to research in higher education. It is hoped that the Commission's existence and efforts will be evident long into the future in a residue of useful, scholarly achievement. It is also an aspiration of the Commission that this legacy might help to set standards of quality and stimulate a continuing interest in higher education in scholars in many academic disciplines.

To achieve appropriate coverage of the broad subject areas under surveillance, the Commission reached consensus on several methodological objectives. First, the attack was to be mounted in an interdisciplinary fashion; this approach not only permitted a variety of perspectives and skills to be brought to bear on the subject, but also attracted fresh minds to the task. Second, fact gathering through hard empirical research was to be the rule, rather than the exception. Third, a problem orientation was to be cultivated. The Commission thus endeavored, wherever possible, to cast research into a policy-oriented mold. Its final methodological concern was to concentrate its resources on those areas of higher education which previously had been sparsely covered or not researched at all, so that some balance might be afforded to the general, overall, research coverage of higher education.

The published output of the Commission has taken two basic forms. One is a series of Carnegie Commission reports on topics of particularly pressing urgency or interest. These reflect the findings and opinions of the Commission itself. The remainder took the form of the sponsored research which is the subject matter of this volume. Over one hundred authorities and experienced observers were asked to bring their professional knowledge and experience to bear on subjects selected, for the most part, by the Commission. In no way did the Commission do more than support these research studies and facilitate their publication. At no time was there any attempt to influence the research outcomes. One result of this policy is that some of the conclusions reached by those participating in the research effort conflict with the official viewpoint of the Commission.

Both the sponsored research and the deliberations of the Commission itself emphasized priorities we identified as vital both to the future of higher education and the purposes of our society. These priorities suggested the major sectional headings in this volume. The first priority was to obtain an accurate reading of the educational system in its present form and dimension. *Looking at the System,* therefore, presents abstracts of the perceptions of the current state of American higher education, as viewed both here and abroad. Research into *Diversity and Options* follows. It has been the strong belief of the Commission, throughout its existence, that the heterogeneity of the nation's total higher educational system must be maintained, at the same time that options for individual institutions and participants are extensively broadened. Selections in this section of this summary reflect that theme. The third section, *Preparing for the Future,* collates those studies that illustrate the Commission's belief that the future should be anticipated and met with active effort both by the public and by the colleges and universities themselves, and not merely by passive, ex post facto adjustment. The priority of *Social Justice* is considered next, and research reviewed here examines how higher education can assist in attaining this long-overdue objective for all Americans. The priority of *Service to Society* is recognized in the next portion of the book. Here some institutional services both to the individual and to society as a whole are examined. Research on the maintenance and improvement of *Quality* is the next priority topic. The final section includes research findings that consider how the various institutions that form the system may be strengthened to meet the challenges of the future.

Readers should not expect the sections of this volume to be either comprehensive or definitive in the discussions of the educational priorities discussed. The Commission has not attempted to synthesize or replicate the great mass of useful research that already exists in thousands of other sources, and the abstracts of our sponsored research that appear here are intentionally brief. Furthermore, the eclectic nature of the tastes and interests of the individual Commission members is to a degree reflected in the topics of research. Some of the effort involved short-term analyses, while other works took a longer-range approach. With these conditions given due consideration, the Commission's goal has been to make a constructive contribution to higher education, either by filling obvious gaps in the literature or by providing fresh approaches to familiar topics.

The impact of the Commission's research reports has been considerable, although varying in intensity from publication to publication. Because the reports stemmed from the thoughts, methods, subject interests, and writing styles of many different authors, it is impossible to say that the total effort has made an impact upon any particular audience. But many of the individual studies have attracted attention, and helped fashion opinion and action among a variety of special audiences. The impact resulting from publication of *The New Depression in Higher Education: A Study of Financial Conditions at 41 Colleges and Universities,* by Earl Cheit, is a useful illustration. Initially, and after wide review in the press, the book appeared to have its main effect on the campuses, where it became "legitimate," in many cases for the first time, to discuss the financial problems of the colleges and universities candidly without inviting accusations that the institutions were either unworthy of trust in fiscal management or overstating financial need to impress prospective donors. Gradually this candid discussion spread beyond the campus boundaries until the nation's lawmakers and the general public became aware that the fiscal crisis that faces many institutions is real and deserves serious attention.

Not all the studies have received nationwide notice. Some of them, for example, *Financing Medical Education,* by Rashi Fein and Gerald Weber and *New Directions in Legal Education,* by Herbert Packer and Thomas Ehrlich, have received serious attention largely from members of a particular profession; others, such as *From Backwater to Mainstream: A Profile of Catholic Colleges,* by Andrew Greeley, have been widely discussed and criticized within the segment of the system about which they were written.

Three of the studies, *Colleges of the Forgotten Americans,* by E. Alden Dunham; *American Higher Education: Directions Old and New,* by Joseph Ben-David; and *Academic Transformation: Seventeen Institutions Under Pressure,* edited by David Riesman and Verne A. Stadtman, have each been selected as "Book of the Year" by the American Council on Education.

The reaction to the reports of the research produced under the auspices of the Commission has not all been favorable. Many small colleges were critical of *The Invisible Colleges,* by Alexander Astin and Calvin B. T. Lee, fearing that it had misrepresented their character and threatened their welfare; others used the occasion of its publication to become more visible and to seek and win extensive press coverage of their goals, facilities, and programs. But all of the reactions have been valuable and seriously considered by the Commission in the course of its discussions.

It would have been too much to hope to please everyone, particularly since many suggestions for reform are included in the research output of the Commission. Human institutions tend toward conservatism. Nowhere is this more seemingly true than in education, whose customary approach to whispers of reform appears to verify the truth of the French maxim that "Nature tends to the right."

More than four hundred years ago, Machiavelli described the loneliness of the leader in the time of crisis when he wrote:

There is nothing more difficult to carry out . . . than to initiate a new order of things. For the reformer has enemies in all who profit by the old order, and only lukewarm defenders in all those who would profit by the new order, this lukewarmness arising partially from fear of their adversaries . . . and partially from the incredulity of mankind, who do not truly believe in anything new until they have actual experience of it.

Such, we fear, was the situation of the authors of many of our research reports. Faced with the perceived present and imminent dangers confronting American higher education in the 1970s and beyond, reformers,

LOOKING
AT THE
SYSTEM

PART

1

commentators, and innovators wrestle with the loneliness of leadership. The research and reflections reviewed here attempt to set American higher education in context and to describe the current state of its development. The Carnegie Commission on Higher Education requested such perspectives to discern where efforts are most needed to determine guidelines for higher education in the future.

The present American system, which has been called the most impressive achievement in higher education the world has ever known, had its beginnings at Harvard College more than 330 years ago. Harvard's Puritan founders drew on their own collegiate experiences, particularly those at Britain's Cambridge University. Early Harvard was closely tied to the church and provided a four-year training in classics, the professions, and theology to the elite youth of the colonies. Although founded by different sects, the other 17 American colleges that appeared before 1800 generally replicated the Harvard model.

By the nineteenth century, some of the European universities had become centers of reaction in their societies, and in France they had been demolished by revolution. They had to change, and Germany led the movement in a new direction. In 1809 the University of Berlin was founded by Wilhelm von Humboldt, and its emphasis was on philosophy and the new science, on academic freedom for both professors and students, and on research and graduate education. Its pattern and direction began to spread throughout continental Europe and eventually beyond.

Young Americans traveling abroad and attending the German universities brought these ideas home with them, and the period between 1810 and the 1860s was marked, in American higher education, by the efforts of George Ticknor at Harvard and Francis Wayland at Brown, among others, to import these ideas. Experiments were tried and dropped. Although Yale awarded its first Ph.D. in 1861, the major breakthrough in graduate education came in the 1870s when, under the leadership of Daniel Coit Gilman, the Johns Hopkins University was founded as a graduate school with emphasis on research. Charles Eliot quickly incorporated these ideas at Harvard, and it was during his term (1869–1909) that Harvard became a university.

Contemporaneously with the successful transplanting of German concepts of the university, an indigenously American creation—the land-grant college movement—grew to maturity. The land-grant movement made such subjects as agriculture and engineering welcome in the university and also diluted the traditional elitism of American higher education by attracting the children of farmers and lower middle-class families to the campus. Although one strain of American higher education was elitist and intellectually centered and the other democratic and more vocationally oriented, they melded to forge the character of the modern American university.

By the early twentieth century, the land-grant movement had developed widely and the "Wisconsin idea," that university activities could and should be extended outside the campus gates, flowered. The University of Wisconsin began to serve the whole state, through extension and other activities, and other universities followed suit. The resulting rapid expansion of university functions was accompanied by a reaction, however, as such educators as Robert M. Hutchins at Chicago tried to lead these institutions back to the Thomism and Aristotelianism of earlier years. They did not succeed; the innovations that they opposed were too widely popular for that. But their efforts did give rise to a revival of interest in the quality of the student existence.

From all of these radically different pressures and experiences has evolved the present system of American higher education with its junior colleges, state colleges and universities, and private liberal arts colleges and universities. The root influences are still identifiable. At the undergraduate level there is extensive British influence, as perceived in residence halls, student unions, and intramural sports. Graduate schools, with their research emphasis, are indebted to the German idea. The incorporation of the professional schools (other than law and medicine) and the emphasis on public service represent purely American inputs. These three basic strands are combined in the generic term, "American higher education." The abstracts that follow put this system into international perspective and examine some of the segments that comprise the whole.

INTERNATIONAL PERSPECTIVES

CHAPTER

Throughout the last two decades, higher education has attracted the attention of an increasing number of professional and lay observers and commentators. Although this scrutiny has sometimes been critical, it has been preferable to the silence of neglect and has made a constructive contribution to problem solving in our colleges and universities.

With this role of enlightened commentary in mind, the Commission asked several informed observers from other countries to assess American higher education. The resulting observations of an Israeli, a Frenchman, a Japanese, and an Englishman make thought-provoking reading either individually or when viewed together—particularly since there are strands of disagreement in their interpretations of what they perceive. By bringing differing cultural perspectives, varying life experiences, and assorted frames of academic reference to bear on their common topic, these authors have provided us with fresh insights and challenging assessments.

Concluding this section is a review of a study of higher education in nine countries around the world. In asking for this study, the Commission was fully aware that cross-cultural comparisons can be misleading. This study attempts to avoid that pitfall and demonstrates that, in terms of broad general categories, many of the problems facing American higher education are shared by other nations, although there may be cultural and national variations that superficially tend to obscure the similarities between these problems as they are encountered in different parts of the world.

AMERICAN HIGHER EDUCATION: Directions Old and New
JOSEPH BEN-DAVID

Three issues important to American higher education are not discussed in this study: there is no discussion of what kind of research should be undertaken at universities, since this is an individual and subjective decision to be made by each institution; the question of federal funding is not explored; and the effects of a technological civilization upon the problems of higher educational institutions are not considered, either in terms of cause or effect.

Even without considering such three basic issues, however, the American system of higher education faces problems which may lead to a modification of its aims and structure to a point where it might be difficult to recognize as the same system that, for the last hundred years, has diffused and marketed liberal, gentlemanly education, specialized knowledge, and creative research. During this period, the different institutions that constituted American higher education were engaged in discovering groups, firms, and governmental or other organizations that would purchase their services and products, that is, advanced secular education and/or scientific research. The principal user of research in this period was higher education itself, since the training of teachers for higher education required that trainees should engage in research (usually leading to a Ph.D. degree) as part of their preparation. Both nonscholarly students and, indeed, nonscholarly intellectual educators presented a chronic problem, but it could be handled if not solved within the collegiate culture. Although the nonscholarly student and his faculty counterpart were often hostile to studies and to research, respectively, they did retain a somewhat self-serving loyalty to the institution.

This balance of forces and pressures, which kept higher education "going and growing until the 1950s," was disturbed in the 1960s. As the collegiate culture declined and expanding enrollments eroded the prestige of going to college, the nonscholarly student lost his loyalty along with his feeling of elite status. Teachers also abandoned institutional loyalty as the disappearance of external threats to academic freedom weakened faculty cohesion. Occurring simultaneously was a third phenomenon: the rising political status of the university made it appear part of the official society, evoking the animosity of those alienated from society and at the same time ceasing to provide, for American intellectuals, their traditional retreat. The basis for the unity of teaching and research has been breached by a rapid rise in university research unconnected with teaching, by the dramatic imbalance in the relative rewards for research and for teaching, and finally, by the sudden burgeoning of graduate studies and the increasing numbers of insecure and marginal intellectuals spawned in the bohemian circles that developed around graduate student communities. These elements contributed to conflict and class tension within the universities.

The ultimate issue under study is whether these problems can be resolved without a change in the purpose and structure of the university, or whether, as a result of the emergence of these crises, the universities will have to alter their fundamental purpose and structure.

Ironically, these problems attest to as well as attenuate the very success of the institution, and the ultimate issue under study is whether these problems can be resolved without a change in the purpose and structure of the university, or whether, as a result of the emergence of these crises, the universities will have to alter their fundamental purpose and structure.

Any examination of reactions to non-teaching-related research inevitably finds widespread prejudice against it on the ground that teaching and research are prima facie incompatible. On the contrary, there is a strong relationship between the two, since researchers consider communication of their results as part of their institutionalized role. Even if researchers are not good communicators, they are unlikely to mislead their students through ignorance, and thus it is concluded that the principle of unity between teaching and research is no mere ideology but inherently true.

On the other hand, it is utopian to believe that all who teach the 50 percent who enter college will also wish to become professional researchers, and the price which has already been paid for attempting to educate all college students as though they were to do research has been out of all proportion to the improvement in faculty competence. The median figure for total years of study for the Ph.D. degree is 8.2 years, which is too heavy an investment for someone who is not going to be a researcher. In addition, the universal requirement of a Ph.D. degree and publications for all teaching careers in higher education has an inflationary effect, since it is enormously demanding of time and money and thus diverts these resources from alternative uses within the system. The creation of a new degree which ensures the highest level of competence without requiring an original dissertation could help solve this cyclical problem but would not solve an attendant problem pertaining to career and rewards. As this study demonstrates, some means other than volume of publications must be sought as a means of evaluating the American professor.

The next problem to be faced is that of the general or nonscholarly student, and the system must discover some way of divesting itself of its function of initiating students into adulthood and also move toward creating courses which will constitute a significant educational experience for the general student.

A further area isolated for consideration in this study is referred to as "the prevention of the potential class conflict inherent in the communities of long-term graduate students and nonstudent bohemians around the universities." The draft-evasion-connected portion of this crisis will ultimately resolve itself, but another portion, concerned with the employment possibilities offered by university-based research, will not. The bohemian enclaves currently encamped around American universities have many attractive features, but "There is a thin line dividing the carefreeness of hopeful youth from the despair of economic insecurity of early middle age. And there is a similarly thin line separating [explorations] . . . to find a fuller life . . . from . . . [instability]. In short, some way should be found, and soon, to eliminate all incentives to stay around universities for those people who have "no aim to study."

Politicization has partially and intermittently occurred as a result of certain "general political circumstances" which "have nothing to do with higher education."

Thus far, all suggestions presuppose that research and education are the purpose of the university. But how, if this is so, has politicization of the campus begun to occur? For the purposes of this study, politicization is perceived as having partially and intermittently occurred as a result of certain "general political circumstances" which "have nothing to do with higher education." Thus the internal condition of the universities themselves merely provided the potential for politicization, a potential that was realized only when students, and others, wished to employ it.

Politicization is not only not inevitable, but also undesirable, for the price of politicization would be the severance of research from university teaching and studies, and quite possibly, the rise of some kind of totalitarianism fostered by the doctrinaire stance of the politicizers.

An alternative to politicization is suggested, and that is "to try to find some way of living with the possibility of it." Some existing academic arrangements will have to be rethought to protect academic freedom from those willing to abuse it for the purpose of denying the freedom to others, but this can and must be done. Student newspapers are a classic example of the genre. Edited by small, self-perpetuating groups who tend to favor the politicization of the university, these organs can monopolize political influence. But there are ways around this—competing newspapers, for example—which must be utilized. This is but one example of the problems emanating from the resistance of politicization, but there are knottier ones. A more complex one might be the attempt to interpret academic freedom so as to prevent its abuse without, in the process, hurting that very freedom itself.

The autonomy and independence of institutions of higher education in America will be an important tool in this struggle, as can be gathered from a brief comparison of the effects of pressures to politicize campuses in America and in France or Germany. Compared with their European counterparts, American institutions have successfully resisted the phenomenon; faculty sovereignty and academic freedom have thus far remained bloodied but unbowed, and academic work has not been seriously jeopardized.

The conclusions of this essay are, therefore, that while there have been recent convulsions, the institutions of higher education in America are trying to pursue the ends of education and research as they customarily have. Indeed, it is prophesied that: ". . . in individual colleges and universities there will emerge a tradition among teachers and students of safeguarding and respecting the autonomy of science and liberal culture even in situations of political conflict and dissent."

(1971)

THE ACADEMIC SYSTEM IN AMERICAN SOCIETY
ALAIN TOURAINE

In this study it is argued that higher education, far from being apart from the rest of society, is very much involved with it. The system of higher education, while always searching to develop its own unity as a social institution, is keenly sensitive and responsive to changing societal need, to the struggles for control over the sources of culture, knowledge, and power within the society as a whole, and to societal attempts to institutionalize, or otherwise repress, class conflict arising from these struggles. This involvement in the life of the larger society is easily seen today, when the dominant areas of knowledge in our society, science and technology, are to a great extent the products of the institutions of higher education. This relationship between society and universities, sharply distinct at present, can be traced throughout the history of American higher education.

The study begins its historical analysis in the middle of the nineteenth century. The period from 1850 to 1917 was one in which the country expanded very rapidly both in terms of population and industrial capacity. During these years our civilization could be called "a civilization of energy." The major sociological function of higher education was to organize these changes, and individuals rather than the various educational philosophies played the key role. Such university presidents as Eliot, Gilman, White, and Harper were the decision makers of the period. As the land-grant colleges were established, and as the seeds of professional training, the hallmark of the university, were sown in the opening of the first business and medical schools, these men, among others, organized strong administrations and set the direction of the entire system of higher education.

The next significant period in higher education occurred between the First World War and 1957, when Sputnik was launched in the Soviet Union. Social and technological sciences began their rise to prominence, and public colleges and universities grew dramatically in importance.

The elitist private universities and liberal arts colleges employed the principles of general education to instill in their students the great ideological themes that would, in due course, permit them, as members of a solidly established ruling class, to set themselves up as heirs to a long cultural tradition.

This study identifies two dominant trends in the academic system that developed during this period. The one was a carry-over from the preceding era and contributed, especially at the middle levels, to a new social order. The second was the development of a social and intellectual elite, at times amounting to a ruling class, which also however engaged in fostering a spirit of critical doubt and intellectual inquiry that had never previously existed. This social and intellectual elite stemmed directly from secularized colleges.

The formation of this elite has effectively contributed to the fact that there is now as much inequality of opportunity as existed before World War II. The table below, from the study by Folger, Astin, and Bayer in 1970 demonstrates this conclusion.

OUT OF 100 MALE HIGH SCHOOL GRADUATES WITH *HIGH* SOCIO-ECONOMIC STATUS AND HIGH ABILITY	OUT OF 100 MALE HIGH SCHOOL GRADUATES WITH *LOW* SOCIO-ECONOMIC STATUS AND HIGH ABILITY
9 do not go to college	31 do not go to college
9 go to junior college, of whom 3 go on to a senior college	17 go to junior college, of whom 5 go on to a senior college
82 go on to a senior college, of whom 63 graduate	52 go on to a senior college, of whom 32 graduate
36 continue immediately into a graduate or professional school	15 continue immediately into a graduate or professional school

Source: John K. Folger, Helen S. Astin, and Alan E. Bayer, *Human Resources and Higher Education*, Russell Sage Foundation, New York, 1970, p. 322.

The figures relating to junior college enrollment are significant and tend to substantiate the argument that these institutions are the mechanism that our system employs to lessen the heavy pressure from the masses of youth who want an education. The mechanism operates to consolidate the social hierarchy by offering some students the limited perspective of the junior college and excluding others. This study therefore finds the junior college a convenient way of appearing to cater to the aspirations of the masses for higher education while actually serving the interests of the leading universities and the social elite.

The period from 1957 to the present is also considered a significant and distinctive era for, during this period, while the old ideology was weakening, the academic system's inability to answer the latest demands of an urban and multiethnic society was increasing. This has resulted in a deep change in the academic system—at least in its main centers.

While the old ideology was weakening, the academic system's inability to answer the latest demands of an urban and multiethnic society was increasing.

To demonstrate the truth of this contention, this study analyzes the nature and structure of our academic system, its social function, the tensions existing within it, and the way in which it has been incorporated into the culture through the production of scientific knowledge. Further evidence is generated by an examination of the relationship between the federal government and the university, from the days of the New Deal, through the GI Bill, the National Defense Education Act, and the growth of and support for scientific research from 1957 to the present. This rapid development in the area of research, it is claimed, unified the academic system and accentuated the hierarchical nature of its structure. With growing independence fostered by the ever-increasing importance of the research laboratory, professors in this period have become considerably stronger as an academic group, and as their involvement with the dominant centers of power has increased with their role as producers of science and technology, so have they developed an ideology and a rhetoric that justify and defend their position. In the early 1950s, this power and strength was both new and untried, and because of their identification with the prevailing social order, this class of professors was unable to counter successfully the "red-scare" tactics of that period. By the 1960s, however, confidence and power had grown, and professors defined themselves purely as professionals, concerned with excellence and academic freedom without considering the students' demands or the impact of the power structure on their own social role.

This study considers the role of the student movement and the relationship between that movement, broader social conflicts, and the current academic crisis. The crisis exists at several interrelated levels, and a comprehension of the student movement is imperative to any understanding of the relationships between the various levels of the American academic crisis.

The student movement in America had its origins in the civil rights actions in the South in the early 1960s, and in the beginnings of the protest against the Vietnamese War. The student movement became aware of its identity in the university, and this identity found its purest expression in the Free Speech Movement. The Negro problem and the black movement superimposed the existence of contradictions and conflicts in society. The war in Vietnam and the campaign against it gave the movement its political dimension.

In the end, the student movement confronted the university not because it was an institution of dubious academic adequacy, but rather because it was a social institution which represented the repressive force of the ruling classes. The comparison made between the situations in America and in France confirm this evaluation; in America, the history of such student groups as the Student Non-violent Coordinating Committee and the Students for a Democratic Society point to a central weakness, namely, that protest has not integrated its components, and therefore has never developed the organization necessary for unified political expression. Despite this flaw it is fair to say that the problems of education have become central social problems, which challenge not only the ideology, but also the political system and the model of production of society.

Some of the outcomes that may result from our academic crisis are considered in the concluding portion of the study. Certain possible reforms are enumerated, and these range from the radical to the more conventional. One outcome might be the abolition of the university, as has happened in the People's Republic of China, but the likelihood of this is not stressed and ultimately only two political choices are suggested as being open to the university: It may reconstruct its present system, or it may diversify its approach to its various functions, and guarantee its own unity by delivering to students and other concerned social agents the opportunity to share in its management and in the management of our system of higher education.

The university should be viewed as an integral part of the larger American society, and we should realize that our system of higher education is just as subject to the power struggles of American society as any other subunit.

The university should be viewed as an integral part of the larger American society, and we should realize that our system of higher education is just as subject to the power struggles of American society as any other subunit. Consequently, the myth of the ivory tower is destroyed, for the institutions of higher education are demonstrated to be participating in societal power struggles both as producers of knowledge useful to the ruling classes and as guardians and reproducers of the prevailing social order. The clashes which are occurring within the university, whether they involve administration, faculty, or students, reflect the social conflicts in American society and can no longer be dismissed as internecine quarrels isolated from the community at large.

(1973)

AN OWL BEFORE DARKNESS?
MICHIO NAGAI

A study of the attitudes of European, North and South American, and Asian youth conducted by the Office of the Prime Minister of Japan in 1972 reveals that most young people today believe that society is materialistic, that governments ignore the needs of individuals, and that, in general, society will be worse, not better, in 30 years. These young people also feel that their education stifles creativity and tend to view schools more as social and career ladders than as institutions of learning. The feelings and concerns of young people should be taken seriously in light of recent events.

Whether one takes a global, international, or national perspective, the 1970s constitute a turning point in world history.

Whether one takes a global, international, or national perspective, the 1970s constitute a turning point in world history. For the first time, all mankind will need to cooperate to solve concrete problems on a global level. Inefficient food production, depletion of natural resources, and pollution, for example, are now receiving unprecedented worldwide attention. Internationally, such changes as the entrance of the People's Republic of China into the United Nations, its announcement that it aligned itself with the Third World, the cease-fire in Vietnam in 1973, and the new sense of independence and national interests of the Arab nations, though seemingly separate events, were all voices of the emerging Third World asking for a readjustment in the relationship between nations of the North and the South. Each nation will also face dramatic social and cultural transformations in the 1970s. Those of the South will be concerned with national sovereignty, economic prosperity, and the cooperation of groups within the country. Industrialized nations of the North will become increasingly responsive to the necessity of preserving natural resources and a healthy environment, and for a slowing of economic growth. Education must take on the task of helping nations cope with these changes.

To do that, the educational system must help to bring about an industrial society that will accommodate a diversity of ideas. Yet it must also help to redesign that society so that it will be able to cope with the problems of a postindustrial age. The difficulties of reconciling these two tasks are very clear in Japan, though they are also apparent in the United States.

Any educational system reflects the values and organization of the society in which it develops. Several traditions in American society have produced three main branches in its higher education: (1) graduate education that concentrates on specialized research, (2) general education based on the British tradition of character-building through the learning of the classics, and (3) professional and vocational training.

According to analyses by Robert Merton and Talcott Parsons, our society and our educational system share several structural characteristics. These include: universalism, "according to which anyone engaged in scholarship will be evaluated by universalistic criteria regardless of race, religion, or any other idiosyncracy"; the communism of ideas, which deems all knowledge to be common property; disinterestedness, or neutrality of affection, in scholarly research; and functional specificity, according to which scholarship is directed toward some specialized subject rather than many different problems. The importance of understanding these and other characteristics lies in their illumination of the relationship between higher education and the American society. These values and the strength of the relationship itself are highly resistant to the radical social changes that must take place if the United States is to handle increasingly international problems.

For both Japan and the United States the following directions for education are proposed.

Organized skepticism—as characterized by Robert Merton—should be regarded as the first principle of all education.

■ Organized skepticism—as characterized by Robert Merton[1]—should be regarded as the first principle of all education. Skepticism is the prerequisite for "the pursuit of truth that is never absolute, but always remains relative, consequently making it necessary for people to engage in ever-lasting exploration." Skepticism also helps man to entertain a liberal and rich culture, the only basis from which man is able to contemplate the possible directions in which human society could be moving.

■ Education must engage in the exploration of the "inner frontier" of man to guide him in finding a meaning of life based on its quality rather than on that which is measured quantitatively.

■ Education must begin to develop an international perspective. The study of foreign languages and cultures should be incorporated into the curriculum, and the importance of nationalism in other countries, especially in the emerging nations, must be recognized.

Other proposed reforms include:

■ A reemphasis of liberal education within higher education. Much more attention must be given to the fields of history and the classics. A strong graduate school curriculum should be developed for prospective teachers of liberal education.

More radically, the gap must be narrowed between information received from the communications media and that received from formal education. Because organized knowledge tends to become stagnant in a rapidly changing world, and because information on world and national events as reported by newspapers and television is extremely fragmented, news reporters should attempt to clarify the historical context of these events and to interpret them within that context.

Journalists should also teach current events classes in schools of primary, secondary, and higher education. Similarly, teachers in the social sciences and humanities might work outside of academe at scheduled intervals. Students would take a break in their formal education to work.

■ More diversity in both the classroom and the system. Teachers should be encouraged to engage in research and in creative teaching experiments. The small, private colleges should be supported by public funds.

■ Consideration of such global problems as pollution, supplies of food and energy, and decreased armament. Serious concentration on these

---

[1] "Organized skepticism involves a latent questioning of certain bases of established routine, authority, vested procedures, and the realm of the 'sacred' generally." (See Robert K. Merton, *Social Theory and Social Structure,* The Free Press, New York, 1968, p. 601.)

problems and their possible solutions will demand an interdisciplinary approach that will break down the barriers between the sciences and technology on the one hand and the social sciences and the humanities on the other.

(1975)

ANY PERSON, ANY STUDY: An Essay on
Higher Education in the United States
ERIC ASHBY

This study is not designed to function as another foreign judgment on the condition of higher education in America. Accordingly, it avoids those areas on which a foreign author is unqualified to comment—for example, the educational problems of religious or racial minorities.

From the viewpoint of this study, the American system did not so much go wrong as it became overtaken by forces external to its control.

The raw materials for higher education are students, faculty, and money; and two problems are identified as besetting the American system. There is a short-term problem: how to plan and finance one last phase of expansion until privileged and underprivileged children of similar ability have similar opportunities to go to college. And there is a long-term problem: how, on the one hand, to preserve innovation, initiative, adaptation, and freshness in a system that has reached its peak in size and in which, by and large, something new can only be done if costs are increased or if something old is discontinued; and, on the other hand, how to reconcile the aspirations of a society in which mobility depends on education with the hard fact that a bachelor's degree is not the birthright of every living American and that, if it became one, the degree would not be worth having.

These two problems are very much intertwined in that the present and the immediate future provide the last opportunity to make preparations for conducting in America—for the first time since colleges were built here—a higher education system at saturation point. The very nature of these two problems illustrates the necessity for examining not only whether the system falls short of its ideals and aspirations, but also whether those ideals and aspirations need revision.

One of the most striking facets of the system is to be found in its wide range of standards and quality, but this range also fosters a weakness in that, at a time when the costs of education are rising faster than the gross national product, it is questionable whether economic investment in low-grade higher education is defensible. As quoted from the Panos and Astin study,[2] the "very high" dropout rate in American higher education, for reasons which are nonacademic, is certainly part proof that the two questions are worth posing. Panos and Astin, using a sample of over 127,000 students, found that academic failure accounted for only 15.5 percent of the men and 5.8 percent of the women who dropped out. Therefore, for the overwhelming majority of those who constitute the attrition rate, withdrawal from the system is voluntary, indicating that for these students at least, higher education did not meet their needs or expectations.

A generally gloomy picture of the American higher educational scene is projected wherein the student bodies are comprised of two-thirds of the college-age group, 18 to 24 years, one in six of whom are on a campus unwillingly, and possibly as many as one in two leaving their institution of first enrollment without any certificate of competence. Teaching these students are the members of a profession whose prime duty is to teach, but whose teaching load is normally in inverse proportion to their distinction, which is itself largely measured by the possession of a Ph.D. and a long list of publications. Both teachers and taught operate within institutions which contain a pervasive streak of frustrated aspiration. Within this system, two-year colleges strive to undertake para-academic work, four-year colleges itch to establish graduate programs, undistinguished universities compete on the open market for academic stars to add to their status, and above all this, at the apex, a few world famous institutions vie expensively to maintain their positions.

Traditionally, higher education has performed a relatively specific purpose within a society, namely, to provide a small proportion of its people with the necessary training to discharge special responsibilities.

Traditionally, higher education has performed a relatively specific purpose within a society, namely, to provide a small proportion of its people with the necessary training to discharge special responsibilities. In a discussion of the function of American higher education, distinctions can quickly be drawn from the traditional model. In terms of sheer size, a far higher percentage of American youth are involved, whether at the undergraduate or graduate levels. This size has been the result of sustained growth in terms of quantity and level and has not been accompanied by any marked decline in quality although enormous variation in quality is a traditional feature of the system. Since World War II, for example, American higher education's share in world production and research (particularly scientific), and in such honorifics as Nobel prizes, has risen to its current all-time high. Coupled with these distinctions is the system's egalitarianism, which differentiates it from others. It is certainly true that socioeconomic status has a significant effect on educational progress

[2] Robert J. Panos and Alexander Astin: "Attrition among College Students," *American Council on Education Report,* vol. 2, no. 4, 1967.

and indeed upon educational success in America, but this factor seems less important in America than elsewhere.

Bearing these chief distinctions in mind, what is the function of the system? Primarily there is consensus and a clarity of purpose in two main areas. The system advances knowledge through rational enquiry, and leads the world in this respect. It also trains young people for an astonishing variety of employments. Once the sanctuary of these two functions is deserted, however, there is a bewildering degree of disagreement concerning the vital area of function. Other goals—general education, the socialization of adolescents to "fit" into society, the transmission of a common core of culture—are far from clear. To say there is no consensus on these points is an understatement; there is dangerous discord.

This confusion and general lack of clarity of perception concerning the functions of higher education is not confined to those who are part of it. There is a rising cacophony of criticism from outside the system which a casual glance at any recent issue of the *New York Review of Books* will confirm.

This criticism, both internal and external, will receive additional fuel rather than abate as this century progresses, because running through the whole system is the awkward fact that "productivity" in education (measured as the number of graduates produced per unit cost) is going down, not up, unlike almost all other enterprises in a market economy. Despite the fact that this trend might be reversed with the aid of massive input from the new technology, steps in this direction are unlikely to be taken because of the well-established and growing revulsion against "dehumanized" education. At a time of rapid expansion, this embarrassing feature of educational economics is concealed; but by the year 2000 there will be no more expansion, and rising costs, essential for innovation and the renewal of scholarship, will reflect falling "productivity." This will become progressively visible because by the year 2000 the funding of this gigantic system will consume about 3 percent of the gross national product. It will be beyond the capacity of private donors to pay for it. The American people will be expected to foot the bill.

By the year 2000 the funding of this gigantic system will consume about 3 percent of the gross national product. It will be beyond the capacity of private donors to pay for it. The American people will be expected to foot the bill.

The unspoken threat contained in this dismal prognosis has direct reference to the problem of delineation of function since it is clear that the survival of the system will be dependent upon the removal of confusions in this vital area and a reconciling of what Martin Trow would term the "autonomous" and "popular" functions of higher education in America.

The system is faced with four alternatives. It may remain as it is. If it does, there will still be outstanding achievements. It will produce great teachers, innovations in thought, citizens who are worthy successors to Jefferson and Franklin and Kennedy. However, should the system remain as it is, the vast mass of "the average" college and professor and graduate may suffer, because there will be brontosaurian cumbrousness and a surfeit of mediocrity.

Or, should the system alter, it might follow the first alternative of imposing a moratorium on expansion. This would not be from above and outside, but from within, from the students themselves. Cartter and Keniston are right in feeling that disenchantment with postindustrial society is not a passing phase. Increasing numbers of youth resent the prolonged adolescence that studenthood confers and that deprives them of adult responsibility, rights, and prerogatives. The corporate and sustained student protest is a struggling for independence, but this time it is independence from the culture and politics of their homeland. The Protestant ethic may change to an ethic which includes work one chooses to do and duty one's conscience demands. Does this perhaps explain the statistic that 15 percent of students are unwillingly on campus?

Compulsory higher education is nonsense and a moratorium on expansion might withdraw from higher education some of those who have no motivation to engage in it, and thus permit the diversion of large amounts of funding from what is generally termed *higher* education into prolonged *further* or even *secondary* education. This does not mean that there should be some gigantic retreat into a Rousseauesque state of nature, but rather that this alternative takes account of the laws of supply and demand and may possibly provide satisfaction, and therefore benefit, to American society.

Another alternative is one that is frequently advocated by political devotees of the New Left, namely, revolutionary change. It should immediately be said that a classical revolution seems unlikely because the student "class" lacks the necessary outside alliance with other "workers." Nevertheless, the numbers of students will have doubled to 14,000,000 by the year 2000 and even now this substantial body of people, when united in common cause, can affect national policy, as witness the events of 1970. With this in mind, there is a slight possibility of the destruction of the system through a series of individual, local, demogogically inspired, institutional revolutions. Furthermore, were this to begin to happen, it would be occurring in an area in which the general public is not immediately and dramatically affected to the extent that reaction to the trend would effectively stop it. On balance, however, this alternative is unlikely to be utilized, both because the present intellectual crisis is not grave enough to make it defensible and because "reason" will ultimately triumph. It is more likely that there will be a mass protest against the pedantic overemphasis on rational thought, and the view that this instrument could satisfy all man's needs. This will probably turn out to be a call not to abandon the examination of nature and man through the generalizations of science, but to reconcile this style of thinking with social concern and a respect for the uniqueness of individuals.

In order to minimize the risks involved, those who adhere to the principles of the moral code of liberalism must declare what they defend and why they defend it, and this challenge leads to the fourth alternative.

What is needed is to navigate the course of higher education to the year 2000 by deliberately adapting it to social change as and when it occurs.

This fourth option is the preferable one and it is, classically, the "liberal's" choice, namely, to navigate the course of higher education to the year 2000 by deliberately adapting it to social change as and when it occurs. Because of its patent sanity this is not only a "hard" alternative but also what should be done. Regrettably, it is the hardest alternative to institute because of its "vulnerability." It is opposed on the left as "mere tinkering with the status quo" and on the right as being too far to the left. It will also take a long time, and thus opportunities for its adherents to be won away, or to drop away through loss of faith, will be many. And there is another, perhaps greater barrier to be crossed: this alternative requires imaginative problem solving because rather than avoiding crises it meets them head on.

If this alternative is adopted, several kinds of core questions will have to be answered, such as: To whom is the university responsible? Is it to the students as consumers? To those who hire the products of the universities? To the public at large? Or to its own guild tradition, providing a service to the state for which it is the sole qualified judge? Whichever answer is ultimately decided upon will determine the source of funding. To opt for pluralism would annoy conservatives; nevertheless, let all interests contribute, and let them all have influence.

A further "typical" question awaiting solution concerns the validity of assumptions made about the purpose of higher education, for this affects both timing and curriculum. If college no longer socializes or endows the young with a cultural tradition essential for their being accepted into adult society, why should full-time college immediately follow high school? While the American system is already permissive concerning the mobility of students in and out of college, a still greater degree of permissiveness might be feasible. The sandwich plan, whereby a student may spend half the year in college and half on the job, is an example of an alternative to present patterns. This solution might help provide the "action" or "relevance" in education so frequently demanded by contemporary youth, and, in time, this might mean that colleges, like libraries and museums, may come to be places that receive students throughout life. Furthermore, institutions of higher education may restrict the educational function to cultivating one way—recognizing that it is not the only way—of reaching conclusions about man, society, and nature.

Further questions that must be confronted concern what should be taught and where. "Hard" subjects must be differentiated from their "soft" counterparts in the same way as "higher" is distinguished from "further" education. The hard subjects will be learned by an elite few undergoing higher education in order to prepare to become part of that thin clear stream of excellence that provides new ideas, new techniques, and the statesman-like treatment of complex social and political problems. The soft subjects will be learned by a larger number and in separate facilities. While this is an elitist conception, it is true that without this elite, a nation can drop to mediocrity in a very short period. Production of this elite is an expensive undertaking also, but it is one upon which America must continue, while at the same time devising a peaceful coexistence between this production and that of the broad mass of the educational population.

The first priority, however, is to restore consensus about the purpose of higher education.

Before anything else is done, however, the alarming disintegration of consensus about the purpose of American higher education must be dealt with. Only self-constraint can restore this consensus, and this must come from within, for it requires a fundamental reevaluation of the relation between universities and the society in which they operate. There is little hope of such restoration until the large academic communities are broken down—preferably by delegation of authority—into self-managing and accordingly, manageable units.

It is foolish at this time to prophesy what the consensus will be, but it is to be hoped that it will include agreement that the prime function of the institution is to teach, and that the prime loyalty of faculty is to the process of education. Ideally agreement should also be reached about the "service" and "advisory" functions of the system as well as the delimitation of university "responsibility."

(1971)

HIGHER EDUCATION IN NINE COUNTRIES: A Comparative Study of Colleges and Universities Abroad
BARBARA B. BURN, with chapters by PHILIP G. ALTBACH,
CLARK KERR, and JAMES A. PERKINS

This comparative study, undertaken between 1967 and 1970, is intended to provide Americans with an opportunity to observe alternative solutions to a variety of the problems that face higher education cross-nationally.

The systems of higher education under study were those of France, Great Britain, Canada, Australia, Sweden, Japan, the Soviet Union, the Federal

Republic of Germany, and India. With the exception of the Soviet Union, all were visited in preparation for this study. Wherever possible, the systems are discussed within a similar structure, although the reader is warned against the difficulties and dangers inherent in cross-national comparative research and the temptations of cultural borrowing.

Of major significance to the study is the fact that there are certain experiences common to all the systems. They all handle vast numbers of students with less than adequate resources, even though facilities have radically expanded in all nine systems. Democratization in secondary education has led to increased demand for college and university entrance, and the need for trained manpower serves to heighten the demand. All the systems, therefore, have also had to resort to new and possibly uncomfortable financial policies merely to keep abreast of the demands and to meet the costs that accompany expansion and growth.

Increases in numbers and costs in all the countries studied have necessitated a variety of public and private systems for planning and coordinating the growth of higher education.

Increases in numbers and costs in all the countries studied have necessitated a variety of public and private systems for planning and coordinating the growth of higher education. While no individual report indicates that these systems are working well, they are all trying, similarly, to deal with the problem of allocating resources in a way that serves both the public purpose and the preservation of institutional autonomy.

In addition to these three general experiences, the study presents certain points of interest from each of the nine national systems of higher education. In Great Britain, the general shift seems to be toward a consolidation of all postsecondary institutions into a national system, with increased control over the universities accruing to the University Grants Commission, and over the total system to the Department of Education and Science. The proper balance between academic freedom and public accountability is clearly a matter of growing concern in Britain, easily understood in light of the fact that the higher education budget is of sufficient size to awaken public awareness and become an issue of public policy.

The three countries with federal systems—Australia, Canada, and Germany—display individual differences but also share certain problems related to their style of government. The relationship between federal and state governments, and the conception of universities both as a system and universities as individual entities give rise to certain problems. In the area of federal-state relationships, Australia's situation is typical. Educational innovation in Australia has normally come from energetic state leadership, with the result that while the system is financed both by the commonwealth and by the states, commonwealth government control has been resisted. The key problem area relates to the maintenance of this balance between funding, planning, and coordinating needs on the one hand and flexibility for the states and for the individual institutions on the other.

Canada further exemplifies the pressures of operating within a federal system. Canada has four separate geographical areas with respect to higher education, and there has been a culturally based resistance to approaching national problems in a national way. Resolution of the fundamental French-English division in the country must be achieved before much progress can be made, although the study demonstrates that there is much innovation and experiment going on within the decentralized Canadian system.

For Germany, also a federal system, the traditional controls exerted over the system of higher education by the states and over the universities by the full professors are breaking (if they are not already broken). The difficulties of preserving local autonomy, both political and academic, while planning nationally, are exemplified here where the recommendations of the Wissenschaftsrat, and more recently of the Federal-Länder Commission for Educational Planning, increasingly threaten and diminish the traditional system of virtually exclusive jurisdiction of the Länder over educational affairs.

Sweden demonstrates features of a relatively centralized system of colleges and universities, with higher education governed through an alliance between the Education Ministry and the Office of the Chancellor of Universities. Recent reforms have expanded student and faculty participation in policy making and planning. Despite an increase in enrollment of over 600 percent in 20 years, the system has adjusted competently, as this study reveals. With a close-knit, single-state system, and a philosophy to which all major interests tend to be committed, Sweden demonstrates a high degree of consensus on planning and a high degree of effectiveness in the execution of those plans.

France contrasts with the Swedish picture. Despite being a centralized state, examination of the French experience since 1950 reveals insufficient central planning to meet developing needs, as the events of May 1968 demonstrated. French higher education reflects the consequences of a democratization of access without appropriate adaptation of the system. The results for France have been swollen enrollments and confusion over the role and direction of higher education. However, with the implementation of the Faure Legislation of 1968, the universities have now gained more autonomy and flexibility, decision making has been broadened, and new efforts are under way to relate university education more effectively to France's needs for highly trained manpower.

In the Soviet Union, the one country not visited, there exists an obvious parallel with Sweden in that detailed planning is accompanied by general public acceptance. Many problems remain, but they are dealt with away from the forum of public discussion, and in common with all planners, Russians have yet to devise reliable means for projecting future manpower needs. The Soviet universities constitute only a limited segment of all postsecondary institutions, and in addition to full-time study, part-time and correspondence study have been extensively developed. It is interesting to note that despite the tight control exercised over higher education by the government and the Party, Soviet higher education shares with systems in the West problems of student alienation, low success rates (for students in part-time and correspondence courses), inefficient use of resources, inadequate articulation between secondary and higher education, and unequal access to higher education.

Despite the tight control exercised over higher education by the government and the Party, Soviet higher education shares with systems in the West problems of student alienation, low success rates (for students in part-time and correspondence courses), inefficient use of resources, inadequate articulation between secondary and higher education, and unequal access to higher education.

Next to the United States and the Soviet Union, India is third in the number of students enrolled in universities. There are roughly 2 million students, and the study indicates that Indian higher education has two principal problems. The first is that 85 percent of all students involved in higher education are enrolled in private affiliated colleges, of which there are almost 1,700. Private institutions are not easily susceptible to public direction, a fact of great significance at a time when the colleges and universities are changing the priorities of their attention. It is important that the Indian system of higher education reflect India's changing needs, and this will be difficult to engineer in a federally decentralized system in which such a high percentage of students are enrolled in private institutions. India possesses a University Grants Commission, but lacks any individual body or group with sufficient interest and power to weld the public and private sectors of higher education into a planning and decision-making unity.

The private sector is also much in evidence in Japan, where 75 percent of all students in higher education are enrolled in private institutions. One outcome of this phenomenon has been to make individual universities largely autonomous, with the result that there has been an inability to deal with such national crises as student unrest with any satisfactory degree of consistency. It is true that a largely private system, with its greater measure of institutional independence, offers a potentially greater degree of flexibility, but it also can result in a stronger resistance to change. As in India, the examination of Japan does not reveal any strong indications that those closely concerned with higher education are organized to offer effective guidance and control to either public or private authority, and it is obvious that no more urgent task than that of remedying this situation faces the system of higher education in either country.

Support for higher education and research is continuing to shift from local to central governments, from state to federal authorities, and from private to public funding.

This survey of higher education in nine countries suggests certain conclusions: With respect to the financing of higher education, it is noted that support for higher education and research is continuing to shift from local to central governments, from state to federal authorities, and from private to public funding. In the United States the fact that this shift has not been more marked may be explained by the relative wealth of the country, the strong tradition of private higher education, and the vitality of the concept of federalism. Since 1965, however, the federal budget for higher education has expanded rapidly, and will probably have to continue to do so.

Increased central governmental funding could drastically alter the balance of responsibility between federal and state governments and, if foreign experience is a guide, there will be a strong reaction on the part of state and local governments aimed at maintaining control, if not financial responsibility, over higher education. Individual institutions will increasingly be called to account for the spending of centrally granted funds, and there will be an enormous impact on the traditional business methods of American higher education generated by this shift in fiscal responsibility from the periphery to the center. Overall, it is clear that when the drive toward national integration is accompanied by a demand for equality of opportunity, the central government is increasingly expected to offset inequities.

Across almost the whole panorama of this study one detects a tendency to widen the range of admissions through increased financial aid, new institutions, and broader programs. Furthermore, although the United States has been among the leaders in developing flexible and differentiated modes of higher education, there is still profit to be made from the experiences of others.

The efforts of other nations to coordinate attempts both to reduce costs and to equalize educational opportunity should be studied by the United States, for coordination and cooperation are big factors in ensuring success in these areas. The British involvement of faculty and the German experiment with both faculty and informed laymen acting with government officials in the area of coordination are worthy of close examination, for both reveal an acceptance of the often ignored fact that coordination is much more than mere administration.

While this study cannot and does not provide instant answers to all of the questions confronting American higher education, it does provide valuable information about the methods being employed in other parts of the world to enable systems of higher education to deal with pressing concerns which sometimes bear a marked similarity to our own.

(1971)

DOMESTIC PERSPECTIVES

CHAPTER

The research studies from which the six abstracts in this section are taken represent the findings of American social scientists who were asked by the Commission to ascertain certain dimensions of the nation's higher educational system by empirical means. The methodologies varied, but results take the form of unemotional, factual representations of the past and present condition of the system, and of the state of scholarship concerning it.

Warren Martin and Dale Heckman's inventory of research in the field up to 1968 is annotated and arranged to provide access to information concerning which subjects had been researched, by whom, and in how detailed a manner in the period that immediately preceded the establishment of the Commission. Perusal of this work will provide an understanding of the apparent unevenness of the spread of the Commission's own sponsored research. We strove, within finite fiscal limits on our research capability, to cover areas which had received little attention in the past and to avoid duplication of major effort recently completed or under way.

Seymour Harris' complex and detailed *Statistical Portrait of Higher Education* constitutes what may be the most solid and extensive source of factual reference on higher education in existence.

The research undertaken by Martin Trow draws upon a massive survey of higher education's constituent groups undertaken by the Carnegie Commission on Higher Education with the assistance of the American Council on Education and the U.S. Office of Education. The survey employed questionnaires administered to 70,772 undergraduates at 189 institutions; 33,963 graduate students on 158 campuses; and 60,028 faculty working in 303 colleges and universities. It is the largest and most detailed survey of this kind ever undertaken in higher education in this country. Two of the resulting reports are represented in this section. The first, edited by Martin Trow, consists of a series of essays based upon the survey findings. The second, a monograph by Martin Trow and Oliver Fulton, concentrates on the survey data about the faculty members on America's college and university faculties.

The ambitious work of Roy Radner and Leonard Miller is designed to estimate statistically several aspects of demand and supply in higher education in the United States and to illustrate the possible uses of the resulting econometric models for policy research.

The staff of the Carnegie Commission provided another perspective on the nature and scope of American higher education with its classification of institutions of higher learning. The definitions adopted in this project are increasingly used by other organizations and many individual scholars in the analysis of national data on different kinds of institutions.

INVENTORY OF CURRENT RESEARCH ON
HIGHER EDUCATION, 1968
DALE M. HECKMAN and WARREN BRYAN MARTIN

The Carnegie Commission on Higher Education—soon after beginning its deliberations in 1967—asked the Center for Research and Development in Higher Education (CRDHE) at the University of California, Berkeley, to undertake an inventory of current research on higher education. The inventory was to supplement work being done by the Educational Resources Information Center (ERIC), the Science Information Exchange (SIE), and others, at a time when social malaise and rapid educational changes made the need for information, and for sources of information, crucial to everyone concerned for the future of higher education.

The plan called for concentration on current research on higher education. "Current" meant research for which no final report was yet available. "Research," for the purpose of the inventory, was described as careful or studious inquiry, usually employing the methodology of the behavioral sciences, yet including qualitative as well as quantitative consideration, developmental or demonstration models as well as empirical data. "Higher education" was defined as postsecondary education in institutional and noninstitutional forms, but with emphasis on junior colleges and four-year colleges and universities; undergraduate, graduate, and professional programs; and educational agencies, institutes, and centers.

The need to put current research on higher education into a context that would provide both foreground and background prompted inventory personnel to add three features to the inventory: First, an attempt was made to probe research on higher education that had been carried out in the academic year preceding the year of the inventory. Subsequently, 135 research projects completed in 1966–67 were compiled and prepared for inclusion in this report. Those actually used appear under the appropriate categories and subsections.

Second, to provide a longitudinal perspective for the inventory, a historical statement on the development of research on higher education in this century was to be included as a part of the total effort.

Educational research in other nations was the third dimension of the inventory. While it was understood that it would be impossible in one year to do more than sample the work under way, it was thought important to supplement ERIC's coverage of research in many nations. Therefore, contact was made with 311 researchers in 60 countries, and the inventory contains 90 projects ongoing in various parts of the world.

During the year of the inventory (July 1967–June 1968), 921 projects of current research on higher education were cataloged. The total number of "principal researchers" listed was 1,020.

For the purposes of this report, projects have been grouped under eight subject categories that conform roughly to the way current research projects tended to cluster. There are also subdivisions of most categories. Chapters 1, 2, and 3 feature research on students, faculty, and administrators. While most of the projects listed in these sections of the report are associational in emphasis, relating the person or group to social and organizational factors, the main emphasis of the research in these categories was understood by inventory personnel to be on personalities more than on programs. Or, to put it another way, the emphasis is on the effect of programs on personalities.

> While most of the projects listed in these sections (on students, faculty, and administrators) of the report are associational in emphasis, relating the person or group to social and organizational factors, the main emphasis of the research in these categories was on personalities more than on programs.

The information in the description of individual research projects was normally provided by the principal researcher(s). However, in some cases information was compiled from alternative sources and without direct contact with the researcher. In a majority of instances the project summaries included were checked by project participants. What is recorded here, therefore, may be regarded as representative of current research emphases but not comprehensive in scope, essentially accurate in content but not fully descriptive.

(1968)

A STATISTICAL PORTRAIT OF HIGHER EDUCATION
SEYMOUR E. HARRIS

This portrait is a 978-page reference volume of statistical data drawn from official and private sources. There are more than 700 tables and a 60-page introduction that gives an overview of the entire study and summarizes the various sections of the report. The main text is divided into five parts: Students, Enrollment, Faculty, Income and Expenditure, and the issue of Productivity.

Overall, the most striking aspect of higher education has been the enormous increase in enrollment, especially since World War II. During the 130 years from 1840 to 1970, enrollment in institutions of higher education became 417 times greater, in contrast with the population, which became 12 times greater. The spectacular rise in enrollment is due, in large part, to the steady rise in the number of high school graduates over the years. Also, there has been an increase in the total college-age population, and an increase in the percentage attending institutions of higher education. Family incomes are at a level which permits increased expenditures for education, and student aid is more plentiful. The rise of community colleges and large urban universities, and a tendency for students to go on to graduate education, have also supported enrollment increases.

Part I of the main text looks at the data on students. Students of higher education are characterized by such factors as occupation and income of parents, aptitude and scholastic record at high school, and environmental conditions, including the size of a student's home town. Select institutions, especially select private institutions, tend to attract more able students from wealthier home backgrounds. Graduate students in arts and science tend to come from families with lower incomes, lower occupational status, and lower educational achievement than law or medical students.

The question of student costs is examined, and it seems these costs have not always correlated with families' capacity to pay. In fact, student costs bear important relations to the numbers who attend institutions of higher education. It is often said that highly talented students have no trouble in getting to college, yet the Wolfle study[1] showed that 45 percent of the top 8.8 percent of high school graduates did not attend college. One reason for nonattendance is an inability to pay the costs of higher education.

Student loans, which have the advantage of spreading the cost of higher education over a period of many years, have increased. Still, students from the lowest socioeconomic quartile accounted for only 7 percent of the total full-time undergraduate population.

However, over the last 25 years the number of student stipends increased three times, and the average amount of stipend increased from $133 to $339. In 1966–67, 44 percent of the financial needs of students from families in the lowest socioeconomic quartile were covered by grants, and 94 percent of students in this quartile received one or more of these forms of aid. Student loans, which have the advantage of spreading the cost of higher education over a period of many years, have also increased. Still, students from the lowest socioeconomic quartile accounted for only 7 percent of the total full-time undergraduate population.

Enrollment in higher education is the subject of Part II. Enrollment in two-year institutions between 1960 and 1970 rose 2.6 times as much as undergraduate enrollment in four-year institutions, and there was a general rise in the average enrollment per institution. Also, between 1960 and 1970, the increase in graduate students was slightly less than 33 percent, and there has been a rise in the proportion of nonwhite graduate students—a trend likely to persist over the next 30 years or so.

Internationally, North America has an especially high ratio of enrollment to population—3.25 times the ratio for the world as a whole. Data for 1965 indicate that United States enrollment in higher education

[1] Dael Wolfle: *America's Resources of Specialized Talent,* report of the Commission on Human Resources and Advanced Training, Harper & Brothers, New York, 1954.

amounted to 41 percent of the relevant age group, while Western European countries had proportions ranging from 10 to 15 percent. The United States led the Western Europeans in the proportion of the relevant age group qualified for admission to higher education and the number of higher education entrants. But the United States also had the highest attrition rate.

The relation of the number of degrees awarded to enrollment (D/E) has declined steadily since the nineteenth century. There are many reasons for this: an increase in part-time and two-year enrollments are two very important ones. There has also been an increase in dropouts.

Part III deals with faculty. The number of scientists has been increasing at a very rapid rate in the last few decades, and the share employed by institutions of higher education has risen steadily. Between 1962 and 1966, for example, the proportions of all scientists employed by higher education rose 30 percent while the proportion in industry declined by 25 percent. And the highest quality institutions tend to have the largest percentages of Ph.D. faculty members.

Faculty members spend 3½ times as much time teaching as on research and 17 times as much time on instructional activities as on public service.

Faculty members spend 3½ times as much time teaching as on research, and 17 times as much time on instructional activities as on public service. Average outside earnings for faculty members are a little over $2,000—approximately one-fifth of average compensation in a year.

Part IV discusses the income and expenditures of institutions of higher education. The main sources of income are state and local government, federal government, private sources, and tuition. In 1963–64, 46 percent of educational and general income of institutions of higher education came from private sources; the market value of total endowment is estimated at $12 billion. Appropriations from state funds in 1964–65 was $2.44 billion and the federal government outlay was $6.2 billion (in 1966–67). Tuition rose as a proportion of educational and general income from 1920 to 1950, but after that it declined. From 1959–60 to 1965–66, the annual average rate of increase in tuition income per student was 4 percent for public and 8 percent for private institutions.

Though the relative importance of endowment as a source of income has declined steadily since the turn of the century, it is still of great importance for those institutions that have relatively large endowments, notably large private universities and the relatively selective liberal arts colleges. But competition for private gifts between private and public institutions is on the increase, and the large rise of GNP and family income should encourage more private giving.

The issue of tuition is important for both private and public institutions. The annual rate of increase in tuition and fees of private institutions was twice that of public institutions between 1955–56 to 1965–66, which helps explain the declining competitive position of private institutions. But it is possible to increase the yield from tuition without increasing the burden of tuition on students and their families by tying tuition increases to increases in per capita disposable income. Increased tuition could then be explained by the increased capacity to pay.

The second section of Part IV looks at university expenditure. The value of buildings and facilities in higher education increased by about $30 billion in the 57 years ending in 1966–67. Library expenditures represent only about 3 percent of higher education outlays, yet in recent years the great increases in book prices and burgeoning operating costs have caused considerable financial difficulties for libraries. Of more than $1 billion expenditure on research (1959–60), only 26 percent came from university funds, with the federal government providing most of the support. Relative expenditures on research were considerably higher in the Northeast and the West than in other regions.

One criterion of productivity is an institution's ability to boost students' intelligence and scholarship; another is the rise in income for individuals with postsecondary education.

Part V turns to the issue of productivity in higher education. One criterion of productivity is an institution's ability to boost students' intelligence and scholarship; another is the rise in income for individuals with postsecondary education. Trends in enrollment provide useful information on unit costs. For example, it has been established that the number of students at institutions has been rising rapidly—but so have unit costs. This finding conflicts with the economic theory that larger numbers make for greater economies.

Several means of improving productivity are examined. Optimum size of institutions is related to the number of institutions of higher education, and the distribution of facilities among small, large, poor, and rich institutions.

(1972)

TEACHERS AND STUDENTS: Aspects of American Higher Education
edited by MARTIN TROW

This volume of essays was written by members of the research team that designed and administered the 1969 Carnegie Commission Survey of Faculty and Student Opinion. This survey, the largest ever carried out in American colleges and universities, was sponsored by the Carnegie Commission and American Council on Education and financed by the Commission and the U.S. Office of Education. The survey data yield information available for the first time on a variety of academic and related issues from a large, representative sample of American college students

School Retention Rates, Fifth Grade Through College Graduation, 1959–1971

For every 10 pupils in the fifth grade in 1959–60

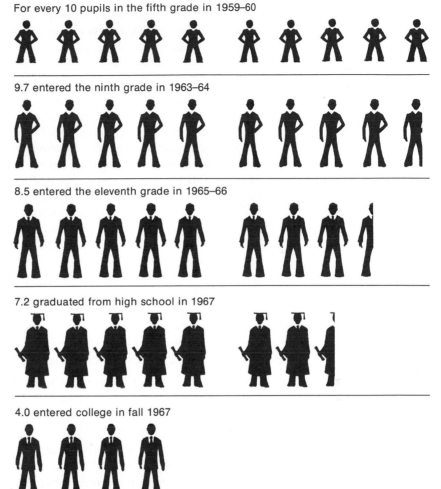

9.7 entered the ninth grade in 1963–64

8.5 entered the eleventh grade in 1965–66

7.2 graduated from high school in 1967

4.0 entered college in fall 1967

2.0 are likely to earn four-year degrees in 1971

Source: U.S. Office of Education, *Digest of Educational Statistics, 1968,* p. 8, 1968.

and teachers. The essays in this volume focus on some of those issues: research activity in American higher education, academic women, black students in the United States, religion and scholarship among American academics, marital constraints on women in American higher education, undergraduates in sociology, and peer influence and student norms. A technical report on the design of the survey concludes the volume.

The introductory essay, "Students and Teachers: Some General Findings of the 1969 Carnegie Commission Survey," by Oliver Fulton and Martin Trow, presents some basic descriptive data of the institutions, faculty, and students covered by the survey. The essay thus provides a general context within which the more detailed analyses of the other chapters may be interpreted. The authors divide the institutions into a total of seven quality levels: high-, middle-, and low-quality universities fall into levels I, II, and III; high-, middle-, and low-quality colleges fall into levels IV, V, and VI; and junior colleges comprise level VII. (This classification is used throughout the volume.) The authors then trace the distribution of faculties across quality levels by such characteristics as degrees held, age, socioeconomic background, publication record, and orientation to research and teaching. Similar information is given for graduate students and undergraduates.

The attitudes and opinions of faculty and students on a series of selected topics are also summarized and grouped by institutional quality level. The topics cover such issues as the legalization of marijuana, campus governance, and faculty unionization.

"Research Activity in American Higher Education," by Oliver Fulton and Martin Trow, looks at one of the core functions of American higher education. The term *research* here refers to scholarly work in both scientific and nonscientific disciplines.

American universities and colleges judge themselves and each other in their quest for prestige on the basis of research productivity.

American universities and colleges, which for the most part are intensely competitive, judge themselves and each other in their quest for prestige on the basis of research productivity, although interest and activity in research varies, of course, in different institutions. Variations in research activity by subject field, academic rank, and age are examined across institutional quality levels. In addition, a wide range of correlates of research activity are studied with special attention being given to the competitive demands of other academic activities, such as administration and teaching, and to the differential rewards associated with research activity as opposed to these other activities.

Several findings of the study bear on one of its central themes, the division of labor between and within the institutions of American higher education. There is, for example, a high level of research activity in elite liberal arts colleges. Another finding is that in the leading universities, where almost all the faculty do research, the academic role includes the expectation of continuing research activity; in weaker universities, where some faculty do research and others concentrate on teaching, it is accepted that the role may or may not include active research work; in the middle-level and other colleges, research is not a usual part of the academic role. There are, of course, exceptions to this general scheme of things—faculty in the performing and fine arts are not expected to do conventional research work, nor are those marginal teachers who hold nonprofessorial appointments: instructors, lecturers, and those in other rankings.

"Religious Involvement and Scholarly Productivity among American Academics," by Stephen Steinberg, focuses on the thesis that on an individual level religious involvement tends to be inimical to science and other scholarly concerns. The author first analyzes the nature and extent of faculty religious commitment and then the consequences of religious commitment for scholarly orientation and research productivity.

Religion and scholarship, in general, are incompatible for most faculty in the limited sense that stronger degrees of one tend to be accompanied by weaker degrees of the other. Among faculty as a whole, however, 78 percent retain at least a minimal religious identity (which of course varies in intensity) and many of the more successful and productive scholars retain strong religious commitment.

Religiosity generally has little effect on Jews, but Catholics and Protestants with strong religious attachments are considerably less likely to achieve a position in ranking universities. Protestants and Catholics with strong religious commitments are also less likely to have scholarly orientations or to publish regularly.

Faculty with strong religious commitments have a special view of the purposes and functions of education.

Faculty with strong religious commitments have a special view of the purposes and functions of education. They place a greater emphasis on teaching than on research and are committed to the spiritual as well as to the intellectual development of their students. Clearly, the incompatibility of religion and scholarship does not take the form of a crude anti-intellectualism, but is grounded in values that are legitimate and valuable in the institutions of American higher education.

"Black Students in Higher Education" by Judy Roizen focuses on the patterns of recruitment and self-recruitment of black undergraduate and graduate students to institutions of higher learning during the last decade. The paper gives particular attention to the relationship between socioeconomic status and the type and quality of institution entered.

The 1960s brought enormous gains in access to higher education for black Americans. It is nevertheless necessary to examine whether the criterion of proportional representation that is often used as a measure of equity in assessing minority access is useful or valid. To answer that question, three areas have to be examined: the kinds of institutions blacks (and other minorities) have access to; the departments and programs within those institutions that black students enter; and the social-class characteristics of the students.

Between 1965 and 1969 the proportion of blacks in the undergraduate population increased from 3 percent to over 6 percent. The proportion of blacks among entering freshmen increased between 1965 and 1972 from 4 percent to 9 percent. The black graduate student population, however, did not show such increases, remaining at 3 to 4 percent of the total graduate population.

Typically, students from advantaged circumstances have attended more selective colleges and universities, whether predominantly black or predominantly white. That pattern persists. There is a racial component as well, however. As of 1969, at least, blacks were more likely than whites of comparable ability and socioeconomic backgrounds to attend lower-quality institutions. Once in college blacks maintain high academic aspirations throughout their college careers and are not "cooled out" to particular departments or fields.

Blacks were more likely than whites of comparable ability and socioeconomic backgrounds to attend lower-quality institutions.

Blacks are particularly underrepresented in the general population of graduate students, but the distribution of blacks by quality of institution did not differ greatly in 1969 from that of white students. Among black graduate students there are two quite distinct populations—young graduates, the majority of whom are in academic fields and the old professions; and older graduates, the vast majority of whom are in education and attend four-year colleges. As of 1969, the number of young black students training for academic or professional careers outside the field of education was very small. But the "old professions" appeared to be opening for blacks; proportionately more young blacks than whites were preparing for careers in medicine and law. Few blacks were preparing for careers in business.

To adequately measure minority access to college, it is necessary to disaggregate the student population by age, sex, and social class, and to develop a typology of institutional selectivity. Doing so demonstrates the inadequacy of strict measures of proportionality for determining standards of equity.

In "Undergraduates in Sociology" Joseph Zelan examines what seems to be an inherent tension among the varied goals of undergraduate sociology education: the goals of general education, preprofessional training for sociologists, and preprofessional training for social work and the other professions. The distribution of these goals among categories of students and types of institutions is described, and they are compared with goals that teachers of sociology see as appropriate academic pursuits for themselves. An assessment is then made of the extent to which the various objectives of undergraduate sociology instruction can be met with less tension.

The great majority of sociology majors are women, attend lower-ranking institutions, and have vocational aims—that is, they plan to become social workers. Most men in sociology attend higher-ranking institutions, which only 9 percent of all sociology majors attend, and have general education goals—that is, they plan to get their Ph.D.'s. It would appear, then, that this institutional alignment of interests should lessen the tension between general and vocational education goals.

At first glance, this is not the case because faculty in sociology, no matter where they teach, are overwhelmingly committed to general education goals. A deeper analysis reveals, however, that general education in sociology and preprofessional training for the kinds of vocational students in the field are in harmony, not in conflict. Clearly, undergraduate sociology education should give students the kind of education that assures they will be well-educated sociologists. The graduate departments can see to it they become technically competent sociologists.

"Rewards and Fairness: Academic Women in the United States," by Oliver Fulton, contributes to the growing literature on women's underrepresentation and underachievement in higher education.

Women are clearly discriminated against, in terms of salary and promotion, by universities and colleges.

Women are at present widely, if not fully, represented in different sectors and strata of higher education. Indeed, in net terms there has been an enormous increase in women's participation in higher education, but the proportion of women relative to men has declined. Regardless of their field or rank, women are clearly discriminated against, in terms of salary and promotion, by universities and colleges. In a wider sense, of course, many cultural values discriminate against women, subjecting them to a kind of selective attrition long before they ever become undergraduate students. Inequality exists; it is documented; and it worsened in the 1960s.

When women do gain access to the academic work world, they find places, for the most part, in the humanities (27 percent) and in education and the newer professions (37 percent), suffering in the latter two fields from both lower pay and lower status. Moreover, the proportion of women rises fairly steadily as the quality of institution declines. Since high-quality universities are models for the rest of the system, change at that level could affect the entire system.

Promotion may come more quickly and more often to single women than to married women, but all academic career women, whether married or single, deviate from social norms, however mildly, and pay the consequences. Because of this and because of their marginal status (in less prestigious institutions, in less prestigious fields, in less secure professional appointments) women are often excluded from the scholarly community of their field, reducing their visibility among their fellow scholars and making research doubly difficult.

Although women are unlikely to raise their expectations without fairly substantial social and cultural changes—not only in job opportunities, but in childhood socialization and the structure of marriage—the continuing practice of sex discrimination in educational institutions is indefensible. Statistics for 1972–73 show some improvement in the situation, but universities and colleges can do much more. Institutions of higher education should encourage equality between men and women; until now, they have hindered it.

In "External Constraints: Marital Status and Graduate Education," Saul Feldman examines how the spouse role affects both men and women in higher education. Divorce comes in for special attention, for if there are conflicts between the two roles, abandonment of the spouse role may alleviate or lessen the conflict.

The data show a consistent pattern of conflict between the role of wife and the role of full-time graduate student. Married women students are under greater pressure—because of both marital demands and academic demands—to drop out, and if they remain in school are less likely to participate in the anticipatory or informal socialization that are important facets of graduate student life. Married men, on the other hand, feel little conflict between the roles of spouse and graduate student and, in fact, are the best-adjusted of all graduate students.

Divorced or separated women become fully immersed in the student role and are the most committed and active of all graduate students. This holds true even for women graduate students who have children, as 70 percent of them do. But if divorce becomes a source of liberation for women students, it becomes a source of strain for men, who lose a supportive relationship.

For some women, it appears, the following sequence occurs: role conflict between spouse and student roles, divorce, increased commitment to the student role. Nonetheless, the student and spouse roles for women are neither constant nor independent. In some cases they conflict; in other cases they complement each other. As traditional sex roles become less rigid, some of the conflict between the student and spouse roles should ease.

The debate continues as to whether or not college has an impact on those who attend. In "The Impact of Peers on Student Orientations to College: A Contextual Analysis," Ted Bradshaw accepts the view that some impact does exist and focuses his attention on the nature of the college experiences that exert that impact.

There are three ways in which college may have an impact on a student: through the overall college experience; through courses, programs, and faculty; and through the influence of student peers. Several theories have been advanced about the impact of college. The "noncollege theory," claims that socioeconomic status and background, family, friends, church, and hometown community are the principal shapers of a student's values, attitudes, and orientation, both before and while he attends college, predisposing him to take advantage of certain opportunities and reject others.

The "institutional theory" focuses directly on the impact of the institution attended, its quality, its various major fields and their students, its faculty, and its setting and facilities. The major field is the key factor here, for it introduces the student to his primary peer group.

The "peer theory" focuses on interpersonal relationships among students, regardless of their background or the quality of the institution they attend.

The analysis here follows the "peer theory," examining how group norms affect the rates of persistence or change among group members and on the student's perspective as to what is right and proper with regard to two basic distinctions in American higher education: vocationalism and high culture. Two items were used: "How often do you go to art galleries and museums?" and "The chief benefit of a college education is that it increases one's earning power." For both items, there was a compatibility of student and institutional orientation. The first item, an indication of cultural orientation, scored higher at the more elite, high-quality schools. The second item, a measure of vocational orientation, scored higher at the newer, more vocationally oriented colleges and universities and at lower-ranking universities.

Regardless of the type of institution or major field a student entered, there was a considerable change with regard to these items. Of the students who reported never visiting art galleries or museums when they entered college, 29 percent reported making such visits either occasionally or frequently in December of 1969; 54 percent persisted in such visits; 17 percent changed to never visiting at all. Of those who disagreed that the chief benefit of college was increased earnings, 18 percent changed their opinion to agreement and 59 percent persisted in their agreement. What caused these changes?

The basic factor appears to be the peer group in a student's major field; the greater the percentage of students in a major field who shared a particular orientation, the greater the probability of persistence. The quality of institution and the orientation of the faculty appear to have little influence.

Appendix A to this volume is a technical report that reviews the design and method of the Carnegie Commission Survey of Faculty and Student Opinion, how the sample was selected, the development of the questionnaire, the collection of the data, guidelines for utilization of the data, the weighting procedure, the nonresponse bias, and the quality ranking of the institutions in the sample. It was assembled and written by Martin Trow, director of the survey project, and by the professional staff that worked with him. Appendix B reproduces the faculty, graduate student, and undergraduate questionnaires used in the Carnegie Survey.

(1975)

THE AMERICAN ACADEMICS*
OLIVER FULTON and MARTIN TROW

This book, by the researchers who designed the faculty survey for the Carnegie Commission Survey of Faculty and Student Opinion, uses that survey to provide a comprehensive sociological portrait of the American academic profession. Its central focus is on the diversity and internal differentiation of the profession and on the implications of this differentiation for the functioning of the American system of higher education. Unlike several recent studies, the focus is on the academic profession as a whole—on teachers in all parts of the university and college system, including two-year colleges, and not simply on the staffs of the elite universities. This is not to deny the somewhat one-sided influence that the elite institutions have on institutions lower in the status hierarchy, but one of the key emphases of the book is on analyzing this impact and noting its mechanisms and the consequences of this impact for the interrelationships among different parts of the system.

The foundation of the land-grant public institutions is seen as the starting point for the distinctive American conception of higher education. These institutions embodied a commitment to the democratization

* This abstract was prepared by the authors before the final manuscript for their full report was completed.

of access to higher education even when the students attending them were still few in number. The system was thus able to cope with the transition from elite to mass access without needing to undergo the transformation with which European countries are still struggling. Now, however, the American system is faced with a real problem of transformation, from the level of mass to that of potentially universal access. The latter transition is producing a series of dilemmas (as opposed to the strains and tensions that occur in all systems) with which present institutional forms are trying to cope. A review of the development of the modern system, therefore, provides not only a perspective from which to view and interpret our findings, but also a partial explanation of those findings, both at the level of the system and also at the group level, and helps to explain generational and structural differences in attitudes and values among academic men and women.

Using both the Carnegie Commission's descriptive typology of institutions classified according to a variety of functions, and the more analytical typology developed by the staff of the National Survey of Faculty and Student Opinion, the study draws together basic figures on the various types of institutions comprising the current system—enrollment of graduate and undergraduate students, institutional resources of various kinds, and especially the numbers, qualifications, and experience of the faculty. It then discusses the rank and age structure of the faculty in these different institutions, and their proportions across academic disciplines and professional schools, relating these areas to the historical development of the system.

Although the elite universities at the upper end of the system place great emphasis on the researcher role and institutions at the lower end emphasize the teacher role almost exclusively, members of the profession—from exclusively teachers to exclusively researchers—can be found in varying proportions at every level of the system along the whole spectrum.

The central question of the "division of labor" within the profession, defined primarily in terms of the two core roles of academics, those of teacher and of researcher, is introduced in the fourth chapter. Although the elite universities at the upper end of the system place great emphasis on the researcher role and institutions at the lower end emphasize the teacher role almost exclusively, members of the profession—from exclusively teachers to exclusively researchers—can be found in varying proportions at every level of the system along the whole spectrum. In this analysis, teachers and researchers are defined primarily through their behavior, and it is seen how they are distributed through the component parts of the system.

The patterns of recruitment to different institutions cannot be elucidated without also taking into account the primary role to which academics are recruited or assign themselves. Full statistical detail of the origins and career lines of American academics of both sexes are therefore examined. Origins are discussed with respect to the respondents' social and religious background, as well as their educational experience and qualifications. The patterns which emerge are examined for different age groups and for changes over time to determine to what extent the democratization of student access to higher education has carried with it a comparable democratization of faculty recruitment. Finally, by breaking the faculty population down into a small number of groups distinguished by age, social class, and educational experience, a set of typical "career trajectories" is developed for these groups. These trajectories show the relative chances of faculty ending up with a post and a role in the various sectors of higher education. These trajectories should lend themselves extremely well to replication in future surveys of academics, and to international comparisons.

The career mobility of the sample faculty, not only within the institutions of higher education, but also to and from the "outside world" is also examined. Here again, although the authors search for common patterns and generalizations that can be made about the whole universe of higher education, much of their analysis looks at differences between diverse institutional and disciplinary elements of the system and the profession. But parallel with this concern with differentiation is the problem of integration: To what extent is it nonetheless possible to describe American higher education as a genuinely interrelated system? It is found that one of the key integrative forces is educational experience and recruitment; teachers at every level of the system below the highest are likely to have been educated, at least at the graduate level, at institutions of greater prestige than their present teaching institutions, so that the values and the roles of faculty at elite institutions are, for better or worse, diffused downward.

The academics' attitudes toward research and their actual research involvement are not always consistent. So the authors look further at the relation between orientation and activity, and especially at the large numbers of academic men and women whose attitudes and behavior are apparently in contradiction. Are there in truth substantial numbers of "reluctant researchers" who are required by the nature of their appointments and the reward structures of their institutions to do research when they would rather be doing less or none (and presumably more of something else, especially teaching)? What evidence is there for a widespread doctrine of "publish or perish" that, it is charged, coerces so many reluctant researchers into doing bad research, neglecting their teaching, and resenting their jobs and institutions? Conversely, are there large numbers of "frustrated researchers," strongly interested in research but unable, in their circumstances (marginal or subordinate status, or in institutions which provide no time, resources or rewards for research) to do the research they want to do? Many young faculty, for example, show strong research orientations but relatively low rates of publication.

The choice of research or teaching is not, of course, an abstract preference, with no further consequences for the faculty member. The phrase
"publish or perish" may not be accurate; there are niches in almost all
parts of the system where nonresearch people can be found. But this
choice is highly consequential for academics. In the elite parts of the
system, the nonresearcher is practically cut off from promotion to high
status, higher salaries, and access to power. "Publish and flourish" is,
perhaps, a more accurate phrase. Moreover, those who are most active in
research teach nearly as much as those less active in research, and also
do a good deal more departmental and university administration. Thus
there is not so much a sharp division of labor as a situation where the
choice to pursue research demands extra labor along with its rewards.
By contrast, in the weaker universities and in the better colleges there *is*
a division of labor within the faculty, between those who do research and
are somewhat less involved in administration and other activities, and
those who do not do research. There are marked differences between
academics who carry on research and those who do not: in their conceptions of higher education, teaching and learning, academic freedom, innovation, and college and university governance. They also differ in their
attitudes toward issues apparently far removed from academic life—for
example, broad social and political issues. Differences on many of these
issues arguably originate in the respondents' basic political values,
which may well antedate their academic careers. But some stem also
from researchers' and teachers' positions in the structure of the higher
education system—which are closely linked to their choice of research or
teaching roles. Access to the prestige and power of the elite sectors
brings its own perspectives, at least on academic issues, almost independently of the strength of an academic's research commitment or his political values. Similarly, these academic perspectives are influenced by his
relation to the body of knowledge on which his research draws. For example, members of applied disciplines have different perspectives from
those of their colleagues in the corresponding basic knowledge fields,
while members of professional schools, who face half outward to the
society and half inward to the academy, have special perspectives of
their own.

In a section on administration and governance, the authors direct their
attention more directly to the authority structure of colleges and universities. They address themselves particularly to the uncomfortable question of differential access to academic power and status. Not only age
and minority membership (defined in terms of race, sex, social class origins, and religion) are included in the discussion, but also, for example,
the possibility that certain types of institutions are dominated by certain
disciplines at the expense of those of lower prestige.

**In the elite parts of the
system, the nonresearcher is
practically cut off from promotion to high status, higher salaries, and access to power.**

**Members of applied dis-
ciplines have different perspectives from those of their
colleagues in the corre-
sponding basic knowledge
fields, while members of professional schools, who face
half outward to the society
and half inward to the academy, have special perspectives of their own.**

The large scale of the Carnegie Commission National Survey of Faculty and Student Opinion has permitted, through aggregation of the responses of their members, the development of contextual portraits of some 725 academic departments in a variety of disciplines and types of institution. Using this contextual information, a variety of new questions are raised:

1   What are the characteristics of research-oriented as compared with teaching-oriented departments within institutions of roughly the same quality?

2   Overall, rather sharp generational differences have been found among academic men and women in their views on research and academic issues and on social and political questions more generally. Are these generational differences among academics as a whole reflected also in individual departments, where they would pose special problems for governance, the design of a curriculum, and the socialization of students? More broadly, to what extent is value heterogeneity in a system of institutions compatible with homogeneity *within* component units?

3   What kinds of "role strains" are felt by academics, particularly when the orientations of men and women to teaching or research are at odds with their behavior?

Contextual analysis not only can be used to help in the search for explanations for specific outcomes, such as the research productivity of faculty members, it can also be used to focus on differences between departments and the consequences of the differences. This makes it possible, for example, to compare the characteristics of big departments with small ones; departments heavily weighted with senior and tenured faculty with those with larger proportions of younger and nontenured faculty; and departments of high quality with those whose rankings on a national scale of quality are lower.

(1975)

A CLASSIFICATION OF INSTITUTIONS
OF HIGHER EDUCATION

At an early stage in its work, the Carnegie Commission on Higher Education recognized the need for a classification of institutions of higher education that would be more useful for purposes of analysis than existing classifications. We sought to identify categories of colleges and universities that would be relatively homogeneous with respect to the functions of the institutions as well as with respect to characteristics of students and faculty members.

The classification was developed in 1970 and has since been used in much of the Commission's analytical work. Readers of the Commission's reports will recall its use in enrollment projections by type of institution, in studies of the behavior of costs and of economies of scale, and in the many tables on characteristics and attitudes of students and faculty, based on the 1969 Carnegie Commission Survey of Faculty and Student Opinion. The classification has been generally useful and satisfactory for these purposes.

A classification of institutions, of course, does not remain fixed. New colleges enter the universe of institutions of higher education every year, and others go out of existence. Institutions merge or change their names, or shift from two-year to four-year status, or become more comprehensive, or in other ways create problems for the classifier. In addition, the specific criteria that we have used for distinguishing among our four groups of universities, for example, involve the use of statistics on federal expenditures and on degrees, which change from year to year.

This classification includes all institutions listed in the U.S. Office of Education's *Advance Report on Opening Fall Enrollment in Higher Education: Institutional Data, 1970.* When a campus of a multicampus institution is listed separately, it is included as a separate institution in our classification. In a few instances, the Office of Education includes all campuses of an institution in a single listing, and in such cases the institution is treated as a single entry in our classification. Our classification includes 2,827 institutions, compared with the Office of Education's total of 2,565 for 1970. The difference is explained by the fact that, *for purposes of obtaining the total number of institutions,* we have treated each campus as an institution, whereas the Office of Education treats multicampus systems as single institutions.

Medical schools, schools of engineering, schools of business administration, and law schools are treated similarly. These institutions appear separately only if they are listed as separate institutions in *Opening Fall Enrollment.* Most of these professional schools, however, are not listed separately, and their enrollment is included in the enrollment of the parent university or university campus. This is true even in a number of instances in which the professional school is not located on the main campus of the university, but on a separate campus, for example, Johns Hopkins University School of Medicine.

The classification divides institutions into five main categories and a number of subcategories, or 18 categories in all. They are as follows:

1 DOCTORAL-GRANTING INSTITUTIONS

1.1 Research Universities I These comprised the 50 leading universities in terms of federal financial support of academic science in at least two of the three academic years, 1968–69, 1969–70, and 1970–71, provided they awarded at least 50 Ph.D.'s (plus M.D.'s if a medical school was on the same campus) in 1969–70. Rockefeller University was included because of the high quality of its research and doctoral training, although it did not meet these criteria.

1.2 Research Universities II These universities were on the list of the 100 leading institutions in terms of federal financial support in at least two out of the above three years and awarded at least 50 Ph.D.'s (plus M.D.'s if a medical school was on the same campus) in 1969–70, or they were among the leading 50 institutions in terms of the total number of Ph.D.'s (plus M.D.'s if on the same campus) awarded during the years from 1960–61 to 1969–70. In addition, a few institutions that did not quite meet these criteria, but that have graduate programs of high quality and with impressive promise for future development, have been included in this subcategory.

1.3 Doctoral-Granting Universities I These institutions awarded 40 or more Ph.D.'s in 1969–70 (plus M.D.'s if on the same campus) or received at least $3 million in total federal financial support in either 1969–70 or 1970–71. No institution is included that granted fewer than 20 Ph.D.'s (plus M.D.'s if on the same campus), regardless of the amount of federal financial support it received.

1.4 Doctoral-Granting Universities II These institutions awarded at least 10 Ph.D.'s in 1969–70, with the exception of a few new doctoral-granting institutions that may be expected to increase the number of Ph.D.'s awarded within a few years.[2]

2 COMPREHENSIVE UNIVERSITIES AND COLLEGES

2.1 Comprehensive Universities and Colleges I This group includes institutions that offered a liberal arts program as well as several other programs, such as engineering and business administration. Many of them offered master's degrees, but all either lacked a doctoral program or had an extremely limited one. All institutions in this group had at least two professional or occupational programs and enrolled at least 2,000 students in 1970. If an institution's enrollment was smaller than this, it was not considered comprehensive.

2.2 Comprehensive Universities and Colleges II This list includes state colleges and some private colleges that offered a liberal arts program and at least one professional or occupational program such as teacher training or nursing. Many of the institutions in this group are former teachers colleges that have recently broadened their programs to include

[2] In all cases the term *Ph.D.* also includes the Ed.D. and other doctor's degrees.

a liberal arts curriculum. Private institutions with fewer than 1,500 students and public institutions with fewer than 1,000 students in 1970 are not included even though they may offer a selection of programs, because they were not regarded as comprehensive with such small enrollments. Such institutions are classified as liberal arts colleges. The enrollment differentiation between private and public institutions was made because the public state colleges are experiencing relatively rapid increases in enrollment and are likely to have at least 1,500 students within a few years even if they did not in 1970. Most of the state colleges with relatively few students were established quite recently.

3 LIBERAL ARTS COLLEGES

3.1 Liberal Arts Colleges I These colleges scored 5 or above on Astin's selectivity index[3] *or* they were included among the 200 leading baccalaureate-granting institutions in terms of numbers of their graduates receiving Ph.D.'s at 40 leading doctoral-granting institutions from 1920 to 1966 (National Academy of Sciences, *Doctorate Recipients from United States Universities, 1958–1966,* Appendix B, 1967).

The distinction between a liberal arts college and a comprehensive college is not clear-cut. Some of the institutions in this group have modest occupational programs but a strong liberal arts tradition. A good example is Oberlin, which awarded 91 Mus.B. degrees out of a total of 564 bachelor's degrees in 1967, as well as 31 M.A.T. degrees out of a total of 41 master's degrees. Its enrollment in 1970 was 2,670. Or, consider two Pennsylvania institutions, Lafayette and Swarthmore. Lafayette awarded 113 B.S. degrees in engineering in 1967 out of a total of 349 bachelor's degrees and has been classified in our Comprehensive Colleges II group. Its enrollment in 1970 was 2,161. Swarthmore has an engineering program leading to a B.S. degree, but it awarded only 11 B.S. degrees out of a total of 250 bachelor's degrees in 1967 and had a 1970 enrollment of 1,164. Swarthmore has a strong liberal arts tradition and did not meet our minimum enrollment criterion for a private college to be classified as a Comprehensive College II, but our decisions in the cases of Oberlin and Lafayette had to be at least partly judgmental.

3.2 Liberal Arts Colleges II These institutions include all the liberal arts colleges that did not meet our criteria for inclusion in the first group of liberal arts colleges. Again, the distinction between "liberal arts" and

---

[3] Astin's selectivity index is based on National Merit Scholarship Qualifying Test Scores for all students who took the NMSQT in 1964, classified according to the college of their first choice. From these distributions of scores, it was possible to estimate both the mean and the standard deviation of the scores of students actually entering each college by making certain adjustments in the data. For additional details, see Appendix C of Alexander W. Astin, *Predicting Academic Performance in College,* The Free Press, New York, 1971.

"comprehensive" is not clear-cut for some of the larger colleges in this group and is necessarily partly a matter of judgment.

In addition, many liberal arts colleges are extensively involved in teacher training, but future teachers tend to receive their degrees in arts and sciences fields, rather than in education.

4 TWO-YEAR COLLEGES AND INSTITUTES

5 PROFESSIONAL SCHOOLS AND OTHER SPECIALIZED INSTITUTIONS

5.1 Theological seminaries, bible colleges, and other institutions offering degrees in religion (not including colleges with religious affiliations offering a liberal arts program as well as degrees in religion).

5.2 Medical schools and medical centers As indicated in our previous discussion, this category includes only those that are listed as separate campuses in *Opening Fall Enrollment.* In some instances, the medical center includes other health professional schools, for example, dentistry, pharmacy, nursing, etc.

5.3 Other separate health professional schools

5.4 Schools of engineering and technology Technical institutes are included only if they award a bachelor's degree and if their program is limited exclusively or almost exclusively to technical fields of study.

5.5 Schools of business and management Business schools are included only if they award a bachelor's or higher degree and if their program is limited exclusively or almost exclusively to a business curriculum.

5.6 Schools of art, music, and design

5.7 Schools of law

5.8 Teachers colleges

5.9 Other specialized institutions Includes graduate centers, maritime academies, military institutes (lacking a liberal arts program), and miscellaneous.

(1973)

Note: Extension divisions of universities and campuses offering only extension programs are not included.

DEMAND AND SUPPLY IN U.S. HIGHER EDUCATION
ROY RADNER and LEONARD MILLER

For econometric modeling, higher education can be viewed as if it were a giant industry and studied in terms of inputs (students, teachers) and outputs (graduates). At the heart of any industry is transformation, here meaning education. This study is concerned with the allocation of human resources in relation to transformational processes. The study provides statistical estimates of certain aspects of demand and supply in higher education, develops a set of related econometric models, and illustrates how the models can be applied to policy research and debate. Thus estimates are built up for future demand for freshman places, for the relationship between faculty-student ratios and other institutional characteristics, and for the total "stocks" of educated persons, categorized by age, sex, field of specialization, and highest degree obtained. To illustrate the use of quantitative models for policy purposes, three issue-laden problem areas are examined: academic demand for new Ph.D.'s, the universal two-year college program, and compensatory education in the primary and secondary schools and its effects on higher education.

Previous econometric models have lacked two criteria of importance. First, a model should describe "joint demand" for different types of higher education. In other words, it should reflect the fact that potential students choose from a discrete set of alternatives rather than from one homogeneous commodity. Thus an increase in the relative demand for one option will decrease the relative demand for all other options, and vice versa. Second, a model should offer a satisfactory solution to the "identification problem"—that is, it should distinguish effects of varying demand behavior by students from effects of varying supply behavior by institutions of higher education. The model developed here, a "conditional logit" model drawn from stochastic choice theory, fulfills these criteria.

Higher education options available to high school seniors are grouped into 10 type-classifications including as Type 1 "no higher education" and ranging from Type 2 (low-cost/low-selectivity) through Type 10 (high-cost/high-selectivity). Which option will a student choose? In the model, the four key factors in the choice are: family income, cost of the option, academic ability of the student, and academic selectivity of the institution. From these, two ratio coefficients are derived: the *cost-to-income ratio* and the *academic interaction ratio*. Using these coefficients, the model's equations predict the probability attaching to each option. Take as a simplified example the case of a senior with an SAT average of 575, and a family income of $12,000. What is his or her most likely choice? The model predicts a probability of .223 for a Type 4 institution (low-cost/high-selectivity), and .206 for a Type 7 institution (medium-cost/high-selectivity). Now take the same family income but reduce the SAT by 100 points to 475. What choice is now most likely? Predicted here are .212 for Type 1 (no higher education) and .182 for a Type 2 institution (low-cost/low-selectivity). (Probabilities for all applicable options are shown.)

The more able the student, the more his family is willing to pay for his education.

Of the two coefficients employed by the model, the *cost-to-income ratio* works in a straightforward manner with good and direct explanatory power. As one might expect, the "financial burden" of higher education is important in explaining demand. The economic variable seems to affect choice behavior fairly uniformly throughout the ranges of cost and income. Its importance does, however, vary with ability—the more able the student, the more his family is willing to pay. The *academic interaction coefficient* (ability, selectivity) is more complicated. In brief, the achievement effect works as follows: For students of the highest ability, the higher their ability, the more they are attracted to highly selective institutions. For students of medium ability, ability and selectivity are not significantly related. For those in the lowest ability quartile (who are generally restricted to junior colleges, unselective private colleges, or no college), the most able prefer no postsecondary education.

The model does not, of course, generate a perfect fit between predicted and observed relative frequencies of choice. Differences are known in the econometric lexicon as "response residuals." These can be reduced, it is found, by taking into consideration such factors as the students' stated aspirations and parents' educational aspirations for their children. (However, whether or not the student perceives the parents to be "concerned" about his or her *current* education does not seem to matter.) Taking account of the sex of the student did not improve prediction of total demand, but did for demand among institutions of higher education.

This study predicts demand for freshman places in United States higher education from 1975 through the year 2000 at five-year intervals. Several cases are computed and shown in order to demonstrate the model's sensitivity to changes in the variables or, as they are termed here, the coefficients (cost-to-income ratio and academic-interaction ratio). For example, as applied to the year 2000, when there will be an estimated 4.2 million high school graduates, the basic case—coefficients unaltered from "best estimates"—shows the following pattern of demand: Type 1 (no higher education), 1.7 million; Type 2 (low-cost/low-selectivity), 867,800; Type 3 (low-cost/medium-selectivity), 187,700; Type 4 (low-cost/high-selectivity), 41,700; Type 5 (medium-cost/low-selectivity), 500,700; Type 6 (medium-cost/medium-selectivity), 267,000; Type 7 (medium-cost/high-selectivity), 133,500; Type 8 (high-cost/low-selectivity), 175,200; Type 9 (high-cost/medium-selectivity) 196,100; Type 10 (high-cost/high-selectivity), 125,200.

Interest in forecasting demand for teachers leads naturally to interest in the patterns of variation in faculty-student ratios among institutions and through time. The period studied is 1950–1967. Variations are studied as a function of the institution's size (enrollment), ratings of graduate schools, faculty salaries, type of control, and so on. For exploration of these factors, the study develops a "variable input coefficient" model. Overall results, in summary, show a picture of declining faculty-student ratios in undergraduate schools and public universities and of fluctuating or increasing ratios in private universities and two-year colleges. Downward pressures seem most pronounced in public institutions, at whatever level. Faculty-student ratios vary widely among institutions, even within each major category of institution, though this is less dramatic in the undergraduate categories. Of particular interest in connection with faculty-student ratios are the "marginal increments"—the ratios at which additional faculty are hired as additional students are enrolled. For graduate programs in private universities, the incremental ratio is 1:5; for public universities, 1:8.3; and for undergraduate programs, public or private, 1:17.

Overall results show a picture of declining faculty-student ratios in undergraduate schools and public universities and of fluctuating or increasing ratios in private universities and two-year colleges.

Over the years, studies of human capital have generally concentrated on the *level* of educational attainment. But educational characteristics of jobholders have not remained constant; there has been continuous upgrading. Hence the need to fill the striking gap in information about the *composition* of the stock of degreed manpower, by educational specialty and additionally by vintage (age).

Degreed manpower now comprises 10 percent of the population aged 19 through 70. Overall, the degreed stock grew at a 5 percent rate throughout the period 1930–1971. About 24 percent of the stock is qualified at the master's level and 2.5 percent at the doctorate level. More than half of the men and more than a third of the women bachelor's degree recipients currently will go on for advanced degrees. The time lapse between degrees is typically longer for women than for men at all degree levels. (Qualitative developments overall were not in the direction of greater equality during this period.) Finally, the median age of the overall stock—37 in 1971—stayed relatively constant over the entire period.

The projections offered by Allan Cartter in 1970, which, in brief, forecast that demand for new Ph.D.'s will decline, become negative in the mid-1980s, and slowly rise thereafter, are reexamined here. If stringent financing conditions prevail in the 1970s, academic demand will be below that projected by Cartter. Under revised assumptions as to enrollment, finance, staffing standards, and hiring practices, however, demand could exceed Cartter's estimates by a factor of two or even three.

This study makes projections of sector-by-sector demand for new doctorates, based on judgmental assumptions about the distribution of future enrollment. In summary, these projections show a declining share of aca-

While the enrollment expansion of the 1970s implies considerable growth in faculty numbers, the composition of this expansion compels reexamination of present patterns and objectives of doctoral training.

demic demand for doctorates by universities, and a large percentage increase by public four-year colleges. Public two-year colleges will have only slightly higher demand for Ph.D.'s (historically they have hired only a small proportion) even though their enrollment growth will be enormous. Overall, while the enrollment expansion of the 1970s implies considerable growth in faculty numbers, the composition of this expansion compels reexamination of present patterns and objectives of doctoral training.

Whatever projections are used, there will be a marked "trough" in demand for new Ph.D.'s in the mid-1980s. Can this be avoided? Several techniques for "smoothing" the peaks and troughs of demand are suggested. For example, by allowing student-faculty ratios to rise considerably in the 1970s and then reducing them in the 1980s, annual doctoral faculty hires could be held constant for a 20-year period. At the federal level, adoption of a steady, long-range policy of financing gradual enrichment of student-faculty ratios would help, as would a policy of substantial aid to students in order to bolster enrollment. All in all, under the conditions of policy decentralization prevalent in United States higher education, demand smoothing will be very difficult to achieve. Individual institutions, unable by the mid-1980s to hire new, young Ph.D.'s, will undoubtedly turn to devices such as early retirement to open additional vacancies beyond normal attrition.

A decline in the *rate of increase* for faculty stock will cause an *absolute* decline in demand for new faculty. Yet the prolonged enrollment expansion that is only now ending in higher education has generated an increasing supply of new and aspiring Ph.D.'s. On the other hand, should total enrollment rise sharply, effects are reversed. Demand for new faculty leaps upward, but stocks are not available unless that upturn has been anticipated well in advance. Of course, similar considerations apply to supply and demand for any highly educated group; higher education is, however, the most difficult case, since it "feeds on itself" for its supply of human capital. In such a situation, a dynamic model can provide a useful tool for analysis of changes in inputs and outputs required to bring about prescribed changes in activity at different levels. Thus the model developed here can be used to calculate the dynamic implications of changes in enrollment and in faculty-student ratios. Indirect as well as direct effects can be predicted; moreover, changes in dynamic requirements that are implied by alternative plans can be calculated with a minimum of information about the system.

As an exercise, the model is applied to explore the consequences, in teacher requirements and costs, of introducing a "universal two-year college program." This is defined as raising enrollment in the first two years of college to a level of 90 percent of all high school graduates. Plans are presented for 5-, 10-, and 15-year start-up times; all plans are based on a single educational technology, defined as a teacher-student ratio by faculty degree, for each higher education activity. In total, the program would produce an increase of about 1.5 million students enrolled in higher education, and an expansion of about 13.5 percent in undergraduate education. Graduate enrollment increases required to service the plans are relatively small—by the time of full operation, an expansion of only 0.5 percent would be required. Manpower feasibility problems would be minimal. In the long run, increased costs would be $1.5 billion per year, or 18.5 percent of educational costs in 1967.

A second exercise applies the model to calculate the impact on higher education of introducing a plan of compensatory education in the primary and secondary schools. Compensatory education is defined here simply as reducing student-teacher ratios for disadvantaged children in the schools to 6:1 (a dramatic change from the present). Again, 5-, 10-, and 15-year start-up times are tested. By 1987, the time of full operation under the 15-year plan, some 1 million additional schoolteachers would be needed (half again the 1969 stock). Costs would be stabilized at $12 billion per year higher than at present (excluding capital costs), of which about $1.0 billion would represent costs induced in the higher education sector. Functioning compensatory programs would be much more complex than those described in the exercise; it appears, however, that the dynamic input-output model could be extended to cover these complexities.

(1975)

MAJOR SEGMENTS AND FUNCTIONS

CHAPTER

The five abstracts that follow are drawn from the studies undertaken for the Commission on various parts of our higher education system and on some of its major functions.

Jack Morrison documents the recent and continuing rise of the arts to respectability nationwide, Everett Hughes and his co-authors document the state of professional education, and Richard Storr examines the history of the graduate school of arts and science, establishes the causes of its current malaise, and suggests what must be done if it is to retain its prominence in the American university. Earl Cheit gives us a profile of schools for the industrial professions, and the collection of essays edited by Carl Kaysen provides insights into the origins, development, and problems of curricula, teaching, and learning in the American university.

Shifting priorities in society generate shifts in emphasis on campus. The institutions of higher education reflect as well as refract their environment. These studies tend to suggest that nowhere is this phenomenon more perceptible than in the recent histories of those portions of the institution which concern themselves with its original function—the teaching-learning process. Although, increasingly, teaching has had to vie with research for funding on many campuses, its importance remains fundamental and there is some evidence that this function may be of increasing concern in the years ahead.

THE RISE OF THE ARTS ON THE AMERICAN CAMPUS
JACK MORRISON

The rise of the arts on the American campus is the result of a long and constant, if not consistent, battle of the natural inclination of human beings against the forces of puritanism, the work ethic, and narrow scholasticism. On the campus, however, the tide of battle has turned for the arts and is unlikely to recede. Susan Langer's remark that the discursive symbol does not encompass the full range of human expression is a strong intellectual rationale for the arts in the curriculum, and more recently, psychologists have indicated that a fully functioning human being does not mature without the afferent as well as the cognitive, the emotional as well as the intellectual modes of learning. Daniel Bell sees the artist as vital to the interpretation of life now and in the future.

In 1970, the American Art Directory listed 605 four-year colleges and 74 two-year institutions that offer a major in art. These do not include institutions which offer joint programs with a degree-granting institution. It has been projected that, by 1980, enrollments and graduations in fine arts will increase significantly.

To survey the arts in higher education, Dr. Morrison undertook case studies of 17 degree-granting institutions in the United States. The "arts," for the purposes of this questionnaire, consisted of architecture, dance, film, music, theater, (poetic) writing, and visual arts (including crafts). The structure of the survey provided information for a preliminary statement of the dimensions of the arts in academe. They do not represent one school of thought or "best way."

The 17 institutions interrogated were Antioch College (Washington-Baltimore campus), Bennington College, Carnegie-Mellon University, Dartmouth College, Duke University, Earlham College, Fisk University, Harvard University, Indiana University, Jackson State College, New York University, Pasadena City College, Pennsylvania State University, University of California at Los Angeles, University of California at Santa Cruz, University of Georgia, and the University of New Mexico.

According to the study, students in the arts appear to fall into five groups. There are those who have made a commitment to a particular art; those who are "shopping" around the arts; those who have chosen the arts as a means of fulfilling college education; those who take a minority of arts courses "because they like them"; and those with minimal talent who attach themselves with great protestations of zeal to "the arts." Many teachers report these categorizations and find them generally helpful and useful in their work with students. This study finds that few students of the arts earn a living as professional artists after graduation; some teach, and the majority use their training as sound general education.

The study also considered the question of resistance to and support for the arts in academe. The finding that emerges is that reaction to the arts varies from campus to campus, dependent usually upon the opinion-forming sentiments of some strong leader in the institution's history. Generally the arts are in favor on the campuses, although there are "still some pockets of resistance."

"Some administrators feel that the rate of growth of the last 15 years reflects not a fad, or a phase of interest that will level off, but a trend that will continue and increase."

The rate of enrollment in the arts is reported as increasing, and "some administrators feel that the rate of growth of the last 15 years reflects not a fad, or a phase of interest that will level off, but a trend that will continue and increase." Because of this, funding and space allocation may become a major problem in the 1970s.

Certain recommendations emerge from this survey: Each institution should define its policy concerning the arts, and, complementarily, each department, school, and college of the arts must define its approach to the rest of the campus and to the community. Further, bigger is not necessarily better and an optimum number of majors in each of the arts must be discerned for each institution so that students and faculty may have optimal conditions for growth. Each institution is also urged to "establish a professional follow-up study of its graduates and dropouts to find out, "What do they do afterwards?" And each institution is urged to campaign for more arts-conscious regents or trustees.

With change so rapid in this field, many departments are bogged down. To ease this condition, specific criteria are suggested for use in self-assessment and self-study. The study also advises that each campus set up an organization to provide information on likely sources of funds, to guide preparation of proposals, and to seek individual and collective donors.

Outside the campus, the study proposes the establishment of a commission at a national level for reordering the teaching of the arts and the creation of "a task force to seek and preserve the aesthetic component in architecture and planning as they relate to the other arts and to the curriculum at all levels." Also at a national level, the study recommends "a causal-comparative study of graduates and dropouts in all the arts . . . because students in the arts appear to be noticeably different from those in any previous generation."

"Students in the arts appear to be noticeably different from those in any previous generation."

Establishment of campus-based research and development centers for the arts are also recommended. The arts have traditionally refused to be ignored, and it is reasonable to believe not only that their current position on the American campus is permanent, but that their sphere of influence in higher education will grow in the decades to come.

(1973)

EDUCATION FOR THE PROFESSIONS OF MEDICINE, LAW, THEOLOGY, AND SOCIAL WELFARE
EVERETT C. HUGHES, BARRIE THORNE, AGOSTINO M. DEBAGGIS, ARNOLD GURIN, and DAVID WILLIAMS

Those occupations called professions are entered after a long period of formal schooling. The number of years of schooling varies, but the sequence is fixed: high school, college, professional study. During or after completing the standard sequence required for admission to a particular profession, the candidate may be required, or may choose, to engage in supervised practice; he may also study for certification as a specialist. This is the fixed order of American professional education, although the length of the stages varies.

In the American system, the longer one has to go to school for a profession, the higher that profession's standing. Medicine (four years of college, four of medical school, and one or more of internship) takes highest honors. Its practitioners also have the highest median income. Law (four years of college and at least three of law school) comes next. Theology of the "accredited" sort gives some prestige, but not necessarily a secure or high income. Social welfare, in part because of its newness, still has uncertain status and economic returns.

The length, and in large part, the quality of professional education in the United States is determined not by law, but by voluntary professional associations, specialty bodies, and associations of professional schools. The movement for accreditation has been generally led by people devoted to the raising of standards of education and practice, although there is often some orthodoxy or rigidity in their programs. The success of the movement varies by profession. Thus, while the standard education for these professions is the bachelor's degree plus some years of professional school, this standard has not been completely realized in any profession quite so completely as in medicine. And, it has no sooner been achieved in medicine, and nearly achieved in other professions, than it is being attacked.

The professions deliver advice and other services to individuals or to social bodies. Their services are paid for in fees and paid by individuals or organizations, by gifts and titles, by large philanthropic grants from social agencies and foundations, or by taxes levied on individuals and businesses. The means of support affects the distribution of services, and distribution is considered, by the professions, as a matter over which they should have control. Control over distribution is, however, in fact shared by other bodies that either pay for the services or believe that they should share in control over distribution of services. Students have now joined the debate over distribution of services, especially as it affects the cost of schooling itself. Costs, in turn, affect the social and ethnic mix of those entering the professions.

Students have now joined the debate over distribution of services, especially as it affects the cost of schooling itself. Costs, in turn, affect the social and ethnic mix of those entering the professions.

The general labor force is becoming professional to an unprecedented degree, and the establishment of paraprofessional employment accompanies this process. An elaborate work system surrounds each profession with an ever-changing division of labor. Simultaneously, professional specialization is on the increase, bringing with it demands for more narrow and advanced training.

Although professional schools tend to center around the university, they increasingly rely on government agencies and private institutions to aid them in the training of students for modern practice. Although they need, request, and utilize this outside help, the schools continue to resent anything resembling outside interference or control, and in this hotly contested area, many outside voices, including those of students, are raised.

One example of a traditional process currently under fire is that by which the professions select recruits for training, and great pressure is being applied to facilitate the broadening of the professions by admission of greater numbers of members of racial and ethnic minorities, women, and those of low socioeconomic status. Another complaint is that services are not distributed according to need, but instead, according to capacity to pay, and thus the accepted canons of professional success are under attack. Additional questions are being voiced about the length, content, and methods of professional training, in light of the rapid increase in the amounts of both theory and practical skill that must be taught and learned prior to practice.

There seems to exist a genuine difference between the values espoused by different generations, and this is not peculiar to professional education. We are clearly in a period when the balance between theory and practice and the whole economy of emphasis in higher education are matters of general public concern.

Thorne contributes the study of professional education in medicine. Since publication of the Flexner report in 1910, a homogeneous program of study has evolved in medical education which typically involves three to four years of general study and additional years of internship and residency. This structure, and its accompanying priorities, are currently subject to widespread criticism and proposals for change. Since the early twentieth century, medical knowledge, technology, and specialization have expanded rapidly. Paramedical or submedical occupations have also proliferated. Based on the homogeneity of the Flexner model, however, medical schools and the everyday world of health problems and practice have steadily grown apart. Simultaneously, the academic elite has assumed a central role in shaping the profession of medicine, challenging the dominance of the American Medical Association.

Changes are likely in the near future [in the medical profession], particularly as the rate of technological advance favors the young, with older professionals becoming obsolete faster (thus losing rational authority more quickly) than in the pretechnological era.

The medical profession is currently divided on the issues of structure and responsibility, and three main factions are involved: the politically conservative AMA, representing generally the interests of the traditional entrepreneur; the "academic" practitioners, with their complex affiliations and sources of power; and the emerging "health movement" of radical professionals, consumers, community workers and student groups. The conflict raging over the profession, and its education and purposes, is, in part, one of generations, perhaps because younger professionals and students have less invested in traditional practitional forms. The fact remains, however, that changes are likely in the near future, particularly as the rate of technological advance favors the young, with older professionals becoming obsolete faster (thus losing rational authority more quickly) than in the pretechnological era.

Thorne also writes on professional education in law. Legal education, which for decades has remained substantially unchanged, is now being critically evaluated. The curriculum committee of The American Association of Law Schools recently made recommendations for change in the organization, length, and content of legal education, concluding that "legal education is in a crisis and fundamental changes must be made soon. The idea that law is a homogeneous profession has now become an illusion, and law schools must diversify their curricula content and methods in order more closely to reflect the increasing heterogeneity and specialization of professional practice." One method suggested to bring training closer to professional reality involves the concept of clinical education, which tries to break down the isolation of the law school from the realities of professional practice through student involvement in preprofessional, on-the-job training.

"Law schools must diversify their curricula content and methods in order more closely to reflect the increasing heterogeneity and specialization of professional practice."

A large proportion of the criticism of the legal profession's system of training comes from law students who voice concern about recruitment policies and professional access for hitherto underrepresented groups, as well as distaste for the divisive effects of law school competition. Students are particularly pressing for grade reform and a generally less achievement-oriented preprofessional training.

Additionally, and here they are joined by other critics from both within and outside the profession, students debate the mandate of the profession—who should be served and in what ways. Many schools are expanding, but the rising demand for places outruns supply. Theoretically, the need for more lawyers is there, but the clients whose needs are unfilled are precisely those who are "legally indigent" and cannot afford legal services as they are currently organized. Resolution of the debate over professional mandate will have enormous consequences for legal education in the years ahead.

Writing on theological training in the United States, Hughes and DeBaggis divided institutions offering training for the clergy into three types: the prestigious graduate professional schools; the undergraduate professional schools (chiefly fundamentalist Bible colleges); and the proprietary schools (generally cultic in character). Traditionally, the theological schools have provided a training which is now at variance with the contemporary conception of church and church institutions in America. Each type of religious organization has developed its own system of training correlative to particular conceptualizations of the ministerial role within the overall social organization, and to its concept of "vocation." The major Protestant denominations train their ministers in seminaries, largely at the graduate level, for three years before ordaining them. Increasingly, however, specialized courses now prepare paraprofessionals, without ordaining them, for the professional age has come, and professional services of many kinds are demanded of theologians. At this vital period, however, the profession which has historically provided "social services" is in crisis. Alone among the professions, the church and the ministry are declining in significance. No other profession is being subjected to the radical questions concerning validity that confront the church and the ministry, which are dogged by uncertainties of function and problems of impending obscurity. There is a crisis of confidence at all levels within the profession, and this is reflected in professional recruitment. In 1956, there were 20,720 students enrolled in member schools of the American Association of Theological Schools. In 1960, there were 19,976. By 1970, although enrollments had substantially increased, they had not kept pace with the rates at which enrollment was increasing in schools for the other professions. In the Roman Catholic Church, the situation is bleaker still. Since 1963 the number of seminarians had decreased by 50 percent. Unlike other professions, theology possesses neither a common body of knowledge nor a common code of practice. Advancement therefore depends on the consensus of widely differing groups. With this in mind, theology educators had better keep a close eye on the religious weather.

Alone among the professions, the church and the ministry are declining in significance. No other profession is being subjected to the radical questions concerning validity that confront the church and the ministry.

Gurin and Williams, writing about social work education, point out that the present period is one of great ferment surrounding both practice and the education for practice. Neither education nor practice emerges as a clear leader in this matter; they both interact with the larger forces affecting them. The sense of being "arriviste" continues to haunt the profession, although its history now goes back three-quarters of a century.

The intellectual climate of the schools, however, is changing, and for several reasons. First, there is the widening mandate imposed upon the profession during the past decade by a growing public pressure to deal with social evils of many kinds. Second, faculty and students brought a wide variety of new and unorthodox experiences to the schools during the 1960s, which created a heightened urgency for "broader and more sophisticated understandings of causation and action strategies." Third, the schools in this period became more closely merged with the general fabric of the universities of which they are part.

At present it is difficult to predict future directions in social work education. There is a downward turn in the current labor market for social workers after a decade of rapid expansion in demand, and even if this decline is short-term, it seems likely that the character of the demand, and therefore the nature of both professional practice and education, will be vastly different in 1980 from what it was in 1960. The major transition, the establishment of a bachelor's degree as the first professional degree, has already taken place, and whatever else happens must take into account that professional education in this area is no longer the monopoly of graduate schools. If this were not sufficient confusion, there is a growing commitment, within schools, to part-time, nondegree, or sub-degree training for many different kinds of practitioners at various levels of practice.

As social work education be-comes increasingly diverse, it becomes harder to define—as does social work practice. The dominant issue con-fronting the field is whether to define its essential profes-sional contribution and com-petence in clinical or adminis-trative terms.

As social work education becomes increasingly diverse, it becomes harder to define—as does social work practice. The dominant issue confronting the field is whether to define its essential professional contribution and competence in clinical or administrative terms. Social work education has recently moved away from the clinical model, and it is dramatically apparent that it is now very difficult to establish what the alternative approach really means.

The situation is highly volatile, and in the light of these and other uncertainties, the best prospect for the immediate future would seem to be the continuing development of the profession along its present diffuse organizational lines together with the increasing linking of social work with other professions such as medicine, law, and theology that also aspire to contribute to the personnel needs of the human service field.

(1973)

THE BEGINNING OF THE FUTURE: A Historical Approach to Graduate Education in the Arts and Sciences
RICHARD J. STORR

Throughout the short history of graduate education in America there has been a strong connection between innovation and vitality. Today because of the expansion of knowledge, the growth of interdisciplinary fields, the shrinking job market for postgraduate degree holders, and the blurred meaning of graduate degrees, it has become imperative that wise direction be given the innovative process. What is done now will influence the future of higher education for years to come.

A sharper, more subtle comprehension of the options academics faced in the past can liberate our considerations of future choices. To discern the relation of substance to form in graduate education the history of higher education in the United States must be reviewed.

Pride in one's university, for many Americans, is associated with the university's imagination and determination to try institutionally what had not been done before. The germ of graduate studies may be detected as early as the 1780s, when Ezra Stiles was president of Yale. Stiles perceived distinctions between grammar school, college, and university—as did Thomas Jefferson in Virginia—and advocated professorships in arts and sciences as well as in law and medicine. These proposals reflect a desire to plan institutions grander and more intrinsically American than the existing colleges of the period.

Not only would a national university provide a monument to nationhood but, as George Washington and others envisaged, it would provide a common training for the brightest youth in the nation. And this perhaps provides a clue to why higher education in America has always reflected a degree of political purpose.

Similar sentiments may account for the proposals for a national university, which appeared occasionally from this period onward. Not only would a national university provide a monument to nationhood but, as George Washington and others envisaged, it would provide a common training for the brightest youth in the nation. As this study shows, the idea of a national university has never died, and this fact perhaps provides the clue to why higher education in America has always reflected a degree of political purpose.

In the early nineteenth century a trickle of young Americans began to go to Europe to study, and some of them were inspired by the idea of establishing graduate education in America. George Ticknor, teaching at Harvard after his return, for example, is remembered for reforms that embodied a principle of organic growth and established the elective system. Gradually the college widened its concept of higher education, and the Yale report of 1828, although mainly conservative, did contain a section in which President Day "looked beyond the undergraduate course." Day outlined a scheme wherein the unitary curriculum of the college should stand, but with a faculty of philosophy erected above it.

The mode of instruction in college at this time was not designed to promote inquiry. Piety took precedence over intellect. The advancement of knowledge and the promotion of disciplines appropriate to it were not the goals of the college. One possibility that remained open, however, was to make room for truly higher education by pushing up the ceiling on time spent in study. George Pierson describes this as "the vertical university" and, in America, this school of thought favored study after college graduation. By 1849, with the establishment of the Harvard Scientific School and the Yale Department of Philosophy and Arts, something very like graduate work existed in America. Both schools adumbrated graduate studies in the arts and sciences but at the same time represented the horizontal expansion of higher education to serve persons and often studies classifiable as neither undergraduate in the then conventional sense, nor graduate in our developed sense.

A decade of increasing interest and pressure for conceptual expansion followed these developments, but more than half a century of debate and experiment had not produced an institution that either challenged the hegemony of the college or created a demand for graduate education. The need was constantly reiterated, however, and finally, in 1860, Yale instituted the Ph.D. degree.

The period after 1861 in American higher education is called "the age of universities." As this study shows, before 1861 no foreign observer would have reported that the university existed save in name. By the turn of the century, however, the university's characteristic feature was a graduate school with a Ph.D. program, and the question would have been how the American university, like the British, embraced the college. Charles W. Eliot, the president of Harvard, did not speak of a graduate school of arts and sciences, but adhered to the credo that "no subject of human enquiry can be out of place in the programme of a real university . . . it is impossible to be too catholic in this matter."

Andrew White at Cornell, Henry Tappan at Michigan, and Eliot were among the foremost university builders of the period, but it was the Johns Hopkins University, opening in 1876 under the leadership of Daniel Coit Gilman, that gave the American Ph.D. its momentum. The Johns Hopkins University represented the conjunction, for the first time, of a venturesome board, a substantial amount of uncommitted capital, and a president who was ready to devote a major part of his energy and thought to the establishment of graduate studies in fields other than the existing professions. Johns Hopkins put other institutions on their mettle, and the creation of graduate schools continued as a sense of common interest grew.

By the twentieth century, what defined a university had become the offering of graduate work and the granting of the Ph.D. degree. But college and university did not become different worlds, for as Woodrow Wilson at Princeton stated, "There should be a constant, conscious, intimate action, interaction, and reaction, between graduates and undergraduates in the organization of a university."

As early as 1932, Dean Mc-Bain of Columbia University stressed that "every graduate school is a teacher's college. . . . the Doctor's degree has come to have high commercial value . . . pursued by large numbers who have high interest in the degree but little or no interest . . . in genuine research."

Between 1900 and the 1960s a massive proliferation both in numbers and in fields of study occurred. By 1961, the centenary year of the American Ph.D., more than 300,000 students were in graduate school and about 10,000 received a doctorate. Some part of this growth resulted from efforts to provide graduate study on a geographical basis, but there was no master plan, and with expansion came a subtle change in the substance of graduate education. As early as 1932, Dean McBain of Columbia University stressed that "every graduate school is a teacher's college. . . . the Doctor's degree has come to have high commercial value . . . pursued by large numbers who have high interest in the degree but little or no interest . . . in genuine research." There are elements of truth in that statement; and it is not wholly wrong to say that youth moved from the family, the fields, and the workshop into formal education and ultimately into the graduate school.

In the 1930s, President Atwood of Clark University spoke for a gradation in doctorates, favoring the establishment of a doctor of arts degree because, "We have no degree now that is exclusively held by men who are devoted to research in various academic fields." The substance had departed the form of the Ph.D. degree. Not that research languished. On the contrary, research came into its own after the First World War as research funding expanded. Form and substance, however, had separated, and by 1955 this problem had been recognized in suggestions that Ph.D. programs should educate the scholar-teacher who could both teach and do research.

The reading of the past indicates that the Ph.D. has been less the villain than the victim of the piece in the history of graduate education.

The permutations of substance and form that are possible in graduate education constitute a great web of choices, but from the review of graduate education afforded by this study, certain propositions emerge which should be considered when planning for the future.

First, graduate education is essentially a vehicle of inquiry, which leads the mind out and therefore should be thought of as education rather than as training. Second, as a governing force in education, the possibilities of inquiry should have higher claim than existing professional demands. Third, the graduate school should foster the advancement of inquiry, both intensively and extensively. Fourth, programs of study should be defined primarily by arriving at the closest match possible between the intellectual bent of the individual student and the whereabouts of the knowledge to which clusters of professors are drawn by their questioning. Additionally, graduate study should carry the student, with the least avoidable delay, to attack the questions that are most worth answering.

These propositions yield no single table of degrees, but they suggest two patterns. In the first, which is closer to current practice, two master's degrees, one certifying professionalism, the other completion of a program of postgraduate studies with no particular professional base, would underscore a Ph.D., which would stand for full competence, both in a mode of inquiry and a field of knowledge. Perhaps in rare cases, to reward particular contributions, a Ph.D. with honors might be awarded, but this, it is warned, could merely serve to aggravate an already tense "obstacle race toward academic preferment."

The other pattern is based on the premise that a master's degree should stand for mastery and thus requires stiffening the current master's to protect the Ph.D. In this case, however, would the Ph.D. be rendered superfluous? Perhaps not if it could be removed from the system by which careers are advanced, and reserved for inquirers at any stage of life who demonstrate possession, in the highest degree, of the power to *teach mankind philosophy,* using all three words in their most comprehensive sense.

In conclusion, this study stresses that if graduate education is to be freed of the burden of convention, the public attitude must shift dramatically. Degrees as a form of social currency are in need of deflation; and even more importantly, the pricing of intellectual ability in that currency must be restricted to the markets where such calculations reflect the real needs of the buyer and the particular capacity that the seller supplies. Until then, it is neither fruitful to criticize some students for becoming grinds nor intelligent to wonder why other students rebel. The university must remodel its own arrangements to alter public opinion, for what is in the future will be heavily influenced by the choices made now between the goals, policies, and devices of graduate education. Standards must be made subject to consistent and continuous audit and what is at stake is deeply informed understanding *of* the university, *across* the university. What we think of the university, past and present, constitutes the beginning of the future.

(1973)

Degrees as a form of social currency are in need of deflation; and even more importantly, the pricing of intellectual ability in that currency must be restricted to the markets where such calculations reflect the real needs of the buyer and the particular capacity that the seller supplies.

THE USEFUL ARTS AND THE LIBERAL TRADITION
EARL F. CHEIT

At a time of declining rates of enrollment growth in higher education, study related to work is on the upturn, and professions, new and old, are forcing a reexamination of the relationship between higher learning and useful work.

Although it was long assumed that liberal education was the paradigm of higher education, the rise of a new vocationalism is calling that assumption into question. As a result, the issue of whether "liberal" or "useful" should be the primary aim of higher learning is again, as it has been at various times in the history of education, in the forefront of discussion about the direction institutions of higher learning should be taking.

The premise of this study is that the experience of the new professional schools is highly relevant to that discussion. If the new interests of students and the evolution of the curriculum require that new educational models be developed, the academic experience of these old useful arts should be made part of that work.

When the understanding was finally reached that higher education could be both practical and diversified, a reconsideration of the old question about the tension between useful and liberal was undertaken.

This volume examines the origin and direction of four of these new professional schools (agriculture, engineering, business administration, and forestry). Their history shows that from the very first efforts to bring these fields onto college campuses debate was intense and continuing about the relative worth of "applied" and "pure" subjects. The useful arts first encountered resistance, and subsequently separatist attitudes, until long after the period of dramatic growth of professional schools, brought about in part by the Morrill Act. When the understanding was finally reached that higher education could be both practical and diversified, a reconsideration of the old question about the tension between useful and liberal was undertaken.

In the 1950s considerable study was made of professional schools and their relationship to the rest of the campus. These studies revealed that professional study was becoming well established and accepted in liberal arts colleges as well as in universities and that concern about the resistance to the newer professional schools was diminishing. In fact, the professional fields have, in recent years, become increasingly attractive to new campuses and are regarded on established campuses as a source of stability, innovation, and campus leadership.

The numbers of graduates in the four fields studied in this book rose from less than 10 percent of all graduates in the early 1900s to about 33 percent in 1950. While the relative numbers declined to about 22 percent in the 1960s, all available evidence today indicates that the trend has been reversed. Whether motivated by idealism or the need to compromise with an ideal, it is clear that large numbers of today's students want professional and occupational study.

The volume concludes from the experience of these four fields that there is a "professional model" now available for liberal education that is responsive both to classical aims of education and to the current needs of students. The review of these four fields also reveals that each has developed its own internal tension between "useful" and "liberal," that instruction in these fields did not develop in the form anticipated by the Morrill Act; and finally that their ability to contribute to the renewed discussion about the aims of education requires a restatement of their own liberal requirements for instruction.

(1975)

CONTENT AND CONTEXT: Essays on College Education
edited by CARL KAYSEN

This collection of essays was originally conceived as an examination of what the college student does and should learn in terms of liberal education rather than professional training. Liberal education continues to hold a central position in the concept of higher education—both in the public and in the academic mind—although, at the first-degree level, it has ceased to be the major program of undergraduate students.

From the outset, however, it became clear that any useful discussion of the content and prospects of undergraduate liberal education required explicit consideration of the context in which it takes place. Accordingly, of the ten essays contained in this volume, six deal directly with the substantive content of the undergraduate curriculum, and the remaining four with the institutional, social, and intellectual context in which it is presented.

The first essay, by Laurence Veysey, stands apart from the others; it views curricular development across the last century from a historical perspective. The period 1870 to 1910 witnessed the first major reformation of American higher education, and nowhere was this more keenly felt than in the undergraduate curriculum. During this 40-year period, the traditional narrow and rigid classical curriculum was modified, and there emerged a broader and more flexible one that included many "modern" subjects and permitted a wide element of student choice. Veysey's account of these developments and those that followed sets the scene for the remaining essays.

Four essays are grouped around the various major divisions of the undergraduate curriculum. Roger Shattuck establishes the place of the humanities and suggests that although they no longer enjoy virtual monopoly on higher education they still carry a special responsibility for evolving and carrying out an educational contract which would cast the universities in the responsible role of assessing and criticizing the social institutions which shape our lives.

The humanities still carry a special responsibility for evolving and carrying out an educational contract which would cast the universities in the responsible role of assessing and criticizing the social institutions which shape our lives.

Neil Smelser delineates the scope and functions of the social sciences, from what he stresses is a subjective point of view. He gives particular attention to the educational impact of the social sciences as they are currently taught to undergraduates in America. The question about total impact is answered through a series of subquestions designed to probe what is being taught in the social sciences, where and by whom they are being taught, and how they are taught. For the future, Smelser recommends separating professional education and research in the social sciences from the undergraduate curriculum, holding that only by such structural changes in higher education can the vital activity of liberal undergraduate education be restored to its appropriate position.

The role of the natural sciences is examined by Paul Doty and Dorothy Zinberg. Science is the newcomer in the American university, and in its short lifetime it has enjoyed dramatic expansion in terms of its importance, although it is currently undergoing a slightly leaner period than it is used to. Currently, both the demand for scientists and the demand of students for natural science courses are decreasing, and this essay stresses that in the immediate future science in the university faces a period of evolution and consolidation of course design. The outcome of this should be curricula that encourage deliberate and searching enquiry, not only into the main subject areas of the natural sciences, but also into the complexities of the science-society interface, and the range of conditions under which science can serve the society that supports it.

James S. Ackerman's essay "The Arts in Higher Education" concludes this section. It deals with another curricular area which has experienced rapid growth. For example, a majority of this year's college seniors, when interviewed as freshmen, indicated that they would prefer a career in the arts to one in law or medicine. Despite this boom in interest, however, funding remains meager. Ackerman points out that financial support and public awareness of the arts must be expanded, for unless they are, he warns that an education in the arts, in which eccentricity and absurdity tend to be either encouraged or ignored, may well become training for alienation. To facilitate the changes necessary in this area it is recommended, among other things, that the various campus-based arts be incorporated into the curricula of other fields; for example, painting and drama into the study of history and literature.

Financial support and public awareness of the arts must be expanded, for unless they are . . . an education in the arts, in which eccentricity and absurdity tend to be either encouraged or ignored, may well become training for alienation.

The context of liberal education provides the axis for the next four essays, and Everett Hughes discusses professional education in the first of these. Here, we see that the massive increase in the proportion of the labor force engaged in professional and allied service occupations makes the place of professional education crucial to our total system of higher education. The transition and expansion of professions into modern service systems has involved higher education at all levels. The medical profession, for example, is now incorporated into a system that delivers health services, and at every rung of the hierarchical health services ladder, there is reliance upon higher education. For example, the postgraduate university teaching hospitals produce the surgeon, and the local community colleges have trained some of his nursing staff. The rise to prominence of professional education has contributed largely to the lessening in popularity of liberal studies.

The university is attempting to do too much for too many different constituencies.

James S. Coleman expands the theme of societal demands upon the university in the next essay, raising the question of whether the variety of new tasks that the university has assumed in recent years is helping or hurting undergraduate education. Concluding that the university is attempting to do too much for too many different constituencies, Coleman recommends both an organizational and conceptual change. The organizational change would separate undergraduate education from graduate training and from training for research and development. The conceptual change involves the dismantling of the ideal of the university. The resultant institutions would have coherent and focused conceptual foundations, so that liberal education, training in vocational and professional skills, and training in research for scholarship, could all flourish independently of one another.

A broad view of the relationship between the new electronic technologies and teaching and learning is taken by Anthony Oettinger. The question of whether to rely on custom-tailored, or on standardized learning situations, is crucial in the short term. This analysis suggests that if maximum return from investment in technology is to be achieved, this decision should be made before a technology is selected. However, institutional choices yet to be made in areas remote from higher education will influence the uses of these new technologies, and so mediate their influence on the formal structure of education.

The liberal university, which transmitted a culture in which knowledge and a moral conception of its use were joined, is dying.

Norman Birnbaum examines the university as an institutionalized social critic and assesses the relation between that role and the teaching role in his chapter "Students, Professors, and Philosopher Kings." Discerning a contradiction between the legacy of the university and its present functions, the author concludes that the liberal university, which transmitted a culture in which knowledge and a moral conception of its use were joined, is dying. The inexorable growth of knowledge, and the change from a market to a bureaucratic society, has altered the university: It has become technocratic, speaking not to an educated coterie, but serving specific markets, groups, and clients. More importantly, it has abandoned its notion that it is the custodian of a coherent high culture. Unless the idea of the public education role of the university can be given new historical context, the institution is likely to lack clarity as to its political and social functions.

The final essay in this collection is contributed by David Hawkins. The title warns that this is a modest polemic, and the underlying thesis is that our institutionalized education presupposes levels of experience, conceptual development, and motivation that the education itself does not foster, and often discourages. In providing evidence for this, the essay concerns itself with the procedural rather than substantive, and emphasizes mode of learning rather than any particular content. From this broad examination of the current condition of education, Hawkins evolves a speculative vision of one kind of liberal education around which the future college could be constructed.

(1973)

DIVERSITY AND INCREASING OPTIONS

PART

American higher education is characterized by a diversity that was inevitable as institutions were established to serve a variety of religious, ethnic, class, and occupational interests. Such diversity is not invulnerable to social change, however, and in the last 20 years there has been a tendency for some of the components of the system to become homogeneous. But the tendency has not yet totally obscured the richness of variety that distinguishes the institutions that provide our nation's youth with their many options for postsecondary learning.

The Commission's report *Reform on Campus* was concerned with preserving this diversity and also with increasing the variety of instructional options available within the various institutions. There, we endorsed such concepts as the cluster and theme colleges within large institutions, and urged that state plans and multicampus system plans provide for specialization of instruction in certain fields and for differentiation of general functions among campuses and groups of campuses. We also have urged that admissions policies be consistent with the diversity in American higher education.

Our report entitled *Less Time, More Options* also addresses itself to this realm of concern. It explores the possibilities of shortening the duration of formal education, of providing more options to increase the relevance of educational opportunities to the lifetime needs of people in a changing society, of making degrees more appropriate to the positions to which they lead, and of making opportunities to attend colleges and universities more available to more people regardless of income, age, or sex.

In *New Students and New Places,* we presented forecasts that enrollments will increase by one-half in the 1970s, remain steady in the 1980s, and increase again by one-third in the 1990s. By the year 2000, we estimate that the percentage of college-age youth enrolled on a campus of a higher learning institution will have climbed from the 35 percent enrolled in 1970 to 50 percent. Additionally, higher education will increasingly welcome participation of all people over 17 years of age. If our recommendations in this area are implemented, the Commission projects the following enrollments:

YEAR	TOTAL ENROLLMENT
1980	12,500,000
1990	12,300,000
2000	16,000,000

The pressures of the future will be many and varied, but we are convinced that whatever their directions may be, the preservation of institutional diversity and the expansion of educational options for the American people must remain one of our major policy priorities.

INSTITUTIONAL COMPONENTS OF THE SYSTEM

CHAPTER

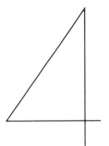

To define the parameters of the institutional variety in American higher education, and to estimate the current condition of the various parts of our system, the Commission sponsored the preparation of a series of profiles of distinctive types of colleges and universities. A list of the studies prepared under that program is almost self-explanatory and may illustrate better than any other description the wide range of institutional types in our higher educational enterprise. Colleges founded for black Americans are portrayed by Frank Bowles and Frank DeCosta in *Between Two Worlds.* Catholic institutions of higher education are the subject of Andrew Greeley's book, *From Backwater to Mainstream,* while the Protestant liberal arts colleges are studied in *Education and Evangelism* by C. Robert Pace. Morris Keeton surveys the private liberal arts colleges in *Models and Mavericks,* and those with limited resources are explored by Alexander Astin and Calvin B. T. Lee in *The Invisible Colleges.* Leland Medsker and Dale Tillery provide timely information concerning the most rapidly growing segment in higher education, the two-year community colleges, in *Breaking the Access Barriers,* and E. Alden Dunham gives a lively profile of state colleges and regional universities in *Colleges of the Forgotten Americans,* a book selected as the American Council on Education's "Book of the Year" for 1970.

On the basis of the profiles prepared for the Commission, augmented by data on student opinions, C. Robert Pace undertakes a review of eight distinct types of institutions and, in *The Demise of Diversity?,* concludes that they are moving away from diversity and toward conformity under social and economic pressures.

BETWEEN TWO WORLDS: A Profile of Negro Higher Education
FRANK BOWLES and FRANK A. DECOSTA

As recently as a decade ago the hopes of most black youth for education beyond high school centered of necessity on the colleges founded for Negroes after the Civil War. For many years the historically Negro colleges and universities were the major custodians of black literacy, history, and aspirations. Except for the few Negroes who could afford to enter Northern colleges, the old Southern institutions provided the only access for black Americans to higher education and professional life.

Aside from a few students who entered law, medicine, or the ministry, however, teaching was the only profession open to them. This imposed heavy limitations on the black colleges—now numbering more than 100—which in their isolation came to rely on didactic methods, handing down knowledge that was often obsolete. In a self-perpetuating cycle of poverty, they taught students to teach in schools operated with meager support, in old and inadequate facilities. The intellectual effects of these limitations, combined with chronic shortages of money for books, equipment, and salaries for the faculty, resulted in weaknesses that were almost insurmountable.

But by the late 1960s, the historically Negro colleges were no longer the predominant institutions of higher education for black people that they had been earlier. Out of a total black enrollment of about 267,000 in 1967–68, they enrolled 134,000. Other Southern institutions, formerly segregated, enrolled 38,000; and nearly 95,000 black undergraduates were enrolled in colleges, universities, and community colleges outside the South.

There is the melancholy fact that the great problem facing both the black student and the college he enters is that of underpreparation.

Against today's promise of increasing freedom of choice and movement for black students, there is the melancholy fact that the great problem facing both the black student and the college he enters is that of underpreparation. At the college level, the black student, like any other, is expected to be able to demonstrate the skills to learn; the college is expected to stimulate, guide, and help to develop him. Yet neither the black students who have entered predominantly white colleges nor the colleges they have entered have yet learned to play their assigned roles. The problem is complex.

The historically Negro colleges have not been unready in terms of understanding the problems of limitation and discrimination imposed on black students, but they have been unready in terms of modernization of programs and extension of services to the black community. Part of their unreadiness was related to the shortage of funds, but also, until recently, the black colleges had not seen the need for modernization. They have experienced confrontations, some of them violent, and it is predictable that there will be more, for these institutions are moving from a stable past into an unstable future.

The small size of the Negro professional class is probably the greatest single handicap the black community faces in its effort to raise standards of living, production, consumption, and education.

The small size of the Negro professional class is probably the greatest single handicap the black community faces in its effort to raise standards of living, production, consumption, and education. The principal obstacles now in the way of professional entry for black citizens are (1) the lack of adequate recruitment and preparation of students in both high schools and colleges, and particularly in the science-based fields of medicine, dentistry, the paramedical fields, engineering, and teaching and research in pure science; and (2) money. Two steps need to be taken: a counseling service should be provided for black students considering professional education; and a broadly based, federally supported, professional school scholarship program should be established. In addition, the historically Negro colleges should join in efforts to recruit able students to go on to graduate and professional schools. This study suggests that a target be set to accredit one million black professionals by 1980.

Existing historically black colleges could double their enrollment without great difficulty, provided additional operating costs were covered either by subvention from tax funds or by tuition. What they need above all else is a student body large enough to fill their classrooms and well-to-do enough to pay fees and charges. If a federal "education salary" were made available to any student who wished to claim it, enrollment would rise rapidly and the black colleges would soon be able to markedly improve their offerings, administration, and general condition. A 1964 study of the graduates of predominantly Negro colleges showed that 62 percent owed money for college expenses as compared with 36 percent of white students.

The future of the historically black colleges will be determined in part by America's political readiness to support them as educational assets, including building them up to the strength needed to compete with predominantly white schools in preparing students for graduate study. It will also depend on a continuing demand within the black community for such colleges as a supportive ambience for black students.

It is clear that if adequate student and institutional support programs are provided, the historically black colleges will grow in size and influence up to a point and then level off—becoming a permanent group of special-purpose institutions not unlike the Catholic colleges and universities, that is, following the central pattern of American education but tacitly reserved for a defined clientele.

If such programs are not established, or if they are delayed by more than ten years, the black colleges will be severely damaged by the competition of the major white colleges and universities, which will siphon off some of their best students.

There is an appalling lack of hard facts about the Negro in America, including a lack of agreed-upon statistics as to the number of Negroes enrolled in higher education —and this despite all the emotion-laden material written about the problem.

There is an appalling lack of hard facts about the Negro in America, including a lack of agreed-upon statistics as to the number of Negroes enrolled in higher education—and this despite all the emotion-laden material written about the problem. There have been all too few real studies of Negro life and institutions. It would be very useful to the black colleges, for example, to have an approximation of the size of the black middle class and of its mean income and growth rate.

Furthermore, there are no research and development centers attached to the historically black institutions, although we could have expected this to be one of the first moves for institutions deeply involved in urban problems, such as Howard, Fisk, Atlanta, and Dillard.

There has also been a surprising failure of teacher-training departments in the black colleges to publicize the problems of preparing teachers for segregated ghetto schools, which is in fact where most of their graduates will teach. Such schools require both dedication and expertise; hence it would have been entirely reasonable to publicize the training problems and seek federal aid in solving them. Improving the colleges will have little significance, however, unless the lower schools are improved; and, in turn, the lower schools cannot improve until the conditions of Negro life are improved. This study urges, among other steps, the formation of a planning and consultant body for Negro education—to be established with a financially guaranteed life span of at least ten years—to undertake both spot and longitudinal studies and to supply consultant services for black schools and colleges.

(1971)

FROM BACKWATER TO MAINSTREAM:
A Profile of Catholic Higher Education
ANDREW M. GREELEY

By now it is no longer a secret that Roman Catholicism is not the massive, smoothly organized, and efficiently operating monolith that many of its writers and defenders have thought it was. Whatever remnants of the monolith myth may remain are quickly put to rest by investigation of the 350 colleges and universities affiliated with the Roman Catholic Church in the United States.

There are some general similarities, to be sure: the presidencies of most of the schools are still held either by priests or nuns. The schools are subsidized, in some fashion or another, by the Church—either through the contributed services of the religious or through direct financial support from a religious community or a diocese. They all represent some kind of commitment to the Roman Catholic faith, though the nature of this commitment varies from school to school, both in theory and in practice. Almost without exception, they were founded to serve the Catholic immigrant population and are now going, willy-nilly, through the process of adjusting to the needs of the Catholic population that is emerging from the immigrant experience. None of them is of the highest quality, as American standards go, though most would claim that they aspire to some kind of excellence which is simultaneously Catholic and American. Almost all of them are going through a period of questioning and self-doubt, and most have serious financial problems. Many, and probably most, feel inferior, at least at the subconscious level, to their non-Catholic competition.

Approximately three-quarters of the Catholic schools have been founded

Almost without exception, they were founded to serve the Catholic immigrant population and are now going, willy-nilly, through the process of adjusting to the needs of the Catholic population that is emerging from the immigrant experience.

in the present century, and more than 100 of them since 1950. With one exception, the largest institutions, however, those with over 5,000 students, date to the last century. Most of the schools which have proliferated since 1950 are either junior colleges or the so-called sister formation colleges.

The 350 schools that have survived into the present are but a minority of those that were founded; 68 percent of the Catholic colleges founded for men prior to 1956 are no longer in existence. The highest casualties were in the early 1900s, from which period only 4 of 35 schools survived to the present, and 24 were closed down by 1920. But the survival rate in every decade of founding has been less than 50 percent. In 1940, the founding of colleges for men evidently tapered off.

There is a subtle atmosphere which enables the sensitive observer to know rather quickly that he is on a Catholic college campus. Perhaps the most important contribution to the different atmosphere is the dedication of the religious. It is not at all improbable that the greater loyalty of Catholic alumni, despite a realistic appraisal of the weaknesses of their schools, is directly related to many warm and satisfying relationships between students and members of the religious orders. But one of the great weaknesses of Catholic higher education has been its failure to create a culture and a structure which would maximize the benefits of these relationships.

It is not at all improbable that the greater loyalty of Catholic alumni is directly related to many warm and satisfying relationships between students and members of the religious orders. But one of the great weaknesses of Catholic higher education has been its failure to create a structure which would maximize the benefits of these relationships.

While there are some 350 institutions in the Catholic higher educational "system," 21 of these schools with enrollments over 5,000 have more than 40 percent of all students in Catholic colleges. Catholic schools are concentrated in the Northeast and North Central parts of the country, and generally within the standard metropolitan statistical areas. The most important block within the system consists of 28 Jesuit colleges and universities. Lay faculty predominate numerically over clerical faculty, but the clergy still have most of the important upper-level administrative positions. Faculty salaries are about average when compared with the rest of American higher education as, apparently, is faculty course load. The students at the Catholic schools are not greatly different from other Americans in socioeconomic background, though they are less likely to marry in college or immediately after graduation.

The financial problems of Catholic schools are probably no more acute than the problems of American private higher educational institutions in general, and, in some respects, are less acute. Catholic schools, in all likelihood because of the contributed services of members of the religious community, are, as a "system," able to operate in the black while the rest of private higher education has been in the red. They are also getting a better rate of return on some of their auxiliary revenues for higher educational enterprise. Their administrative costs seem perhaps a bit too high, and they are deficient in obtaining revenue from federal research projects, although presumably only a small proportion of the large private non-Catholic universities in the country are obtaining much income from such projects. Despite the popular myth to the contrary, Catholic schools are no more deficient in endowment funds than the rest of American private higher education.

Historically, the Catholic higher educational "system" arose as part of the comprehensive ghetto which was the inevitable response of the Catholic immigrant groups in the early phase of their adjustment to American culture. The schools trained lay and clerical elite, reassured parents and clergy that the faith of the young was being protected, provided an "intellectual" communications network within the Church and a status and prestige system not available to Catholics outside of the comprehensive ghetto. As the immigrant experience recedes into the past and the post-Vatican modernization of the Church continues, many of these functions are no longer accepted or relevant, and the question of what is distinctively Catholic about Catholic higher education becomes, at least on the rhetorical level, crucial. No matter how the question is solved, many if not most Catholic colleges and universities are likely to continue (given federal assistance) and continue in one way or another to be distinctively Catholic. But the rhetoric about goals and purposes is not unimportant, particularly if the question is phrased in such a way as to refer not to what must be preserved out of the past, but to what contribution, if any, the Catholic religious vision can make in the future to the total American higher educational enterprise.

The rhetoric about goals and purposes is not unimportant, particularly if the question is phrased in such a way as to refer not to what must be preserved out of the past, but to what contribution, if any, the Catholic religious vision can make in the future to the total American higher educational enterprise.

In the vast amount of National Opinion Research Center research material on the graduates of Catholic colleges, there is almost no confirmation of the theory that the graduates of these colleges are academically or socially inferior to the graduates of any other American college. It appears that the colleges do have religious impact on students, though it is difficult to filter out the self-selection factor. It also appears that a considerable proportion of the lay and religious elite of American Catholicism are trained in Catholic colleges. On balance, Catholic colleges and universities are in some instances worse and in a few instances a little bit better than average.

Judging from the response of 1961 alumni to the survey, a Catholic educator might take reasonable encouragement from the finding that his former students do not think he did badly, and apparently have by no means rejected the idea of such an educational experience for their

It might be said that the alumni seemed to be rather more confident of the future of Catholic higher education than many Catholic educators themselves.

children. It might be said that the alumni seemed to be rather more confident of the future of Catholic higher education than many Catholic educators themselves.

Among the core problems are:

Public image Not the least of Catholic higher education's problems is that so little is known about it by those outside the Church.

Sponsorship Most Catholic colleges and universities in the country are sponsored or owned outright by dioceses or religious orders. Until recently, therefore, the boards of trustees of such institutions have been rubber stamps either for the president of the college or for the religious superior who, in fact, is the major decision maker for the college.

Relationship with the Church A more generalized version of the problem which exists between a Catholic college and the sponsoring religious community is the question of the school's relationship to the whole Catholic Church.

Faculty In common with most small and medium-sized private institutions with limited budgets, Catholic schools have difficulty recruiting and maintaining the quality faculty that they feel is appropriate for their ambitions.

Administration In a survey by the National Opinion Research Center, it was concluded that the most serious operational problem that Catholic schools face is the recruitment of competent and effective top-level administrative personnel.

Students There are two major problems that Catholic higher education faces with its students. The first is the replacement of the traditional compulsory religious life that marked Catholic colleges and, until very recently, was taken for granted. The second is the difficulty that these schools may face in years to come in finding an appropriate clientele.

Interinstitutional cooperation A very simple answer can be given to the question of whether there is much cooperation among Catholic colleges. The answer is "no."

The author has no doubt that the Catholic vision of the meaning of man, particularly as it is being reinvigorated in the present transitional crisis in Catholicism, has much to say that would be extremely important to American higher education. Whether there is the courage and imagination to put aside the concerns of the immediate past and attempt to implement the Catholic vision of the future in Catholic colleges and universities remains to be seen.

(1969)

EDUCATION AND EVANGELISM: A Profile
of Protestant Colleges
C. ROBERT PACE

There are between 450 and 600 colleges in the United States associated with Protestant Christianity. These include:

■ All those universities and colleges which have historical links with the Protestant religion, but are no longer Protestant in any legal sense today.

■ Most of the Ivy League institutions, and such other major universities as Boston University, Syracuse, Baylor and Southern California.

■ Those colleges and universities which have retained their connection with Protestantism (though some are on the verge of disengagement).

■ Colleges and universities associated with evangelical, fundamentalist, and interdenominational Christian churches.

Within the past 20 years, higher education has become so dominantly secular that there is a tendency not to recognize the overwhelming influence the Protestant Church has had on higher education. From the mid-seventeenth to the mid-twentieth century, higher education was mainly private and mainly Protestant. But since 1950, when for the first time students enrolled in public institutions equaled those in private ones, the proportionate share of total student enrollment at Protestant colleges has dropped considerably. Today they enroll about one-tenth of the college-student population.

What are the Protestant colleges like today? The results of a questionnaire, developed by the author and administered to 100 institutions of different types, including 20 Protestant colleges, show that Protestant colleges are characterized by a general atmosphere that is friendly, supportive, and congenial. Yet there are striking differences between the different groups of Protestant colleges.

The evangelical and fundamental groups are most distinctive. Their campuses are polite and considerate, with an absence of assertive, demonstrative activities. There is a strong feeling of cohesiveness and group-orientation. Campus life is structured but unrepressive.

At the Protestant-independent colleges—colleges with only historical connections to the Protestant religion—campus life is generally indistinguishable from that at other liberal arts colleges of comparable size. But in comparison with other types of Protestant colleges they are more scholarly, provide greater opportunity for creative and appreciative activities, have a higher concern for the welfare of mankind, and a greater awareness of self, society, and aesthetics.

In comparison with other types of Protestant colleges, Protestant-independent colleges are more scholarly, provide greater opportunity for creative and appreciative activities, have a higher concern for the welfare of mankind, and a greater awareness of self, society, and aesthetics.

Although most mainline Protestant colleges—those colleges with loose associations to Protestantism—are similar to other liberal arts colleges, some of them are characterized by low energy, low exposure, and low involvement. They rank low on faculty demands, quality of class discussions, preparation and study effort, and intellectual challenge. Energies

Lacking strong commitments to the church and to spiritual experience as well as to scholarship and the world of ideas, the atmosphere at some of these mainline Protestant colleges might be described as "tepid."

that might be devoted to activities directed at social reforms or political programs are devoted instead to new fads and phrases, pennants and pin-ups, and knowing the right people. In short, lacking strong commitments to the church and to spiritual experience as well as to scholarship and the world of ideas, the atmosphere at some of these Protestant colleges might be described as "tepid." However, mainline Protestant colleges vary more widely than the Protestant-independents and evangelical-fundamental colleges, and it would be unfair to describe the entire category in this way.

A questionnaire survey of alumni from 88 colleges and universities, among them 19 Protestant colleges, showed that college influence on values and attitudes varies by type of college. For example, graduates of Protestant-independent colleges feel they have gained from their alma mater an awareness of different philosophies and ways of life, an ability to think critically, and appreciation of individuality and independence. They are most willing (compared with alumni of other types of Protestant colleges) to accept blame for discrimination against blacks and are most likely to believe that not even hard work can overcome the handicaps of prejudice. They believe strongly in freedom of expression. In general, their attitudes are similar to those from other small, nonurban, liberal arts colleges. Graduates of evangelical-fundamental colleges have been influenced mainly in their appreciation of religion, in vocational training, in their tolerance of other people, and their friendships. They have very strong attachments to their alma mater. Like alumni of other Protestant colleges, they are pro-business and pro-competition, but are more inclined to feel that big may be bad. They are the least likely to support women's liberation, and least willing to accept the charge of white racism. They are also the least willing to condone free expression if it advocates unpopular or extreme ideas or if it is critical of basic moral concepts. The mainline Protestant alumni are the least distinctive in their attitudes and personal traits, and do not stand out from college and university graduates as a whole.

A questionnaire identical in most respects to the one filled out by the alumni was given to upperclassmen at most of the colleges that had participated in the alumni survey. The patterns of response are nearly identical to that of the graduates. Students of the mainline denominational colleges are like students in general. The Protestant-independent students are more "liberal" and do not differ very much from other liberal arts upperclassmen. Evangelical-fundamental college students adhere most firmly to the morality of hard work and belief in God.

Yet there are also differences between the students and alumni. Students

The evangelical-fundamental students are exceptional in that they tend to express beliefs and attitudes most commonly expressed by the alumni.

are more likely than alumni to support free expression, regardless of the popularity of the views expressed. They are more skeptical than the alumni about minority-group advancement through hard work alone. The students also give stronger support to the notion that more money and effort should be spent on education, welfare, and self-help programs for the culturally disadvantaged. The evangelical-fundamental students, however, are exceptional in that they tend to express beliefs and attitudes most commonly expressed by the alumni. For this group, apparently, there is no generation gap.

In general, personal visits to a number of Protestant colleges confirm the results of the various questionnaires. There is wide variation in the educational programs, physical plants, and student behavior at the various colleges. In nearly all cases the campuses are friendly and neighborly. The Protestant-independent colleges are not much different from other types of liberal arts colleges, and their future seems to depend more on the quality of their educational programs than on the strength of their ties to religious groups. This is not the case for the evangelical-fundamental colleges, whose place in American education seems assured through private giving by alumni and friends who believe in the virtues of institutions of this type.

It is likely that the "in-between" mainline denominational colleges, having neither a reputation based on their educational quality, nor great support from the churches, will turn towards the Protestant-independent model and further away from their religious links.

(1972)

MODELS AND MAVERICKS: A Profile of
Private Liberal Arts Colleges
MORRIS T. KEETON

In its first report in 1968 the Carnegie Commission on Higher Education stated, "What the American nation needs and expects from higher education in the critical years just ahead can be summed up in two phrases: quality of result and equality of access." Subsequently, Howard R. Bowen spelled out in *The Finance of Higher Education* the objectives he felt national policy embraced: rich opportunities for personal and vocational development of individuals, with priority for the advancement and dissemination of learning; a system of maximally autonomous public and private institutions providing a diversity of programs for different types of students and different regions, with sources of support of the colleges sufficiently different that no interest group can dominate the whole; access for all to higher education within their capacity, regardless of barriers of finance, race, national origin, religion, place of residence, or background; and free choice of programs and institutions for students, within the limits of their qualifications.

The achievement of these objectives will require a substantial increase in the volume and variety of opportunities for higher education, with constant culling and refinement of programs to assure efficiency and responsiveness to changing social purposes and new circumstances. This new volume and variety imply a need for both increasing financial resources and greater efficiency in their use. To justify the claim on these resources, institutions of higher education will have to achieve a more sophisticated division of labor than they have today and develop both more substantive cooperation and a degree of competition that gives students a greater choice. Implied in turn are changes in planning, financing, governance, and management of colleges—which will be enormously difficult. It is by no means settled that changes implicit in this transformation will gain either a timely public acceptance or be welcomed by the institutions.

Private colleges as a group should undertake a part of each of the two main services suggested by the Carnegie Commission's phrase, "quality and equality." First, they should accept a share of the increase in the numbers of students who will demand higher education within the next decade, and should do so on terms clearly advantageous to taxpayers and state governments. Second, they should undertake ventures in qualitative achievement for which the private colleges are particularly qualified.

The burden of making the needed transformation cannot and should not be borne entirely by public colleges and universities. Private colleges as a group should undertake a part of each of the two main services suggested by the Carnegie Commission's phrase, "quality and equality." First, they should accept a share of the increase in the numbers of students who will demand higher education within the next decade, and should do so on terms clearly advantageous to taxpayers and state governments. Second, they should undertake ventures in qualitative achievement for which the private colleges are particularly qualified. Each of these qualitative ventures should derive from one or another of the advantages inherent in the nature of the particular private college. Such advantages, for example, are the freedom to orient life and curriculum to a philosophical or religious perspective inappropriate or illegal for a state-supported college; the opportunity for curricular and instructional achievements that derives from distinctive student characteristics, capital resources, or other assets of particular private colleges; and the freedom open to certain private colleges to undertake socially needed but risky or unpopular innovations, a freedom deriving from the distinctive control of these colleges.

It is often supposed that religious or philosophic commitment severely inhibits a liberal education, and that only neutrality with respect to value issues is compatible with genuine and effective inquiry. Evidence suggests that we should not endeavor to erase philosophic distinctiveness from every university, but to assure awareness of both the dominant and alternative outlooks, to provide options for students and faculty within the nation's system of colleges, and to use the resources for communication within our society to further the testing of these outlooks. From the perspective of optimizing learning and offering a spectrum of intellectual outlooks to test, the United States is fortunate to have institutions of higher education that differ markedly. We should sustain and enrich this variety.

A second type of qualitative venture derives from distinctive student characteristics, critical resources, faculty, and other assets of particular colleges that have a unique opportunity to be models of excellence. Reference here is to the same kind of excellence sought by public colleges and universities, not "excellence" made possible because of philosophical or religious distinctiveness. In this context the mix of students and even the distinctive local or regional setting is a resource to be weighed in planning for effectiveness in achieving the college's purpose. Do private colleges have the unusual resources prerequisite to this function? Some do, others do not. The evidence on this point is twofold: (1) results already achieved and (2) data that appear to correlate with these results and give some hints of the dynamic underlying the results.

Some private colleges have striven for a unique form of excellence and have become clearly outstanding in liberal education. Other colleges not as outstanding nevertheless offer alternatives that should interest legislators, trustees, and members of college staffs who seek to understand the opportunities and hazards of undertaking a unique service. Concerning the provision of socially needed but unpopular ventures, times may be changing. Large universities may become able to support small ventures that earlier could not have survived in a public context. A substantial sharing of authority and governance with students could contribute to such programs.

Private colleges must prepare to accept in the next decade an increase in enrollment (which, at the same time, will allow a 5 to 8 percent decrease in the overall proportion of private to public college enrollment). This may seem a strange recommendation at a time when many observers are prophesying the demise of private higher education. But most private colleges are viable, and with greater sustenance can become still more productive. Higher education as a whole will also be more effective and more efficient if a dual system of private and public colleges is fostered under conditions favorable to a healthy competition in the public service. Such competition would help to eliminate the private colleges that do not deserve to survive.

Higher education as a whole will be more effective and more efficient if a dual system of private and public colleges is fostered under conditions favorable to a healthy competition in the public service. Such competition would help to eliminate the private colleges that do not deserve to survive.

To implement the recommended growth in enrollment and improvements in quality of education, private colleges should undertake substantial change of internal government and management. These changes should include: (1) a sharp realignment of rights in the determination of college purposes, the definition of problems and of the priorities to be followed in their resolution, and the definition of the prerogatives of those who constitute the college—trustees, administrators, faculty, students, alumni, parents, and others; (2) an improvement of communications on campus, with particular stress on the climate and mechanisms of informal communication; and (3) division of labor and decentralization in the governance and management of colleges, with a view to increasing the capability of effective action by subcolleges or programs.

To enable private colleges to perform the proposed task, leaders of public opinion and institutions' governing bodies should weigh the following recommendations for public policy:

■ Legislators should view higher education as a joint investment by individual students and the general public.

■ Legislation and administrative priorities in government—federal and state—should focus upon enabling qualified students to afford the higher education of their choice without delays based upon difficulties in financing.

■ Federal and state effort should give priority not to meeting all current costs of any particular subset of institutions of higher education (such as community or four-year colleges), but to capitalization of the needed quality, types, and amount of educational services in the system of higher education as a whole.

■ Rather than try to control quality or enforce standards directly, federal and state efforts should be directed toward providing a high quality of education by offering the public and private colleges and universities incentives to compete with one another.

Policy should aim at substantially increasing borrowing and earning possibilities for students in such a manner that a parity is achieved between costs of public and private institutions. Thus, a student would be able to obtain the best possible buy in his particular field of interest.

■ Policy should aim at substantially increasing borrowing and earning possibilities for students in such a manner that a parity is achieved between costs of public and private institutions. Thus, a student would be able to obtain the best possible buy in his particular field of interest.

■ Charges to students should enable colleges to achieve a balance of income and expenditures. Colleges should do true cost accounting on a program basis to facilitate elimination of economically and educationally unsound programs and to provide adequate support to sound ones.

■ Public policy should encourage substantial efforts to achieve gains in the productivity of teaching and administration and to apply a part of such gains to the arrest of rising costs.

■ Colleges should rely for long-range solvency upon the growth of tuition income and upon assured forms of public support (such as grants to the institution per student graduated or grants to students that follow automatically from need and qualification) rather than upon unpredictable private and public financing.

(1971)

THE INVISIBLE COLLEGES: A Profile of Small, Private Colleges with Limited Resources
ALEXANDER W. ASTIN and CALVIN B. T. LEE

Although most Americans know the names of the prestigious private universities, the state universities, and the distinguished private colleges, few realize that one of the largest segments of American higher education—at least one-third of all the four-year institutions—consists of relatively little-known private colleges. These would be worthy of study simply because of their large number, but the added fact that some of them may face extinction makes a thorough examination of their problems and prospects imperative. The term "invisible" is more descriptive than evaluative, and focuses attention on what is possibly the main problem facing this section of the educational establishment, namely, obscurity.

The invisible colleges should not be treated in isolation from the remainder of higher education; thus, in much of this analysis, they are compared both with institutions at the elite end of the status scale and with state colleges, from whom the invisible colleges face increasing competition for faculty and students.

Inclusion of institutions in this study was determined by their low selectivity in admissions and small size; using these criteria, a group of 494 colleges which "few people know about and perhaps even fewer care about" was selected for the survey. Admissions selectivity was assessed from the data on the aptitude test scores of entering freshmen from four sources. These scores were then converted into a common scale. Data concerning size were obtained from U.S. Office of Education statistics. Only some 20 percent of over 2,000 colleges founded during the nineteenth century survive today, and many of these survivors are just hanging on.

As the nature of higher education has changed, so have the invisible colleges. For example, 12 percent have changed their name, while many others have been pressured into curricular change and religious disaffiliation over the years. The portrait this study presents is of institutions in a constant state of flux, which frequently requires fundamental change in their whole raison d'être. Unlike the elite colleges, invisible colleges have

The primary concern, therefore, of this sector of the higher education industry is survival, whether the institution be sectarian or nonsectarian, and the national trend toward nonsectarian, state-supported, tuition-free higher education does nothing to relieve the gloom cast by this eternal shadow.

faced a situation in which the ability to survive has always been a moot point and it is difficult to live from day to day in such doubt. The primary concern, therefore, of this sector of the higher education industry is survival, whether the institution be sectarian or nonsectarian, and the national trend toward nonsectarian, state-supported, tuition-free higher education does nothing to relieve the gloom cast by this eternal shadow.

These institutions exist in all but three of the 50 states and enroll approximately 15 percent of all students attending four-year colleges. A higher percentage are church-related. They receive substantially less money from all sources than do other private colleges.

The time-worn phrase, "the plight of the small college," gains real meaning when applied to the invisible colleges. They worry not about attracting students of any specific type, but about attracting enough students, particularly as their student bodies, socioeconomically so similar to those of the tax-subsidized public colleges, are now being tempted away by virtually free public education.

Role and identity confusions lie at the core of the invisible colleges' dilemma, and no strategy for salvation has yet been devised which does not jeopardize either their small size or their private status. Increasingly, attempts—largely unsuccessful—have been made to "ape" the elite colleges by "upgrading" student and faculty quality, and by disaffiliating from founding churches. At present the invisible colleges are plagued by inadequate federal and state aid and the minuscule nature of their endowments, which have held them to an increasing dependency upon tuition and fees for income. The data in this study reveal that public colleges are competing much more successfully for the lower-income students, while elite colleges compensate, with prestige, for higher tuition charges. Other than raising their charges, the alternatives for these invisible colleges are unattractive, consisting of such courses of action as cutting faculty salaries, or raising student-faculty ratios. These alternatives lack appeal either because they are not likely to work or because even if they do, they will be self-defeating and may well lead to erosion of the special qualities and essential contributions of the invisible colleges.

One does not have to push the virtues of diversity and heterogeneity to the absurd extent of maintaining that demonstrably inferior institutions should be maintained purely to provide options; indeed, the study challenges the view that the invisible colleges as a group are "of poor quality," "inefficient," and "redundant," simply because they operate under standards different from those of the elite colleges.

American education has long prided itself on its diversity, which springs from the assumption that there are important individual differences between students. In support of that assumption it is logical that small colleges, which may be church-related and which are not intellectually selective, will better satisfy the needs of some students than any other kind of institution. One does not have to push the virtues of diversity and heterogeneity to the absurd extent of maintaining that demonstrably inferior institutions should be maintained purely to provide options; indeed,

The invisible colleges are currently an "underutilized" educational resource, for they can help accommodate the increasing demand for open admissions in already overloaded public colleges, while simultaneously alleviating their own financial problem.

the study challenges the view that the invisible colleges as a group are "of poor quality," "inefficient," and "redundant," simply because they operate under standards different from those of the elite colleges. This study presents data which indicate that elite colleges bestow no specific educational advantages, although they have social benefits which can affect career plans. Additionally, elite and invisible colleges perform different functions, neither of which is undesirable in the career area, the former tending to produce graduates interested in the humanities and the latter tending to produce graduates who function in the physical sciences and health professions. Public four-year colleges perform different functions in a different way also, so that invisible colleges are not redundant. Perhaps the greatest educational justification for the invisible colleges is that they possess the special expertise required to provide appropriate learning opportunities for certain students now composing a large segment of the expanding college population. From a policy standpoint, therefore, this study indicates that the invisible colleges are currently an "underutilized" educational resource, for they can help accommodate the increasing demand for open admissions in already overloaded public colleges, while simultaneously alleviating their own financial problem.

By and large, then, the invisible colleges do justify their existence in helping to maintain the diversity of the American system of higher education. Having established this, there is then the problem of keeping these institutions solvent, and therefore functioning. State aid is considered the most likely answer, despite the thorny problem of granting public money to church-related education. Indeed, there is evidence that among the 50 states, much consideration is being given afresh to the notion that, in the long run, the public interest might best be served by utilizing and augmenting the resources of private institutions. This method would finally "lay the ghost of unfair price competition" to rest and is recommended by the study.

If the invisible colleges are, to some degree, to be publicly supported, the issue of inefficiency due to small enrollment must be faced. More than 70 percent of these colleges have fewer than 1,000 students, and data from this study suggest that no major detrimental institutional effects would be felt should they enlarge to a 2,500-student level. Thus, most invisible colleges could absorb enrollment expansions of over 150 percent without suffering grave institutional damage.

Should this expansion be carried out nationally, it is mathematically shown in this study that, with each invisible college taking 100 more students each year, public institutions would not have to expand at all to absorb current projected freshman enrollments.

A further recommendation in respect to funding is that such public money as is forthcoming should be awarded in such a way as to preclude the invisible college's aping its elitest confreres. This could be achieved by granting public funds only to preserve and strengthen the unique institutional features of low selectivity and small size. This was achieved with reasonable success under Title III of the Higher Education Act (1965) and it is reasonable to hope that similar success might be achieved here.

These recommendations should not suggest that no improvements are needed with the invisible colleges. What is intended is that the focus of improvement should be placed on the teaching and learning process, particularly for disadvantaged students.

What is finally recommended, therefore, is a thorough examination of the invisible college's mission, role in higher education, and strengths, both by the academic world and by those concerned with public policy at the state and federal level. Perhaps such scrutiny can lead to a wider view of the constituent elements of institutional excellence, one based on educational values rather than on tradition, sentiment, and academic snobbery.

(1972)

BREAKING THE ACCESS BARRIERS:
A Profile of Two-Year Colleges
LELAND MEDSKER and DALE TILLERY

Almost 40 percent of all entering college students in the United States now begin their work in community colleges. The phenomenal development of the two-year institutions and their projected enrollments for the next decade—between 3 million and 4.4 million students by 1980—identify them as the fastest-growing segment of higher education.

They serve two dominant roles. An increasing percentage of recent high school graduates enter these colleges either with the expectation of continuing their education later in a four-year institution or of finding employment after leaving. The demonstrated ability and willingness of community colleges to serve older youth and adults enable many individuals to pursue an educational interest at will, and thus reopen the doors that often close when a person terminates his formal, full-time education. A delineation of the community college's role would be incomplete without reference to its democratization of postsecondary education. An open-door policy, proximity to clientele, low cost to students, and a multiplicity of programs all combine to make the community college potentially effective in extending educational opportunity. The authors are concerned, however, about the gap between expectations for universal college education and fulfillment.

The problem obviously is not that the community college lacks general acceptance by the nation—its rapid growth to date indicates its popularity. But the serious question is whether, in a period of belt-tightening, it will have sufficient public understanding and support to enable it to serve the increasing number of students who heretofore have not gone beyond high school and who will be served best by institutions with unconventional functions and practices.

Some of the rhetoric about universal higher education deludes both policy makers and educators and makes false promises to those who have yet to enter the mainstream of American life. This is particularly threatening to community colleges, which are emerging as the target institutions to do those things which other colleges and universities cannot or will not do. Unfortunately, it is widely assumed that community colleges can succeed in educating great numbers of new students at less cost than other agencies and that they will have the personnel and freedom from tradition to do the job.

Equal opportunity involves more than merely lowering the barriers to college admission. There is ample evidence that postsecondary education is not meeting the needs of many students, particularly those below the median in financial resources, traditional measures of academic achievement, and interests and values usually held in American colleges. The challenge to the community colleges to be relevant seems to have been accepted, but new talents, new resources, and new programs are necessary.

Equal opportunity involves more than merely lowering the barriers to college admission. There is ample evidence that postsecondary education is not meeting the needs of many students, particularly those below the median in financial resources, traditional measures of academic achievement, and interests and values usually held in American colleges. The challenge to the community colleges to be relevant seems to have been accepted, but new talents, new resources, and new programs are necessary.

Some students are deprived of opportunity because of where they live, their racial and ethnic background, their financial resources and because of nonacademic interests and school histories. And even though barriers are being systematically lowered through widespread development of two-year colleges and changing concepts of financial aid, large sections of the country (particularly the Eastern seaboard and the South) lack adequate low-cost, comprehensive institutions. There are few states which recognize in their financial aid programs the importance of forgone earnings to the decisions of sons and daughters of the poor to go to college or not. Not only do heavy work schedules, family indebtedness, and economic pressures contribute to the vulnerability of many who enter junior colleges, but many young people under such pressures choose not to try college at all. Low tuition, then, is not enough to remove the economic barriers to education.

The continued emphasis on traditional academic criteria in preparing students for college discourages those with nonacademic talents and interests. Such practices are reinforced by college admissions requirements, and together they result in restricted opportunity for the children of the poor and minority groups. Negative attitudes toward vocational education and the lack of programs for career development are byproducts of the academic syndrome in American higher education.

Perhaps one-third of the students who enter junior college find themselves in limbo and are soon on their way out—dismissed for low achievement in programs they could not handle, turned off by instruction that is irrelevant to their interests, or overwhelmed by financial pressures.

Perhaps one-third of the students who enter junior college find themselves in limbo and are soon on their way out—dismissed for low achievement in programs they could not handle, turned off by instruction that is irrelevant to their interests, or overwhelmed by financial pressures. It is likely that many of these students find no hospitable place—either in the high-status transfer program or in the highly selective technical and semiprofessional curricula of the contemporary community college. This gap in program comprehensiveness, when combined with deficiencies in guidance and developmental education, means that many students find no programs which offer opportunities for them.

The particular components of the comprehensive junior college program that are generally underdeveloped are career guidance, special help to the undereducated, and community service. Compared with other functions, these three lack full staff commitment, effective planning, and adequate resources. Transfer education consumes the lion's share of the instructional budget. This is so in spite of the modest rates of transfer to senior institutions, irrational counselor-student ratios, and heavy dropout rates for the very students whom the community colleges claim to serve.

Whether the community college can and will maintain a sufficiently comprehensive program as a means of serving its diverse student body is still an unanswered question. There is by no means universal commitment, either at the faculty or state planning levels. While most states now have specifications for the development of two-year colleges, the plans frequently are not well integrated with an overall plan for education beyond the high school. They too often deal with broad generalities and do not provide enough guidance to help the community college achieve its assigned mission. It seems inconceivable that, with nearly 40 percent of all beginning college students entering such institutions, almost every state would not by now have taken firm steps toward planning.

It seems inconceivable that, with nearly 40 percent of all beginning college students entering such institutions, almost every state would not by now have taken firm steps toward planning.

Difficult problems lie ahead in recruiting, training, and providing in-service assistance to community college teaching and counseling staffs. An important factor is to identify staff members whose interests and backgrounds will enable them to relate meaningfully to the increasing number of students who are "new" to postsecondary education. Since the majority of such students will fall below median academic aptitude as measured by conventional means and many will come from poor homes, the staff will need a deep commitment and a strong orientation to the special situations involved in working with students from minority groups.

There are strong arguments in favor of increased state support for community colleges: it tends to equalize the burden of community college support; it draws on funds from sources other than property taxes; and it places the funding of community colleges on somewhat the same footing as other public higher education. Undoubtedly, a greater portion of revenue will come from the state in the future, and probably from the federal government as well.

At present there is no agreement on the ideal method for planning and controlling community colleges. Both state and local involvement in decision making is desirable, but there is need for mechanisms of joint control.

(1971)

COLLEGES OF THE FORGOTTEN AMERICANS: A Profile of State Colleges and Regional Universities
E. ALDEN DUNHAM

Until fairly recently, many of the state colleges and regional universities have been relatively sleepy, single-purpose, teacher-training colleges. Having acquired a taste for higher status and strong ambitions, they are now at various stages of movement along a spectrum from their single-purpose origins as teachers colleges toward multipurpose university status and prestige. Emerging colleges, developing colleges—different descriptions are used for these schools. Basically, they are the 279 institutions that make up the membership of the American Association of State Colleges and Universities (AASCU).

Individual histories of state colleges and regional universities differ, but there is a general pattern. If the institution is very old, it is likely that it was founded as an academy or seminary and then evolved into a normal school during the period when most other normal schools were being founded—usually prior to the turn of the century. The religious schools and those under the auspices of the YMCA also became normal schools when they came under state control, principally because of financial pressure. A few of the agricultural and technical institutes, mostly those founded for Negroes, likewise became normal schools, but most expanded their offerings and skipped over the normal-school phase. Some junior colleges became state colleges without going through the normal-school phase at about the same time the normal schools and teachers colleges were becoming state colleges and expanding their curriculum. Today, new state colleges are being founded as many existing state colleges are becoming universities.

The 279 state colleges and regional universities are spread widely around the country. Fifty of them are in the South Atlantic area—far more than the average of about 30 found in other sections of the country. The Mountain states are low with 18. Though leaders in the number of institutions, the South Atlantic region lags behind in total enrollment because the colleges are not large. The North Central area leads in number of students.

Nationwide in 1967, there were 1.47 million students enrolled in state colleges, or 21 percent of all students in higher education. And this figure is fairly consistent across the country, though low in New England and the Middle Atlantic area. Nationwide, 42 percent of the students in public four-year institutions are in these state colleges and regional universities. Residential, full-time students comprise most of the enrollment.

Twenty-four of the 279 institutions have enrollments under 1,000 and account for only 1 percent of the enrollment in state colleges and universities. Twenty-seven percent of the enrollment is found in the 144 colleges with 1,000 to 5,000 students. Eighty-two medium-large places with enrollments of 5,000 to 10,000 have 41 percent of the students. The 29 large institutions with enrollments over 10,000 have 31 percent of the students. These large places are mostly on the West Coast and in the eastern part of the North Central region.

Overall, these colleges enroll 53 percent men and 47 percent women, or just about the national average. Bearing in mind the heavy predominance of women in the early history of most state colleges, this change in the sex balance is a noteworthy development. It reflects the move from the preparation of elementary teachers to secondary teachers as well, the gradual development of liberal arts and applied programs as these colleges became multipurpose institutions, and in recent times, the heavy demand for and short supply of space in the colleges.

The most salient characteristics of state colleges and regional universities are rapid change of function and astounding growth. These factors complicate decisions about what the functions of these colleges and universities ought to be.

The most salient characteristics of state colleges and regional universities are rapid change of function and astounding growth. Rapid growth in itself produces all sorts of strain in the network of relationships involved in the running of a college or university. Then there is the complication of deciding just what the function of these colleges and universities ought to be, the "identity crisis."

These problems would be difficult enough if each institution were to make its own decisions, but increasingly, institutional decisions—whether at the faculty, administrative, or trustee level—must dovetail with the overall interests of the state as determined by boards of higher education, coordinating councils, and the like. In turn, these state agencies must make decisions bearing in mind the total financial resources of the state and the competing demands from every side. All of these elements are entangled with one another, and it is difficult to pull them apart. But when one adds the traditions, folklore, and legalities of 50 individual states as well as the idiosyncratic behavior of thousands of individuals looking at higher education from particular points of view, one despairs of any form of reliable generalization.

In any case, because of the enormous cost of graduate education, it is understandable that the established universities and statewide boards look with great concern at ambitious state colleges wishing to take on university status. With that status inevitably comes a desire for doctoral programs and, just as inevitably, vast increases in expenditures to maintain a very low student-teacher ratio at the graduate level and to provide the highly expensive facilities, equipment, and library for advanced work. Additional money going to a regional university to inaugurate a doctoral program may mean less money going to the state university for its programs.

Concerning students of the state colleges and universities, aggregate statistics do not say very much about who they are, where they come from, what they look like, how they dress, or what their ambitions are in life. They are the sons and daughters of the "Forgotten Americans," the phrase coined by President Nixon in his 1968 campaign to describe the millions of Americans who elected him, people whose way of life is summed up by a term that is pejorative in liberal intellectual circles but that still reflects much of what the nation is all about: middle-class values.

The faculties of the state colleges are restive. They jealously look over the fence at the university, where generally higher salaries, better fringe benefits, lighter teaching loads, and greater opportunities for research prevail. Rifts often occur within college faculties as institutions expand their programs beyond teacher education and as enrollments begin to bulge. The old-guard education faculty loses its influence, and the same kinds of splits between academics and educationists occur in the former teachers colleges as has been evident for years in more established universities.

In the area of curriculum, at the undergraduate and master's levels, programs of all descriptions can be found. In teacher education some truly innovative approaches are being tried, but many of the state colleges apparently have not caught up with improvements in secondary education and are teaching the same thing year after year. The rapid growth of community colleges across the nation and the increasing numbers of transfer students will call for a new look at institutional structure and purpose. A new look is needed at curriculum as well. Implications are that there will be more concern for the development of a student's moral, aesthetic, and creative qualities than for his rational skills. Education of the "whole man" will become more than a cliché on the front page of the catalogue.

Recognizing the magnitude of the urban challenge, these institutions have begun to look at how they can better serve the cities. A number of them give considerable attention to inner-city teacher training. Special programs exist at both the undergraduate and graduate levels. There are several relevant observations about these efforts: Many of the programs are in colleges that are not in urban areas, and the programs, for the most part, are special in the sense that they do not represent the main thrust of the college. The categories of programs promulgated by AASCU do not include all that might be done. Also, urban programs involve risk at every step. A different approach is institutions that are dedicated to urban needs. Federal City College in Washington, D.C., and Metropolitan State College in Denver are two examples.

But the greatest single problem facing these colleges that make up the AASCU membership is the question of institutional purpose. Many of the 279 institutions are quickly moving along a spectrum from single-purpose teachers colleges to multipurpose universities. Very few, however, will ever become first-rate universities. They will not attract enough money, top-flight research faculty, or academically oriented students.

Even if the stated goal of state colleges is to become multipurpose teaching institutions educating teachers, businessmen, engineers, civil servants, homemakers, nurses, and so on, it is being subverted by the very nature of the system. The graduate school and the Ph.D. are the culprits. A Ph.D. is a research degree and a union card which means acceptance among one's colleagues within the guild, the academic discipline. So long as the only sources of respectable faculty are the leading graduate schools within major universities, state colleges will automatically be led toward these institutions as models.

State colleges and regional universities should take the lead in establishing a new and different doctoral degree specifically focused on the preparation of undergraduate teachers, with special concern for lower-division teaching, whether in two-year or four-year institutions.

State colleges and regional universities should take the lead in establishing a new and different doctoral degree specifically focused on the preparation of undergraduate teachers, with special concern for lower-division teaching, whether in two-year or four-year institutions.

One thousand junior colleges enrolling 25 percent of all students in higher education are crying out for faculty members, persons with training beyond the straight master's degree, but different from the research Ph.D. The market for such people would be enormous in liberal arts colleges as well. And in the emerging state colleges and regional universities there would be an almost limitless opportunity for such people, provided that the stated purposes of these institutions are meant to be implemented.

Intermediate or truncated Ph.D. programs are not the answer. There should be a new and different doctoral program and degree for the preparation of college teachers in the arts and sciences. I propose the title Doctor of Arts, which is the degree given graduates of a program begun recently in a limited number of fields at Carnegie-Mellon University and recently authorized at the University of Washington. The doctor of arts is a terminal degree. It is not a consolation prize for losers en route to the Ph.D., nor is it a beginning step for people aiming at the Ph.D. Also, to say that the Ph.D. is a research degree and the D.A. a teaching degree is an oversimplification. The Ph.D. emphasizes research and the D.A. emphasizes teaching.

State colleges and regional universities are full of vitality, enthusiasm, and dedication. What is needed is bold imagination and self-confidence to strike out in new and uncharted directions. Indeed, there should be much more emphasis on diversity; each college should aim at development of uniqueness, its own personality. Enough has happened in higher education within recent years to convince even the most conservative educators that we haven't come close to finding answers to what education is all about. Now in a state of flux, developing state colleges can do one of two things: strike off in new directions or follow in the weary footsteps of those very institutions where many of the current problems are the most evident.

(1969)

THE DEMISE OF DIVERSITY?   A Comparative Profile of Eight Types of Institutions
C. ROBERT PACE

Conflicting social and economic pressures have alternately pulled higher education in the United States toward and away from diversity and conformity since its earliest history. Colonial colleges and the frontier colleges of the nineteenth century were nearly all liberal arts institutions founded by Protestant sects. Since then, the educational landscape has been filled with state universities, women's colleges, theological seminaries, vocational and technical institutes, teachers colleges, Catholic schools, military schools and, most recently, junior colleges. Clearly, the system did not grow by merely providing the same kinds of programs for larger numbers of students. Rather, by introducing programs in engineering, agriculture, business, and other fields, colleges and universities attracted students who would not have gone at all if courses had been limited to the classical program of moral philosophy, mathematics, literature, and Latin.

This study examines eight types of institutions "whose historical development, programs, and clientele have given them a distinctive character or personality" and discusses the ways in which each type may be gaining or losing its distinctiveness. The institutional typology was derived from results of the College and University Environment Scales, used to survey students' opinions on campus facilities, rules, customs, courses, faculty, events, activities, and other conditions that make up the academic environment.

Liberal arts colleges—mostly small, privately supported, and residential—are divided into three categories: *selective liberal arts colleges* are usually nonsectarian, with a strong intellectual emphasis; *strongly denominational liberal arts colleges* have a Catholic or evangelical Protestant religious atmosphere; *general liberal arts colleges* are those that do not clearly fall into either of the former two divisions. Universities—large, comprehensive, and complex—are also divided into three categories: *selective universities* are mostly private and nonsectarian; *state colleges* (and other less comprehensive universities) are typically larger in size and scope than liberal arts colleges, but not as comprehensive as the major universities; *general universities* are more comprehensive than the state colleges, but not as selective as the selective universities. *Teachers colleges* and *colleges of engineering and science* compose the final categories.

It was assumed—and confirmed by data analysis—that the educational environment of an institution has a definite and measurable effect on the attitudes and activities of its students.

It was assumed—and confirmed by data analysis—that the educational environment of an institution has a definite and measurable effect on the attitudes and activities of its students. The study bases its further analysis on a questionnaire administered in 1969 to alumni (class of 1950) and upperclassmen (class of 1970) of institutions across the country. The questionnaire was designed to determine the characteristics of the student bodies and the environments of different institutions and to see if and how they had changed in the 20-year period. Respondents were measured on their involvement in civic and cultural affairs; on their awareness of, knowledge about, and attitudes toward certain major issues in American society, including the economy, science, government, the role of women, free speech, and civil rights; and on the extent to which their education had benefited them in such areas as vocational training, social development, awareness of different philosophies and ways of life, improved writing and speaking, increased understanding of science and technology, and critical thinking. These measurements of civic and cultural activity, educational benefits, and attitudes may be referred to as educational outcomes. In addition, the direct educational experience of the respondents was measured through data on college residence, major field, academic performance, nature and extent of discussions with faculty members and counselors, and aspects of the college experience that were particularly memorable.

Detailed factor-analysis procedures identified several major dimensions of the college experience for both alumni and upperclassmen and facilitated comparisons between institutional types. For example, along the alumni dimension of "faculty and counselor discussions of personal and financial problems," considerable homogeneity of scores occurred within the state colleges, selective universities, and colleges of engineering and science. The strongly denominational and selective liberal arts colleges ranked high on this measure; the universities and colleges of engineering ranked low. Comparing the results for alumni and upperclassmen on all measures, the study found less institutional diversity and distinctiveness in 1970 than in 1950.

Similar analysis was applied to measures of educational outcome. In contrast to the ranges of educational experience, the ranges of difference between institutional types in the outcome measures were somewhat greater for upperclassmen than for alumni. In addition, the ranges themselves were quite a bit greater for both the alumni and upperclassmen than they were in the college experience factors. There is, in other words, greater institutional diversity in what comes out of the college experience than there is in the nature of the college experience itself.

The statistics do not unimpeachably demonstrate a loss of diversity or distinctiveness within the educational system in the United States. Beneath the data, however, are indications of important social trends that are pulling the system toward greater conformity. The growth of the junior colleges and of part-time and commuter enrollment and the increased emphasis on vocational and technical training have reduced the proportion of students who experience a campus life rich in interpersonal relationships, campus activities, and associations with faculty. As the data show, a rich academic life—a trait of institutional distinctiveness—is closely related to the attainment of such outcomes as personal and social development, liberal interests and attitudes, and involvement in civic and cultural affairs. But the enrollment in the general liberal arts colleges, which promote such an academic life more than any other

Comparing the results for alumni and upperclassmen on all measures, the study found less institutional diversity and distinctiveness in 1970 than in 1950.

The growth of the junior colleges and of part-time and commuter enrollment and the increased emphasis on vocational and technical training have reduced the proportion of students who experience a campus life rich in interpersonal relationships, campus activities, and associations with faculty.

institutional type, is declining. The selective liberal arts colleges, the denominational liberal arts colleges, and the colleges of engineering and science, the most distinctive types in terms of intellectuality, religion, and science, respectively, also have declining enrollments, while the least distinctive institutions—the general universities and state colleges—are growing. Moreover, the opportunities for institutions to be different have been curtailed as financial support has fallen more heavily upon state taxpayers and as the federal government continues to allocate grants and contracts according to its research and training priorities. The diversity of the higher education network has thus been, and may continue to be, diminished—a loss to students, to the educational system itself, and to society.

(1974)

PREPARING FOR THE FUTURE

PART

Time is a tripartite constant: the present as we experience it; the past as a present memory; and the future as a present expectation. By this Augustinian criterion, the future world has already arrived because its basic design is constantly framed by the decisions we make now. Just as the railroads and the concept of the city block in the nineteenth century shaped the growth of our twentieth-century cities, so the developments in instructional technology, and the revamping of graduate school curricula, will help frame educational patterns for the twenty-first century.

The first source of change will be technology. The impact of the computer on higher education will be vast. The possibility that we may eventually have a national information-computer-utility system, with terminals in homes and offices, could have enormous effects on the structure of intellectual life and organizations devoted to the discovery, preservation, and dissemination of knowledge. Indeed, as our report *The Fourth Revolution* anticipates, the computer and other electronic media will bring to education its first great technological revolution in five centuries. The nature of technology itself is also changing with a machine technology slowly being replaced by an intellectual technology that facilitates decision making with the use of such tools as operations research and model construction.

A second source of change is found in the shifting structure of our society. Our political system is becoming more centralized and we are becoming, with the aid of the mass media and advanced transportation, a national society. Additionally, we have become economically "postindustrial" as the emphasis of the economy has shifted from goods to services, and the sources of innovation have become increasingly based in our intellectual institutions, notably the universities and research organizations.

Changes in the distribution of goods, whether they be tangibles or social claims on the community, will have dramatic effects. When this distribution accelerates, as it recently has in higher education, it modifies the essential character of the institutions where the acceleration occurs.

The Carnegie Commission believes that it is not only possible but essential to direct some of this change and thus to help shape the future rather than wait passively and merely meet it with reaction and adjustment.

For all of these reasons, a substantial part of the Commission's sponsored research concerns the methods by which the institutions of higher education are altering and adjusting to face their changing environment.

Projections of College-age Population, High School Graduates, and Full-Time-Equivalent (FTE)
Enrollment in Higher Education (in thousands)

	18–21 AGE GROUP	HIGH SCHOOL GRADUATES	TOTAL FTE ENROLLMENT	ENROLLMENT INCREMENTS (2-YEAR AVERAGE)
1960	*9,168*	*1,864*	*2,835*	
1961	*9,945*	*1,971*	*3,092*	
1962	*10,493*	*1,925*	*3,322*	*244*
1963	*10,879*	*1,950*	*3,539*	*224*
1964	*11,088*	*2,290*	*3,924*	*301*
1965	*11,880*	*2,665*	*4,443*	*452*
1966	*12,546*	*2,672*	*4,792*	*434*
1967	*13,098*	*2,680*	*5,168*	*363*
1968	*13,773*	*2,702*	*5,594*	*401*
1969	*13,654*	*2,839*	*5,891*	*362*
1970	*14,541*	2,978	6,242	324
1971	14,864	3,090	6,666	385
1972	15,297	3,210	7,008	386
1973	15,621	3,306	7,373	354
1974	15,966	3,389	7,722	357
1975	16,346	3,563	8,131	379
1976	16,602	3,589	8,491	385
1977	16,796	3,634	8,825	347
1978	16,889	3,633	9,110	310
1979	16,855	3,705	9,338	257
1980	16,755	3,669	9,528	209
1981	16,596	3,658	9,648	155
1982	16,408	3,588	9,678	75
1983	16,007	3,428	9,546	− 51
1984	15,503	3,256	9,264	−207
1985	14,953	3,162	8,934	−306
1986	14,394	3,083	8,597	−334
1987	14,183	3,237	8,470	−232
1988	14,076	3,259	8,473	− 62
1989	14,297	3,361	8,605	68
1990	14,664	3,416	8,826	177

NOTE: Figures in italics are actual as estimated by the Office of Education. See "Projections of Educational
Statistics to 1979–80" (OE-10030-70).

INSTITUTIONS UNDERGOING CHANGE

CHAPTER

For many years, colleges and universities have been regarded as bastions of the traditional and as temperamentally resistant to change. Harold Hodgkinson's survey of 1,230 college presidents, which provides the background for *Institutions in Transition,* indicates that this may no longer be true. Hodgkinson's five case studies, and the comprehensive self-studies of institutions analyzed by Dwight Ladd in *Change in Educational Policy,* demonstrate that the colleges and universities emerged from the turbulent 1960s with at least a deepened sensitivity to the need and demands for reform. The success with which they brought about change was often imperfect and fraught with frustration, but the willingness to consider and even to embark upon new programs and procedures was clearly present. Lewis Mayhew's examination of planning in *Graduate and Professional Education* provides a closeup of this sensitivity to change as it is evident in one highly specialized part of higher education.

To shed light on whether changes are recognized as necessary by those within education, Edward Gross and Paul Grambsch, who had made a study of *University Goals and Academic Power* in 1964, conducted supplementary surveys in 1971 to produce *Changes in University Organization, 1964–1971.* They concluded that "there are signs of genuine changes, some startling, all worthwhile."

The idea that colleges and universities have resisted experimentation with new structures and procedures is rendered almost obsolete by the inventory of innovations compiled by Ann Heiss. While it concentrates on the new and different, and thus tends to ignore the traditional, this work serves as a selective catalog of alternatives to be considered by higher education planners.

In addition to reform in university structures and curricula, the sixties also witnessed efforts to reform the national collegial associations of faculty, researchers, and practitioners—the learned societies. The efforts were largely led by internal radical caucuses of faculty disenchanted with the theoretical and methodological perspectives of their disciplines advocated by traditional learned-society leadership, and with the relationship between these organizations and the larger society. In *American Learned Societies in Transition,* Harland Bloland and Sue Bloland chronicle the brief period of caucus activity in the learned societies and review its present decline and the growth of a new faculty organization—the union.

An analysis of the political ideologies of graduate students in the late sixties is carried out by Margaret Fay and Jeff Weintraub, who use data derived from the 1969 Carnegie Commission Survey of Faculty and Student Opinion. They conclude that those students most interested in politics (both liberals and conservatives) were most ideologically consistent. In addition, the relationship between most attitudes of graduate students and a given political self-label varied systematically and was affected by the prevailing ideology in a given department.

After 1964, there were many observers who believed that our colleges and universities had been so torn by dissension and turbulence that they would never be the same again. This thesis is examined closely in the vignettes compiled for *Academic Transformation: Seventeen Institutions Under Pressure,* edited by David Riesman and Verne Stadtman, which won the American Council on Education's Book of the Year Award for 1973. A similar examination, with only one institution as its focus, is made in essays on Harvard University, by Seymour M. Lipset and David Riesman. Ironically, this study of America's oldest university tends to show that the change that seems so new in the 1970s has ancient antecedents—and, indeed may be, in reality, a part of the tradition of American higher education.

INSTITUTIONS IN TRANSITION: A Study of Change in Higher Education
HAROLD L. HODGKINSON

The study from which this book emerged concerned itself solely with American higher education, but certain caveats concerning the nature of change should be borne in mind throughout. There are two vital points to be made in this regard. First, man normally perceives change only after it has occurred, and second, man's perspective concerning change is almost invariably too narrow.

The task for this study was to describe the changes that have taken and are taking place in American higher education in terms of institutions, individuals, and systems, in order that some projections for the immediate future may be tentatively made.

Using statistics garnered by the U.S. Office of Education, the research team compiled what had never previously existed, a "statistical history" of changes in institutions of higher education over the last several decades. After employing this to identify trends and tendencies, a questionnaire was constructed which extracted further information from the 1,230 presidents of institutions of higher education who replied to it, thereby eliciting information about what had been going on in terms of more subtle dimensions than the U.S. Office of Education statistics could provide. These answers were placed on a grid which sorted the 1,230 institutions by 112 categories to discern whether certain segments of higher education were moving in different directions from others.

The next stage concerned the development of a series of five case studies of institutions which "had gone through changes which seemed from our research to be formative in determining what an institution will become. Unlike many case studies which provide no basis for comparison these cases were built about a common grid so that each case presents similar characteristics."

During the past five decades the pattern of leaving school after the completion of eighth grade has all but ceased, and completion of high school has become the norm.

Before enumerating the major conclusions reached by this study, attention should be drawn to a "fragmentary" sketch of the context within which America's system of higher education currently operates. The first point is that the past five decades have witnessed revolutionary changes in both the nature and the duration of formal education. During this period the pattern of leaving school after the completion of eighth grade has all but ceased, and completion of high school has become the norm. Indeed, whereas at the beginning of this century only 20 percent of the appropriate age group entered ninth grade, some 50 percent of high school graduates currently go on to some type of further education, and in California the figure is as high as 80 percent. While on this subject, it should be noted that a vastly important input to this development is being provided by what may be termed "the educational periphery—that is, education often for credit which is taking place through the surveillance of industries, the various proprietary institutions, correspondence courses, T.V., etc." Further elucidation of this topic is as follows: "In 1965 there were 57 million Americans in some form of education from pre-primary through graduate school. In that same year 44 million . . . engaged in education through one of the peripheral formats. In 1970 there were 63 million Americans on the periphery. . . ." Thus, by concentrating only on the educational core of formal institutions, it would be very easy to miss the salient fact that education has become a national resource and "is thus too important to be left entirely to the educators at the core." By 1976 the projection is that 150 million Americans will be taking part in some sort of formal educational experience for which "credit" may be given, and this proportion of formal educational involvement "has never been achieved by any other society in the world."

This evidence prompts the researchers to surmise that "we are clearly approaching a proletarian era in American education," for just as 40 years ago the junior high school evolved as a bridging institution to facilitate the expansion from an eight-year educational program to one taking twelve years, so the 1960s witnessed the dramatic advances made by the phe-

Another societal trend has been the growing tendency of industries and other institutions to certify their own brands of instruction to meet their own needs, with these certifications increasingly being handled independently of the college or university.

nomenon known as the junior college, which is "moving us now from a high school diploma for everyone toward a college degree for everyone." Concomitant with this has been another societal trend—the growing tendency of industries and other institutions to certify their own brands of instruction to meet their own needs, with these certifications increasingly being handled independently of the college or university.

This egalitarianizing of education indicates that such questions as open admissions and even open graduation may soon dominate faculty meetings throughout the country. In fact, it may be forecast that a major task of higher education in the 1970s will be to develop more flexible and adaptive means of meeting the needs of large segments of the population as these needs appear while abandoning the rigid, arbitrary, and depersonalized means which are all too frequently currently employed.

A review of the nature of the changes which have taken place reveals the following major conclusions:

■ More students graduate and more continue their formal education in graduate school, to the extent that overproduction of Ph.D.'s could become a national malaise. Additionally, they have gained more control over institutional policy making and in academic decision making, while they also wield greater power over the creation and maintenance of social regulations.

■ In general, the faculty involved in the formal higher educational process are teaching fewer hours, demonstrating a heightened interest in research, and expressing a slightly increased interest in teaching. Furthermore, they are much less loyal to their institution, obtain tenure at a younger age, speak out more frequently on issues of national policy, and support students who oppose the administration. These trends are strongest in large institutions offering advanced degrees, regressing in a linear fashion to the point where small colleges offering the B.A. do not significantly reflect these trends at all.

■ The vast numerical increase in college students has been handled by the public sector through the construction of many new community colleges and by expansion of existing public colleges and universities, often to enormous size.

■ The greatest increase in institutions awarding the Ph.D. degree is in public institutions, especially in state colleges which have been transformed into state universities. This trend is even more marked in degree programs than in institutions.

■ Almost all higher education is now conducted coeducationally.

■ In the opinion of the presidents consulted by the study, the most important changes in their institutions, in order of magnitude, have been increases in faculty and student power, changes in academic programs, and changes in the composition of the student body.

■ The presidents further estimate that by 1975 more than 20,000 faculty will be employed solely to undertake research in over 300 institutions.

■ One of the most important factors in describing an institution is its size. The larger the institution, the more diverse, alienated, and transient is its student body; the more research oriented its faculty, the lower the degree of loyalty granted to it and the poorer the network of communication within.

■ Geographical region and control exert relatively insignificant effects in determining what changes will occur in institutions.

■ In general, the degree of institutional diversity in American higher education is decreasing, due partially to the pervasive nature of a single-status system. This system has at its apex the prestigious university offering a wide selection of graduate programs and preoccupied with research. So few alternative models to this system are now functioning that they may be regarded as exceptions to this conclusion.

Perhaps the depressing reality of this last conclusion can be altered, and remedy of another glaring fault in American higher education would contribute to that alteration. The fault is to be found in the general area of communications. As identified by the study there is "no single comprehensive information network for higher education in America."

Only because higher education involved a relatively minor percentage of the population and was, to a degree, "sacrosanct," could it survive with such a slow-paced and casual information network. With the changes identified in this study has come a concomitant requirement that objective information concerning what is going on be available to everyone on the campus and indeed beyond it. Only if and when both those involved with higher education and those who are not directly involved are regularly and reliably informed can there be realistic expectation that the reasons for the changes identified within this study will be understood and the changes themselves supported.

(1971)

The larger the institution, the more diverse, alienated, and transient is its student body; the more research oriented its faculty, the lower the degree of loyalty granted it and the poorer the network of communication within.

CHANGE IN EDUCATIONAL POLICY: Self Studies in Selected Colleges and Universities
DWIGHT R. LADD

In the atmosphere of pressure for change which developed in the early 1960s, a number of colleges and universities undertook wide-ranging reviews of educational policies and processes. A tremendous amount of energy and time went into these studies, in institutions as diverse and generally influential as Duke, Berkeley, Swarthmore, and Michigan State.

The studies, in one way or another, were responses to several striking and rapid developments in the general environment of higher education: "The Academic Revolution," with its emphasis on professionalism and meritocracy; the knowledge explosion, which seemed to be destroying confidence in the traditional, humane ideal of the educated man; the compound growth in student population, which brought with it so many qualitative changes as well as the obvious quantitative ones; and the rapid development of the student movement, with its challenges to the traditional values and structures underlying educational policy making.

These environmental factors gave rise to the several educational policy issues with which the studies were concerned: teaching and advising, independent study, freshmen seminars, pass-fail grading, the nature of general education and the balance between it and specialized education, and the shifting to the academic departments of the balance of power in decisions about faculty and curriculum.

Reports which formed the principal base for this study were:

■ *Education at Berkeley:* Select Committee on Education, Academic Senate, University of California, Berkeley, March 1966.

■ *Interim Report and Recommendations:* Special Committee on Educational Principles, Brown University, April 1969.

■ *The Reforming of General Education: The Columbia College Experience in its National Setting:* Daniel Bell, February 1966.

■ *Varieties of Learning Experience:* Subcommittee on Curriculum, Undergraduate Faculty Council, Duke University, March 1968.

■ *Report:* Committee on Academic Innovation and Development, Academic Senate, University of California, Los Angeles, November 1967.

■ *Improving Undergraduate Education:* Committee on Undergraduate Education, Michigan State University, October 1967.

■ *Toward Unity from Diversity:* University-wide Educational Policies Committee, University of New Hampshire, February 1967.

■ *Study of Education at Stanford:* Steering Committee of The Study of Education at Stanford, Stanford University, November 1968 *et seq.*

■ *Critique of a College:* Commission on Educational Policy, Swarthmore College, November 1967.

■ *Undergraduate Instruction in Arts and Sciences:* Presidential Advisory Committee on Undergraduate Instruction, Faculty of Arts and Sciences, University of Toronto, July 1967.

■ *The Study of Educational Policies and Programs at Wesleyan,* Wesleyan University, May 1968.

On the whole, there was a great deal of similarity in the solutions proposed by the several studies: greater rewards for teaching as opposed to other professional activities, smaller classes, lessening or elimination of curriculum requirements except for the major, student-designed majors, deemphasis of grades and various organizational structures intended to affect the hegemony of departments over curriculum and teaching. In the context of the extreme changes in the environment of higher education, these policy proposals, on the whole, seem neither very imaginative nor very radical. Real change in educational policy will require significant reallocation of resources, and at present resource allocation is controlled, primarily, by those who most benefit from the status quo.

Real change in educational policy will require significant reallocation of resources, and at present resource allocation is controlled, for the most part, by those who most benefit from the status quo.

For the most part, changes proposed and generally accepted were those which would have little effect on the behavior patterns and value systems of most individual faculty members. Conversely, those areas where little concrete change was proposed, and even less generally accepted, were areas where professorial behavior patterns and value systems would have been significantly affected had consequential change occurred.

Except for student-initiated changes at Brown, all proposals were developed and acted upon collegially, as the academy has conducted its business for so long. *Collegiality* assumes that everyone in the community will have a voice in all of its important decisions, and that these decisions will reflect a broad base of acceptance. This, in turn, implies a general willingness to devote time and energy to the often tedious process of achieving such general acceptance. Collegiality as a system of self-government is well-described by the term, "community of scholars." The model looms large in the rhetoric of the academy and was—ritualistically, at any rate—followed in all of these studies.

There seems, at this time, a consensus that such things as lessening requirements and student course loads, deemphasizing grades and reducing the size of classes—all of which were proposed and generally accepted—have educational merit. It is also true that these are changes which can be made without much effect on what most faculty members do or on how they do it. Conversely, if some of the problems of teaching, advising, and control over the content and structure of education are indeed as great as several of the studies state them to be, it would be hard to deny educational merit to proposals intended to resolve them. Nevertheless, these matters were mostly dealt with in a most tentative fashion. The results of these studies do suggest, however, that the conditions necessary for effective functioning of the collegial systems were not

Faculty members seem not to have primary concern with the college or university and its character, value, and goals; educational policy making has been fragmented by departmental power, and it seems structurally impossible for large numbers of people collectively to consider basic educational policies.

present in most institutions. Faculty members seem not to have primary concern with the college or university and its character, value, and goals; educational policy making has been fragmented by departmental power; and it seems structurally impossible for large numbers of people collectively to consider basic educational policies. Consequently, there is a need to attempt to re-create the conditions which permit a collegial system to function or to accept that some institutions are not and cannot be collegial, and to search for new ways of decision making in such institutions.

The several moves toward cluster colleges and satellite colleges around the country should be encouraged. New institutions, Santa Cruz or Hampshire, for example, can readily develop in ways which support collegiality. Buffalo's example suggests that an expanding institution can channel its growth through small, relatively homogeneous units. Michigan State has created such units in an institution which is neither new nor any longer expanding rapidly. In short, situations in which collegiality is viable are regularly brought into being; more should be encouraged.

Ultimately, however, the organizational and financial problems involved in any such wholesale restructuring of our educational institutions are enormous. The answer to this problem lies, it is suggested, in the development of a system akin to the responsible government of the parliamentary democracies. Utilizing such a system would recognize that, after appropriate consultation, someone must have the power to make decisions. Those affected would select the person or persons to whom the power of decision would be granted and could, with due cause, take back that power.

(1970)

GRADUATE AND PROFESSIONAL EDUCATION, 1980: A Survey of Institutional Plans
LEWIS B. MAYHEW

Graduate and postbachelor professional training will remain the fastest growing segment of American higher education, expanding at an even more rapid rate than junior college enrollments.

In 1969, about 400 institutions responded to a questionnaire asking how many degrees of various types were awarded in 1968 and how many they expected to award in 1980. In applying those rates of increase to the total degrees awarded in 1968 by all institutions, estimates were obtained of 344,000 master's degrees and 67,519 doctor's degrees to be awarded in 1980. Still another projection resulted in an estimate of 77,000 doctorates.

This report on the future of graduate and professional education, up to 1980, is an interpretation based on campus visits and interviews and the examination of planning documents as well as analyses of the questionnaire responses.

Not all institutions which now offer or anticipate offering postbachelor's degree work will expand in similar ways. There are some "developed" institutions such as certain prestigious private universities with a reasonably complete range of professional schools and a large graduate enrollment. These universities do not anticipate adding new schools or making any significant increase in undergraduate enrollment. Their graduate enrollments will expand, but much more slowly than previously. The public-developed institutions typically will accept a steady and substantial increase in graduate and professional enrollments, at least on the parent campus.

"Developing" private institutions are typically changing from a local or regional undergraduate clientele to a national or at least a transregional one. While they may seek some expansion of undergraduate enrollment, a substantial increase in graduate work is anticipated.

"Developing" public institutions are quite heterogeneous, but they all expect a rapid expansion of new professional schools, master's-level work, and relatively quick entry into doctoral work. While hoping for increased federal support, they are inclined to assume that state appropriations will provide not only for the educational programs but for faculty research as well.

If all American colleges and universities proceed with their plans for expansion, the first and most obvious implication is the possibility of an oversupply of potential college teachers holding the doctorate.

If all American colleges and universities proceed with their plans for expansion, the first and most obvious implication is the possibility of an oversupply of potential college teachers holding the doctorate. Already institutions are reporting heavy, unsolicited applications from recent Ph.D. awardees, even in fields for which no applicants could be found as late as 1966 or 1967. Given the continued high regard for the Ph.D. in comparison with other types of doctorates, this phenomenon of surplus is likely to foreclose any widespread adoption of special kinds of doctoral programs for the preparation of college teachers unless, of course, the expanding capacity for graduate training is modified for such a purpose.

Developed institutions of high prestige, not expanding at a fast rate, should be able to maintain experienced faculties, but this may result in an even wider gulf than now exists between holders of "good doctorates" (i.e., from prestige institutions), and holders of "mediocre doctorates" (those produced by the lesser-known developing institutions).

Within the developing institutions, aspirations to increase graduate education will also produce internal tensions for at least part of the decade of the 1970s because of their mix of faculties. It seems likely that graduate instruction will be offered by many relatively young and inexperienced Ph.D.'s and by older senior faculty, appointed when institutions concentrated on teaching, who have done little or no research after they completed their own theses toward the end of World War II. Block voting by these two groups on such matters as representation on academic senates, with the resultant power struggle between constituencies, is already reported in several cases.

There may also be tensions with statewide coordinating agencies. These have been created to achieve a better, more economical deployment of state resources for higher education and to prevent unnecessary duplication of high-cost programs. But once the virus of graduate and advanced professional work strikes an institution, it will oppose efforts to contain its ambitions, whether the efforts are made by the state's senior institutions or by a coordinating body. By 1969 there were a number of cases of controversy which could be prelude to serious problems in the future.

But once the virus of graduate and advanced professional work strikes an institution, it will oppose efforts to contain its ambitions, whether the efforts are made by the state's senior institutions or by a coordinating body.

Graduate and professional work is presumed to be considerably more expensive than undergraduate education. Many of the hopes of developing institutions to offer or expand graduate work are based on the expectation that the federal and state government and philanthropy will support their expanded programs. But financial support of the magnitude needed has begun to weaken. Federal appropriations are curtailed, states question escalating budgets, and private institutions find themselves forced into deficit spending or retrenchment. Many factors, including student protests, are involved in this "end of a bull market."

There are serious implications for federal policy on science and research. Assuming that the production of doctorates proceeds at expected rates, federal agencies must review and revise plans for research programs and criteria for awarding support. Revised plans could curtail trainee support, distribute available research more broadly, or try to redirect energy from the production of Ph.D.'s to other professional fields, where it is perhaps more critically needed, such as medicine. The only certainty is that the policy will change.

(1970)

CHANGES IN UNIVERSITY ORGANIZATION, 1964–1971
EDWARD GROSS and PAUL GRAMBSCH

The distinctive features of American institutions of higher learning—their size, range of quality, diversity, and high degree of autonomy—have been subjected to increased research attention in recent years. Although universities comprise a scant 6 percent of such institutions, this study is concerned solely with them.

This limitation is less restrictive than it might appear, for universities contain within them much of the variety offered by the remaining institutions. For example, whereas most liberal arts and comprehensive colleges give no more than a B.A. and M.A., universities award these and also a variety of doctorates. Many also offer the A.A., frequently thought to be solely within the province of the community college.

Ben-David[1] described three strategies that institutions of higher education variously employ to attract students—the cultivation of prestige, the establishment of a service tradition, and the nurturing of an emphasis on research. Universities seek to employ all three of these. Furthermore, at a university, it is possible to find all the student types identified by Trow[2] as existing in the various segments of higher education—those with a strong academic interest, the fun lovers or "collegiate" students, and those oriented to occupational careers.

Universities are a microcosm of the larger set of institutions of which they constitute only one type. They enroll about 30 percent of all students in higher education, include most of the celebrated centers of student unrest, train most of the scientists as well as a high proportion of all American professionals, and may thus reasonably be expected to shed light on the broader category of all institutions from which they are selected.

In all these senses, then, universities are a microcosm of the larger set of institutions of which they constitute only one type. They enroll about 30 percent of all students in higher education, include most of the celebrated centers of student unrest, train most of the scientists as well as a high proportion of all American professionals, and may thus reasonably be expected to shed light on the broader category of all institutions from which they are selected.

Despite their obvious importance, universities were strangely neglected as objects of serious study until the outbreak of the student "troubles" in 1964. Institutional and general histories to the contrary, this neglect was partially due to the fact that universities did not attract much public attention until World War II, when government turned to them for help, and shortly after, when the universities experienced massive growth in enrollments. Another reason stems from the fact that organizational development has only recently become a subject of scientific interest to social and behavioral scientists. For all these reasons, it was not until even more recently that both the interest and the methodology necessary to study universities empirically have existed.

Such considerations led the authors to undertake a study of some 68 universities in 1964. At that time there was no inkling of the great crises that were about to convulse those institutions. Their interests were largely scientific, seeking to describe the social structure of universities

[1] Joseph Ben-David, *American Higher Education,* McGraw-Hill Book Company, New York, 1972.
[2] Martin Trow, "Reflections on the Transition from Mass to Universal Higher Education," *Daedalus,* vol. 99, Winter 1970, pp. 1–42.

in a way that would furnish illustration of one more type of organization, the university, to the burgeoning literature on formal organizations. Events and crises since then led to a decision to replicate the study in 1971, to see whether significant changes in the university's social structures had occurred.

This study therefore is an analysis of change in the organization and power structure of American universities between 1964 and 1971. It is based on replies to a lengthy questionnaire obtained from 7,200 persons in 1964 and 4,500 persons in 1971, in 68 universities. It was felt that such replication would shed light on whether the major events of the 1960s had merely shaken American universities or whether they had led to structural change. The findings tend to support the latter supposition, for there are signs of genuine changes, some startling and all worthy of close examination.

Very little change was detected in either the goals or the values of universities or the persons in them. Universities remained, in 1971, what they had fundamentally been in 1964: institutions oriented to research and scholarly pursuits, set up to provide comfortable homes for professors and administrators, and according a distinctly secondary position to students and their needs.

Above this fundamental level, however, important changes had taken place. Professors and administrators both felt (in 1971) a stronger congruence between the actual emphases in their universities and the kind of emphases they felt proper. Universities had grown more stratified to the point of fragmentation. Private universities—already differing from public institutions in 1964—were even more distinctive in terms of their goals; highly "productive" universities were increasingly differentiating themselves from less "productive" universities, and the more prestigious universities were even more distinctive than they had been in 1964. In essence, distinct "leagues" were being carved out, with decreasing competition between them.

Private universities—already differing from public institutions in 1964—were even more distinctive in terms of their goals in 1971; highly "productive" universities were increasingly differentiating themselves from less "productive" universities, and the more prestigious universities were even more distinctive than they had been in 1964.

As regards the power structure, this study discerned little change between 1964 and 1971. Higher administration was still dominant, with professors occupying a middle position, and students and various "outsiders" (parents, alumni, citizens of the state) at the bottom. Despite this retention of the status quo, everyone, except departmental chairmen, felt he had more power than ever, reflecting a growing confidence in the ability to take control over his own professional life. However, with regard to "outside" power holders (as personified by regents, legislators, and citizens) and "insiders" (as personified by chairmen, deans, faculty, and students) an ominous cleavage had taken place. This situation has very much affected the goals of universities.

The power struggle between "insiders" and "outsiders" showed evidence of a shift from the national to the local level, with concomitantly strong implications for the internal structure of universities.

The power struggle between "insiders" and "outsiders" showed evidence of a shift from the national to the local level, with concomitantly strong implications for the internal structure of universities. Partly as a consequence of this battle, administrators and faculty members were seen to be forming an increasingly cohesive alliance, and this in turn resulted in the resolution of many of the mutual antagonisms and suspicions which traditionally have marked interaction between these two groups.

Overall, this study effectively countermands the conventional wisdom that universities, as human organizations, are capable of change only at a glacial pace. In the light of these findings, such conventional wisdom, so frequently mounted as an accusation, is both inaccurate and unfair. As Gross and Grambsch stress, given that this study covers a scant seven years, and given the existence of some powerful forces that would be expected to resist change, the results of this study give impressive and optimistic evidence of the adaptive and robust character of America's universities.

(1974)

AN INVENTORY OF ACADEMIC INNOVATION AND REFORM
ANN M. HEISS

Pressures for reform in colleges and universities in the United States have varied with the character of American society and with the intensity of demand for educated manpower or an informed citizenry. Current pressures began immediately after World War II, when a compelling need for space, personnel, educational facilities, and other resources was felt by colleges and universities that were faced with obligations to accommodate an enrollment that was expected to double in the 1960s.

In the 1960s there were new problems. The "new" students, and their large numbers, introduced a broader cultural diversity to the campuses. Some of the students began to complain of the impersonality of the instruction offered them, and then, as America's social and cultural unrest spread, many turned their campuses into centers of dissent, and sometimes, disruption. During the decade, academic development virtually came to a standstill as faculty, officers, and other campus personnel became preoccupied with the administration and resolution of protest.

The new discourse that emerged exposed the nature and intensity of student discontent with available academic programs. A number of influential institutions mounted self-studies to discover ways to adjust to the criticism. As implementation of the recommendations emanating from these self-studies began, the stage was set for widespread academic

It has become evident that the 1970s will find colleges and universities occupied with planning, implementing, and administering academic innovation, renewal, and reform.

change. It has become evident that the 1970s will find colleges and universities occupied with planning, implementing, and administering academic innovation, renewal, and reform. This inventory describes the most recent characteristics and the current pulse of that action.

Although, conceptually, *innovation* and *reform* have common elements, and the terms are often used interchangeably, this inventory gives them distinct meanings. *Innovation* means that a contemplated change is new for a particular institution or for particular individuals. *Reform* applies to those changes which an institution might introduce to redirect its goals, reorganize its structure, or revise or eliminate part of its tradition.

For the most part, this compilation lists innovations or changes which, during the past six years, have been adopted by accredited institutions, proposed by members of the academic community, and critically reviewed by persons knowledgeable about higher education. In a few cases the time span has been increased to include changes introduced during the early 1960s. In several other cases the change cited has been approved, but has not as yet been implemented.

Originally this inventory was undertaken as an appendix to the Commission report *Reform on Campus: Changing Students, Changing Academic Programs,* which was published in June 1972. Some institutional changes are not recorded here. And some that are listed may have been altered or abandoned since the list was compiled. Given the extreme state of flux and the extensive scope of higher education today, such discrepancies are unavoidable.

Chapter 1 collates new innovative institutions and describes them under generic subheadings: Four-year colleges and universities; New graduate institutions; New two-year colleges; and External-degree colleges. In Chapter 2 the inquiry moves inside the institutions, and is concerned with such phenomena as cluster colleges, federated colleges, mini-colleges, optive colleges, and the "extended university" of California.

Innovative changes wrought by academic subunits within conventional colleges and universities are next described. There are many of these, including living-learning units; work-study off campus; courses by newspaper; and courses for minority students. Experimentation is currently under way with the internship and the apprenticeship, or practicum (which illustrates that not all change must involve new ideas); field study programs; study abroad; and even traveling campuses, which are considered under the heading, "Afloat Colleges."

Experimentation is currently under way with the internship and the apprenticeship, or practicum (which illustrates that not all change must involve new ideas); field study programs; study abroad; and even traveling campuses, the "Afloat Colleges."

Procedural innovations are next considered, and provide examples of ways in which institutions have adjusted to the rapid increases in numbers of students. There have been changes in the academic calendar; changes in methods, as well as in time blocks, for teaching and learning; innovations in admissions and in counseling; structural changes in the alignment of disciplines; and changes in general education. Additionally, colleges and universities are experimenting with new degrees and changes in course and degree requirements, as well as new fields of study, variations in grading systems, and course-credit policies. Policies are also currently being subjected to experiment and evaluation.

The inventory concludes with four case studies of institutions which have recently engaged in the agonizing exercise of detailed self-study. Although all are in the Northeastern region of the United States, they are sufficiently varied institutionally to render their findings and recommendations significant to those seeking a better understanding of change on the modern American campus.

(1973)

AMERICAN LEARNED SOCIETIES IN TRANSITION: The Impact of Dissent and Recession
HARLAND G. BLOLAND and SUE M. BLOLAND

Primarily an in-depth portrayal of the actors and events of the recent caucus movement in American learned societies, this report also details the history and traditional functions of the societies and speculates on the possible effects of the present academic recession upon their character.

Learned societies in the United States have always been closely related in values and orientation to the major universities, and until the caucus movement of the late 1960s they stubbornly clung to an ivory-tower commitment to "the advancement of knowledge for its own sake." In following their commitment, the societies played a critical role in formalizing the academic disciplines and establishing new ones. And as disciplines developed theory and methodology, academicians began to identify themselves professionally with their specialties rather than with their academic institutions. For their members, learned societies provided national career systems in which recognition (and advancement) could be secured through publication in association journals, awards, and association officerships. By allocating these rewards to those who performed research in tacitly sanctioned areas—and research, or "scholarly accomplishment," was the main criterion for recognition—the societies were able to wield increasing control on the directions and emphases of their respective disciplines.

Learned-society leadership generally used this power to bolster the status quo. The governance structure of most societies comprised committees of eminent scholars who nominated other such scholars for officerships. Annual business meetings ostensibly provided opportunities for the memberships at large to participate in governance procedures, but members rarely attended, and control rested with council officials. This structure survived even during the unprecedented, postwar expansion in membership and learned-society activity.

During the postwar period, increasing federal support for scientific research and the employment of scholars by nonacademic institutions sowed fears within the academic community that the imposition of lay standards would impinge upon research autonomy. By the mid-1960s, learned societies, particularly those in the social sciences, had begun to take steps to defend their interests to government. Internally, these societies also began to formulate codes of ethics for their members who were funded by nonacademic agencies. Learned societies in all disciplines grew dramatically, and the formerly homogeneous memberships splintered into groups with diverse, though not generally hostile, interests and specialties.

Under the added burden of federal relations and the demands of a highly diversified membership, association administration became more complex and required more organizational skill. The "eminent-scholar" criterion remained intact, however, as society leadership garnered increasing power. In the late 1960s, the traditional governance and reward structures came under heavy attack from newly formed radical caucuses. Because recognition devolved exclusively upon "value-neutral" research —that is, research detached from political and social issues—radical activists saw the established reward structure as constraining social criticism and supporting the dominant ideological interests of American society. In addition, women, minority groups, and members from small or nonprestigious institutions were severely underrepresented in positions of authority. These constituents and the radical activists thus developed a two-fold objective: to democratize the governance structure, and to focus learned-society attention and resources upon the country's political and social issues.

There were several groups of participants within the caucus movement. Radical activists, "the most visible and vociferous dissidents," were committed above all to political activism, a stand that sometimes conflicted with their pursuit of an academic career. Much activist strategy took shape at meetings of the New University Conference, a national organization of academic radicals. Although less militant than the activists, radical intellectuals also urged more consideration of social issues in aca-

In the late 1960s, the traditional governance and reward structures came under heavy attack from newly formed radical caucuses. Because recognition devolved exclusively upon "value-neutral" research—that is, research detached from political and social issues—radical activists saw the established reward structure as constraining social criticism and supporting the dominant ideological interests of American society.

demic research. But in relying upon the established scholastic mode, they stressed the importance of developing a theoretical foundation for social programs within an insular academic setting. The setting itself, according to this view, was to be altered to accommodate research in radical theory. Left-liberal reformers, more closely akin to the radical intellectuals than to the activists, possessed a narrower vision than either radical group of the range of possible (or desirable) reform. They directed their major energies toward creating special committees that would investigate political and social issues and introduce them into learned-society affairs.

Another category of caucus participants was the "disinherited"—women, blacks, minority ethnic groups, and members of the academic proletariat. These members were more concerned with alleviating inequalities in the academic career system than in restructuring it, although many of these members were also committed to radical activism.

Early coalitions of these groups in caucus activity were stabilized by widespread antiwar sentiment, general dissatisfaction with the elitist governance of learned societies, and the success of the simple strategy of attending business meetings en masse to affect important policy decisions. Later, as radical activists gradually fell away from caucus activity and began to organize independently, the caucus movement was largely directed by those who remained willing to work within learned-society channels.

The general history of the caucus movement is illustrated by three detailed case studies. The American Political Science Association, the Modern Language Association of America, and the American Physical Society were chosen to represent the social sciences, the humanities, and the natural sciences, respectively. Although the caucuses in these societies had separate and varied histories, they shared several basic characteristics. Each was founded in 1967 or 1968, at the time of massive national demonstrations against the Vietnam War, race riots, and the Democratic convention in Chicago; each criticized the governance of its learned society and the dominant theoretical emphasis of its discipline; and each attacked the concept of "value-neutral" research and, particularly in the sciences, insisted upon moral responsibility for the results of research. In all three learned societies, radical caucuses successfully wedged themselves into "legitimate" society activity: caucus panels were incorporated into society business meetings and financial resources were allocated to caucus activity. The caucuses were most successful in generating wider participation in learned societies and in chipping away the traditional insularity by bringing social issues into open discussion.

A waning commitment to activism and the unfavorable job market of the 1970s prompted a shift in radical attention from reforming the learned societies to organizing faculty unions.

A waning commitment to activism and the unfavorable academic job market of the 1970s prompted a shift in radical attention from reforming the learned societies to organizing faculty unions. "Competing for membership from the same general population, unions represent egalitarian norms that are almost diametrically opposed to the professional and scholarly norms and values of disciplinary associations." And because untenured faculty, women, and minority groups find greater advantage in joining faculty unions to improve conditions of their employment, learned-society membership may well revert to the eminent scholars and scientists from the nation's elite universities. The implications of such a trend include fewer learned-society activities, partial dismantling of governance structures, and a return to research as the exclusive professional commitment of learned-society membership.

(1974)

POLITICAL IDEOLOGIES OF GRADUATE STUDENTS: Crystallization, Consistency, and Contextual Effects
MARGARET A. FAY and JEFF A. WEINTRAUB

This report is based on an analysis of a random sample of approximately 2,000 of the 32,963 completed questionnaires from graduate students that were part of the comprehensive Survey of Faculty and Student Opinion conducted jointly by the Carnegie Commission on Higher Education and the American Council on Education in 1969. Specifically, the analysis identifies some factors that tend to influence the political ideologies of this sample of graduate students.

The respondents in the original survey were asked to characterize themselves as politically "left," "liberal," "middle-of-the-road," "moderately conservative," or "strongly conservative." The distribution of the sample on this item was as follows: liberal, 40 percent; middle-of-the-road, 27 percent; moderately conservative, 23 percent; left, 7 percent; strongly conservative, 3 percent. Compared with the national population, both left-of-center categories were disproportionately large, there being twice as many leftists as strong conservatives. Liberals were by far the largest single group, and together with the leftists made up nearly a majority.

The self-labels were examined to discover what ideologies they signified, to what extent there was uniformity in the meaning attached to them, and what conditions altered or influenced this meaning.

The basic technique used in the study was to analyze the relationship between an individual's political self-label and his or her response to 33 selected attitude items that dealt with four broad areas of opinion: (1) national political and social affairs; (2) university controversies; (3) the unionization of university personnel; and (4) the status of minority groups in the education system. The researchers then tested the influence on these relationships of each of their major variables—political interest and academic context.

For each attitude, the responses were divided into "agree" or "disagree," and the "left" position was identified as that position which was taken by a higher percentage of left-of-center individuals than of right-of-center individuals (conversely, the "right" position was designated as that position which was taken by a higher percentage of right-of-center individuals than of left-of-center individuals). The correlations between the political self-characterization item and the set of attitude items demonstrated that the five political categories formed an ordinal scale.

For purposes of analysis, the sample was classified into four political categories: left, liberal, middle-of-the-road, and conservative. In the first part of this report, respondents were ranged on a scale according to their expressed interest in national politics (high, medium, and low). It was found that *ideological consistency* was a function of the degree of interest in politics. The hypothesis was that greater interest in politics produced clearer *crystallization* of attitudes, and that, therefore, in each political category those persons most interested in politics were also the most ideologically consistent. This hypothesis was confirmed both by analysis of the sample as a whole and by a more detailed examination of individual political categories.

The hypothesis was that greater interest in politics produced clearer *crystallization* of attitudes, and that persons most interested in politics were also the most ideologically consistent.

A supplementary hypothesis was developed during the testing of this central hypothesis to account for certain anomalies. It appeared that on certain issues, the "left" position coincided with the "sophisticated" view, and that therefore, on those issues, greater interest in politics increased the probability that persons in all political categories would support the "left" position. In the conservative category, this "political sophistication effect" resulted in canceling or reducing the relationship between political interest and crystallization. Further analysis supported this supplementary hypothesis, although it was not possible to test it as rigorously or confirm it as decisively as the central hypothesis.

The second part of the study examined variations in the meaning of the political label in relation to the respondent's social context, in this case his or her academic department. The findings here suggest that, for any political self-label, the ideology associated with it varied in conformity with the ideological complexion of the student's academic department, so that individuals in different departments who adopted the same political label could not be regarded as necessarily holding the same views.

The item on the questionnaire discussing "Department in which you are studying" was tabulated with the political self-characterization item. Subtracting the percentage of right-of-center respondents from the percentage of left-of-center respondents generated a "Political Complexion Statistic" for each of the 71 "department" response categories provided on the questionnaire. The researchers then developed a ten-category "political complexion" scale of academic departments, which ranked from the most liberal to most conservative departments as follows: (1) social sciences, history, philosophy; (2) psychology, social work; (3) humanities, fine arts; (4) law, medicine; (5) economics, mathematics; (6) education; (7) physical sciences, biological sciences; (8) health fields, home economics, library science, physical education; (9) business administration, educational administration; (10) engineering, agriculture, forestry.

For purposes of further analysis, these ten categories were collapsed into three: "Very liberal" (1, 2, and 3), "Moderately liberal" (4, 5, 6, and 7), and "Conservative" (8, 9, and 10). The relationship between this three-category scale of academic departments and a set of 25 selected attitude items was examined, holding constant the individual's political self-characterization. A *contextual effect* pattern became evident in a majority of the cases for all four political categories; that is, the relationship between most attitudes and a given political self-label varied systematically according to academic context, showing that this relationship was affected by the prevailing ideology in a given department. Further examination showed that the effect operated most frequently for liberals and middle-of-the-roaders, less often for leftists, and least of all for conservatives.

The relationship between most attitudes and a given political self-label varied systematically according to academic context, showing that this relationship was affected by the prevailing ideology in a given department.

Extensive and detailed statistical data are included, as well as a reproduction of the original questionnaire.

(1974)

ACADEMIC TRANSFORMATION: Seventeen Institutions Under Pressure
edited by DAVID RIESMAN and VERNE A. STADTMAN

American colleges and universities will remember the 1960s for a long time. Campus disruption, abandonment of traditions, and seemingly insatiable demands for change brought tension into the academic atmosphere, exposed serious weaknesses in campus policies and procedures, and aroused public suspicion where there had been acceptance and approval.

This study was undertaken to discern whether there were common elements in the crises experienced by hundreds of American colleges and universities between 1964 and 1971. In selecting institutions to be included, there was no effort to predetermine some master theme or grand design, for although the outward signs of the collegiate crises were similar, they did not share uniform causes and were not susceptible to uniform solutions. As can be seen from the following titles, the selection was made on the basis of variety, not similarities.

The 17 institutional accounts are titled:

■ "A Network of Antiochs" by Gerald Grant

■ "Berkeley in Crisis and Change" by Neil J. Smelser

■ "City College" by Nathan Glazer

■ "Federal City College" by Irene Tinker

■ "After the Bust: Student Politics at Harvard 1969–1972" by Marshall Meyer

■ "Change Despite Turmoil at MIT" by Benson Snyder

■ "Michigan Muddles Through: Luck, Nimbleness, and Resilience in Crisis" by Zelda F. Gamson

■ "Old Westbury I and Old Westbury II" by John A. Dunn, Jr.

■ "A Profile of the University of Pennsylvania" by David R. Goddard and Linda C. Koons

■ "Princeton in Crisis and Change" by Paul Sigmund

■ "Rutgers: The State University" by Richard P. McCormick

■ "San Francisco State College: A Tale of Mismanagement and Disruption" by Algo D. Henderson

■ "Stanford's Search for Solutions" by John Walsh

■ "Swarthmore Knocks on Wood" by Paul Mangelsdorf, Jr.

■ "Academic Change and Crisis—Canadian Style" by Jill Conway

■ "The Wesleyan Story: The Importance of Moral Capital" by Burton R. Clark

■ "The Champagne University in a Beer State: Notes on Wisconsin's Crisis" by Philip G. Altbach

It is now clear that what began at Berkeley in 1964 was a style of confrontation rather than a trend in institutional transformation.

The commonly accepted "beginning" of this period occurred at Berkeley in 1964. In planning this volume that date was used, although it is now clear that what began at Berkeley in 1964 was a style of confrontation rather than a trend in institutional transformation. Earlier, Zelda Gamson relates, the first tremors of rebellion had been heard at Michigan in the 1950s, and Goddard and Koons inform that the University of Pennsylvania had begun a self-study in 1953, some ten years before that exercise became generally fashionable. At Antioch, the existence of almost continuous innovation is traced by Gerald Grant, while Algo Henderson discovers the seeds of San Francisco State's problems in the Master Plan for Higher Education adopted by the State of California in 1960. According to Benson Snyder, MIT has been reforming for over a century, and Philip Altbach reminds that Madison was a center of student radicalism in the 1930s and was one of the few bastions of student radicalism during the apathetic 1950s.

Any notion of when the crisis began must depend largely on which aspects of the crisis are being traced. Despite this caveat, it is possible to construct a crude chronology from the vignettes themselves.

In 1964, there was the Free Speech Movement at Berkeley. The original issue was the extent to which campus facilities could be used for personal and political expression.

In 1965, Michigan students and faculty members held a "moratorium" to protest the war in Vietnam. Opposition to university contracts with the Department of Defense found students and faculty members in unaccustomed agreement at Pennsylvania that year. (It is evident that the "war issue" was alive on many of the campuses prior to this date, but these are the first events specifically mentioned in the vignettes.)

In 1966, disruption was again related mainly to the war issue. At Berkeley there was an incident involving the picketing of a marines' recruiting table. Wisconsin had its first disruptive protests—against selective service and recruiting efforts by Dow Chemical Company. At Michigan that year, students voted 2 to 1 against disclosing student's academic ranking to selective service offices. This was also the year at Michigan when an issue rooted in pre-1964 times emerged. It involved a protest of the transmission of the names of 65 students and several faculty members associated with radical groups to the House Committee on Un-American Activities.

In 1967, the war continued to be the focus of campus demonstrations. At Wisconsin, police were called to remove students from the Commerce Building, where a sit-in to protest recruiting by Dow Chemical Company was under way. A "small demonstration" against Dow recruiters occurred at Pennsylvania. At Rutgers, police were called to unblock the entrance to the ROTC building, and at Princeton, in October, there was a sit-in in the Institute for Defense Analysis.

At San Francisco State, the first violence associated with racial tensions occurred (although Algo Henderson suggests that racial tension had been building for some time prior to the incident).

In 1968, Martin Luther King was murdered and race-related incidents generated crises for several institutions represented in this volume. At Rutgers, demonstrations followed King's assassination. At Wesleyan, black students demanded that a Malcolm X and Martin Luther King "day of education" be held. A black student shot at a white student at Antioch. And at Princeton, students suggested that the university divest itself of investments in South African holdings.

In November of that year, San Francisco State's prolonged strike occurred in which demands for black studies and improvement of the lot of black students on campus were major issues. The student strike was followed in December by a faculty strike that was apparently supportive of the dissenting students, but overtly related to working conditions and other bread-and-butter issues.

Continued concern with the war was evidenced in 1968 by a confrontation with a Navy recruiter at Wesleyan and occupation of buildings and vigils in protest against ROTC and on behalf of sanctuary for an AWOL soldier at City College.

In 1969, the lot of the black student remained a key issue. The strike at San Francisco State continued until early spring, although there were mass arrests in January. In February, a black students' strike at Wisconsin grew to such dimensions that the police and national guard were called in. At the University of Pennsylvania, College Hall was occupied to protest the clearing of university-owned land for a city high school and other contested uses. The protesters claimed that the demolition would destroy the homes of the poor and the blacks in the area. In April, students seized the South Campus of City College to demand, among other things, proportional representation of blacks and Puerto Ricans in the state university system. The whole college was closed as a precaution against massive violence. Building occupations and demonstrations seeking concessions for black students also occurred at Berkeley, Princeton, Rutgers, Swarthmore, and Wesleyan.

At Harvard, in October 1969, the racial issue was raised in the form of protests that a number of blacks hired for work on the campus were paid as painter's helpers although they were doing the same work as journeymen. The dispute evolved eventually into demands for a 20 percent quota of "Third World" representatives among the workers employed on Harvard construction sites.

On the front of campus action directed against the war in 1969, the issue of institutional involvement in defense-related research was the focus of the first severe disturbances at Harvard, Stanford, and the Massachusetts Institute of Technology.

On the front of campus action directed against the war in 1969, the issue of institutional involvement in defense-related research was the focus of the first severe disturbances at Harvard, Stanford, and the Massachusetts Institute of Technology.

1969 was also a year for maverick issues—the bookstore sit-in at Michigan that resulted in the arrest of 107 persons, and the massive Berkeley riots that occurred when students and "street people" attempted to occupy university-owned land as a "People's Park."

1970 was a climactic year for major campus disturbances. The racial issue was critical at Michigan for the first three months of that year as the university sought to deal with demands of BAM—the Black Action Movement.

References to campus demonstrations following the Cambodian invasions in April 1970 are surprisingly subdued in these vignettes, either because the authors regarded them as occurrences too common at that time to note individually, or because, in contrast to the horror at Kent State and Jackson State, the demonstrations for the most part took non-violent forms. The trashing of Harvard Square in April 1970 was a notable exception. Protest of university engagement in defense-related activities persisted during this year, however—notably at Harvard and most shockingly at Wisconsin, where a saboteur's bomb exploded in the Army Mathematical Research Center and killed a postdoctoral fellow in physics.

Riesman is at pains to warn against explaining campus unrest in America in terms of one or two social or psychological variables, and also against assuming that such unrest is necessarily a thing of the past.

In the concluding chapter of the volume, Riesman is at pains to warn against explaining campus unrest in America in terms of one or two social or psychological variables, and also against assuming that such unrest is necessarily a thing of the past. In contrast to many other industrialized societies, America lacks one single dominant metropolitan center from which political and cultural movements spread to the provinces. Britain has London and France has Paris, but the United States has New York, San Francisco, Washington, and others, and compared with its counterparts in other parts of the world, American campus unrest reflected this difference.

From the institutional case studies, it is seen that changes in campus climates have occurred in such areas as residence, racial integration, and curriculum. These changes owe a lot to activism germinating from differing motivations. The first, the urge to purify the particular institution, has been an essential element of a great deal of activism, often with the consequence of increasing group isolation and conflict within the walls, even while hoping for a greater sense of community. The second motivation identified by Riesman is less frequently discussed. It is animosity, however concealed. After examining campus unrest from a perspective larger than these specific institutional vignettes, Riesman is satisfied that, on the larger, more radicalized campuses many activists have acted as geologists in prospecting for emotion-laden issues on which to mobilize and attack within the somewhat protected university precinct. As he points out, politicians generally proceed in this way—by prospecting for issues.

Neither the hopes of the anti-academic wing of the radical movement in the 1960s nor the fears of their opponents have proved predictive.

On balance however, although the wounding divisions within academic liberalism have not yet been healed, there are modest grounds for optimism concerning the future of American higher education. Neither the hopes of the antiacademic wing of the radical movement in the late 1960s nor the fears of their opponents have proved predictive. The curtailment of public support for higher education—resulting from public disenchantment and occurring while demands for higher education increase—has been less severe than was anticipated. This may well mean that the hostility generated toward the campus by the general public during the period with which this volume deals has abated. It is to be hoped that this partial restoration of faith and pride in our system of higher education will be accompanied by a corresponding thoughtfulness on the part of academics as they utilize the degrees of freedom permitted them by the larger society.

(1973)

EDUCATION AND POLITICS AT HARVARD*
SEYMOUR MARTIN LIPSET and DAVID RIESMAN

"Political Conflict at Harvard, 1636–1974" by Seymour Martin Lipset is concerned with the history of political controversies at Harvard from its founding in 1636 to the present. It deals with varying sources of conflict, including tensions with external political and religious authorities, and internal conflicts among the various estates of the universities, that is, students, faculty, administrators, and governing boards.

The early Harvard story has a number of unique elements stemming from the fact that its main governing board, the Corporation, was designed to be a faculty board, somewhat along the lines of those at the Oxford and Cambridge colleges, though modified by the existence of a second board, the Overseers, given review power on behalf of the religious and political authorities. Some of the struggles at Harvard up to 1825 revolved around the efforts of the faculty either to maintain or to regain a major element of control. And though the faculty lost their battles for membership on the Corporation, they secured more power over the internal life of the institution than was true for most other American colleges before the twentieth century.

The historical record suggests that politically relevant tensions are endemic to the nature of a university. The university's insistence on scholarship inevitably generates conflicts with extramural powers, who want colleges to advance their interests and sustain what they hold as their secular and religious truths. Fundamental to Harvard's emergence as a great university was the triumph of liberal religion within the Boston-area elite and religious establishment who controlled, for more than two centuries, one of its governing boards, the Overseers. Thus, the struggles over religion, which affected faculty, students, and governing boards, are a major aspect of Harvard's development. Equally important is the extent to which the commitment of the Puritans to education remained vital in Massachusetts during these religious changes.

The link to the state through the Overseers, however, also exposed Harvard to the uncertainties of shifting political fortunes in the state. Since the university was regarded as an expression of the Unitarian and afflu-

* This abstract was prepared by the authors before the final manuscript for the full report was completed.

ent classes, as an elitist school it was repeatedly under attack by Calvinist and allied populist Democratic forces who sought to get control of it so as to change the direction of its teaching. It was the Populist opponents who undercut the state financial contributions, which formed an important part of the university's income, thus forcing the university to become a private institution, in the contemporary sense of the term.

The final severance from any vestige of state control, which occurred at the end of the Civil War, almost coincided with the beginning of the successful effort under the presidency of Charles Eliot to make Harvard a great research and graduate institution by recruiting faculty from an international pool. This commitment to intellectual creativity carried with it an emphasis on academic freedom for both faculty and students and an enhancement of faculty power.

The atmosphere of the research university, open to ideas from everywhere, stimulated the involvement of segments of the faculty and students in critical, reform-oriented politics.

The atmosphere of the research university, open to ideas from everywhere, stimulated the involvement of segments of the faculty and students in critical reform-oriented politics. From the 1880s on, the Harvard faculty, particularly in economics, faced charges from alumni and others that they were fostering radical programs. And from the beginning of the twentieth century, some Harvard students were involved in the various waves of radical and other protest politics.

It is striking that every radical movement, from the Intercollegiate Socialist Society of the early part of the century down through the Students for a Democratic Society (SDS) of the late 1960s, had its largest chapter at Harvard.

It is striking that every radical student movement, from the Intercollegiate Socialist Society of the early part of the century down through the Students for a Democratic Society (SDS) of the late 1960s, had its largest chapter at Harvard. Innovative intellectual tendencies seem to have begun frequently among undergraduates exposed at Harvard to a free, stimulating, and intellectually critical atmosphere.

The image of Harvard as encouraging liberal social tendencies was reversed during the 1920s, when the school attempted to segregate black students and to set limits on the number of Jews it would admit. Although these policies occasioned considerable internal controversy and official reaffirmation of egalitarian principles, discrimination remained as unofficial policy until World War II.

During the McCarthy period of the early fifties, Harvard was the Wisconsin Senator's leading symbolic target in his campaign against intellectual dissidents and Communists. Reaction to his charges helped to politicize faculty at Harvard and other leading schools, who became involved in politics on an unprecedentedly large scale. Such involvements helped pave the way for the growing wave of political protest on American campuses in the 1960s.

Harvard was deeply involved in the protests through a number of student-based movements—TOCSIN, an antiwar group of the early sixties, the Maoist May 2nd movement, founded at Harvard, and finally, the SDS. The groups helped stimulate a growing wave of incidents of civil disobedience, culminating in a take-over of the administration building in the spring of 1969. This incident, which resulted in police being called by the administration to retake the building, led to a massive student strike and the repudiation of the administration by the faculty.

As at other universities, these events culminated in the ultimate resignation of many administrators, including the president and the dean of faculty, and the enactment of a number of policies favored by the student militants. It also led to a serious split in faculty ranks and the formation of two formally organized political parties, termed liberals and conservatives.

As campuses quieted across the country, Harvard also gradually entered the postcrisis "calm." By 1973, political controversy had almost disappeared among faculty and students. Faculty meetings, once large mass meetings, once again had difficulty in assembling a quorum and were frequently called off.

As noted in studies of faculty behavior generally, there is a strong correlation between scholarly creativity and eminence and a propensity for supporting antitraditional positions in other areas of life.

The more than three-century history of Harvard suggests that there is an inherent relationship between the conditions that make for academic excellence and political controversy. As noted in studies of faculty behavior generally, there is a strong correlation between scholarly creativity and eminence and a propensity for supporting antitraditional positions in other areas of life. Hence the involvement of Harvard in successive waves of political protest may be expected to recur in the future.

The second part of this book, "Educational Reform at Harvard College: Meritocracy and Its Adversaries," is a personal essay in which David Riesman focuses on the rise of meritocratic values in undergraduate education, in America in general and at Harvard in particular. It begins with a brief review of the "genteel" Harvard of the 1920s, when the author was a student there, and then takes a longer look at Harvard after 1950, when he returned as a teacher. *Meritocracy* is defined here as educational or occupational selection by some more or less formal process, based on judgments as to qualifications. It is distinct from historically earlier forms of selection such as lineage, patronage, or the personal impressions of evaluators.

In the 1920s Harvard was not overapplied and remained relatively open to virtually all applicants. When the author arrived at Harvard in 1927, President Lowell had been edging toward more demanding admission standards, hoping to recruit forceful, intelligent young men who would take part in the major institutions of American life. The Harvard Houses, for example, enhanced the possibility of students to participate in social and intellectual life without the need to join either a Final Club or one of Harvard's rather low-status fraternities. In addition, the Houses provided an atmosphere in which adults could give support to students' intellectual and cultural interests, support that was hard to find among peers who were largely Republican and unconcerned about social problems.

The atmosphere at Harvard began to change during the 1930s when the scholarly work of faculty members was encouraged by Lowell's successor, President James B. Conant, who gave strong support to graduate and professional schools, encouraged the recruitment of students on a national scale, and created financial-aid programs that enabled any qualified, but needy, applicant to come to Harvard.

The influx of returning veterans after World War II further changed the academic atmosphere. Older and more purposeful, these new students insisted on being treated as adults and were not interested in traditional collegiate activities. Under Conant and his successor, Nathan Pusey, Harvard encouraged more democratic and meritocratic admission standards, turning away from the aristocratic kind of meritocracy that favored the specially chosen, glamorously talented, and well-sponsored.

The faculty counterpart to this national recruiting of undergraduates was the Ad Hoc Committee system set up by Conant. Any department that wanted to appoint someone to a permanent chair on the faculty had to submit the candidate's qualifications to a committee of faculty, both from Harvard and from other institutions, from within the candidate's field and from outside it, that was appointed solely for this task. The system no doubt advanced meritocracy in its democratic version. Nonetheless, the search for the best possible person for a department may overlook the need to find a cadre of people who can work well together and with other faculty and students. It can also lead to self-destructive departmental microclimates.

It is easier to escape Harvard meritocracy academically than psychologically, and the self-regard of many students, high-risk or low, is often grievously wounded during their undergraduate years.

Pusey's appointment led to an effort to balance the claims of the undergraduate college and the graduate and professional schools. New programs, for example, Freshman Seminars, Independent Study, and expanded tutorial programs, while giving students greater access to faculty, in some ways increased the pressure on them for performance, and thus eventually led to demands for easing of academic restraints. Throughout this period, and continuing to the present, there has been a lack of effective counseling for undergraduate students who were having academic difficulties. It is easier to escape Harvard meritocracy academically than psychologically, and the self-regard of many students, high-risk or low, is often grievously wounded during their undergraduate years.

Teaching assistants, junior faculty, and teaching fellows bear the brunt of teaching undergraduates but, concerned with the work they must do to keep up with their peers, they do not have the time or energy to give adequate attention to students who are having difficulty, either academically or in a more personal sense.

During the 1960s meritocratic values began to be seriously questioned (honors program, for example, and the pressure to be "grinds"). In the wake of the civil rights movement and antiwar activity, the author says, "Meritocratic selectivity, earlier, of course, seen as the path of equity, became in the eyes of many just another form of racial discrimination, once it was evident that equality of opportunity produced anything but equality of results." Meritocracy lost the support of the Protestant Ethic and came to be criticized for its focus on specialized work and its resultant hierarchies of expertise. Part of the criticism of the meritocratic system was based on the conviction that in a highly competitive society the losers condemn themselves for nonachievement, the winners for manipulativeness. The greater variety of programs and courses, the visible cadres of black students whom some faculty felt could not always be rigorously graded in their underclass years (though, of course, Harvard has always had black students who could be as rigorously graded as anyone else and white students who could not), the introduction of pass-fail courses, and the Freshmen Seminars all contributed to lessening the competitive atmosphere for undergraduates.

At the same time the power of the departments was weakening for a number of reasons. University Professorships were established for scholars who wanted to cross traditional boundaries to find the constituencies for teaching they preferred. In addition, collegewide committees were set up to decide some matters that were formerly decided by departments; the Harvard Graduate and Teaching Fellows Union was organized in the spring of 1972; women and black students wanted to pursue interests that cut across departmental lines; and finally, students became increasingly uneasy about academic careers and were more and more reluctant to play academic games.

Yet many academic reformers at Harvard believe that all the changes are mere tokenism—the "system" goes on as before. In recent years, feeling the pressure of a more static and hence more competitive employment market, students have either become more concerned with grades or give up, and in following countercultural lifestyles, drop out, at least temporarily, sometimes actually and sometimes only metaphorically. Academic reform no longer interests students very much, either at Harvard or at other American universities. Some faculty at Harvard believe that the changes that were made allow many students to slip by without ever doing anything that requires long-term diligence.

Feeling, perhaps, less pressure to measure up to parental expectations, students at Harvard may now be even more vulnerable to the ideology of their peers. Although student life at Harvard today seems more relaxed and less competitive than heretofore, inward anxieties remain: Can I love? Am I fully human? Am I sufficiently independent? Where can I find meaningful spiritual guidance? All these questions are of continuing importance to students.

As for the faculty climate, that too has seen some changes. Chances for promotion from within are small. Although it is now easier for students to shape their own programs, to do so they need more knowledgeable counseling from faculty members, who, to do such counseling effectively, must be aware of all the various programs and aware as well of the individual student's talents and goals. Some faculty want to continue efforts at curriculum reform, in spite of countermeasures, and thus would like to do away with such admission criteria as SAT scores, favoring more "human" measures. Both the needed counseling and the proposed admission changes demand much more time and energy for personal student-faculty contact than is now available. But it is a kind of contact students want.

This need for personal student-faculty contact is also a factor in the problems of teaching an extremely diverse student body, for it is difficult to balance a concern for the student's personal growth with a concern for conveying didactic information, especially in the large lecture courses.

"The older convictions as to what is excellent have become attenuated," Riesman observes, "though the Harvard faculty have not found anything to take the place of those convictions within the institution which gave them form. It is hard to imagine Harvard going on as before," he concludes, but "an institution like an individual can continue to live with a lot of ruin within the system."

(1975)

Feeling, perhaps, less pressure to measure up to parental expectations, students at Harvard may now be even more vulnerable to the ideology of their peers.

DIRECTIONS OF FUTURE CHANGE

CHAPTER

The studies abstracted in this section by no means cover all anticipated future changes. In sponsoring research related to the priority of preparing for the future, we saw some matters to be in more immediate need of review and modification than others. The studies presented here were selected with that criterion in mind.

Richard Peterson's analysis of trends in enrollment in 1971 was inspired by reports of falling enrollments—for the first time in several decades—in some sectors of higher education that year. His study not only confirmed the reports, but identified the trends of the enrollment changes and helped us to check the reliability of our own projections of future enrollments.

The examination of *Academic Degree Structures: Innovative Approaches* by Stephen Spurr provided the basic documentation for many of the proposals made by the Commission in *Less Time, More Options.* Spurr's was a timely and badly needed analysis of degree-granting procedures which had become cumbersome and chaotic by the end of the 1960s. The study concludes with the author's own synthesis of "an idealized and generalized system of degree structures for American higher education."

The potentials of computer technology for revolutionizing higher education is analyzed in the study done for the Commission by the RAND Corporation under the direction of Roger Levien. *The Emerging Technology: Instructional Uses of the Computer in Higher Education* is the result of that study. It offers both a primer for computer use on campus and a sophisticated analysis of the steps required to accelerate the rate of computer use for teaching and learning.

The critical area of management efficiency in higher education—a subject of growing importance as resources for institutional operations become more and more limited—was surveyed for the Commission by a team of scholars under the direction of Alexander Mood. From that study, Professor Mood extracted some of the more speculative sections and combined them into a provocative essay called *The Future of Higher Education: Some Speculations and Suggestions.*

Forthcoming change in the professions is discussed by Edgar Schein in *Professional Education: Some New Directions* and by the late Herbert Packer and Thomas Ehrlich in *New Directions in Legal Education.* The authors of these studies make similar pleas for greater diversity in professional education so that new features of practice, and the changing expectations of professional students, may be reflected in the training that is offered.

The increasing number of alternatives to traditional, full-time higher education include extension programs, the minicampus, instruction by correspondence and electronic delivery systems (radio, television, micro-wave links, communication satellites, and telephone services), the university without walls, and the off-campus learning center. Thomas Karwin concentrates on a possible model for developing and equipping a learning center.

A second study of computer-assisted education, *Computers and the Learning Process in Higher Education,* by John Fralick Rockart and Michael S. Scott Morton, develops a model of the learning process as the first step in determining the place of technology-based learning aids in higher education. Acquiring different kinds of knowledge (facts, skills, or concepts) requires different learning and teaching techniques—and thus different learning aids. The authors prescribe a variety of traditional and computer-based learning aids for each stage of the learning process, but note that, for various reasons, computer-based aids will be introduced into higher education much more slowly than is technically feasible.

AMERICAN COLLEGE AND UNIVERSITY ENROLLMENT TRENDS IN 1971
RICHARD E. PETERSON

American colleges and universities are presently experiencing enrollment patterns that break significantly with trends that have held since World War II. Following a decade of spectacular growth, the annual enrollment gain in the public institutions is now much smaller than before; that of the private sector has ceased to grow at all. This study provides a fairly detailed description of these changes between fall 1970 and fall 1971 and notes the implications of the trends observed.

Following a decade of spectacular growth, the annual enrollment gain in the public institutions is now much smaller than before; that of the private sector has ceased to grow at all.

In October 1971 the registrars of 2,417 colleges and universities throughout the country received the study's questionnaire. Parallel, though differing, forms were sent to four-year and two-year institutions, and both requested fall 1970 and fall 1971 data in a variety of categories, including total undergraduate and graduate enrollment and applications, numbers of new freshman and graduate students, breakdown in these categories by sex and for black and Spanish-surname students, and numbers of new students applying and entering a variety of academic and professional fields. The report is based on information from a 48 percent sample—the 1,158 replies received from the campuses contacted.

Total undergraduate enrollment in all four-year institutions increased by 2.5 percent over the 1970 figure, with private universities reporting a slight decrease in enrollment. The increase in total graduate enrollment was 4.4 percent, with public and private colleges receiving the bulk of these additional students. First-time transfer students increased by 7.1 percent, and while enrollment increases for women were generally greater than for men in all categories, women scored their greatest gains in graduate school. Minority-student enrollment increased at a much higher rate than enrollment in the total student population, with Spanish-surname students making larger gains than black students. Public institutions received the bulk of these new minority-group students.

Data concerning movement of new undergraduate students in and out of academic fields in four-year institutions showed that the ecology-related fields of forestry, biology, and agriculture were favored by incoming students. At the graduate level, psychology, ethnic studies, and nursing scored highly.

Information concerning applications to four-year institutions indicated that, overall, undergraduate applications decreased, particularly at the private universities (8.1 percent). Graduate applications in general, however, increased—particularly at private colleges (27 percent). Both law and medical school applications climbed substantially, but engineering school applications declined by 7.9 percent.

In 1972 a total of 55,200 unfilled freshman places were reported by 572 four-year institutions, up 24 percent from 1970, and about half of these were in the private colleges.

Altogether a total of 55,200 unfilled freshman places were reported by 572 four-year institutions, up 24 percent from 1970, and the study estimates that about half of these were in the private colleges.

Annual tuitions rose an average of $19 in the public universities, $50 in the public colleges, $165 in the private universities, and $136 in the private colleges. This may well have affected applications, particularly to the private sector.

The reports from the two-year institutions revealed a different profile. Total enrollment increased by 8.4 percent in the public sector and decreased by 2.3 percent in the private two-year institutions, but part-time enrollment significantly increased at both. Minority-student enrollments were up at both, with the public colleges showing an increase of 15.7 percent blacks and 17.6 percent Spanish-surname students, and the private schools showing an increase in black students of 26.7 percent and in Spanish-surname students of 14.6 percent.

Despite a slowdown, the public junior colleges are still the fastest growing sector of higher education in the United States, and registrars most often cited "increased public awareness of educational opportunities" and "changing student interests" as partial explanations for this phenomenal growth, which continues even though tuition costs are also rising in two-year institutions.

From the data in this study, there is little doubt that the educational and career interests of college-age youth are rapidly changing. Increased numbers are electing not to attend a college or university, and particularly not in a lock-step manner. The chief reasons seem to be financial difficulties, desire to do something different, and desire for "no-nonsense" job training. Thus, the leveling off in enrollment can be attributed not only to general economic circumstance but also to a growing feeling that a college degree may not be the only key to the good life. This latter trend, it is stressed, may not be temporary.

Students also are emigrating to new fields from old ones in large numbers. Since the new fields cluster around ecology, this may mark a "faddishness" in student thought similar to the "lemming" run to the natural sciences which occurred in the post-Sputnik era.

Students also are emigrating to new fields from old ones in large numbers. Since the new fields cluster around ecology, this may mark a "faddishness" in student thought similar to the "lemming" run to the natural sciences which occurred in the post-Sputnik era. Similar to their sensitivity to well-advertised national currents, however, students are also demonstrating cognizance of job market conditions, which may help explain declines in enrollment reported in engineering, teacher education, and the graduate divisions of the humanities. Additionally, women are shown in rapidly growing numbers to be breaking out of the roles to which they were presumably socialized. There is, for example, increased female interest in law, architecture, medicine, engineering, and forestry.

All four types of institutions have a spotty record of response to these shifts in student interests and applications, but at a time when finances are low, it is not easy to produce new programs or change old ones. Some reforms could and should be easily, and cheaply, instituted. Students can be allowed to "drop out" more easily, and to lengthen or shorten their time for attaining a degree without major institutional upheaval. Women should be accommodated with greater alacrity than is at present being shown. So should minority-group students who, having been admitted, require certain skills and interests from faculty members who up to now have been loath to show either quality.

Institutions should also speedily facilitate desires of students to carry either heavier or lighter than traditional course loads, or to transfer from one school to another.

What is to be done with "new" students who, because of their backgrounds and styles, do not share traditional academic values? New conceptions of the meaning of "competence" will have to be found and internalized by the institutions of higher education.

In addition, more thought should be given to the ramifications of the "open-access" policies of admission. What is to be done with "new" students who, because of their backgrounds and styles, do not share traditional academic values? New conceptions of the meaning of "competence" will have to be found and internalized by the institutions of higher education. Policy regarding fiscal support of private colleges and universities, traditionally a bitterly contested issue, will have to be settled soon, as will the time-worn arguments about the extent to which colleges and universities should be responsive to the educational interests of students (the "consumers"), merely in order that America's system of higher education survive the coming decades.

More specific policy questions also require answers. At the graduate level, for example, should programs proliferate regardless of manpower-needs projections, or further, should lesser institutions operate lesser programs while, at the same time, identical programs at the major universities are operating at reduced capacity?

Currently changing enrollment patterns should hasten action on several questions which hinge on the fundamental purposes of higher education in the United States. For example, some observations of the data seem to assume that the college experience must be job-relevant. Need it be? Can it also be a period of self-discovery and improved human relating, of developing leisure skills, of experimenting with differing lifestyles, of acquiring humane values? Can it also be a base from which stems useful public or social service?

The nation's system of higher education needs to be an increasingly open system, capable of providing a great range of flexible learning experiences in the interests of individuals, groups, and the nation, in order to move toward the achievement of a society celebrated for, among other things, a commitment by its people and institutions to constant learning. As this study concludes: "It would be well indeed if higher education policy and practice were informed by a comprehensive conception of the good society."

(1972)

ACADEMIC DEGREE STRUCTURES: INNOVATIVE APPROACHES: Principles of Reform in Degree Structures In the United States
STEPHEN H. SPURR

The present academic degree structures in western Europe and the United States have descended with remarkably little change from those of the Middle Ages. When the concept of degrees was created in the thirteenth century at the original universities (Paris and Bologna) the three titles—*master, doctor,* and *professor*—were synonymous. A bachelor was initially a student allowed to teach in a master's school, that is, a teaching assistant. When students seized power at the Medieval University of Bologna, the *doctor,* or teacher, was shorn of his prerogatives and the title came to represent not an office but merely a distinction. The same transformation occurred with respect to the title of *master.*

In the United States, the bachelor of arts was the only degree awarded until the Civil War period. Today, however, there are many degrees and the once simple pattern has become immensely complicated. From the student's viewpoint, degree programs form the structure of higher education; and degrees simply and directly characterize an academic program in terms of generally accepted admissions standards, curriculum, duration of effort, and level of accomplishment.

Five general degree levels are recognized, the first three being consistently named *associate, bachelor,* and *master.* The fourth, covering intermediate graduate degrees, is in a state of development and flux. The term *specialist* is accepted in professional education and *engineer* is standard in that field. In the liberal arts, *candidate* has the widest current usage, although *licentiate* has much to recommend it. The fifth and highest level is *doctor.* Law schools are rapidly moving from the bachelor of laws to the juris doctor at this level, and theological seminaries are considering a similar move from the bachelor of divinity to a doctoral degree.

In fields where the first professional degree is the doctoral, the need exists for higher scientific or professional degrees. In medicine and dentistry, the path from the professional doctorate in science is recognized by the M.S. and the Ph.D. Advanced clinical accomplishment is recognized through certification by specialty boards established by the profession rather than by academic degrees. In law, advanced professional degrees are the master of laws and the doctor of juridical science. In theology, they are master of sacred theology and doctor of theology.

There is no reason why a student should not be recommended for the bachelor's degree with fewer formal credits as soon as he has met the levels of academic attainment set for the general education (distribution), specialization (concentration), and other curriculum standards.

As to possible innovations, there is no reason why a student should not be recommended for the bachelor's degree with fewer formal credits as soon as he has met the levels of academic attainment set for general education (distribution), specialization (concentration), and other curriculum standards. Moreover, advanced credit toward the master's degree should be available in the last year to advanced students wishing to enjoy the four-year undergraduate experience while pursuing graduate studies.

Much of the criticism of American degrees is leveled at a relatively few titles, for example, the master's program in the liberal arts. The master of arts and master of science degrees too often are awarded for the mere accumulation of additional credits, of which many represent work of only undergraduate caliber. And they are often awarded as a consolation prize to those who cannot continue on for the doctorate. It is recommended that all students wishing to continue beyond the baccalaureate pass through the master's stage and not be admitted to study for more advanced degrees until they do—making the master's a mark of successful forward progress or an appropriate stopping place for those who do not wish to go further. It should have a finite time—probably one year for the student en route to a doctorate; and at the other extreme, students might well earn the master's degree at the same time that they complete the requirements for the baccalaureate. The requirement for a master's thesis should not be universal.

The fourth level involves the intermediate graduate degree or certificate, which requires one academic year's work past the master's and may take as much as two years. Among the most widely used titles: candidate in philosophy, master of philosophy, and specialist in education. Licentiate in philosophy or diplomate in philosophy, however, would seem more specific and less misleading. The intermediate degree should represent an affirmation of accomplishment to date rather than an implication of failure to complete the dissertation.

The student who elects to carry out independent scholarly research beyond the intermediate graduate stage and to prepare the dissertation, would receive the doctor of philosophy degree. The doctor of education could well be granted to the student who elects an individual project that is essentially pedagogical or professional as opposed to individual scholarly research. Others could write an expository thesis for the doctor of arts degree. Still others could submit creative literary projects for the doctor of literary arts degree.

The great value in the doctor of arts programs would be to offer parallel and respectable alternatives to the doctor of philosophy in the liberal arts.

The great value in the doctor of arts programs would be to offer parallel and respectable alternatives to the doctor of philosophy in the liberal arts. A one-year minimum is probably attainable in the doctor of arts program, but two years would often be required in Ph.D. programs.

It is to be expected that postdoctoral studies will attract increasing numbers of scholars either in the formal sense of full-time postdoctoral study at a university or in the informal sense of continuing postdoctoral education throughout a scholarly career. The possibility exists, therefore, of recognizing accomplishment at this level with a higher doctorate, given in recognition of distinguished published creative activity over a period of years. We opt for the generic title *doctor of natural philosophy* for this highest-earned degree.

There is much merit in reducing the number of degrees if the surviving degree levels can be handled so as to meet the multiple needs of our student population. A number of alternatives suggest themselves.

To begin with, the bachelor's and doctor's level are so well entrenched as to warrant their inclusion in any set of structures. Greater flexibility should be introduced into the bachelor's degree, both in terms of providing opportunities for earlier completion of the degree and for advanced study applicable to graduate credit. For the Ph.D., major efforts must be made to encourage more students to finish in less time.

If the master's level can be strengthened and made a requirement, and if the doctor's level can be tightened up, the existing three-stage structure would serve us very well. The bachelor's program would require three to four years, the master's program one-half to one year, and the doctor's program from two to three years—a span of six to eight years in all. Today the modal period is nine years.

But, since this system is probably not sufficient to deal with the complexities of contemporary higher education, we must introduce into our pattern one or more of the additional three stages that have actually evolved: the associate stage, which the four-year colleges can do without, but the omission of which would make it more difficult to integrate the two-year colleges into a single system of higher education.

For graduate education, the master's and the intermediate graduate level could well be combined into a single two-year program for all students at this level. This, however, should constitute a regular phase through which all doctoral students would pass.

Whether or not a formal higher doctorate should be established in the United States hinges upon the effect such a doctorate would have in streamlining the Ph.D. But we emphasize that the formalities of our academic degree structures are important only to the extent that the form can influence the educational process itself.

The formalities of our academic degree structures are important only to the extent that the form can influence the educational process itself.

(1970)

THE EMERGING TECHNOLOGY: Instructional Uses of the Computer in Higher Education
ROGER E. LEVIEN

When it undertook its examination of higher education, the Carnegie Commission on Higher Education recognized that the computer might have a major impact on the form, quality, and cost of education in the future. To provide a basis for further deliberations on this potential, the Commission asked the RAND Corporation to undertake a study of the present state of computer use and its future prospects in higher education. This book reports the findings of that study.

Whereas in 1950 there were about a dozen computers in the United States, by 1970 there were almost 80,000 and their manufacture, service, and use employed nearly one million people. Estimates that these numbers will double by 1975 and redouble by 1980 are widely accepted, and it is reasonable to believe that the computer will very shortly be an everyday necessity for many people.

With the advent of this kind of service, the computer will affect higher education in three distinct roles: as the subject, tool, and agent of change. Of the campus's three principal functions—research, administration, and instruction—research was the first to be affected by the computer, and research uses have spread from engineering and the physical sciences to the social sciences, humanities, and the arts. Computer application has spread within disciplines too, and the influence of this technology has even induced change within the various academic disciplines themselves.

These innovations have made the computer so essential to many campus disciplines that, even where on-campus research is minimal, new faculty members are more and more likely to expect a computer to be available to serve their limited uses and support their teaching. The computer's use in a discipline affects not only research but also what can be taught and how it is taught.

In campus administration, the computer can assist with the management of all the main administrative concerns—finances, personnel, programs, and facilities. Whether keeping the payroll, registering students, scheduling classes, or cataloguing library books, campus administrators are placing growing reliance on the computer, and management methods are being influenced by it.

In 1968–69, about $100 million was spent on instructional use of the computer by almost 600,000 students in over 15,000 courses, but almost none of this was for instruction assisted by the computer.

Research and administration uses account for the largest part of higher education computer use to date, but instructional use may have the greatest long-run effect on higher education. The instructional uses conveniently break down into instruction *about* and instruction *with* computers, and this report primarily concerns itself with computer-assisted instruction, although the greatest portion of current instructional use involves instruction about computers. Using Southern Regional Education Board data, it emerges that there is "an image of widespread computer access, but considerable lack of access at the private, the smaller, and the two- and four-year institutions." In 1968–69, about $100 million was spent on instructional use of the computer by almost 600,000 students in over 15,000 courses, but almost none of this was for instruction assisted by the computer. A smaller study carried out in California served to confirm these findings.

Attempts to examine the capability provided by computer technology or the technology of current instructional uses are impaired by the lack of adequate data. However, even if the data were accurate, a confusing picture would emerge because the definition of what is possible differs from campus to campus as equipment or "computer environment" alters. The picture is further distorted because the computer offers some capacities for application which, thus far, have been barely tested or tested not at all. There are also differences not only in computer "environment," but in the various types of institutions in which the "computer environment" exists.

The general picture presented, however, is one of many capabilities available and few being utilized. Costs are part of the problem, but access to adequate instructional materials is as large if not larger a part, for almost all materials are "homemade," and thus little cumulative "know-how" is being built up throughout higher education as a whole.

"The picture is one of a technology poised on the edge of fruitfulness, held back not so much by limitations of its technique as by limitations of the institutions that must provide for its use. Until means to facilitate the production and distribution of instructional materials develop, the computer's full instructional potential is not likely to be achieved."

"The picture is one of a technology poised on the edge of fruitfulness, held back not so much by limitations of its technique as by limitations of the institutions that must provide for its use. Until means to facilitate the production and distribution of instructional materials develop, the computer's full instructional potential is not likely to be achieved."

During the next two decades, however, the computer will participate widely in most fields of human activity, and higher education can ill afford to ignore this development. The study concludes that many influences will determine the outcome of this critical concern. The changes in higher education itself, under social, economic, and political pressures, may be the most significant influences. The institutions will likely differ in their sources of support, clinetele, and governance, and in the way they structure their programs. Although the computer may facilitate or enable certain of these changes, the institutions will establish the context within which the computer must find its role.

Other influences will include rival innovations ranging from cable television to credit for work experience and open universities, so that the only available present conclusion is that the computer's place as an instructional tool will be shaped by the extent to which its use competes with or complements these other changes as well as its relation to traditional instruction.

Additionally, change and developments in computing itself will wreak their effects on the "uses" to which the technology is put; thus the future in this area depends on the disparate nature of advances in higher education, instruction, and computing.

Although the above factors will be influential, it is nonetheless possible at this stage to guide future developments to serve our objectives. The principal objective of the nation concerning instruction about the computer should be to ensure that higher education is providing adequate training to a sufficient number of persons to meet national needs for computer specialists, users, and literates and to improve the efficiency of computer use through instruction about the computer.

With regard to instruction with the computer, the main point of interest for this study, no national interest exists save in the general area of improving instructional efficiency in higher education. In this area, therefore, the prescriptive golden rule must be to ensure that access to the computer and associated instructional materials is possible whenever its use would be cost-effective and to improve the cost-effectiveness of instruction with the computer where such improvement will lead to a consequent improvement in the cost-effectiveness of higher education.

The study recommends that the natural growth of instructional computer uses through the development of a competitive market for computer-based instructional materials should be encouraged. This would be the most effective way of satisfying national objectives within the range of possibilities defined by economics, technology, institutions, and attitudes.

Government agencies, industry, and the higher educational institutions themselves, however, will have to act to implement this strategy. Research and development, and certain experimental programs, might receive government funding to induce the desired market to form. The input desired of industry is that it pay far greater attention than at present to the potential of this market, and that it perceive the difference between this market and those of computer-assisted research and computer-assisted administration in eduction. Finally, higher educational institutions themselves have a role to play. Administrators must create an environment wherein the computer's potential to assist the instructional process may be fully explored; faculty must seek to develop and exploit effective instructional computer uses; and students must demand that the faculty and administration perform their functions as outlined above.

Administrators must create an environment wherein the computer's potential to assist the instructional process may be fully explored; faculty must seek to develop and exploit effective instructional computer uses; and students must demand that the faculty and administration perform their functions as outlined above.

We can ill afford not to develop the uses of the computer in instruction, and this study provides not only the reasons why, but also rational insights into how the goal of harnessing the computer to assist instruction in higher education might be facilitated.

(1972)

THE FUTURE OF HIGHER EDUCATION:
Some Speculations and Suggestions
ALEXANDER M. MOOD

If the future of higher education is to be set in perspective, some hypothetical future society must be envisioned. This essay is prepared from the point of view of one such perspective—admittedly optimistic—that anticipates that by the year 2000 we shall be much further along the road toward elimination of social injustices and that there will have been a steepened decline in the kinds and degrees of inhumanity. Further, society will have solved those problems that currently derive from maldistribution of information, and will have altered, but not lessened, the degree to which work is a part of the life of mankind. Careers will not necessarily be connected with earning a livelihood, and this change is symptomatic of a deeper revolution in attitudes. Young people today are the harbingers of that revolution; many of them would prefer to be loved and/or healthy than, for example, to be rich, and by the year 2000 we shall see a much wider and more careful calculation of the pros and cons of these values being demonstrated in personal decision making. Additional growth in government is also forecast, for as people become relatively well supplied with personal goods and services, they will demand more public goods and services—both nationally and internationally. Science and technology (biochemistry excepted) will probably advance more slowly than other areas of human achievement. The big difference in the future is more likely to be made by changes in personal philosophies, fundamental changes in attitudes of people toward each other, changes in social institutions, and the creation of new social institutions.

These societal changes are bound to affect subsystems of society and one subsystem, higher education, is already feeling their effects. The very functions of higher education are already changing; service to the elite, for example, has been replaced with service to the broad mass of the populace. Several forces operate in this situation and these are identified so that reasonable guesses can be made about what higher education will do in the future. One such force is the natural tendency of bureaucracies to grow. By this growth, bureaucrats achieve status, but part of such growth, particularly budgetary growth in higher education, is through enrollment increases. Enrollment increases mark the bringing of the masses to higher education, but these increases have also engendered problems, for the system is not really geared to deal with universal access in a meaningful way. There is already a glaring mismatch between what today's students need and what higher education provides, and this portends major changes for higher education in the near future.

One solution to today's problems lies in improving educational technology. We are still basically operating at the same technological levels as the medieval universities, and improvements in this area could cut costs and improve quality. This improvement can be gained by changing education from a labor-intensive enterprise to one that uses capital judiciously, that is, by doing only those things with humans that cannot be done by machines. Teachers assist the learning process in two ways: by providing an imitatable model to the students and by diagnosing and correcting errors in student performance. Machines can perform these functions, and it is not too farfetched to foresee a video university which would operate entirely through the medium of video cassettes attached to television sets, thus dispensing entirely with the need for campus and faculty. The technology of computers can be harnessed to facilitate this process. A computer network for testing and curriculum design is possible. Computer terminals could become as common in a household as the telephone.

After a sizable initial capital investment, a video university would pay for

Enrollment increases mark the bringing of the masses to higher education, but these increases have also engendered problems, for the system is not really geared to deal with universal access in a meaningful way. There is already a glaring mismatch between what today's students need and what higher education provides.

itself and, though chartered as a national university and federally funded, there is no reason why it should become a monopoly. It would, however, require operation on the assumption that the general public is simply one great body of students who require the continuous availability of large quantities of information.

The value of academic credentials is diminishing. Large numbers of college students are already quitting college before graduating. Frequently they are right; their time could be better spent in other pursuits. Along with accrediting organizations and grades, credentialing as a function of higher education could decline in overall importance.

Our educational system does not prepare its students for the world they must live in. This will change when people are prescribing their own education. Freed from the emphasis on credentials, learning will change radically and increase spectacularly.

The future college student body will be different—not just high school graduates selected by various criteria, but the entire adult population. Higher education will be spread out over one's lifetime as an occasional part-time activity because as society changes more rapidly so will careers, and in the future, people will have to be prepared to learn throughout their lives. What is worth learning will be decided by the student rather than by someone else. Our educational system does not prepare its students for the world they must live in. This will change when people are prescribing their own education. Freed from the emphasis on credentials, learning will change radically and increase spectacularly.

With these anticipated changes in mind, an alternative system of higher education may be hypothesized. The main features of the rearrangement would be as follows: First, the vast majority of students would attend college initially on a full-time basis for only one year instead of two or four or more. Additional higher education would always be available according to need and desire, but as a part-time activity extending throughout life. Second, almost everyone would attend college for a year, regardless of whether he or she had graduated from high school. Furthermore, the roles of residential and community colleges would be essentially reversed: the one year of full-time attendance would be at a residential college, and the part-time lifelong learning would be more in the domain of the community college. The public subsidy that now supports students who attend college for more than one year could be withdrawn and used to support the one year of residence for those who do not now go to college.

In order to move higher education toward this conception of the future, several courses of action are recommended. At an international level, the "global village" would benefit from a number of international universities which could operate free of national biases. In the United States, the government should fund the video university, for this is the most cost-effective method of bringing educational opportunity to all citizens at all levels

Our system of financing higher education should be overhauled, particularly at the state level, so that all tax support is parceled out both to high school graduates and high school dropouts, in the form of education grants, to equalize their financial capacity to purchase advanced education.

of preparedness. Additionally, our system of financing higher education should be overhauled, particularly at the state level, so that all tax support is parceled out both to high school graduates and high school dropouts in the form of education grants, to equalize their financial capacity to purchase advanced education. Simultaneously, public institutions would raise their undergraduate tuitions to compensate for this loss of tax revenue.

As far as specific curricular changes are concerned, institutions should concentrate on providing off-campus learning to students while recognizing that many careers of the future will not be primarily income oriented. If these suggestions are followed, as well as those concerning such reforms as the elimination of entrance requirements, the abandonment of the certification function, and the abolition of faculty tenure, there is every hope that higher education will be able to deal with enrollment increases despite budgetary stringencies. The foundations and research organizations should help in this adaptation of our system to the future. They can provide much needed studies, projections, and funds with which to aid in the transformation of higher education.

In conclusion, several strategies to accomplish change are suggested. Higher education can be dragged into a new era kicking and screaming by the budget, as would be the case if public support were to be channeled through students. Alternatively, a competing and more efficient structure could be built to chip away at the domain monopolized by the present system. Further, the students could adopt the well-tried strategy of organized labor and withdraw their "labor" en masse for a year or so—which would have the effect of "strengthening their voice in the future operation of the system."

This essay suggests that a coalition of students, workers, job seekers, the courts, employers, and the educators be immediately formed to get the educational system out of the credential business so that it may concentrate on the real business of education. Only by concentrating on this "real business" can our educational system come to terms with such demands as will be put on it in the next 30 years.

(1973)

PROFESSIONAL EDUCATION: Some New Directions
EDGAR H. SCHEIN

This 150-page report, based on interviews with 75 men and women associated with the professions and professional education, is in two parts.

The first describes those forces of change that demand a redirection in professional education; the second deals with the question of how professional education is to respond to these changing conditions.

Perhaps the greatest evolution in the professions is the shift away from the autonomous practitioner working with a single fee-paying client, to one who is for the most part an employee of a large group or organization. The new professionals are more likely to be working for a salary and to function in a corporate atmosphere. The distinction in work-setting is important because it strongly influences the professional's self-image, his definition of the client, and his conception of the proper ways to relate to the client.

Often, by working for a large corporation the professional not only loses direct client contact, he also loses control over his professional output. Once the engineer, scientist, or architect has produced a solution to a problem his employer, who now becomes the immediate "client," may do what he wishes with it; the modifications or alternative uses to which his work may be put are beyond his control. The professional is seeing areas of his autonomy ebb away as organizations become more powerful in dictating what they want the professionals to do.

Regrettably, most professional schools today still base their program on the assumption that the professional is, and will remain, an autonomous expert. The attitudes and skills needed to work in collaboration with others have been largely ignored.

Increased specialization—one result of the great knowledge explosion—again points to the need for teamwork and the learning skills that will help professionals to work together in interdisciplinary teams. For many of the pressing problems that society faces today there is no *single* profession that can hope to deal with them effectively. It will not be enough for the psychiatrist to collaborate with the social worker, or for the architect to work closely with the planner. If the problems of the city, of environment, education, health, and international relations are to be solved, interprofessional teams must be developed and the abilities needed to work within a team must be given prominence in the professional's training.

Specialization also presents particular problems to the professional educator. Unless the length of training is to extend indefinitely, there will probably have to be a reduction in the "core" curriculum. (However, this must be balanced against the danger of overspecialization, which could lead to early obsolescence.) Clients are often bewildered by the number of related specialists, and the question arises: "How does a layman determine which specialist can best deal with his complaint?" A new type of general practitioner must be trained, one who can serve as the initial diagnostician to help the client select the appropriate mix of specialists. And there must be training for manager-administrators who can lead the professional teams effectively.

Among the strongest voices for change are those of the professional students. Their criticisms of professional education and early career training reflect a change in social values and changed expectations about career opportunities.

Among the strongest voices for change are those of the professional students. Their criticisms of professional education and early career training reflect a change in social values and changed expectations about career opportunities. Young people are asking whether the right sets of clients are being served—that is, is it right that members of higher socioeconomic strata should receive better medical, psychiatric, and legal care only because they are in a better position to pay the professional fees? They criticize the early years of practice, which are often stultifying, unchallenging, and more like an initiation rite than good preparation for later years. Young architects reject the licensing requirement of a three-year apprenticeship; engineers leave large corporations because their jobs are too circumscribed; and lawyers reject law firms with too rigid an apprenticeship system. The professional schools are criticized for their rigid admissions policies. There is criticism of the "fixed sequence curriculum"—beginning with a large common core, offering only a few electives in the middle of the program, and ending with clinical or practicum courses—because it does not take into account individual learning rates and interests. And there is criticism of the too-few provisions for smooth transition to professional practice.

In view of the far-reaching criticisms of professional education as it is and looking ahead to future developments, the report makes the following four general recommendations:

■ More flexibility in the professional school curriculum, in the number of paths available through school, in the number of electives available to students inside and outside the school, in the pacing and sequence of courses, in the required length of time needed to go through school, and in the degree or certification process used by the school.

■ More flexibility in the early career paths of professionals, more differentiated rules for licensing to reflect different kinds of professional careers, and more support of role innovation of various kinds by the professions themselves.

■ New curricula and new career paths which are inter- or transdisciplinary and which may lead eventually to new professions.

■ Greater integration of the behavioral and social sciences into the professional school curriculum, particularly applied behavioral science dealing with the theory and practice of planned change, the diagnosis of complex systems, and the analysis of the client-professional relationship.

The study of behavioral science might also prove useful for developing insight, learning how to work in and lead professional teams, and in learning how to learn.

If professional education is to adapt to the changing conditions in a reasoned and logical fashion, it must undergo a *planned* change of direction.

But if professional education is to adapt to the changing conditions in a reasoned and logical fashion, it must undergo a *planned* change of direction. It is not going to be easy. There is bound to be resistance among the older professionals to greater flexibility in career paths—it may threaten their own specialty—and they may object to basic changes in the traditional curriculum which, by remaining tedious and uninspiring, deters the less-than-committed student from rising up through the ranks. There will be objections to the additional educational costs of offering more electives and individualized training. And the inclusion of behavioral sciences may be seen as a seduction to pull students away from basic knowledge and skills.

Planned change, the theme of Part II in the report, means learning new ideas, attitudes and values, and new patterns of behavior and skills. Such change can occur only when there is a feeling of psychological safety in overcoming present obstacles to innovation. Given the resistance to basic innovation among established professionals, a realistic way to bring about educational change is to find innovations that can be fitted into or around the present system, innovations that will encourage a more flexible approach. Examples of such innovations may be found in the new kinds of undergraduate programs that have sprung up both in new colleges and within more established institutions. The "self-paced" elementary physics course taught at MIT offers a number of prepackaged, self-contained units of material that are administered by a professor and guided by tutors who are students roughly two or three years ahead of those taking the course. Another innovation is the "independent study program" that provides the student with a vastly greater degree of freedom in following his interests and finding novel ways to attack problems.

The new professional school would integrate the basic sciences, applied sciences, and professional skills. There would be a small permanent faculty and a large part-time adjunct faculty to permit the offering of a wide range of classes.

Other examples of innovative approaches to professional education include more use of small-group and seminar-tutorial methods, work-study programs and off-campus study. Innovative postgraduate activities include career halfway houses and interdisciplinary service centers and workshops. In all cases these methods and ideas have been used successfully in professional schools throughout the country.

The final chapter of the report, "Some Bold Horizons: A New Kind of Professional Education," goes from what is to what might be. The new professional school would integrate the basic sciences, applied sciences, and professional skills. A variety of professional degrees would be offered, requiring different lengths of time to complete. There would be a small permanent faculty and a large part-time adjunct faculty to permit the offering of a wide range of classes. The adjunct faculty would function like consultants, teaching several different schools and possibly maintaining some private practice as well; they would have power in determining school policy and the design of the curriculum. Physically, the new professional school would be organized around a "learning-resource center" that should include as many laboratories and "application-oriented subcenters" as possible, much like a teaching hospital that is tied closely to various community activities.

Administratively, the school would be highly decentralized. It would deliberately avoid the search for standardized solutions to curriculum questions, engaging instead in a perpetual process of self-diagnosis and research on the outcome of its educational efforts.

(1972)

NEW DIRECTIONS IN LEGAL EDUCATION
HERBERT L. PACKER and THOMAS EHRLICH with the assistance of STEPHEN PEPPER

This study draws attention to the fact that legal education must alter to accommodate the changing nature of American legal practice. The American bar has generally reflected middle-class values and problems and thus it is no surprise that, in the face of growing societal heterogeneity, the legal profession has become so heterogeneous that the homogeneity assumed by legal education, bar admissions, and bar organizations is by now wholly spurious.

Believing that the future of legal education is inextricably entwined with the future of the profession, the authors identify certain trends which are affecting the course of the profession. First, certain legal fields both old and new seem to be expanding rapidly. Such areas as criminal law, problems of poverty and the consumer, and problems emanating from the environment and the reconstruction of government are generating a need for expanded legal services that will have to be met. Second, there is a growing demand for change in the mechanism and organization of the profession. Increased specialization in practice is resulting both in pressure for specialty licensing and in a growing clamor for group legal services. Concomitant with these developments is a need for a cadre of trained, specialized paraprofessionals, the emergence of which will lessen the number of squabbles over "unauthorized practice."

Identification of the key problem areas, however, merely serves to raise further questions, for educational arrangements will have to be made to accommodate the aforementioned developments. For example, who will train specialists and paraprofessionals? Where on the formal educational ladder will these new forms of training occur? How will the future legal educational structure be financed?

As America grows steadily more urban, more postindustrial and more service-oriented, it seems clear that the legal task will grow both qualitatively and quantitatively. The term "legal task" encompasses all that lawyers, both as architects of order and as advocates, might do to help reconcile the interests of people and institutions. As a necessary response to the crisis in the availability of legal services, the authors prophesy a cluster of developments that will make legal services more available and less expensive. Primary responses to the crisis will be the development of sublegal and paralegal personnel, group legal services, and certified specialists. In brief, the stage is currently set for a dramatic expansion of needed legal services and for equally drastic changes in the skills required to provide these services. Both of these phenomena will have far-reaching implications for legal education.

As a necessary response to the crisis in the availability of legal services, a cluster of developments will make legal services more available and less expensive. Primary responses to the crisis will be the development of sublegal and paralegal personnel.

Operating at its best, legal education is good, but the authors aver that serious problems do exist. Although there are wide variations in the quality of law schools today, legal education has a unitary nature, being inextricably bound to the profession of law and its unitary admissions standards. Because of this, law schools are more alike than they are different. For example, their primary mission is the education of students for entry into the legal profession; the faculties of none are primarily engaged in research; none engages in undergraduate education; and none offers its professional degree (LL.B. or J.D.) in less than three years. American law schools share a common structure, and in schools where the student-faculty ratio does not exceed 25 to 1, most instruction in the first year is carried on through the case method. The Socratically oriented case method was developed at Harvard in the nineteenth century and involves the learning of law through the study and discussion of appellate decisions. The method dominates the curricula of American first-year students across the spectrum of legal education and, by providing embryonic lawyers with a common cultural base, it has been far more the strength than the weakness of the first year in American legal education. It is currently receiving criticism, however, as being hostile to student initiative and emotionally stifling, although the first year for most students is reported to be an exciting and challenging experience.

Beyond the first year, curricular rigidity eases, and recent developments include a trend toward seminars and other forms of small-group instruction, as well as an increase in "jointwork" of an interdisciplinary nature.

Another identifiable trend has been the increased interest in "clinical" programs, the methods of which reflect a debt to the Deweyan concept of "learning by doing." Despite these, however, an air of discontent hovers over the second and third years of legal education, and the authors believe that "secularization of the law" is the prime intellectual cause of the malaise. Acknowledging their debt to Calvin Woodard, they maintain that law schools, which have so far focused their curricula largely on the practical realm, now need to pay much more attention to the collective aspect both in the areas of curriculum and of legal scholarship.

One way in which it is frequently urged that this broadening of the philosophical base of legal education can be facilitated involves the concept of "clinical education." Three reasons contribute to the current popularity of this teaching method. It helps assuage the demand that education become more relevant to social needs; it operates programmatically outside the law school and thus can be incorporated without involving fundamental intramural change; and it is actively encouraged by the Council on Legal Education for Professional Responsibility Inc., which, backed by the Ford Foundation, has funded many experiments with this method at various law schools. While allowing that there are many benefits to be derived from clinical education, doubt is raised that it is the ultimate solution many of its proponents claim it to be or that it should dominate legal education in the future. These doubts hinge upon the anti-intellectual nature of the method, which seeks relevance at the expense of rigor, and its operating costs, which are substantially higher than those of the case method.

While allowing that there are many benefits to be derived from clinical education, doubt is raised that it is the ultimate solution or that it should dominate legal education in the future. The doubts hinge upon the anti-intellectual nature of the method, which seeks relevance at the expense of rigor, and its operating costs, which are substantially higher than those of the case method.

With regard to curriculum, this study discusses the suggestions made in the 1971 report to the Association of American Law Schools entitled "Training for the Public Professions of the Law." Known as "The Carrington Report," it is reproduced in full as Appendix A to the study. The Carrington Report hypothesizes a number of model curricula for law schools and moves toward creative innovation from a generally conservative position. Various curricular models are suggested that permit the necessary diversification by such means as changing the rigid three-year requirement for the first professional degree; positing means for the training of paraprofessional personnel; and enabling part-time preservice and in-service education within the aegis of university-related law schools.

Professors Packer and Ehrlich point out that secularization of the law has led to much confusion in law schools. This is particularly regrettable because the law school traditionally provides to the American university a valuable form of general purpose—advanced higher education. Two ex-

Two extensions of this traditional role of law schools are urged: the promotion both of extensive scholarship in macrojustice and of law as a humane study for undergraduates.

tensions of this traditional role are urged: the promotion both of extensive scholarship in macrojustice and of law as a humane study for undergraduates. The implications of these various suggested reforms and extensions of traditional legal education are far reaching indeed, but one of the major obstacles to their being implemented, even on an experimental basis, is financial.

Legal education is now so inexpensive, relatively speaking, that "almost all reforms . . . will raise unit costs." The problem is exacerbated because, in terms of their fiscal structures, law schools—whether they be private, public, non-elite, elite, university-affiliated, non-university-affiliated, etc.—already enjoy a wide-ranging diversity. All have differing fiscal needs and opportunities, and diversity in this area is only the beginning. If legal education develops along the lines predicted in this study, law schools will also cease to have structural similarity. Two factors, however, have combined to precipitate the current fiscal crisis in legal education. The first is the general depression in higher education identified and described for the Carnegie Commission by Earl Cheit, and the second concerns the various changes which have already taken place in law schools, but without any dramatic alteration in the traditional structure of legal education. Many new areas have developed in American law, and while some curricular change has occurred, much more is needed, and that will require money. This study suggests fresh potential sources of funds and intimates that although a comparatively small amount is needed nationwide ($100 million would double the present aggregated budget of law schools) it must be sought now. The sources which are detailed in the study as ripe for harvesting include the legal profession itself, employers of law school graduates, individually wealthy lawyers, lawyer-suggested bequests, corporations, foundations, and federal support. Two other sources of financial help are suggested. The first involves increasing the incidence of student loans to cover cost increases. The second is more intriguing: a schema of institutional borrowing whereby law schools might maneuver both in the money market, and also, significantly, by issuing bonds for sale to the general public. The future development of legal education depends directly on the provision of substantial new funding, and this suggestion regarding the employment of income tax-exempt bond issues makes much sense.

Tied closely to the fiscal issues are suggestions relating to the length of preprofessional training. There is no reason why all students should take seven years to qualify for the profession, and thus schools are urged to experiment with accepting undergraduates who have completed three years of college and graduating them after two years in law school. The American Bar Association has no rules forbidding this, and while some

The unitary bar is crumbling, and while structural change may almost sound like heresy to some ears, institutional diversity in all areas will occur increasingly throughout the next generation.

students may take three or four years in law school, two years is seen as the minimum time in which most could achieve a working level of competence. The unitary bar is crumbling, and while structural change may almost sound like heresy to some ears, this study attests that institutional diversity in all areas must and will occur increasingly throughout the next generation.

The remodeling process has started, not by discarding old patterns completely, but rather by building on those patterns where new development is called for. Different schools will employ various approaches and techniques in legal education, and this the authors welcome because no single schema is yet sufficiently tested to be imposed on all schools and all students. As is rationally argued, a diversity of approach will yield—over time—real evidence upon which to make the considered judgments that are necessary to ensure the fullest contribution of law schools both to the profession and to American society.

(1973)

FLYING A LEARNING CENTER: Design and Costs of an Off-Campus Space for Learning
THOMAS J. KARWIN

This report is essentially a blueprint for creating a learning center to accommodate degree-seeking, part-time students who are unable to attend classes on a campus at prescheduled times or whose goals cannot be achieved through conventional instruction.

The study touches only briefly on instructional techniques and lightly on the problems of transition from traditional to innovative instructional practices. The intention of the proposed planning is to interrupt the cycle of designing spaces to support established instructional designs and then limiting instructional designs to those for which appropriate spaces are available. It is hoped that this detailing of a new facility will encourage academic planners rather to build a facility and then adopt the instructional practices that the facility was designed to support.

Currently, the most widely available alternatives to the traditional model are:

1   Extension programs, which provide flexibility of content and location, but fall short of the goal of expanding educational opportunity by adhering to traditional academic calendars, course schedules, and instruction methods, when what students need is more flexible access to learning opportunities.

2 The "minicampus" concept which offers certain advantages to part-time students living beyond "reasonable" commuting distance from a home campus, and holds promise of extending instruction to the urban ghetto, but has limited potential for expansion. Professors are not likely to warm to the notion of "circuit riding," and the practice is certain to make uneconomical use of valuable faculty time.

3 Correspondence instruction which does provide nearly complete flexibility of time and place of study, but is limited to learning goals that can be achieved through reading and writing in relative isolation. Cable television holds promise of extending the range of resources available to the correspondence student at home or at work, but development of various proposed broad-band and narrow-band systems is still in the drawing-board stage.

4 Electronic delivery systems, such as radio, broadcast television, microwave links, communication satellites, and telephone services, which can reach large audiences through commonly used and widely available equipment and require no significant departures from established teaching methods, but are limited to scheduled instruction, thereby ignoring much of the research on learning and the desirability of flexible access to learning opportunities.

Given the weaknesses of these familiar models for reaching the off-campus student, the university-without-walls idea and the learning-center concept are attractive. A prototype of the latter is described in detail.

A *learning center* is conceived as a base for guided individual study, rather than a place for conventional meetings between students and instructors. It is designed to provide students, who are either geographically or socially remote from the campus of their choice, with all the resources and facilities needed to achieve their academic goals. The learning-center concept encompasses use of learning modules, local resources, learning contracts, field studies, work experience, and materials shuttled from the home campus.

A *learning center* is designed to provide students, who are either geographically or socially remote from the campus of their choice, with all the resources and facilities needed to achieve their academic goals.

The instructional program provides contact with home campus faculty, resident tutors, and learning facilitators. Lectures by audiocassette or videocassette are envisioned, but not live televising of lectures or other forms of home campus instruction.

While existing learning centers, such as those in public libraries in the Study Unlimited program cosponsored by the City Colleges of Chicago and the Chicago Public Library, may prove effective, they involve highly variable costs and depart from ideal design. Karwin's projection, assuming new construction of a facility designed specifically as a learning center, permits a reliable estimate of capital and operating costs and provides an idealized center as a basis for more concrete planning.

The prototype learning center is a wood-frame structure of quality construction providing 6,000 assignable square feet of space (8,000 square feet for the outside dimensions) on a one-acre site designed to accommodate 500 students. Adequate parking space is provided.

The main facilities include:

Individual study room: central and largest space in the center, combines individual study spaces and multimedia library and is furnished with carrels for videocassette and audiocassette players, graphic computer terminals, desk-top computers, a wide range of learning modules available on shelves, and spaces for 100 students.

Seminar rooms: two informal seminar rooms, accommodating 20 students each, located near the individual study room.

Tutorial rooms: four tutorial rooms adjacent to the individual study room for brief meetings between tutors and students and other small-group uses, including testing.

Counseling offices: two offices for counseling of students and meetings with prospective students.

Administrative office: a large office for a manager-librarian who has responsibility for running the center and liaison with home campus.

Receptionist-clerk station.

Typing rooms: 10 soundproof cubicles for typing study reports, for individual study, or for listening to audiocassettes over loudspeakers.

Child-care center: supervised playroom and play yard where students may leave their children during study periods.

Parking facilities: experience indicates that about 80 parking spaces are adequate for an anticipated 500 students.

Instructional equipment: individual study carrels (custom-built for electronic gear), videocassette and audiocassette players, color TV receivers, desk-top computers, hand-held calculators, electric typewriters, microfiche viewers, and cassette-to-cassette duplicator.

Staff: a manager-librarian and an assistant, four counselors, eight tutors, a senior electronics technician, two clerk typists, and a half-time custodian-groundskeeper to support a 12-hour-per-day operation.

Using a construction cost per outside gross square foot of $42, a total of about $336,000 would be required for the learning center, excluding land acquisition, equipment, furniture, and parking facilities.

Using a construction cost per outside gross square foot of $42, a total of about $336,000 would be required for the learning center, excluding land acquisition, equipment, furniture, and parking facilities. Parking facilities would add $42,000; instructional equipment $52,950; and furnishings $20,160. This brings *total capital costs* to $451,340 (plus land). No estimate is given for land acquisition since prices vary so widely.

Operating costs per year, including staff, amortization of instructional equipment and contingency, supplies and expenses, are set at $215,785, to provide a six-day week schedule of operation.

Planning for networks of learning centers, rather than for only one or a few, is suggested.

Ideally, a center should be located within 30 minutes' travel time of prospective students, although this may not be economically feasible because the viability of learning centers depends on their use by some minimum number of students.

Social distance between prospective students and the campus should also be considered. Many people who would find a main campus unappealing might be attracted to a learning center that had a familiar neighborhood ambience.

Social distance between prospective students and the campus should also be considered. Many people who would find a main campus unappealing might be attracted to a learning center that had a familiar neighborhood ambience.

Locating "learning pavilions" in metropolitan libraries and on the campuses of community and comprehensive colleges, as was suggested in two earlier reports of the Carnegie Commission on Higher Education, has merit.

(1974)

COMPUTERS AND THE LEARNING PROCESS IN HIGHER EDUCATION
JOHN FRALICK ROCKART and MICHAEL S. SCOTT MORTON

Studies of computer-assisted education to date have answered only one of three significant questions: Can it be cost-effective? (The answer is yes.) Two additional, and now more significant questions are: In what specific ways will the computer affect the learning process in higher education? and, How should a faculty member approach the selection of a mode of computer-based instruction for a particular course of study?

In answering these questions, this study focuses upon the teaching-learning interaction, an area central to the university's purpose and an area in which little innovation has yet taken place. Computer-based education comprises some techniques with great potential and other techniques with virtually none; both are delineated here. For only when we understand both the teaching-learning interaction and the characteristics of different computer-based learning mechanisms can we begin to determine what the place of technology is in higher education, and what it is not.

First, there is clear need for a robust model of the learning process. Only through the development and use of such an explicit model can we predict the possible impact of any particular type of technology upon segments of the learning process. The model developed here embraces two sets of variables: four stages of learning and four kinds of material to be learned. The learning stages are (1) acquiring, (2) embedding, (3) integrating, and (4) testing. The materials are (1) facts and definitions, (2) skills and procedures, (3) established concepts, and (4) frontier concepts. Thus we have a "learning matrix" containing 16 cells, each of which is determined by the interaction of a stage and a material. For example, cell 1-1 is "acquiring facts," and cell 4-4 is "testing frontier concepts." From cell to cell among the 16, learning processes differ, and the mechanisms used to aid the learner must reflect these differences. Some cells are impregnable to "technology" as we understand it today; others are ripe for it.

Which are which? Where does the computer fit? For each cell in the learning matrix, the authors define the attributes of an effective learning mechanism. They then assess both traditional and computer-based learning mechanisms in light of these attributes to determine which mechanisms should be used in which cell.

When the learning stage is *acquiring,* cost-effectiveness attributes are the most important. Traditional methods, therefore, are appropriate. The textbook dominates this stage, followed by the programmed text. As acquisition moves from "facts" to "frontier concepts," the lecture becomes the learning mechanism best fitted to convey knowledge. Only in limited cases of acquisition, such as remedial education, does it appear that the computer may become the mechanism of choice.

When the learning stage is *embedding,* feedback is the significant learning requirement. This attribute is possessed most by computerized drill-and-practice and problem-solving devices. Though traditional homework and written assignments prevail at present, coming decreases in computer costs will stimulate growth of computer-assisted instruction—to the benefit of the student.

When the learning stage is *integrating* or *testing,* the learning process has traditionally been left to the student, because traditional mechanisms are inadequate. In the future, the development of "enrichment" attributes, through computerized simulation, games, inquiry, and problem solving, will receive increasing attention, and will ultimately dominate educational effort.

In the future, the development of "enrichment" attributes, through computerized simulation, games, inquiry, and problem solving, will receive increasing attention, and will ultimately dominate educational effort.

Analyzing the learning model leads to clear understanding that no single technology can adequately serve the learner in all stages of the learning process—or across all types of materials. This study, therefore, prescribes using a variety of learning mechanisms, with refinement of each mechanism in areas where it has a clear comparative advantage. Diversity is not only desirable, it is necessary for effective learning assistance. At the moment such diversity must look like a *smorgasbord*—an array of teaching devices from lecture, film, and television, to multimedia computer-based labs. In time, the collection will take on aspects of a *portfolio,* a set of learning mechanisms gathered together for a purpose.

Turning to cost trends and equipment configurations, the study concurs with predictions that hardware costs will diminish radically, and by 1980 will represent only a small fraction of what they were in 1970. Because of inflation and increasing program complexity, software costs will increase, and will become the most expensive components of computer-instruction systems. Overall, however, *computer costs per program will decrease.* Configurations of hardware can be put together in three basic ways: "batch" systems, "remote job entry" systems, and "on-line interactive" systems, listed here in order of increasing expensiveness *and* increasing effectiveness in the learning process. Recent technological advances, it should also be noted, have split the available configurations of computer power into three size classes: "mini" (special purpose), "maxi" (general purpose), and "midi" (combination).

The term *courseware* refers to systems that deal directly with the subject being taught. Tutorial and drill-and-practice modes of computer-based instruction are by far the most common (and have absorbed 95 percent of available government and foundation funding, with results that, at least on the university level, are ambiguous). The authors believe that the Skinnerian model of learning—which leads to prevalence of fill-in-the-blank-computer-page-turner modes—has dominated for too long. At the university level, the Skinnerian view seems appropriate only for a small subset of the materials, some of the facts, and only certain of the students. Dialogue systems, which combine "presentation" and "enrichment" modes, are at present purely experimental. A third category of systems deals, as noted above, entirely with "enrichment." This area is growing rapidly, operates without government subsidy (a fact that suggests it really is useful), and embodies a shift toward greater "learner control" and away from "author control" (thus aiding the learning process more effectively). For almost all kinds of materials, problem solving, games, and simulation can provide the learner with better means of integrating and testing knowledge than can other technologies. Looking at evidence from around the country,[1] and extending the insight gained from the learning model, the study argues that the computer's unique ability to provide low-cost enrichment represents the most underexploited aspect of educational technology. It follows that the real impact of the new technology will be for the most part adding to, rather than replacing, current learning mechanisms.

The real impact of the new technology will be for the most part adding to, rather than replacing, current learning mechanisms.

[1]The study examines, often in detail, computer-assisted learning projects at Stanford, Florida State University, University of Illinois, MITRE, Ohio State Medical School, MIT, IBM Educational Research Department, Dartmouth, Montana State University, and North Carolina State. In addition, a full chapter is devoted to the authors' survey of computer applications in 73 Massachusetts institutions of higher education (offering a B.A. and above) representing a total student population of more than 260,000.

These developments will take much longer than is technically possible. The reasons are many, but what they boil down to is that the forces favoring further efforts to design and implement learning systems technology are not nearly as powerful as the opposing forces. On the positive side are such forces as student pressures, innovative tendencies of faculties, the availability of better technology, external competition, and some demonstration effects. None of these is terribly powerful. Negative forces include such factors as a possibly decreasing number of students, tightness of funding, the relative weakness of university administrators vis-à-vis the faculty, increasing external regulations and internal unionization, and a faculty reward system that discourages innovation in educational technology.

The availability of educational technology is currently motivating researchers to refocus effort on understanding more precisely—from either a fundamental or a behavioral standpoint—how the learning process works. This by itself can be a major contribution of the new technology. And as educators determine more specifically in what areas of the learning process efforts should be focused, as efforts are focused on the proper areas and positive results are achieved, and as the absolute and relative cost of learning technology decreases, technology will take greater hold in the learning process.

(1975)

SOCIAL JUSTICE

PART

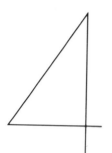

One of the more urgent problem areas with which the Commission was concerned was that of social justice. This problem is still evident in our nation nearly two centuries after the Declaration of Independence asserted that "all men are created equal and endowed by their creator with certain inalienable rights." The clamor for social justice has heightened markedly during the last 15 years, and the pressure upon higher education to play a larger role in facilitating the realization of this goal has also intensified.

ACHIEVING SOCIAL JUSTICE

CHAPTER

7

A substantial portion of the Commission's research resources have supported studies concerned with equality of educational opportunity and the improvement of social justice through practices on the nation's campuses. The studies ranged from the impact of "open access" programs on ability levels of student bodies to the role of religion in colleges and universities.

In 1900, 4 percent of the 18- to 21-year-olds in the United States were enrolled in higher education. By 1970 the percentage had risen to 40. Paul Taubman and Terence Wales' study, *Mental Ability and Higher Educational Attainment in the 20th Century,* discerned that this enormous expansion had not only been achieved without any significant decline in the quality of students, but had actually led to an increase in the percentage of the most able high school graduates who went on to college. At the same time the Commission report *A Chance to Learn* examined the extent to which barriers to admission to colleges and universities still exist. Such factors as low family income, ethnic grouping, geographic location, age, quality of early schooling, and sex constitute formidable handicaps for many Americans who might have a need and desire to seek a college education.

The Carnegie Commission recognized community colleges as central to the eventual solution of the problem of access. By 1969, almost 2 million undergraduates, who formed nearly 30 percent of the national undergraduate population, attended the two-year institutions, and in our report *The Open-Door Colleges,* we recommended that as many as 280 additional community colleges be established by 1980. (In a subsequent report, *New Students and New Places,* this number was reduced to between 175 and 233). With their open-admissions policies, their wide geographic distribution, and their generally low tuition costs, they tend to offer widely varied programs and a chance for students of all ages and interests. In *Where Colleges Are and Who Attends,* C. Arnold Anderson, Mary Jean Bowman, and Vincent Tinto suggested attacking the problem from another angle. This study established that the geographical proximity of a college does not have particularly significant impact on whether a student enters higher education, and its authors support the idea that social justice can best be served by increasing the quality of early schooling. By whatever means, however, solutions must be found, for inequality of opportunity is still present in American higher education, particularly for members of ethnic minorities and for women.

The Commission report *From Isolation to Mainstream* drew attention to the plight of the colleges and universities founded for black Americans. An adequate response by American society to the needs of these institutions that are already combatting inequality is of high priority in the overall struggle for social justice. These institutions must be brought into the mainstream of higher education so that they can make a maximum contribution to the need to accommodate the rising demand of Americans for higher education. The work and problems of those colleges are reported in detail in *Between Two Worlds,* which was reviewed in Section 4.

With regard to women, colleges and universities exhibit a wide range of discriminatory practices. As is suggested by *Escape from the Doll's House,* a study by Saul Feldman, our institutions view women primarily as wives and mothers, and there is evidence of overt discrimination against them by faculties, deans, and other officials. More insidious, however, are the institutional discrimination resulting from rigidity in admissions requirements and the paucity of specialized facilities and services that would help to make higher education compatible with the other interests and activities of women.

In one area, efforts to achieve social justice have met with success. Discrimination on religious grounds has been all but eliminated from the nation's system of higher education. The religious factor is, however, the subject of Stephen Steinberg's contribution to our analyses. He first examines the positions of the Jew and the Catholic from a historical perspective and concludes that their early socioeconomic status contributed heavily to discrimination against them. As their position in the class system improved, discrimination against the Jew and the Catholic abated to the point where today, Steinberg asserts, religious discrimination is of constantly declining significance in American higher education.

When the many-faceted problems of social injustice are closely studied, it is clear not only that higher education has an invaluable role to play in their solution but also that it must play that role fully if the goal of social justice is ever to be secured.

MENTAL ABILITY AND HIGHER EDUCATIONAL ATTAINMENT IN THE 20th CENTURY

PAUL TAUBMAN and TERENCE WALES

This report concerns itself with a long-standing debate in American educational circles that addresses itself to two main questions:

■ Did the expansion in college enrollment, 1900–1961, lead to a decline in the measured average mental ability of the college student population?

■ Did the expansion lead to a reduction in the loss of talent?

Very little research prior to this study has touched on these questions and, indeed, this study is a part of a larger study concerning itself with the rate of return to higher education. The intent of this study is to examine the two questions by determining the relationship, in various samples spanning the twentieth century, between the percentage of high school graduates who enter college and their mental ability at the time of college entrance. The samples used are drawn from the Project Talent Study and the studies done by Barker, Berdie, Berdie and Hood, Benson, Little, O'Brien, Phearman, Proctor, Wolfle and Smith, and Yerkes. These studies present information on the number of high school graduates entering college by IQ or aptitude test score.

In any empirical study, it is necessary to define and delimit the terms which are to be employed, and in this case a definition of *mental ability* is relevant. In common with the field of psychology, this study accepts the theoretical definition of mental ability as the capacity to retain ideas and comprehend and solve abstract problems, and observes that while there is no perfect empirical counterpart to this theoretical definition, there are measures on which differential performance is partly determined by the theoretical construct. The more that differences on the measure are determined by mental ability, the more appropriate is the measure as proxy.

The two most obvious measures relating to mental ability are the rank in high school class and scores on a standardized set of tests. Standardized tests may themselves be separated into IQ tests, which purport to measure general inborn ability independent of previous schooling (although certain evidence counters this claim), and aptitude or achievement tests, which measure the degree of knowledge acquired, primarily in school, in particular subject areas. Since the evidence suggesting that IQ test scores depend at least partially on school-related factors is strong, this study intermixes information from both kinds of tests, holding that the typological difference is probably not of kind but of degree.

Severe difficulties emerge when rank in class is used as a measure. First, its value will probably not remain constant from school to school, and second, rank may depend less on objective criteria than on such factors as the importance placed on docility in class, individual capacity for memorization, and rewards for regurgitation of facts.

More severe difficulties emerge, however, when rank in class is used as a measure. First, its value will probably not remain constant from school to school or even from grade to grade within the same school, and second, rank may depend less on objective criteria than on such factors as the importance placed on docility in class, individual capacity for memorization, and rewards for regurgitation of facts. Therefore, despite the fact that most studies find that knowledge of both IQ and rank in class significantly improves the accuracy of predictions about college attendance, this study relied solely upon test scores.

The scores from various instruments were made comparable after being converted to percentiles, with the "norm" being the population of high school graduates. This method has the added advantage of permitting the use of results provided by other investigations in which data were presented only in percentile form. Primarily interested in analyzing post-high school educational achievement, the authors assumed that the average ability level of high school seniors in the population has remained constant over time and distinguished two stages in the formal educational process: entrance into college and length of stay in college. They concerned themselves with the former, since the necessary data on that stage were more readily available. Additionally, in terms of their methodology they excluded consideration of vocational education from this study for lack of available data. This, they warn, may have slightly tainted their findings regarding loss of talent because an unknown proportion of high-ability students who do not attend college are engaged after high school in vocational or other peripheral further education.

From 1900, did the expansion in college enrollment lead to a decline in the average mental ability of college students? The general pattern for college entrants was as follows: During the 1920s their average ability was at its lowest value—approximately 55 percent. During the 1930s it rose to about 58 percent, and reached a peak of 63 percent in 1946. It remained at approximately this level through 1961.

The data show a downward pattern in the average ability of those not going on to college, and the conclusion drawn is that the quality of college students through the period 1920–1960 has noticeably improved.

While the average ability of college entrants was changing, there were also shifts in the fraction of high school graduates entering college, with the 1950s to 1961 witnessing a larger entering fraction than the 1920s (or 1930s, which actually experienced a slight decline). The data show a downward pattern in the average ability of those not going on to college during the period, and the conclusion drawn from all this evidence is that the quality of college students through the period 1920–1960 has noticeably improved.

With regard to the question of talent loss, the study produces equally encouraging results. The selected values of average ability are: .25, the less gifted; .50, the median of the distribution; .75, which is well above the mean IQ percentile of college entrants; and .90, which includes the most talented members of this population. Manipulation of the variables suggests that at both the 90th and 75th percentiles, college entry has substantially increased over time. At the 50th percentile, the 1960 values are slightly superior to those of the 1920s, while those for the 1930s and 1940s are markedly lower. At the 25th percentile, after a dip during the 1930s and 1940s, the fraction of high school graduates entering college climbs back by 1960 to the 1920s level.

Based on the percentage who enter college at various IQ levels, it is clear from the study that in the 1950s and 1960s there was less loss of talent than in earlier decades, and the authors' speculations concerning the reasons for this phenomenon fasten onto the relaxation of financial constraints as a prime cause. In the middle 1920s, a period of prosperity, the high school population and the middle and upper classes grew rapidly. Partially because income permitted it and partially for reasons of social status, children from these groups tended to attend college. The 1930s ushered in the depression, but still the high school population expanded faster than the national population as employment availability declined. Since World War II, the percentages of students continuing to college rose sharply in the upper IQ brackets and more slowly in the lower ones, perhaps reflecting an increasing capacity on the part of middle-class families to provide a college education for their more gifted children, combined with an increase in the general faith in education as the road to socioeconomic advancement.

Any alteration in graduation requirements or course offerings stimulates substantial debate and opposition. Scratch a liberal academic where the preservation of his own bailiwick is concerned, and you will frequently discover a most conservative tartar preparing to defend his own.

Human institutions seldom react easily to change, and perhaps this is nowhere better exemplified than in higher education, where any alteration in graduation requirements or course offerings stimulates substantial debate and opposition. Scratch a liberal academic where the preservation of his own bailiwick is concerned, and you will frequently discover a most conservative tartar preparing to defend his own.

It is fervently hoped that this study will contribute to depriving the forces of academic conservatism of one of the more mindless objections to expansion, in that it has now empirically shown that expansion does not necessarily result in a loss of quality, but conversely, has led to a diminution in loss of talent.

(1972)

WHERE COLLEGES ARE AND WHO ATTENDS: Effects of Accessibility on College Attendance

C. ARNOLD ANDERSON, MARY JEAN BOWMAN, and VINCENT TINTO

With the increasing drain upon public resources for postsecondary education and projected remedial programs, it becomes more essential every year to reexamine aims and means in relation to policy options. Within the sphere of higher education, the scope for choice among alternative arrangements may in fact be wider now than in 10 years hence. What happens today will condition future options.

This monograph explores from many sides the evidence relating to one general question: Does immediate geographic accessibility to a college increase the proportion of high school graduates who will embark upon some form of postsecondary schooling? Subordinate questions are: What is the response to an accessible college among subpopulations defined by sex, ability, or parental background? Is it possible to construct hypotheses about the factors determining college attendance which may be tested empirically?

The statistical data for this study were originally collected by investigators examining quite different topics.

One set of data concerns Wisconsin high school graduates who were originally surveyed by Professor J. Kenneth Little in 1957 and followed up by Professor William H. Sewell in 1964. This survey made data available for a whole state, a sociolegal entity which provides the money, the students, and the jobs for most college-going youth of the area. The second set of data came from the SCOPE Study (School to College: Opportunities for Postsecondary Education), which was made available by Dr. Dale Tillery and which afforded information on college-bound high school seniors of 1966 in California, Illinois, North Carolina, and Massachusetts.

For the purposes of this study "accessibility" is defined in the layman's geographic sense, and the analysis uses comparisons across towns or communities (whether a village of a few hundred people or a metropolis). Accessibility within large metropolitan conurbations could not be considered because such analysis requires special sorts of data which were unavailable.

The data were analyzed in the context of three increasingly complex models. These provided the appropriate framework for hypothesizing particular determinants of the response to varying degrees of college accessibility. The simplest conclusion from this analysis is that spatial accessibility to one or more colleges has little effect, for most youth, on whether they will attend college—be the accessible school a junior college, an open-door four-year college, or a more selective institution.

Spatial accessibility to one or more colleges has little effect, for most youth, on whether they will attend college—be the accessible school a junior college, an open-door four-year college, or a more selective institution.

This conclusion has large practical implication; ". . . at a minimum, the case for implanting junior colleges thickly over the landscape will have to stand on other ground." However, ". . . there are important exceptions to that conclusion for particular categories of youth who live in particular settings. . . ." Response to accessibility varies with ability and family background, and also with the structure of higher education within a given state. In Wisconsin, for example, "about one-eighth of the boys and one-sixth of the girls obtained some sort of noncollegiate instruction within seven years after finishing high school. They represented respectively one-fourth and two-fifths of all who received any formal postsecondary instruction."

The propensity to stay in school for more and more years has been permeating progressively deeply into the general population, and into particular various subpopulations once they have begun to use collegiate services. To what extent colleges have induced this, or merely reflected it, cannot be ascertained from this research, but the study stresses that "it would be difficult to support the assertion that spreading attendance at college among the nation's various subpopulations should be attributed in major degree to the greater local availability of colleges. . . . Indeed, family status and personal ability outweigh accessibility in explaining variations in college attendance rates, despite large overlapping in the ability distributions for college and non-college youth."

College accessibility does, however, play some part. Schools render their services mainly in a particular location, and the families of potential students are also distributed in particular settlement clusters. "The composition of these settlements varies in distributions of measured ability of youth, the quality of previous schooling, the education or social status of the parents, and so on." In this situation, educational space may be looked at either from the viewpoint of the planner: How can we attract students? Or from the viewpoint of the student: Should I go to college, and to which one? This study took the second stance and tried to ascertain whether the presence of a collegiate institution of one kind or another in the community increases the proportion of that community's youth who go to college, and to what extent the response might be a substitution of local attendance for what would have been attendance farther from home.

The basic questions about the effects of college location are these: When a new (or branch) institution of a particular kind is established in a community, what effect does its presence have on where young people of the vicinity go to college? To what extent will local attendance be a net addition to, or a substitution for, attendance elsewhere? And lastly, what are some of the implications, for individuals or society, of one pattern of migration or the other?

There is a "weak" preference for the nearer option in attending college, but what happens depends on the characteristics of the colleges in the immediate vicinity and the traits of the potential students and their families.

The data do indicate that there is a "weak" preference for the nearer option in attending college, but what happens depends on the characteristics of the colleges in the immediate vicinity and the traits of the potential students and their families. When viewed as channels to future jobs and earnings, colleges differ in what they seem to promise youth of varying characteristics. For example, the study demonstrates that the more able youth from advantaged homes are most prone to seek prestigious colleges, often in other states. On the other hand, it emerges that many youth who grow up in remote areas express a strong preference, regardless of their sex, for the security of a "local" environment. Similarly, youth who, because of meager parental means, regard cost as a high-priority item in college selection, tend to live at home and attend "local" institutions.

Both low-cost tuition and the elimination of ability constraints emerge from this study as being more important factors in college attendance than the proximity of a college.

Both low-cost tuition and the elimination of ability constraints emerge from this study as being more important factors in college attendance than the proximity of a college. In particular, evidence that a new local college will increase college attendance among the disadvantaged is weak, although there is evidence that local open-door colleges will sometimes increase college attendance among youth of below-average ability and socioeconomic status.

Placing a new college in a particular location will have different implications for those who attend it instead of going elsewhere—depending on the nature of the college, the nature of the community, and the nature of the communications which that community has with other places. For example, to grow up in Madison, Wisconsin, and to attend the local university is to participate in a broadening experience which a "local" college cannot offer. Accordingly, this study suggests that introducing colleges into the depressed mountain communities of Appalachia, or the slums of a major city, may in fact deprive rather than contribute to local youth who, but for that college, would have traveled elsewhere to school.

Introducing colleges into the depressed mountain communities of Appalachia, or the slums of a major city, may in fact deprive rather than contribute to local youth who, but for that college, would have traveled elsewhere to school.

The arguments both for and against dispersal of colleges widely over space are actually very different according to the kind of college considered and whether it is an intervening link in a regular academic sequence, or a community institution serving many people, old and young, through diverse educational activities attuned to many interests. Does deliberate localization serve the interests of either the students or the society? And more crucially, what services should be developed to serve a local community and raise its quality of life? These are questions which must be faced by educational decision makers, for while schools might be defensibly located where demand is strong, there can be no defense for a policy of creating colleges and then creating demand for them. Equalization of opportunity will not have been achieved in a situation where a large majority of high school graduates continue through to the fourteenth year of formal education only to find, at the point when they might extricate themselves from the mass, a closed door. It is not accidental that in California, with its immense establishment of free-access junior colleges, the bottleneck to opportunity is a stage further along.

"Inevitably," the authors maintain, "we must ask also whether the junior college will come to be conceived of mainly as an extension of secondary education," and again, "whether the junior college, using this term generically, is viewed mainly as a form of remedial education for students who were sluggards in earlier years of school, even though of high potential."

Extrapolating from the findings of their study, the authors close on the issue of priority in educational funding. They maintain that "with . . . justification, one might contend that higher education now receives a sufficient proportion of the education dollar. . . . The major holdup in educational progress for most youth occurs during the earliest grades. . . ." Equality of opportunity "is not served merely by lower qualifications or by providing open entry. . . . Investment of resources for the purpose of thickening the network of colleges . . . is indefensible. . . ."

There is an opportunity now for education policy makers to consider options in aims, but intellectual fads must be resisted in planning for the future so that major decisions made now, on less than careful research, will not unduly preclude better decisions in the future.

(1972)

ESCAPE FROM THE DOLL'S HOUSE: Women in Graduate and Professional School Education
Saul D. Feldman

For over 200 years after the founding of Harvard College, the doors to higher education in the United States remained closed to women. Underlying most of the objections to opening these doors were fears that a college education would render women unsuitable for marriage and childrearing. In addition, women were considered too weak, in body and in mind, to bear the rigors of advanced schooling.

In spite of these objections, early advocates of women's education established female seminaries during the 1820s. Glorified high schools at their inception, these seminaries slowly introduced more rigorous courses into their curricula, without ever rivaling the academic excellence of colleges for men. By the late 1880s, however, colleges for women were being founded, and newly formed coeducational institutions, as well as previously all-male colleges, began to make room—albeit grudgingly—for women. At this time, graduate schools admitted women with somewhat less reluctance than the undergraduate institutions did. At both levels of education, however, women were severely underrepresented.

In 1970, women received 43.2 percent of the bachelor's degrees, 34.8 percent of the master's degrees, and 13.3 percent of the doctorates. Female undergraduates are still less likely to enter graduate school than men, and female graduate students are less likely to attain a degree. Furthermore, female students are segregated into academic disciplines that stress teaching rather than research and yield little prestige, power, or economic wealth.

This study clarifies the situation of women empirically by analyzing questionnaire data. First, a sample of undergraduate students was asked to rate 45 academic fields on masculinity or femininity. The results of the questionnaire upheld typical stereotypes: Engineering, physics, and chemistry, for example, emerged as masculine, while art, English, and nursing were regarded as feminine. Taking 1968–69 enrollment figures, the author then shows that the proportion of female graduate students in a discipline corresponds almost exactly to stereotypic views of the discipline's masculinity or femininity. Why this relationship originally developed cannot be determined, but at present a circular process takes place: Women are encouraged to enter fields that are "feminine" by virtue of their predominantly female enrollment.

The balance of the study is based on an analysis of massive data gathered by the 1969 Carnegie Commission Survey of Faculty and Student Opinion. These data reveal that fields considered feminine differ significantly from those considered masculine or even "neutral," both in their own characteristics and in those of their students. As perceived by both male and female students, feminine fields command less respect, foster less exciting developments in research, and attract fewer of the best students than masculine fields. Faculty in these fields tend to receive lower salaries and to do less paid consulting and, since feminine fields cluster in the humanities, they are teaching- rather than research-oriented.

More important to women's status within academia, however, is the strong prejudice, especially within masculine fields, against female graduate students. Particularly in masculine fields—mainly the "hard" sciences and such professions as business, law, and medicine—students sensed that faculty do not take women students seriously. Both students and faculty were more likely than those in other fields to feel that women lack the same dedication to graduate study as men. Such a belief naturally affects peer interaction as well as the manner in which professors relate to their female students. Handicapped by a more negative self-image than male students, women also seem to depend more on support from their professors and tend to falter without it, both in confidence and career aspirations. The absence of professorial support is evidently a main factor in the choice made by graduate women to teach in a junior college rather than embark on the more prestigious careers of university teaching or research. In any case, academically inclined graduate women

As perceived by both male and female students, feminine fields command less respect, foster less exciting developments in research, and attract fewer of the best students than masculine fields. Faculty in these fields tend to receive lower salaries and to do less paid consulting.

opt for junior college teaching far more often than men even when they score equally high on such variables as degree attainment, involvement in professional activities, and article publication.

The pressures of graduate school alone do not hinder academic progress for women: marriage places an "external constraint" upon their graduate education. Almost three-fourths of the married female graduate students enroll only on a part-time basis, and married and divorced women—probably for childrearing reasons—also defer their education, so that they tend to be older than other graduate students. Divorced women, however, achieve far greater success (that is, they commit themselves more strongly to graduate study and are more likely to take satisfaction in the student role) than their single or married female counterparts.

The analysis of the data does not substantiate contentions of outright discrimination within higher education. Rather, it documents patterns of sex-based inequality—an inequality that nonetheless reflects differential treatment from professors and fellow students.

The analysis of the data does not substantiate contentions of outright discrimination within higher education. Rather, it documents patterns of sex-based inequality—an inequality that nonetheless reflects differential treatment from professors and fellow students. But the inferiority of the position of women in higher education will not change decisively even with improved counseling, enlightened faculty attitudes, or even equal enrollment of men and women. Long before they come to college, students have shaped their lives and feelings in response to society's expectations. Thus, until differential socialization and stereotypic thinking disappear throughout society, patterns of inequality in higher education will continue.

(1974)

THE ACADEMIC MELTING POT: Catholics and Jews in American Higher Education
STEPHEN STEINBERG

Until the twentieth century, American higher education had an unmistakably Protestant cast. Most of the leading colleges had been founded by Protestant religious denominations, the intellectual and moral climate was heavily tinged with Calvinism, and the great majority of students and faculty were also Protestant. However, the influx of millions of Catholic and Jewish immigrants during the great migrations of the nineteenth and early twentieth centuries set the stage for the ultimate de-Protestantization of higher education.

The educational history of Catholics and Jews in America is one of striking contrasts. At a time when Jewish immigrants were eagerly sending their children off to college, Catholic leaders were issuing warnings about the dangers of secular schools. Even when threatened with restrictive quotas, Jews rejected the idea of building their own colleges, while Catholics chose to develop an elaborate system of parish schools and Catholic colleges. Jews have produced a disproportionate number of scholars and scientists, whereas Catholics historically have been underrepresented in these spheres.

Jewish immigrants entered a situation of expanding educational opportunity. Despite the problems they encountered in the elite colleges, where religious quotas were instituted in the form of regional quotas and other subterfuges, few obstacles successfully blocked the paths of aspiring Jewish students. The structure and content of higher education were changing in directions that corresponded with Jewish interests and talents, and Jews quickly became established in the social sciences and certain of the professions. Concentrated in the urban Northeast, they were in the "right" place at the "right" time. No other ethnic group in America has found itself in such fortuitous circumstances when it was prepared for its breakthrough into higher education.

Despite the problems they encountered in the elite colleges, few obstacles successfully blocked the paths of aspiring Jewish students. The structure and content of higher education were changing in directions that corresponded with Jewish interests and talents.

The Catholic story is quite different, although in the past half-century, American Catholicism has undergone dramatic change in its relation to the larger society. Protestant-Catholic conflict, once intense, continues only at minimal levels. The weight of historical evidence suggests that Catholic problems with American educational institutions were not expressions of a native anti-intellectualism emanating from Catholic religion, but rather the result of conditions associated with the position of Catholics in nineteenth-century America. Most of the factors that once resulted in Catholic separation have now disappeared or lost their force, and Catholics have accommodated themselves to the secular currents in American society.

Catholic problems with American educational institutions were not expressions of a native anti-intellectualism emanating from Catholic religion, but rather the result of conditions associated with the position of Catholics in nineteenth-century America.

Even before their arrival in America, Catholics and Jews differed in their cultural orientations toward education. Indeed, these cultural factors have generally been assumed to be the main source of differences in intellectual achievement between the two groups. The most important theoretical problem of this study, however, was to determine the extent to which these different cultural orientations merely reflected differences in social class. The overall conclusion is that Jewish and Catholic educational values were more than aspects of a culture passed on from one generation to the next, but were solidly grounded in material conditions, particularly those associated with social class.

Jews had experience and skills in middle-class occupations. They were also literate as a group and had cognitive skills to pass on to their children. Catholics, however, were handicapped by factors related to their peasant origins. In short, the value orientations of both Catholics and Jews were congruent with and bolstered by social-class factors.

Changes in these underlying conditions have produced corresponding changes in surface culture. Catholics demonstrate the validity of this proposition. In this century, the bulk of Irish and Italian immigrants have improved their relative class standing, and are fairly well integrated into the nation's economic and cultural mainstream. Data from the 1969 Carnegie Commission Survey of Faculty and Student Opinion were used to determine whether this change increased Catholic representation among scholars, and whether religious values still function as an obstacle to scholarly productivity.

The data indicate a dramatic upsurge in Catholic representation at all levels of American higher education and a leveling off of Jewish representation.

The data indicate a dramatic upsurge in Catholic representation at all levels of American higher education and a leveling off of Jewish representation. While Catholics continue to be underrepresented in high-quality institutions, they are rapidly closing the gap there, just as they are in higher education as a whole.

The problem with cultural theories that explain Jewish success in terms of Jewish values is not that they are incorrect but that they are superficial. They are correct in the sense that Jews did have the benefit of a rich intellectual tradition and did place an unusually high value on education and intellectual achievement. But cultural theories are trivial unless they go on to examine the broad structural factors that buttressed this value system, as well as the favorable structure of opportunity that permitted values to become realities.

Jews did have the benefit of a rich intellectual tradition and did place an unusually high value on education and intellectual achievement. But cultural theories are trivial unless they go on to examine the broad structural factors that buttressed this value system.

Conversely, Catholics had great difficulty in adjusting certain of their core values to the requirements of modern secular education. This value conflict had both cultural and ethnic sources, and was a major factor in explaining, as expressed by Richard Hofstadter, "why Catholicism has failed in America to develop an intellectual tradition or to produce its own class of intellectuals." Several findings of this study offset this harsh assessment.

First, there is the fact that Catholics are belatedly taking their place in the nation's colleges and universities, both as students and as faculty members. Furthermore, on questions of religion, science, and politics, Catholics exhibit a remarkable similarity to Protestants, though both are consistently different from Jews. However, there is no evidence of a special brand of anti-intellectualism among Catholics.

Given the handicaps with which Catholic immigrants started life in America, it is not surprising that they required another generation or two to produce their numerical share of scholars and scientists.

Given the handicaps with which Catholic immigrants started life in America, it is not surprising that they required another generation or two to produce their numerical share of scholars and scientists. The fact that the great majority of Irish, Italian, and Polish immigrants came from peasant backgrounds was of enormous consequence, for not only did high illiteracy levels slow the pace of acculturation, but such Catholic immigrants also lacked the occupational sophistication that accelerated economic mobility among Jews. These conditions presented formidable obstacles to intellectual achievement.

As Catholics have gradually improved their position in the class system, however, their children are increasingly going to college and, as in every group, a certain number of them follow academic careers and become scholars of distinction. The scenario is the same as for other groups. It has only taken longer to play itself out.

(1974)

BLACK ELITE: The New Market for Highly Qualified Black Workers in the U.S.*
RICHARD B. FREEMAN

Despite the popular connection of discrimination with poverty, labor market differentials by race traditionally have been greatest at the top of the economic ladder. College-trained black men, in particular, have long suffered from low incomes and poor job opportunities. In 1959 the income of black and white college graduates differed by 72 percent, while that of grade school graduates differed by just 34 percent. Of new degree recipients young (25- to 34-year-old) black men earned $4,439 compared to $6,356 for white men. With rare exception, black graduates were excluded from high-level jobs in major corporations and concentrated in low-paying professions. Nearly half of black male seniors planned on teaching careers compared to one-seventh of white seniors. The potentiality for black economic progress through additional education and attainment of college and university training seemed small indeed.

In the 1960s these discriminatory patterns underwent dramatic change. The demand for black college graduates increased enormously, with consequent improvement in job opportunities and salaries. For the first time, national corporations began to recruit black men and women for managerial and professional jobs, seeking employees at Southern black colleges that had previously never seen corporate recruiters. Increasing numbers of black college men entered managerial and business-oriented professions, such as accounting and law, rather than the traditional teaching field. The ratio of black to white incomes rose sharply among college workers, reversing the historical pattern of increasing racial income differentials with the level of education. The starting salaries of black college graduates attained parity with those of whites.

This study is a detailed empirical examination of the post-World War II improvement in the labor market for black college-trained and related high-level workers. It documents the extraordinary gain in the economic

* This abstract was prepared by the author before the final manuscript for his full report was completed.

position of these workers, investigates the response of black college students and qualified personnel to the new market setting, and explores the factors that have transformed the market.

The study begins with a detailed statistical analysis of the change in the labor market position of highly qualified black workers. The evidence shows:

A marked convergence in the job distribution of black and white college-trained men, with, for example, the proportion of black graduates in managerial jobs rising from 7.0 (1962) to 13.4 (1972) percent while the white proportion increased by just 2.6 percentage points (21.4 to 24.0)

A jump in the number of corporations recruiting at black colleges from just 4 per campus in 1960 to 287 per campus in 1970

An increase in the ratio of starting salaries of black to white college graduates from .72 to 1.00 in the decade of the 1960s, with a resultant improvement in the rate of return to black investments in college: by 1972 the return to black college training exceeded that to white training

Gains in the relative economic position of black college women so that they earned considerably more over the year than comparable white women in the early 1970s—a difference due largely but not exclusively to differences in hours worked.

This and other evidence indicate the collapse that took place in the late 1960s in traditional discriminatory patterns against starting college-trained blacks.

This and other evidence indicate the collapse that took place in the late 1960s In traditional discriminatory patterns against starting college-trained blacks.

Accompanying the Improvement in the black labor market position was a significant transformation in the educational system. The principal educational developments include: desegregation of public schools; a sharp upswing in the enrollments of blacks in college; a shift in enrollments from Southern black colleges to Northern and traditionally white Southern institutions; an increase in federal and foundation support for the Southern black colleges, which were hard-pressed by the switch of students, particularly the most able, to other institutions. For the first time, the relative number of blacks obtaining college-training is approaching that of whites, with the black as well as the white elite receiving training in the same set of colleges and universities.

The response of black students to new opportunities was rapid and extensive. Career decisions changed greatly in the 1960s, with large numbers of students and related qualified workers shifting from teaching and related fields to "traditionally closed" business occupations. At black Southern colleges, the proportion of men majoring in business administration jumped from 5.4 to 23.7. The changed pattern of career choice appears to reflect exceptional responsiveness to economic incentives and a highly elastic supply of black graduates to professions. Econometric estimates of this supply of black college men to professions reveal an elasticity above unity; a survey analysis of the factors in entering students' decisions shows considerable concern with pecuniary incentives, in part because of the generally low economic background of black college students.

With increased numbers of black youngsters going on to college and entering professional-managerial occupations, traditional patterns of intergenerational social mobility also changed significantly in the 1960s. The probability that blacks with a given family background would rise in the economic hierarchy improved greatly, nearly equaling that of whites. The improvement was greater, though only modestly so, among blacks from relatively better family backgrounds. Even those from broken families experienced a substantial increase in the likelihood of economic progress.

The reasons for the transformation of the labor market are also investigated in the study, though the findings are more equivocal because of the difficulty in pinning down the precise factors and mechanisms underlying a "social revolution." Governmental antidiscriminatory policies associated with the Civil Rights Act of 1964 appear to have had a substantial effect on the market, with the improvement in the position of black male graduates concentrated in the late 1960s, following passage of the act, while the advance of black female graduates was also accelerated at that time. Statistical calculations show that the post-1964 advance cannot be attributed to normal cyclical or trend changes in black/white economic position. Across states, the black position improved especially rapidly in the South—where federal antidiscriminatory activities were concentrated. Additional indication of the impact of public policy is found in the hiring practices of governmental bodies—at the federal, state, and local level. The relative number of blacks in high-level public jobs increased significantly in the later 1960s, with, for example, the black proportion of federal workers with civil service classifications of GS-16 or better rising from less than 1 to 2.5 percent in the late 1960s to the early 1970s. The wide variety of other social changes in the decade of the sixties, however, makes it difficult to quantify the effect of governmental policies, for observed correlations could reflect unmeasured changes in attitudes and the like. Even so, it cannot be gainsaid that governmental policy did improve the economic position of highly qualified blacks in the 1960s.

Desegregation of schools led to a decline in employment of black teachers and, more strikingly, of administrators in Southern states, which was counterbalanced by their increased employment in the North.

The study also investigates the one major job market in which demand for black college graduates worsened in the post-World War II period, namely, the market for black schoolteachers in the South. Desegregation of schools led to a decline in employment of black teachers and, more strikingly, of administrators in Southern states, which was counterbalanced by their increased employment in the North. The employment effects of desegregation were, however, quite different across areas, due, it is hypothesized, to differences in black political power. In border states which desegregated relatively rapidly after the 1954 Supreme Court decision, the ratio of the black share of teachers to pupils in education fell sharply; in Southern states which delayed desegregation, the decline in demand was much less—apparently as a result of increased black voting power.

In sum, this study finds a remarkable change in the market for highly trained black workers in the 1960s which, *if continued,* marks the collapse of market discrimination against highly educated blacks. However, whether black college workers will maintain their relative position in the future, advancing in the job and income structure as rapidly as whites, remains to be seen. The study raises several important questions which deserve additional analysis, namely, those relating to the basic reasons for national antidiscriminatory policies and for the contrast between the improvement in the black position in the 1960s and the previous decades of little relative advance.

(1975)

WOMEN AND THE POWER TO CHANGE
edited by FLORENCE HOWE

This volume of essays represents an attempt by four academic women to chart the changes that have taken place in their lives and thoughts some four or five years after the women's movement began to make its mark on campuses in the United States. The authors begin with two assumptions: (1) In a technological society, the university is a crucially central institution and (2) the university is a male enclave that allows women to function only in closely restricted areas. In addition, the authors are keenly aware that, as Florence Howe notes in her introduction, "Bright women even at women's colleges learned to think as the ubiquitous generic 'man,' and never to consider their histories as women." Thus, the issues that these essays center on are: changing the (male-oriented) curriculum; and changing current practices in the employment, promotion, and tenure of academic women and their recruitment into administrative posts. In developing the theme of change, two of the authors—from different points of departure and with somewhat different conclusions—approach the question of power.

In her essay, "Toward a Woman-Centered University," Adrienne Rich focuses on the male-centered nature and bias of the university and offers thereby a holistic approach to the issues surrounding women in higher education. In Rich's view, there must be a move inside the university, as there already is one outside it, to re-create a feminist history and culture and to serve the needs and interests of women. Women's education is undermined both by the curriculum and by the male-topped hierarchy superimposed on the fragmented lives of women who serve in subordinate positions. Rich recommends revisions in the curriculum and several institutional reforms—chiefly university-supported child care and arrangements for part-time study and work. She envisions a university sweepingly transformed by its consideration for women. Such an institution would refocus not only its course of study and organizational structures, but its research goals and services.

While Adrienne Rich scans the university scene cinematically, Arlie Hochschild closes in to examine the career patterns and daily lives of its faculty. Building on personal experience as well as on the research of the last decade, Hochschild attempts an explanation for the paucity of women in high academic places. She examines the two most common explanations—discrimination and the socialization of women to avoid success and authority—but argues that a third pattern, more massive even than they, controls the lives of academic men and women. In her words, "the classic profile of the academic career is cut to the image of the traditional man with his traditional wife." That is, the university is organized around the employment of males with supportive families—wives who type manuscripts and serve meals and children who are taught to stay out of their father's way. Hence, even if the university were the meritocracy it claims to be and women were not socialized differently from men, radical inequities would persist. Hochschild's solutions, like Rich's, suggest the necessity for institutional change.

The university is organized around the employment of males with supportive families—wives who type manuscripts and serve meals and children who are taught to stay out of their father's way.

In "A View from the Law School," Aleta Wallach focuses on her experiences as a law school student and on her conception of law as "the source of all power, indeed as power itself, conferring or withholding status as it does." As she traces women's presence in and absence from legal training and practice, Wallach builds a case for law being the "rule of men." Males used the "law" to confer "upon women inferior status and upon men preeminent status." Through its curriculum, admissions policies, and institutional style, the law school became one essential tool for this end.

As one of a handful of pioneers, Wallach describes the recent yielding of the law school to feminists' demands for the admission of more women students and faculty and the revision of curriculum. As she turns her attention to the question of equal educational opportunity for women, Wallach argues that so lengthy a period of inequality justifies compensation. Thus, she recommends preferential treatment to achieve parity and

183

concludes that, if equal educational opportunity for women cannot be achieved in the presently male-dominated and biased law schools, separate feminist institutions should be established.

Florence Howe writes about instrumental power—the tool of political leaders, administrators, teachers, and husbands—in her essay, "Women and the Power to Change." Until now, *power* has been carefully avoided as a slogan and a goal within the women's movement. The traditional concept of power as commodity has frightened both men and women in their attempts to understand—and change—male uses of power and has hindered efforts of women to improve their legal, social, and economic status.

Consciousness-raising groups have turned the women's movement into a teaching movement and have developed open forms of leadership and information sharing.

An alternative conception of power promulgated by the women's movement is reflected in the formation of consciousness-raising groups. These groups, which generally function democratically, have turned the women's movement into a teaching movement and have developed open forms of leadership and information sharing.

Howe feels that women can also effect change by teaching in the more structured environment of the university. "Organizing a process and curriculum called women's studies challenges 'traditional bodies of knowledge' not only by replacing them (at least for a while), but more significantly, by attempting to disestablish their authority." Howe offers suggestions for a woman-oriented curriculum and discusses three teaching strategies—working with small groups instead of individuals, substituting the action project for the library paper, and insisting that students keep journals of their class-related experiences. She concludes by arguing that women can work the most change in our society by concentrating major energies on teaching (and other heavily female occupations) to build a base of support and develop leaders for the women's movement rather than attempting more fully to integrate nontraditional fields.

(1975)

ANTIBIAS REGULATION OF UNIVERSITIES:
Faculty Problems and Their Solutions
RICHARD A. LESTER

This study presents an analysis of the complex problem of eliminating racial and sexual bias in the appointment, advancement, and compensation of faculty members of major universities. It takes the form of a critical examination of government programs that enforce "affirmative action" against job discrimination in universities and also of the implications that "compliance" with these programs may have for the future of the country's distinguished universities. Alternative proposals are made to correct what are seen as deficiencies in existing public antibias programs.

The study draws on the experience of faculty members and administrators of 20 universities across the country since 1968, when enforcement of federal antibias regulations first began to be applied to universities. Compliance officials in Washington and in several regional offices of the Department of Health, Education, and Welfare (the enforcement agency), as well as staff members of college and university associations, were also consulted.

Generally, university faculty members and academic administrators can be expected to support appointment, advancement, and compensation of faculty on the basis of merit. However, since opinions may differ on the qualities a particular university needs most in its faculty in general, and especially in a particular instance, it may be difficult in a given case to convince others that the best-qualified candidate was appointed or promoted to tenure.

The quality of a university's faculty is likely to be influenced by the existence of working arrangements that faculty members find congenial and by a system of rewards geared to individual merit as judged by colleagues in the discipline. Distinguished faculty stress self-determination in their teaching and research, departmental self-government through peer sharing of responsibility for departmental management and personnel decisions, and reward for individual merit and performance based on professional evaluation.

Outside pressures are exerted in the name of antibias regulation that undermine a system of faculty work arrangements that nurtures independence of thought, creativity, and work satisfaction.

Although working conditions considered ideal by faculty contrast sharply with those found in business enterprises or government bureaucracies, government programs of antibias enforcement have been designed on the industry-government model of hierarchical personnel practice and authority. It may be that federal and state compliance personnel, with backgrounds in business and government, lack interest in preserving and strengthening the faculty system of governance. Consequently, their inflexible application of rules designed for industry-model situations tends to weaken the faculty system and bolster centralization of authority and control within the university. Thus, outside pressures are exerted in the name of antibias regulation that undermine a system of faculty work arrangements that nurtures independence of thought, creativity, and work satisfaction.

Administrative pressures by HEW and actions by the Department of Labor to make faculty selection and pay systems conform to the industry model take the form of insisting that methods of selection and promotion of faculty be validated on the basis of proportionality of results; attempting, under equal pay enforcement, to use job content rather than intellectual qualifications as a basis for specialized tenure positions; and requiring that affirmative action numerical goals be calculated according to an estimated labor market pool of qualified and available persons applied to all academic ranks and specialties.

Faculty decisions on tenure appointments customarily involve comparative analysis of candidates' résumés; letters or oral communications from faculty in the field about a candidate's relative standing and promise; student appraisals of various aspects of the candidate's teaching performance; critical reviews of published and unpublished scholarly work; and conclusions of department members from personal interviews, a class, seminar, or lecture given on campus, or a paper delivered at a professional meeting. With such information and evaluation as a basis, the tenured members of the department meet, discuss the candidates' relative merits, and make their choice.

It has become increasingly clear to university faculty and administrators that the only intelligent policy is to adhere to the principle of equal employment opportunity.

It has become increasingly clear to university faculty and administrators that the only intelligent policy is to adhere to the principle of equal employment opportunity—to have faculty appointed and promoted who, on the basis of their past performance, are judged by mature teacher-scholars to be the best available in terms of the requirements of the position. Such a policy is also consistent with the most effective pursuit of a university's educational goals.

Seven defects are identified as characterizing the federal regulatory system as it applies to universities and colleges:

■ Failure to recognize that demand for tenured faculty is highly individualistic and selective, based on personal achievement of the highest quality as a teacher-scholar, and stimulated by competition for excellence of faculty

■ Failure to make a proper analysis of supply differences by sex and race for academic disciplines and subfields, and to take special account in affirmative action plans of human-capital development on the job during the five to seven years after receipt of the Ph.D.

■ Flaws in the conception and measurement of discrimination under availability-utilization analyses that result in placing undue blame and remedial responsibility on the demand side and lead to inflated numerical hiring goals

■ Pressures for discriminatory hiring to meet inflated goals, resulting in new discrimination and the likelihood of an increasing number of "mistakes" in the selection of tenured faculty

■ Government application of the industry model of authority and personnel management to university faculty operations, with the consequent threat to the faculty system of collegial decision making based on professional evaluation of merit

■ Increasingly involved and intrusive regulation of faculty decision making, with the negotiation and enforcement of each successive affirmative action plan

■ Inconsistent government policies and regulatory treatment between government agencies and among different HEW offices, opening up added legal liabilities for universities and affecting arbitrarily and unevenly their ability to compete for faculty, students, and resources

The proposed alternative program is designed to improve executive-order enforcement of nondiscrimination in several respects: soundness of conceptions, consistency of policies, suitability for the special needs of higher education, avoidance of adverse effects on educational objectives of institutions, restraint on the regulatory tendency toward undue intrusion, and economy and efficiency of administration.

Experience indicates that the following aims and considerations need to be stressed:

■ Guidelines for affirmative action plans should be based on the facts, well-considered objectives, clear definitions and concepts, appropriate analytical methods, and arrangements for intelligent, sensible enforcement.

■ All parts of the federal effort to achieve nondiscrimination in higher education should be consistent in aim and policy.

■ Stress should be placed on and adequate credit given for developing a larger supply of women and minority-group faculty qualified for tenure appointment at high-ranking universities.

■ The importance of intellectual autonomy for universities should be recognized and care taken to avoid detailed regulation of their internal operations.

■ In the enforcement of equal opportunity for all faculty, due recognition should be given to the primacy of the basic objectives of a major university, namely: the discovery of important new knowledge; the cultivation by faculty instruction of understanding of existing knowledge, ability to use that knowledge, and competence to create new knowledge; and the training of students in professional schools in the understanding and practice of a systematic body of specialized knowledge.

An effective affirmative action program would include

■ A program for increasing the supply of highly qualified women and minority-group teacher-scholars in certain academic disciplines and fields of professional practice where the supply of teacher-researchers is thin.

■ Use of availability-utilization analysis and numerical goals to achieve "proportionality" to be confined to first regular appointments of new and prospective Ph.D. holders to the position of assistant professor or advanced instructor on the ladder of professional advancement. Thus, "affirmative action demand plans" would be focused on those at the same stage of career development, and should be broad enough for the law of averages to apply.

■ For faculty appointments other than first appointment as assistant professor and for promotions within professorial ranks, use of (1) analysis of data in the proposed periodic reports of institutions, (2) field examination of the institution's central information file on each faculty appointment and promotion, (3) the internal procedures of the institution for settling individual faculty complaints, (4) the Equal Employment Opportunity Commission and state agencies for antidiscrimination enforcement, and (5) the courts.

■ Concentration in a single agency (HEW) of the administrative overseeing of affirmative action plans and compliance, which would remove college and university faculty from the Labor Department's jurisdiction for contract compliance.

■ HEW regulation for faculty of major universities that recruit a majority of their faculty from the national market to be handled by one well-qualified unit instead of 10 regional offices.

■ A restricting and strengthening of the staff of the Higher Education Division of the Office for Civil Rights in HEW, so that it is suited to meet its increased responsibilities and functions.

Equal opportunity for students and faculty members to rise to the top on the basis of merit is essential for the healthy functioning of universities. Painful experience in this country and abroad has shown the corrosive effects on the process of creation and cultivation of truth when outside groups—government, business, religious, or other special interests—exert undue pressure or gain significant control over the operation of universities. The professional integrity of the search for and dissemination of truth must be maintained if the intellectual leadership in a country is to be free.

(1974)

HIGHER EDUCATION AND EARNINGS:
College as an Investment and
a Screening Device
PAUL TAUBMAN and TERENCE WALES

The proposition that education can be treated as an investment in human capital—that education teaches marketable skills and produces other monetary and nonmonetary benefits—has recently attracted much attention in economic circles. Most studies of the rates of return to education share two concepts: First, the differences in earnings by education level represent the net effect of education rather than some other personal characteristics that have not been held constant. Second, these differences represent increases in productivity made possible by education. Although some attempts have been made to account for the effect of mental ability and family background on one's lifetime earnings, these have been hampered by insufficient data.

The authors of this study make use of a new and extremely rich data source to obtain better estimates than have previously been possible of the rates of return to education at various levels of ability and education. In addition, they explore the implication inherent in most studies that income differentials are due solely to skills produced by education and concentrate on the possibility that the differentials arise because those who lack ''required'' educational credentials are screened out of high-paying jobs.

Most of the analysis and conclusions in this study are based on a sample of volunteers for the pilot, navigator, and bombardier training programs of the Army Air Corps during World War II. The volunteers were required to pass the Cadet Qualifying Test with a score equivalent to the average for college sophomores (thereby limiting the sample population to one brighter and better educated than the United States population as a whole). A battery of 17 tests was then administered that measured such abilities as mathematical skills, physical coordination, and spatial perception. In 1955, Robert L. Thorndike and Elizabeth Hagen conducted a survey of 17,000 of these volunteers to determine how well the tests predicted subsequent vocational success. In 1969, the National Bureau of Economic Research conducted a follow-up survey of those who had responded in 1955. The results of these two surveys (from some 4,400 respondents) form the data base, to be denoted as the NBER-TH sample, for the present study. In addition, a sample taken in the mid-1950s by Dael Wolfle and Joseph Smith, which included all Minnesota high school graduates of 1938, provides a comparison of results with the NBER-TH sample.

In detailed and skillful regressions analyses, the authors relate earnings in a particular year to a large set of explanatory variables, break up the independent variables into discrete categories, and combine the dummy variables to allow for interaction. The equations include measures of education, mathematical ability, personal biography, health, marital status, father's education, and age.

Within-occupation regressions are calculated to indicate both the extent to which success in different occupations depends on ability and education, and the extent to which education, ability, and prior work experience impart specific skills. The nature of the NBER-TH data also allows the authors to construct time-series profiles to examine several questions about the relative increases in lifetime earnings that generally have been studied only cross-sectionally. The rise in earnings with age, at least until middle age, has been well documented in other studies. Evidence from the present analysis suggests that starting salaries do not generally differ by education or ability level, but that individuals with more education and ability will perform their jobs better and, over time, will be promoted more quickly and receive higher salaries than those with less education and ability. Among the authors' findings is that, for those who are at least high school graduates, ability is a more important determinant of the range of the earnings distribution than is education. The widely accepted proposition that age-income profiles are steeper, the higher the education level, is not entirely borne out by the results in this sample. These are calculated with ability and background held constant, unlike previous results based on mean earnings by age and education level.

For those who are at least high school graduates, ability is a more important determinant of the range of the earnings distribution than is education.

Both the ex post and ex ante rates of return to education (the rate actually received from an investment in education and the anticipated rate over a lifetime) are calculated for all levels of educational attainment, and they are found to approximate each other. The data indicated that ability initially has little effect on earnings by education level, but that its effect grows over time, and grows more rapidly for those with graduate training and high ability. Mathematical orientation was found to be the only type of physical or mental ability that had a significant effect on earnings.

The social rates of return realized in the population (before deflation) were, compared with those for a high school graduate, 14, 10, 7, 8, and 4 percent for two years of college only, an undergraduate degree, some graduate work, a master's degree, and a Ph.D. degree, respectively. The most striking aspect of these results is the general decrease in the rate of return as education level increases. Another, perhaps surprising, result is that in this sample the rate of return to a college dropout exceeds that to a college graduate.

The authors conducted their analysis of earnings differentials and rates of return without considering how education increases income, but they speculate that—for reasons ranging from snobbery to profit-making motives on the part of firms—education may add to a person's income partly because it serves as a credential for high-paying jobs. To test this hypothesis, the authors compare the actual occupational distribution of individuals at various education levels with an "expected" distribution under free entry into all jobs. The basic assumption made in estimating the expected distribution was that each individual selects the occupational category in which his income will be highest. Thus, under free entry into all occupations, very few people at any education level would choose the blue-collar, white-collar, or service occupations. For high school graduates, the actual fractions in these low-paying occupations are considerably greater than the expected fractions; for the group with some college, a similar, but weaker, result occurs; and for those who attained undergraduate degrees, the actual and expected fractions are about the same.

Education is, in fact, used as a screening device.

Since the discrepancy between actual and expected distribution is directly related to education (and not to ability), the authors conclude that education is, in fact, used as a screening device. Existence of screening would imply (since part of the income differential attributed to education arises from restricted entry into high-paying jobs) that the rate of return to education for society is overestimated by conventional measures, although the private rate is not.

(1974)

SERVICE TO SOCIETY

PART 5

The idea that service to society is a major function of an institution of higher education is indigenously American. As early as the 1750s, Benjamin Franklin conceived of such a function for his College of Philadelphia. He was interested in training undergraduates for careers in commerce and agriculture, a radical departure from the European idea, but he believed that education should serve mankind. Franklin's ideas were destined to lie fallow for a hundred years, when they were advanced as part of the rationale for passage of the Morrill Act in 1862, which made higher education available to students from the agricultural and industrial classes and legitimized the function of public service for the American university. By harnessing the function of service, first in agriculture, and later in other fields, to the model of the German research university, universities became increasingly powerful influences on almost all the political and economic strata of American society.

These ideas, which combine American pragmatism with continental intellectualism, have given birth to a social dynamic which has never been experienced before. Over the years, the development has expanded, until now the once radical concept of service to society is accepted as the sine qua non of the American university and has been copied by systems of higher education throughout the world.

In considering the service function, we have focused several Commission reports on specific areas of concern in society. *Higher Education and the Nation's Health* highlights the serious shortage of professional personnel in health services and recommends enrollment increases of 50 percent in medical and 20 percent in dental schools by 1980. Further, these schools, along with educational institutions engaged in training allied health personnel, must be given greatly augmented public financial support so that their educational and service programs may be restructured to meet the national need for a more adequate system of health care delivery.

The Campus and the City explores another area of growing concern and concludes, as does George Nash in his study *The University and the City* (published by the Commission), that institutions of higher education can play a substantial role in solving urban problems. The Commission recommends that a federally sponsored urban-grant program be established to explore this role. This progrm would provide 10 institutions with up to $10 million over a 10-year period, to make a comprehensive institutionwide urban commitment.

The service function is, however, bifocal. The American institutions of higher education not only serve the larger society, but also the individuals who constitute it, and part of the Commission's work was undertaken in studying this area. The report *College Graduates and Jobs* examines the whole area of postcollege employment. The rapid expansion of higher education has affected and is affected by the job market. The market is changing, and temporarily shrinking, although it is anticipated that this recession will abate, partially as a result of new career lines that open up in the wake of advances in technology.

Higher Education: Who Pays? Who Benefits? Who Should Pay? researches the relationship of costs and benefits in higher education. The share of educational expenditures in the gross national product has approximately tripled during the past 15 years, and this report examines how the "users" of higher education (students and their parents) share these costs with taxpayers and with private philanthropy. The Commission recommends that the overall public and private shares in the financing of higher education that have evolved historically should not be greatly altered. It is reasonable that students and their families should continue to bear approximately 30 percent of the direct costs, although we do recommend increasing federal support levels for higher education to the point where, by 1980, half the public contribution will be made by the federal government. Additionally, this report reiterates our recommendation that the federal government charter a student loan bank to serve all students regardless of need. The fund should be self-sustaining and permit borrowing to a limit that reflects both tuition and subsistence costs. These loans should be repaid in amounts which reflect income earned, over a 40-year period if necessary.

The sponsored research in this area divides under the categories of service with a public dividend and service which results in benefits to the individual. As befits the indigenously American nature of the concept of service, the research coverage is extensive.

THE PUBLIC DIVIDEND

CHAPTER

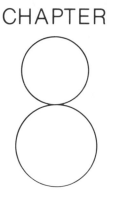

In the modern world of economic industrialization and political democracy, education plays a critical role for society as a source of inspiration, innovation, and renewal.

In *The Home of Science,* Dael Wolfle explains how the impact of science on the traditional American college led to the development of the American university. Wolfle also explores how the advent of science on the campus paved the way to acceptance of the concept of public service and facilitated the research into the practical problems of society that constitutes so much of the public dividend from contemporary higher education.

The modern dependence upon research is further analyzed by Harold Orlans in *The Nonprofit Research Institute.* Since World War II these institutes have dramatically expanded their capability to conduct research to order. In considering their origins, funding, operations, and proliferation, Orlans draws attention to the problems they currently face. If, as seems likely, the quantity of large-scale research conducted on the campuses declines in future years, these institutes will inherit some of the cast-off work load. Before they do, however, Orlans warns that they must demonstrate to the public that they do not consider technological advancement more important than the solution of social ills, and they must demonstrate to the federal government that they can responsibly account for the massive government funding that will support their work.

Two sponsored research studies concern points of topical concern. The overproduction of Ph.D.'s in the 1960s is well documented and contrasts sharply with supply of M.D.'s. Mark Blumberg's work, *Trends and Projections of Physicians in the United States 1967–2002,* considers alternative methods for increasing medical school production of physicians. George Nash, in *The University and the City,* contributes case studies of the interaction between a city and a campus and demonstrates how a university can serve its metropolitan surroundings as an educator, neighbor, social model, and provider of services.

A technical analysis of some of the concepts related to dividends of higher education has been prepared by Richard Eckaus. His papers on *Estimating the Returns to Education: A Disaggregated Approach* consider the efforts of economists to establish the benefits of higher education. He concludes that education may not "pay off" quite as much as we have come to believe it does.

THE HOME OF SCIENCE: The Role of the University
DAEL WOLFLE

That universities are the focal point of scientific research today is a result of the early history of science in the United States. Scientists in the middle of the nineteenth century had no ready and willing source of support for the work they wanted to do. Support was not forthcoming from business or private philanthropy, and government support was erratic. The colleges were poor and often unfriendly to research. So the scientists helped to develop universities. The Johns Hopkins University, Clark University, and the University of Chicago were the first institutions to adjust to the needs of scientific research. Scientific research, particularly agricultural research, was given another boost in 1862 with the passing of the Morrill Land-Grant Act, which established new state colleges and universities. The act had the broad effect of encouraging more research in more parts of the country and of establishing a formal, continuing relationship between the universities and the federal government.

After 1880 scientists in a number of American universities and in other types of institutions as well were competing, challenging, sometimes verifying one another's new findings and sometimes demonstrating error. The American system of higher education, which was decentralized and competitive, stimulated scientific research and development. The universities, organized as a kind of benign anarchy in which merit could be easily recognized, gave scientists freedom to explore ideas to their limits. And just as the university influenced science, so science influenced the university. It helped to break up the classical college curriculum, tempered the emphasis on religion, and opened the way for further graduate work in many fields. It also helped in the fragmentation and dispersal of power within the university. Scientists specialized, and the men to whom they looked for inspiration were other scientists in the same specialties. Scientists required freedom for original research and discussion, and exercise of this freedom weakened the powers of the administrative officers. Programs of practical utility developed in agriculture, engineering, and other fields. In most cases the tendency of professors in these fields was to look to the appropriate professional guilds, not the university, for the setting of standards, the approval of curricula, and accreditation standards. The increase in external funding, such as the Rockefeller Foundation support for research in molecular biology, and more emphatically, the later and larger support from federal sources, also had the effect of undermining centralized university authority.

In the more than two decades since World War II, scientific research has boomed and the universities have remained at the center. The decisive

The universities, organized as a kind of benign anarchy in which merit could be easily recognized, gave scientists freedom to explore ideas to their limits.

In most cases the tendency of professors in these fields was to look to the appropriate professional guilds, not to the university, for the setting of standards, the approval of curricula, and accreditation standards.

scientific contribution to the war effort convinced many people, especially in government, that scientific research could make an equally great contribution to the nation's peacetime welfare. Since 1945, the federal government has spent $200 billion on research and development, and $150 billion more has been provided by industry, the states, universities, and other nonfederal supporters. In the 1950s, American universities were awarding 9,000 Ph.D.'s a year; by 1971 there were 32,000. As of 1969, universities with doctorate programs numbered 220 and employed a total scientific faculty of 146,000 persons.

Much of the growth was due to government support, but in the 1960s there was a growing apprehension on many campuses about the propriety of university involvement in Defense Department research and, morality aside, the economic squeeze in the second part of the 1960s moved many congressmen to oppose further increases in federal spending on scientific research. The system whereby individual agencies support their own basic research—for example, the National Institutes of Health supports research on problems of health and disease and the Atomic Energy Commission supports atomic energy research—was now seriously questioned by more congressmen. And as the total amount of federal research money grew larger, congressmen feared that it encouraged overlap, duplication, and inefficiency.

But the arguments for federal support of university-based research are sufficiently convincing to assure its survival. An apprenticeship in genuine research is an essential part of the education of those students who will become researchers or scientific scholars, and of many of those who will enter the applied science professions. Research activities keep the faculty up-to-date in their fields, and many top scientists would leave the university if the research facilities disappeared. The university has a public duty to conduct research furthering the public interest, and its scientists for the most part provide objective criticism of the use of science in our society.

The university has a public duty to conduct research furthering the public interest, and its scientists for the most part provide objective criticism of the use of science in our society.

There have been moves to create a comprehensive government policy, but none has materialized. There are several trends, however, and it is possible to make some predictions. In the 1970s there will be a slower growth in research funds than in the past decade, for example, and a slower growth of universities due to a less-rapid increase in the number of 18- to 22-year-olds. These changes will reduce the demand for new Ph.D.'s in university faculties. Interinstitutional competition will continue, not simply among universities, but between the universities and the nonprofit and proprietary research institutes.

Research at universities will continue to be financed from endowment income, state appropriations, gifts, and other sources, but principally by federal support, of which three kinds are most desirable: the widely used *project grant* to an individual or small group for support of a specific research project, activity, or development; the *institutional grant,* which delegates to the individual university responsibility for deciding how part of its federal funds for science can best be used; and *university development grants.* They would be highly selective, of substantial size, and granted for periods of several years. In general, federal support for academic research should increase at no less a rate than the increase in the GNP.

In summing up the future and the past, it may be said that since the nineteenth century three features have been operative and promise to continue to be influential: the lack of a master plan, vigorous competition between universities for research excellence and support, and close cooperation of government with private institutions.

(1972)

THE NONPROFIT RESEARCH INSTITUTE:
Its Origin, Operation, Problems, and Prospects
HAROLD ORLANS

Nonprofit research institutes are administratively independent, separately incorporated, and non-degree granting. They have been responsible for such impressive technological contributions as electrostatic copying, the hypersonic shock tunnel, practical magnetic tape recording, the first deep-diving submarine, and super alloys and other new materials. Largely a post-World War II phenomenon, the nonprofit institutes have mushroomed—mainly with federal government support. Between 1951 and 1967, the number of federally sponsored nonprofit research centers nearly tripled, from 23 to 67. By 1968, the annual expenditures of all nonprofit research institutes reached $1,637 million, nearly two-fifths of the total research and development expenditures by all nonprofit organizations (including universities).

There are several types of nonprofit research institutes, broadly distinguished by their system of finance. Most prominent, in terms of number and size, are the federal research and development (R&D) centers. The prototypical center is large, with an annual budget exceeding $500,000, is located off campus, and is staffed mainly by a full-time, nonteaching staff whose appointments are not subject to review by university departments. The initial thrust for their formation came from the World War II involvement of university scientists in defense work. Notable examples of this type of center are RAND Corporation, the Lawrence Radiation Laboratory at Berkeley, and Brookhaven National Laboratory in Long Island.

Other types are the applied research institutes, such as the Stanford Research Institute, which conduct proprietary work for private industry and R&D for the government; operating foundations, such as the Carnegie Institution of Washington, which devote more than half of the annual yield from their endowment interest and principal to research by their own staff; endowed institutes, such as Brookings Institution, which derive less than half but more than a tenth of their annual expenditures from their own endowments; cushioned institutes, such as the Sloan-Kettering Institute, which receive income from membership dues, publication sales, grants and contributions, and clinical fees from physicians and hospitals; and project institutes, such as the Hudson Institute, which subsist on contracts and grants.

Nonprofit research institutes enjoy tax exemption under the 1969 Tax Reform Act for activities "serving the public interest." The financial importance of exemption can lie less in the taxes saved than in the contributions received by exempt organizations which taxpayers can deduct from their taxable incomes. Also, because of their favorable tax status, nonprofit institutes have an advantage when competing with for-profit organizations for important contracts—an advantage that should be considered by contracting officers when evaluating bids.

Because of their favorable tax status, nonprofit institutes have an advantage when competing with for-profit organizations for important contracts—an advantage that should be considered by contracting officers when evaluating bids.

Profit from proprietary research for profit-making companies may or may not be taxable, but the Internal Revenue Service guidelines have been ambiguous. Difficulties in interpretation also arise for those institutes engaged in social science and policy research. For example, proscription of "political activity" (for tax exemption) can pose special problems, i.e., "political," "research," "educational," "propagandistic," and "charitable" actions are not always clearly distinct and can be subject to arbitrary interpretations.

The kind of research conducted at nonprofit research institutes is determined to a large extent by the special conditions that prevail in these sorts of organizations. Unlike a university, an institute has no alumni, citizenry, state legislature, students, or tenured faculty to anchor it to the past and limit its freedom of action. Therefore, in large matters as well as small, the director can impose his judgment, interests, and taste upon an institute to a degree that a president cannot do in his university. The director is undoubtedly the man most responsible for shaping the character of an institute.

Unlike a university, an institute has no alumni, citizenry, state legislature, students, or tenured faculty to anchor it to the past and limit its freedom of action.

Also, nonprofit institutes can assemble interdisciplinary teams of scientists with more ease than can universities because they are more "problem-oriented" and less circumscribed by traditional departmental boundaries. And unlike the university where tenured professors enjoy a good deal of insulation from outside political and financial pressures, an institute's reputation and financial security rest solely on the quality of research by its staff. Applied research and project institutes subsisting on detailed contracts must complete their reports or go out of business, and a staff member who fails to deliver a report will normally be dismissed. It is this combined financial and political pressure to meet deadlines and satisfy clients that gives these institutes their special character and reputation.

In recent years, there has emerged among nonprofit institutes a trend to diversify sponsors and R&D activities. Congressional curbs on Defense Department spending on research, and budget cuts in the federal agencies such as NASA and the Atomic Energy Commission, have accelerated a movement away from military, nuclear, and aerospace technology—a movement also fed by a growing number of scientists and administrators who view these fields as wasteful, destructive, or simply irrelevant to deeper national and human needs.

In their place is a new emphasis on social sciences. A case in point is the diversification of the prestigious RAND Corporation. RAND began in 1946 as an extension of Douglas Aircraft Company, supported entirely by the Air Force to undertake classified and policy research. By 1969, its annual report listed 20 other sponsors, including the City of New York, which funds the New York City–RAND Institute. Staffed and administered by RAND, this institute has undertaken inquiries into such diverse areas as water pollution, drug abuse, the courts, and discrimination in employment.

There is also a movement among nonprofit institutes toward more independence from universities, with which they have had close links in the past. Campus upheavals have in some cases forced the nonprofit centers to break ties with universities opposed to classified research, and in other cases the management of these centers has fallen to a consortium of universities, thereby obviating the political difficulties of choosing a single university as manager. The fact remains, however, that, to date, the volume of Department of Defense research expenditures on campuses has held up remarkably. Of 524 campuses surveyed by the American Council on Education's Committee on Campus Tension, only four reported that they had discontinued any research for the military in the 1968–69 academic year.

Despite the minimal effects of campus protests in preventing classified research on campuses, nonprofit institutes may come to be viewed increasingly as the most appropriate places for applied research and development projects. The nonprofit institutes are emerging as alterna-

Campus upheavals have in some cases forced the nonprofit centers to break ties with universities opposed to classified research, and in other cases the management of these centers has fallen to a consortium of universities, thereby obviating the political difficulties of choosing a single university as manager.

tives to university research centers and are becoming a source of greater competition with higher education for research talent and grants.

A precondition of better policies toward nonprofit institutes is better knowledge about them. The National Science Foundation has statutory authority to publish statistics on most governmental obligations to individual R&D centers and certain other institutes, but the number of institutes surveyed should be increased, and all governmental and nongovernmental obligations should be reported. The Internal Revenue Service should improve its reporting forms, making the questions more relevant to the institutes, and the institutes should answer questions more fully.

The trend away from individual university management of nonprofit research centers to "consortia" control by a number of universities should be examined more carefully. So should the trend to diversify, because in some cases diversification may endanger an institute's financial stability and attenuate its professional competence.

(1972)

TRENDS AND PROJECTIONS OF PHYSICIANS IN THE UNITED STATES 1967–2002
MARK S. BLUMBERG

This study is a report on the methodology used in devising projections, to the year 2002, of the number of physicians in the population per 100,000 people in the United States. Based on differing assumptions about the yearly number of entrants into medical schools throughout the country, an attempt was made to determine the probable influence of alternative plans for increasing the entering capacity of the medical schools on the nation's future supply of physicians. Detailed projections of future needs for medical services are outside the scope of this analysis.

Figures on M.D.'s and Doctors of Osteopathy are combined, and for per capita estimates, physicians are defined as those who are fully active in the 50 states and Washington, D.C. Positing that the number of active osteopaths has remained constant since 1967, the best estimate is that there were 157 active physicians per 100,000 resident population in 1970, indicating an increase of 4.7 active doctors per 100,000 persons in only two years. Although this sharp increase may be somewhat related to an AMA redefinition which changed the status of about 6,000 physicians from inactive to active, there is little doubt that the number of active physicians per capita in the United States has grown substantially, particularly since 1966. About half of the steady growth can be attributed to the moderate increase in entrants to medical school that began in Fall 1960; the other half to the continued immigration, both temporary and permanent, of foreign medical students (FMGs).

Partially because projections of health manpower needs can be made in different ways, forecasts of the future supply of physicians have all tended to be underestimations. And the current perceived shortage relative to economic demand also can be variously estimated: for example, by withdrawing from the accounting the FMGs without permanent visas (in 1968 these numbered between 15,000 and 20,000); by reducing the average reported 60 hours per work week; or by considering that the great reliance on house officers (who constitute 20 percent of the entire supply of physicians and may work an average of 80 hours per week) indicates an inadequate supply of alternate medical services. Acknowledgment of such shortages, moreover, which are calculated on the basis of perceived or effective economic demand, still leaves unexamined the unmet needs of large segments of the population, which vary by locale, socioeconomic class, and the availability of appropriate medical specialists. Overall, the issue of shortages is a matter of widespread concern. Several measures indicate there is good reason to project appreciable increases in effective demand for physicians; Medicare and Medicaid are dramatic cases in point of how mechanisms that facilitate payment for services, for example, can escalate the demand for them.

There is good reason to project appreciable increases in effective demand for physicians; Medicare and Medicaid are dramatic cases in point of how mechanisms that facilitate payment for services, for example, can escalate the demand for them.

With respect to the population, the increase between 1966 and 1975 is expected to be 10 million, or roughly 5 percent. A projection based on the estimated number of physicians in 1966 as 295,000 and the number proposed for 1975 as 390,000, is anticipating a net increase of 32 percent. In contrast, if the projection is based on an estimate of 150 active doctors per 100,000 population in 1966, then the net increase of doctors per capita would be 20 percent, with 180 physicians per 100,000 persons. Previous estimates, none well-grounded in reliable data, do provide rough guidelines for projected needs for physicians per 100,000 population, and these indicate a figure between 164 and 180.

A major source of uncertainty in making projections of future supply is FMGs, defined as graduates of medical schools situated anywhere but the United States or Canada. The number of FMGs who remain in the United States evidently has grown from 300 per year (in 1950) to more than 2,000 per year, although estimates have been made on such inconclusive data as permanent visas granted FMGs each year and FMGs who received their first license to practice in the United States each year. It seems reasonable, however, to expect that solely on the basis of the census projection of 400,000 immigrants per year, a minimum of 600 of these will become permanent physicians in the United States.

The primary objective, to raise the supply of physicians per capita as rapidly as possible, is achievable within the constraints of certain practical considerations: awareness of the limits of available faculty, capital, and planning ability; the necessity to allow for lead time in changing plans; recognition that projections of entrants should be made when total class size is either constant or increasing; and the importance of planning increases in entering classes to medical schools when the number of potential medical school entrants also is increasing.

Consistent with the above criteria, eight alternative projections of graduates from medical schools were made, and these in turn were based on alternative projections of entrants to United States medical schools from 1970 through 2000. These projections were then compared in terms of the maximum increase in students per year, which range from 500 per year in the Medium series to 1,100 per year in the High Rapid series of projections of accomplished growth.

Projections of the future supply of active physicians in the United States were made by first determining how many permanent M.D.'s there were in the United States, by year of graduation. To refine the AMA's list of all M.D.'s on file, certain adjustments were made with respect to: living doctors who graduated before 1915; about 2,000 osteopaths who were granted M.D.'s in 1962; an estimated 10,500 FMGs regarded as being in the United States temporarily as of December 1967; physicians with addresses unknown; and physicians with temporary foreign addresses. The grand adjusted total was 288,616 living physicians in the United States as of 1967.

The most practical way of achieving the necessary per capita increase in physicians is through an accelerated (three-year) program.

The conclusion drawn from the alternative projections of the future supply of active physicians is that the most practical way of achieving the necessary per capita increase in physicians is through an accelerated (three-year) program. By modestly increasing the current entering class from 10,000 to 13,000, 14,000, or 15,000, the desired goal could be achieved by 1977. If the Medium 14 accelerated program, which would require no increase in the size of the entering class after 1976, were adopted, the effect of the augmented supply—174 physicians per 100,000 population—on the national health care system could be appraised by 1980. Subsequent increases in the size of the entering medical school classes could then be planned, if necessary. Even assuming the complete cessation of net immigration of foreign medical graduates after 1978, it is not now clear that the demand for physicians will call for an entering class in excess of 16,000 before 1980.

If the United States were to support nationwide conversion to an accelerated curriculum, 15,000 more physicians could be graduated by 1982, and for considerably less than the approximately $300,000,000, exclusive of capital requirements, it would cost to educate this many medical students by conventional means.

(1971)

THE UNIVERSITY AND THE CITY: Eight Cases of Involvement
GEORGE NASH et al.

The combination of urban ghetto riots and student unrest on campus, both frequently related to university expansion in overcrowded urban settings, has caused great interest to be focused on the relation between the city and the campus in recent years. This study examines that relationship by presenting eight case studies that illustrate the roles the urban university can play. It is a companion piece to the Commission report *The Campus and the City.*

The eight universities studied were selected as a cross section of four-year institutions that were actively involved in areas of urban, community, and minority-group problems in 1969. All eight agreed to cooperate in the study and made documentary materials available describing the histories and substance of their urban-oriented activities, and the administrative structures involved. In addition, each campus was visited a number of times in 1969 and 1970. The authors interviewed students, administrators, faculty members, and community leaders.

At the outset, an overview of community involvement delineates four fundamental ways in which colleges and universities can become involved in the "urban crisis": as an educator, as neighbor and citizen, as a provider of services, and as a model to the rest of society.

There are various ways in which the role of educator may be played: by opening access, as at the City University of New York; by educating people to work on urban problems, as does Fels Institute of the University of Pennsylvania; by providing continuing or extension education, as found at the University of Wisconsin; and by educating the unemployed and paraprofessional personnel, as at Malcolm X College of the City College System of Chicago.

Institutions of higher education can function as neighbors and citizens, as some of them have done, by attempting to rebuild and revitalize the areas in which they are located.

The traditional role of providing services is normally through research on specific problem areas.

Custom has long cast the university in the role of model, or example, to the rest of society.

Fifteen dilemmas and contradictions are identified as standing in the way of colleges and universities which would seek to involve themselves more deeply in community service. These revolve around problems with funding, the nature of the social sciences, and the characteristics of urban students.

Fifteen dilemmas and contradictions are identified as standing in the way of colleges and universities which would seek to involve themselves more deeply in community service. These revolve around problems with funding, the nature of the social sciences, and the characteristics of urban students.

The first case study concerns the University of Chicago and the Woodlawn community. Woodlawn is a low-income, black community to the east of the university. When the community first started to stand up for its rights, the university administration seemed uncooperative and even hostile. Today the university has changed its stance, and its present, mutually beneficial relationship with The Woodlawn Organization (TWO) is based on three elements: the strength of TWO, which combines a sound base within the community with a flexible militancy; the capacity of the university to learn from its mistakes in dealing with the Woodlawn community; and the willingness of the university to allow its projects in Woodlawn to be tailored by TWO.

The university and The Woodlawn Organization have engaged in a number of joint ventures, including a child health clinic and a community school board. The university provides the expertise and sometimes helps to secure the resources, but TWO always makes sure that the program serves the needs of the community. Key ingredients in this story have been pragmatic, forceful leadership both at the University of Chicago and in The Woodlawn Organization.

Delyte Morris is seen as the pivotal figure in Southern Illinois University's growth through service to its surrounding region. Recently designated president emeritus, Morris guided SIU for 21 years. The Community Development Services program was the vehicle for much of the aid to southern Illinois. It was once an active developer of the small, impoverished towns around Carbondale. As the university matured, Community Development Services became more of a research unit and less of a developer. By stressing service to the community and providing open access, SIU has proved its worth to citizens and legislators alike. It grew from 3,300 students in 1948 to 35,000 on two campuses in 1969.

The success of SIU in community development was due to Morris' ability to pick good people without regard to academic qualifications, and to give them freedom and resources. Not all the ventures succeeded, and the most impressive did not endure—which may suggest that the university is better suited to innovation than to long-term involvement in non-educational endeavors.

The third case study highlights two sets of programs at the University of California, Los Angeles: open-access education and the ethnic-centers program. The success of these two interrelated programs has demon-

With a supportive central administration and adequate funding, an institution can survive early storms, make adjustments, and eventually make progress toward its goals.

strated that, with a supportive central administration and adequate funding, an institution can survive early storms, make adjustments, and eventually make progress toward its goals. The four ethnic centers, Afro-American, Chicano, American Indian, and Asian-American, have all been touched by controversy, but the progress of these centers is an excellent example of how pressure for change from within an institution can be accommodated.

About 40 percent of San Antonio's population of 800,000 are Mexican-Americans, and the predominantly Catholic and formerly all-female Our Lady of the Lake has been deeply involved in educating Mexican-American teachers. Project Teacher Excellence began in 1966 and aimed at enrolling Mexican-American students who normally would have been academically ineligible and/or financially unable to attend the college. Starting from a $40,000 Talent Search grant from the U.S. Office of Education, the program grew to nearly $800,000 in 1970. The case study describes the combination of leadership and financial aid that enabled the program to succeed. The Project Teacher Excellence students have done better academically than the traditional students at the college, and they have brought about substantial change in the college's methods of education and community service.

In three distinct ways the predominantly black Morgan State College has contributed to the solution of urban, community, and minority-group problems. It is a first-rate institution for black people in a predominantly white society; it is an outstanding educator of black people; and its faculty and staff serve in leadership positions both in Baltimore, where the college is located, and on the national scene. Its method of involvement differs from those of predominantly white institutions, but its success again is attributable to leadership. Martin Jenkins, the president, steered a forceful, but constructive and pragmatic course, and Morgan State demanded and received its fair share of support from public and private funding sources, and consistently documented the fact that such funding was used wisely and well. Morgan's strategies offer an example to all state-supported institutions which too often fail to demand support or obtain the leadership to innovate wisely.

The sixth case study is of Northeastern University in Boston, a private university which has always aimed to serve the needs of urban students from working-class backgrounds. The Cooperative Education program which began in 1909 is a hallmark of Northeastern, encompassing almost all the day students. The university regards it as the best way to provide both education and work experience to the students it serves. Aside from such overt benefits as meaningful work in a field of interest, earned income, and education, the Cooperative program has a hidden agenda, innovation in curriculum. The Cooperative program makes it easier for Northeastern to be involved in community-centered programs. The laboratory school of the Boston Neighborhood Youth Corps, founded in 1966 for dropouts from high school, was one example, but it was closed due to a shortage of funds. The Lighted School House in South Boston began by providing a full range of after-school programs for children and adults. This program failed due to problems in both the university and the community. Despite these reverses, most departments and schools of the university have become involved with Boston's problems. These efforts have not always been successful, but they do indicate that Northeastern is utilizing Cooperative Education for the benefit of both the community and its own students.

Columbia University's problems with surrounding communities have been well documented, but the case study of Columbia's status as of 1970 indicates that the institution is learning from its errors. Through its Ford Foundation-funded Urban Center, Columbia has been given a new approach to physical expansion and a new sensitivity to neighborhood problems. The expansion problem has not been completely solved, but work continues on it, as it does in such areas as minority recruitment and curricular reform. The study shows how difficult it is to alter the course of a major established university.

It is difficult to alter the course of a major established university.

The final case study is of Wayne State University in Detroit, which has a long-standing tradition of urban involvement. Under the presidency of William Rea Keast, urban involvement was made the major focus of the university. By encouraging minority-student enrollment and developing new methods of giving community service through experimental units such as the Community Extension Center, Keast encouraged this broadening of the focus of Wayne State. Wayne State's involvement in urban community and minority-group endeavors is the most comprehensive of any of the institutions covered in the study.

As has been demonstrated, the key to the relationship between the university and its immediate surroundings is leadership. In conclusion, it may be stated that while the primary goal of institutions of higher education should be education, these examples demonstrate how that goal can be served while simultaneously providing aid, expertise, and service to the inhabitants of the city and the community.

While the primary goal of institutions of higher education should be education, that goal can be served while simultaneously providing aid, expertise, and service to the inhabitants of the city and the community.

This study concludes with a review of the literature on urban involvement. Previous writings are seemingly contradictory, with John Gardner and Jacques Barzun occupying polar positions. Gardner favors involvement; Barzun is concerned about institutional viability. Nash agrees with all the writers that the principal role of the university in the community must be that of education and demonstrates the extent to which there is agreement in the seemingly disparate views.

(1973)

ESTIMATING THE RETURNS TO EDUCATION: A Disaggregated Approach
RICHARD S. ECKAUS

The papers presented here evaluate what has come to be one of the most significant features of the economic analysis of education: the calculation of rates of return to education, treating education as if it were an investment. The objective is to gain additional insights into the economic functions of education and, in particular, to understand better the findings of previous investigations—that education pays off rather well. The research demonstrates that this conclusion is subject to considerable doubt.

There has always been skepticism about the treatment of education as an investment, but the questioning has not successfully challenged the main results—partially because those results seemed so plausible. The folklore has always been that "education pays off," and the impact of previous rate-of-return calculations was to raise this folklore to the level of a scientific maxim. The maxim, in turn, appeared to confirm the power of an indirect approach, via education, to the solution of many of the social and economic problems confronting America. Those studies that appeared to validate the economic value of education also served to reinforce a practical tendency that already existed in our society to place great weight on education as a solvent of social problems.

Higher education in particular benefited from the apparent demonstration of the economic benefits of education; until recently participation in higher education was relatively limited, and the rate-of-return studies seemed to suggest that an important avenue of social progress remained to be more fully exploited.

If, however, the calculated rates of return do not reflect real relative scarcities of the productive qualities of educated labor, then the usefulness of those rates for policy making is called into question. For example, suppose that the rates which have been calculated reflect differences in "innate" abilities rather than levels of education; or suppose that the wage and salary payments on which the rates are computed are not generated by reasonably good labor markets in which income payments accurately reflect the real relative productivities of labor; or suppose that the wage and salary payments and the calculated rates reflect mainly social status or the ability to control labor markets. If these suppositions are correct, the rates do not measure the economic payoff to education and cannot help in making efficient decisions which would maximize the contribution of resources now devoted to education.

The calculated rates of return, and the profiles of the variations of income with age from which they are derived, may provide insights regarding influences determining the personal distribution of income. There is no question of the association between education and income.

Nevertheless, the calculated rates of return, and the profiles of the variations of income with age from which they are derived, may provide insights regarding influences determining the personal distribution of income. There is no question of the association between education and income. These three papers are a contribution to the process of sorting out the influences in that association.

The first paper takes up the issue of the extent to which differences in calculated rates of return to education are a result of differences in hours of work that are also associated with education. The results indicate that standardizing incomes for hours of work does make a significant difference in the calculated rates of return, especially at the high school level of education. The results, however, still cannot be accepted as indicating the "true" rates of return to relative scarcities of educated labor. There are many limitations and restrictive assumptions in this method of estimation. It is not even possible to be certain at this stage whether the differences in hours of work associated with education are wholly the result of individual choice or in part due to differences in opportunities for choices of hours of work.

The second paper delineates the sources of variation in returns to education by making a number of calculations on an occupational basis. This disaggregated approach has a number of potential advantages. It permits the comparison of individuals who are more similar in their personal characteristics than is possible if all college graduates are compared with all high school graduates, as has been done in previous investigations. It also helps identify those sources of differences in return rates that are associated with the characteristics of particular occupations, for example, the normal length of hours worked or the degree of control over the labor market. The results indicate that differences in the payoff to education among occupations are a major source of the individual differences in rates of return. They also demonstrate how crucial are the particular occupational comparisons being made.

Differences in the payoff to education among occupations are a major source of the individual differences in rates of return.

The final paper is a general consideration of the problems of estimating rates of return to education, reviewing in detail conceptual issues and the types of data available. Again, the results of this review indicate that the rates of return which have been calculated here and elsewhere should be regarded with considerable skepticism. There are essential difficulties in estimating which have not yet been overcome.

It is not surprising that a significant proportion of economists should, by

It is not surprising that a significant proportion of economists should, by and large, have first done the easy things in analyzing education and behaved as though the rates of return to education could be identified and calculated.

and large, have first done the easy things in analyzing education and behaved as though the rates of return to education could be identified and calculated. It is an attractive idea that, with a set of not wholly implausible assumptions, could be utilized. Leading practitioners were by no means unworried about the effect of the content of restrictive assumptions on their findings, but managed to overcome their doubts. A major implication of this research, however, is that the doubts should remain. The rate-of-return estimates are not robust and, on intensive examination, are shown to be quite sensitive to the effect of the assumptions made in the calculations, the level of occupational aggregation, and the type of comparisons made.

While calculated rates reveal something about the distribution of income, their full meaning still remains so obscure that they cannot validly be employed to aid in forming policy for the allocation of resources to education.

(1973)

THE PRIVATE BENEFIT

CHAPTER

Throughout its long history, higher education has been a doorway to a world of aesthetic and intellectual appreciation and a route toward advantageous and sometimes privileged occupational status. Some of these private benefits are quantifiable, and the Commission has sponsored research to measure them. Other benefits are more subjective and concern the development of the human intellect and personality. Into this latter category fall the benefits of living and studying in a variety of cultural settings. This particular privilege is afforded students through the international education programs that are examined in *Bridges to Understanding,* by Irwin T. Sanders and Jennifer C. Ward.

A subjective assessment of private benefits emerges from *Recent Alumni and Higher Education.* For this study, Joe L. Spaeth and Andrew Greeley have collected data from 135 institutions on 40,000 graduates of the class of 1961. Surveying them in 1961, 1962, 1963, 1964, and 1968, the authors have compiled a dossier on what those who have recently experienced our system feel about it. They report that 93 percent consider it a sound enough investment to desire higher education for their sons; 86 percent expect their daughters to attend. Stephen Withey directed a study that reports objectively on the effects of college education on the individual. It attempts to synthesize the massive amounts of data on this topic that social scientists have been collecting for more than a quarter of a century.

Two volumes of essays sponsored by the Commission also review attempts to assess private benefits of higher education. In the first, F. Thomas Juster and his colleagues identify a number of unifying themes concerning the nature and extent of education's influence on individual behavior. They conclude that the returns on education are higher than the costs of borrowing to invest in it, and further, that the payoff on higher education is substantial regardless of the social background or ability of the student. In *Higher Education and the Labor Market,* Margaret Gordon has assembled a collection of essays which shed light on an area of growing concern. In contrast to the general predictions which are so liberally made, Gordon concludes, among other things, that while the halcyon days of the 1960s may not be repeated, the job market in the 1970s will not deteriorate disastrously. This is not to say, however, that no problem exists. The volume not only stresses how crucial the relationship is between education and the job market, but also that the nation cannot afford to be indifferent to it.

BRIDGES TO UNDERSTANDING: International Programs of American Colleges and Universities
IRWIN T. SANDERS and JENNIFER C. WARD

Until World War II, what has come to be known as the non-Western world was largely an academic *terra incognita.* But during the war, crash programs and publications were needed to train United States military and civilian specialists in Japanese, Chinese, Russian, Malay, and other "exotic" languages, in addition to French, German, and Italian. With peace, some educational and political leaders recognized that the national interest demanded preparation of specialists on every part of the world on a regular, continuous basis.

Private foundations became seriously involved in the development of non-Western studies, and in 1958, the federal government provided funds through the National Defense Education Act to support non-Western language and area study centers in the major (and many minor) languages and cultures. At present, more than 100 such centers are federally supported at United States universities and, in all, there are more than 400 interdisciplinary language and area studies programs available.

As America's world involvements grew, more and more scholars went abroad to teach and conduct research—encouraged by the Fulbright exchange fellowship program. Students too became increasingly "internationalized." In 1968 alone, 110,000 foreign students attended colleges and universities in the United States. The same year, more than 22,000 American students went abroad to study, through some type of formal arrangement between the United States and foreign universities. And colleges and universities in the United States began forming consortia as an efficient means of making study-abroad opportunities available to increasing numbers of young Americans.

Immediately after the war, many university faculty members had worked on the problems of reconstruction in war-devastated countries. Later they went abroad to help nations emerging from colonial rule develop their own political, educational, medical, and economic institutions. By 1968, through the Agency for International Development (AID), some 70 universities in the United States were engaged in agricultural and many other kinds of technical assistance projects in countries around the globe. In such endeavors the universities also received much support from the large, private foundations such as Ford and Rockefeller. The surge of idealism that was reflected in the support of the Peace Corps by young Americans also brought to many institutions a wider international

The surge of idealism that was reflected in the support of the Peace Corps by young Americans also brought to many institutions a wider international perspective.

perspective. More than 100 universities trained Peace Corps volunteers, and some provided the corps with overseas professional support.

The tide of interest in international programs crested in academe with passage of the International Education Act of 1966, which declared "that this and future generations of Americans should be assured ample opportunity to develop to the fullest extent possible their intellectual capacities in all areas of knowledge pertaining to other countries, peoples, and cultures. . . ."

Congress authorized generous funds for the act but—to the acute disappointment of education—no appropriations whatever were forthcoming. Meanwhile, however, the foundations that had given major support to international programs in the past assumed that the federal government was prepared to undertake much greater responsibility for them. They began to shift their financial support to other priorities.

Caught between the drying up of foundation funds and the failure of the federal government to increase its support, top university administrators tried to incorporate many features of their institutions' international programs into their regular budgets. They found this hard to do in the face of inflated costs and the need to deal with doubling or tripling enrollments.

Further crippling of international studies and exchange came with curtailment of appropriations for the Fulbright-Hays educational and cultural exchange program—from $46 million in fiscal 1968 to $31 million for 1969. This affected most deeply the number of United States citizens receiving grants, which dropped by nearly 15 percent.

Planet Earth is becoming a "global village," and our education needs to reflect this development.

Such unfavorable developments slowed the momentum of international programs which had been building since World War II and which had reached its peak with passage of the International Education Act. Now, with every year that is lost, the greater will be the task of regaining momentum and strengthening and consolidating the effort. Reaffirming the need for continued support of United States international programs in no way denies the overriding demands of domestic problems; but it seems myopic either to refuse to recognize that the United States is still part of an international community or to dismantle through lack of support the resources already developed to prepare young Americans for participation in that community. Planet Earth is becoming a "global village," and our education needs to reflect this development. Many colleges and universities are responding imaginatively to the need, but their number is too few and their resources inadequate for the task they face.

This report is essentially descriptive of international studies on American campuses. Among the authors' convictions is the basic tenet that special international programs and an enhanced international aspect in all areas of study are central to the purposes of higher education for the world of today and tomorrow. It is held that higher education must assume the responsibility of making Americans more at home in the complexities of the modern world, less afraid of diversity, and more understanding of the problems other nations face.

The major findings of the authors' investigation are that international studies are still largely underdeveloped on most college and university campuses, and that even the present levels of activity (or any possibility of meeting the urgent needs for improvement) are in serious jeopardy due to financial, organizational, and other difficulties. A chief tenet of this report is that educational efforts (particularly in the social sciences and the humanities) which neglect international topics are not really high-quality programs.

Federal and state legislators are urged to recognize the national need for a selected number of very strong, well-financed centers which deal with international studies at the undergraduate and graduate levels, promote research as well as training, combine to offer instruction in most of the major languages of the world, and develop effective relationships with educational institutions abroad. Support also should be given to modest programs of international studies in a large number of institutions so that colleges and universities can carry out their responsibility for producing a well-informed electorate which will endorse enlightened foreign policy decisions. Such programs should be as integral a part of the academic offering as mathematics, chemistry, or English composition.

Support should be given to modest programs of international studies in a large number of institutions so that colleges and universities can carry out their responsibility for producing a well-informed electorate which will endorse enlightened foreign policy decisions.

Private foundations should continue to help support certain aspects of international programs. Above all, the plurality of funding patterns should be maintained so that no college or university is totally dependent upon a single external funding source for the operation and improvement of its international programs.

Educational administrators are urged to assure a high place for international programs in the determination of institutional priorities and to encourage faculty development in the international sphere. For the latter, special leaves-of-absence are desirable to help faculty members acquire new knowledge about a geographic area or about an important topic to be incorporated into teaching.

Faculty members should reexamine their courses to see if they can appropriately introduce materials dealing with other countries; they should refer students to foreign publications as assigned or supplementary reading; they should advise students to consider, when this is relevant to their career plans, the possibility of study abroad.

In the last analysis, a college or university will make real progress in broadening the international component of its educational effort only to the extent that a substantial number of individual faculty members feel a responsibility to do so and are prepared to act upon it.

(1970)

RECENT ALUMNI AND HIGHER EDUCATION: A Survey of College Graduates
JOE L. SPAETH and ANDREW M. GREELEY

How do relatively recent alumni feel about current student protests? Do such feelings affect their loyalty to their alma mater? And how good was their alma mater? What were its goals, and how did they mesh with those of the student?

It is widely held that a college education should produce a person who is interested in and informed about literature and the arts. One would expect the better colleges to do a better job of this than the poorer ones. Do they?

Many people believe that higher education prepares one for elite positions in the labor market. How important a function of college do alumni think career training should be? How does this preparation actually take place? To what extent do a person's experiences in college or graduate school change his career plans?

This study attempted to answer questions like these with data collected from persons who graduated from college in June 1961. It is based on a longitudinal study by the National Opinion Research Center, which sampled 40,000 graduates of 135 accredited or large colleges and universities. Data were collected during five years, concluding with 1968. The 1968 survey—undertaken for the Carnegie Commission—sought the views of alumni on their colleges and on higher education in general. It was based on a 30 percent subsample of respondents who had returned all four previous questionnaires. Of the 6,005 persons drawn, 4,868 returned completed questionnaires—a response rate of 81 percent. Fifty-eight percent of the respondents were male, 42 percent female.

Though they have little doubt their children will go to college, they are not sure about which school, or even what kind of school. The attractions of alma mater are by no means overwhelming.

The class of '61 is approaching the midpoint between two rather significant events—the day they graduated from college and the day their children will matriculate. Though they have little doubt their children will go to college, they are not sure about which school, or even what kind of school. The attractions of alma mater are by no means overwhelming.

The educational attainment of this class obviously outstrips that of their parents; only a third of their mothers had gone to college, and of their fathers, 4 out of 10 had. About half the fathers were professionals, proprietors, managers, or officials. Among the class of '61 alumni, however, 71 percent of those working were in professional positions; an additional 19 percent were proprietors, managers, or officials, for a total of 90 percent. Ultimately, 73 percent expect to be professionals and 22 percent managers.

A third of the alumni came from families with incomes of at least $10,000 a year (in pre-1960 dollars); even at this early stage in their careers, three-fourths of the alumni were doing as well as their parents had done. Eleven percent of their parents and 9 percent of the alumni were making at least $20,000 annually.

A third of the respondents held some kind of higher academic degree. Twenty-one percent had earned a master's, 10 percent a professional, and 4 percent a doctoral degree. Even at this seemingly late date, one-sixth said they planned to earn the doctorate; more than two-thirds reported the intention of earning some kind of advanced degree.

Recent alumni certainly expect to be consumers of higher education for their children.

Recent alumni certainly expect to be consumers of higher education for their children. Ninety-three percent expect all their boys to attend college and 86 percent expect all their girls to attend. Ninety-nine percent say they will make at least some contribution to the financing of their children's education, and the median parent thinks that the cost of keeping a child in college for a year will be about $3,000.

The class of '61 is far more concerned with the quality of education their children will get than with cost. Eighty-two percent said very high academic standing was of great importance in choosing a college for their children. Nearly all (98 percent) wanted a college to provide a good general education; 87 percent wanted career training; and 84 percent thought that personality development would be desirable. Only 19 percent thought it desirable that their children attend their own alma mater; in fact, most were indifferent on this score.

When asked in 1968 about their emotional feeling toward their college, 27 percent of the class of '61 claimed a strong attachment and 85 percent (including the former group) said they liked it. However, to the same question asked at graduation, 32 percent claimed a strong attachment and 75 percent said they liked their college. Apparently the years have eroded both strong positive and negative feelings. Whatever their attachment, 37 percent made a modest financial contribution to their college in 1967–68.

Of course, alumni, like other taxpayers, make other contributions. Nearly three in five of the class of '61 agreed that state taxes should be raised to provide more money for higher education. Forty-five percent agreed that *all* colleges should receive federal aid for operating expenses; 61 percent would favor federal aid to institutions with no religious affiliation; and only 17 percent favored no federal aid at all. Opinions on state aid were very similar.

Alumni tend to feel that financial aid to students should be allocated according to criteria of need and ability.

Alumni tend to feel that financial aid to students should be allocated according to criteria of need and ability.

Compared to their own parents, the alumni are a politically liberal group. Just over half classified themselves as liberals, while two in five reported that their parents were liberals. Only 1 percent identified themselves as part of the "New Left." Only 5 percent had participated in an antiwar protest and 9 percent in a civil rights protest. But 15 percent would approve if their children protested against the war and 30 percent would approve if their children took part in a civil rights protest. In Spring 1968, about half thought "the protests of college students are a healthy sign for America."

Among other conclusions, we find that colleges and universities operate as mildly effective sorting and screening agencies, with bright students tending to become oriented to the most intellectually demanding occupations. The reverse is true of students with poorer records. However, career plans are a more important independent influence than academic performance.

Alumni make stringent demands on higher education, expecting it to serve as parent, priest, psychiatrist, master craftsman, confidant, charismatic leader, prophet, social reformer.

Alumni make stringent demands on higher education, expecting it to serve as parent, priest, psychiatrist, master craftsman, confidant, charismatic leader, prophet, social reformer. It is supposed to *do* something to the people who attend it. The authors believe it would be desirable if the demands on the college experience were reduced. They disagree with those who argue that all one may expect of higher education is custody and screening, but neither do they agree with those who think it has failed if it does not produce lots of people with a degree of personal nobility never before seen on a mass basis.

Cognitive development has traditionally been one of education's primary concerns. Alumni of the class of '61 seemed to criticize their colleges chiefly on the grounds that they did not contribute enough to value formation or to the ability to intelligently form and express opinions. The student is neither all intellect nor all emotions, but a complex combination of the two. The college should have an impact on his personality, but it should try to do so largely through its facilitation of cognitive development, a facilitation that ought to take place in the context of a sensitive awareness of the development problems of the people with whom it is dealing.

(1970)

A DEGREE AND WHAT ELSE?:   Correlates
and Consequences of a College Education
STEPHEN B. WITHEY et al.

Some researchers interested in human behavior have divided their find-ings according to level of education and found significant differences between educational groups. But a closer look raises questions about the meaning and interpretation of the findings among the "college" group. What are the characteristics of people who attend college? What happens in the college experience? What predictions can be made about colleges and students in the future?

Colleges and universities in the United States have tripled in number since around 1940. Many have also grown in size; some single institu-tions have more students than all colleges and universities had together before the turn of the century. The pattern of education in institutions of higher education now includes—in addition to training in liberal arts, the humanities, and professions such as medicine and law—instruction in vocations, services, management, new fields of specialization, and tech-nologies. Community and junior colleges are examples of an increasing variety in types of institutions of higher education.

Examining the impact of a college education on the individual, one should expect it to be changing, since colleges are changing. The situa-tion is further complicated by the increase in the proportion, number, and variety of young people who now go to college. Colleges are serving people with goals, abilities, backgrounds, and expectations different from those of students in earlier decades.

And if it is hazardous to apply findings from the past to conditions in the present, it is equally hazardous to project into the future. Studying the characteristics of college graduates, a researcher is tempted to project their attributes into the future as a description of a growing section of the population. But what was true for the youth of one decade may not be as true for youth in a decade of different social, political, economic, and social conditions. And what was true for a small core of institutions of higher education may not be as true for a larger, increasingly varied group. Moreover, what was once generally true for colleges and univer-sities may now be true only of graduate schools.

The existing research literature on college impact provides some in-dicators of the characteristics that derive from higher education. How-ever, there are problems in working with existing data on this subject. One problem is that there are areas in which data from studies of dif-ferent educational groups may not be comparable because of bias. Self-report methodological studies provide an example. It is not surprising that such studies reveal that the higher-educated are more efficient reporters than the less well educated. Much self-reporting requires organizing ideas, retrieval of information from memory, and verbal facility, all training associated with higher education. But such studies have also shown that the higher-educated are poorer reporters of some kinds of information. And there is evidence that on some questions they are more subject to motives that inhibit valid responses.

The higher-educated are more efficient reporters than the less well educated. But the higher-educated are poorer reporters of some kinds of information.

Other self-report studies have shown that respondents who graduated from high school or college were better reporters than those who attended but did not graduate. This suggests that some factor other than level of education may be relevant. It may be that people who perform better at any level in one role perform better in another.

There are other problems. Few systematic survey data exist from before 1940 (most is from the last two decades); the methodology of a given survey may not be duplicated by another; questions used on one study are not frequently repeated on others; and data from studies may sometimes be questionable simply because of the coding and analysis procedures used. So it is often difficult to establish trends.

Careful study of the research literature does reveal high enough correlations in some areas that some conclusions can be drawn. For example, it is clear that parents' education, occupation, and income—or socioeconomic status—play a significant role in determining whether youths ever get to college, as do ability and interest. The encouragement of parents, teachers, and peers influence youths, as do the labor market and conditions of economic opportunity. It is also common to find that the impact of college education cumulates in families over generations. Sons and daughters of college-educated parents have attitudes, behavior, and achievement levels different from those of fellow students who are the first generation in their family to go to college.

Sons and daughters of college-educated parents have attitudes, behavior, and achievement levels different from those of fellow students who are the first generation in their family to go to college.

There is a widening knowledge gap between young people who graduate from college and those who do not. College graduates acquire new knowledge, skills, and interests, and change in their behavior toward information. They use the printed media more—newspapers, books, and magazines. And they know more about how the society works and what is happening in the world.

Although the picture is not entirely clear, there is evidence that particular institutions of higher education have specific impact on students and more on some students than others, depending on the goals of the college and what it chooses to emphasize in its "local climate." It is also apparent, however, that a college education has a general impact that cuts across institutions and students.

The college experience appears more likely than not to make students more open-minded and liberal, more concerned with aesthetic and cultural values, more relativistic and less moralistic, and more integrated, rational, and consistent. Students also become less concerned with material possessions. College students tend to change in their traditional values and behavior. They also become less authoritarian, although this may be related to the social climate at the time of their education. They become more aware of interpersonal relationships and show a greater readiness to express their emotions. There is a lessening interest in job security and growing interest in the challenging aspects and meaningfulness of a job.

But this is not true for all. Some students and institutions show different patterns. Vocationally oriented students seem to make fewer changes in college. Students in engineering, business administration, and natural sciences show fewer changes than those in the social sciences or humanities, but it may be that the social sciences and humanities were chosen by students with particular interests originally.

Traditionally, students have changed little in political participation during the college years, but apparently this is changing. The vote for 18-year-olds may have further effect. In their postcollege years, college graduates, more often than others, inform themselves politically, turn out to vote, participate in campaigns, and run successfully for political office.

College graduates have advantages in monetary terms. They have more opportunities, more job security, and better working conditions. They make fewer job changes and are more satisfied with their jobs. College graduates are more optimistic about their personal situation and the national economy. They save more, are more future-oriented, plan more efficiently, and take fewer risks, such as not taking a chance on going without health insurance.

For the individual, college attendance makes for a better life through a network of effects over the years. College graduates have advantages in monetary terms. They have more opportunities, more job security, and better working conditions. They make fewer job changes and are more satisfied with their jobs. College graduates are more optimistic about their personal situation and the national economy. They save more, are more future-oriented, plan more efficiently, and take fewer risks, such as not taking a chance on going without health insurance.

College graduates are more likely to belong to organizations and more likely to go to church. They hold more positions of leadership than those with less education. They are more introspective and concerned about personal and interpersonal aspects of life, but relish more of the pleasures of interpersonal living. They have a greater sense of well-being and tend to feel more socially efficacious and personally competent.

Although there are these indications of the impact of higher education in existing literature, it is clear that data are incomplete. Studies are needed to update findings in light of present conditions. Studies are also needed on the methodology of comparing information from people with different levels of education. Projects need to focus on differences between institutions, programs, and students. Researchers also need to widen their

Total family income—within various groups (percentage distribution of families)

EDUCATION OF FAMILY HEAD	MEAN INCOME IN 1968	TOTAL	LESS THAN $3,000	$3,000 –4,999	$5,000 –7,499	$7,500 –9,999	$10,000 –14,999	$15,000 OR MORE	NUMBER OF CASES	MEDIAN
0–5 grades	$4,000	100	52	22	13	7	4	2	143	$2,920
6–8 grades	6,300	100	33	16	19	14	13	5	410	5,170
9–11 grades, some high school plus noncollege	8,820	100	17	15	20	17	22	9	402	7,260
12 grades, completed high school	9,480	100	6	12	18	24	29	11	415	8,940
Completed high school plus other noncollege	9,890	100	5	14	18	20	31	12	264	9,060
College, no degree	10,830	100	14	9	12	17	31	17	329	9,610
College, bachelor's degree	13,030	100	6	10	14	13	29	28	239	11,240
College, advanced or professional degree	16,460	100	3	6	6	15	31	39	109	13,120

Source: Katona, George, et al.: *Aspirations and Affluence,* McGraw-Hill Book Company, New York, 1970.

scope to include social issues surrounding the college, the complex interaction of many variables, and the extended consequences of a college education. Although it is clear that higher education has significant social impact, colleges and universities can better serve society if the patterns and scope of the impact are better and more widely understood.

(1971)

EDUCATION, INCOME, AND HUMAN BEHAVIOR
edited by F. THOMAS JUSTER

The papers in this broad-spanning book fall into two major categories: one group of essays deals with the degree to which educational attainment produces higher annual and lifetime earnings; the other focuses on the monetary returns to education as they are manifested in a spectrum of social, political, and economic attitudes. To explore these issues, the following related matters were examined:

Does the contribution of ability to income vary with the level of formal schooling and other factors, or is it independent of such factors?

What specific types of formal schooling or ability influence earnings, and how can these influences be measured?

What are the effects of formal schooling and informal training and learning on lifetime earnings?

If education enhances productivity, what other areas of behavior does it also influence?

Part One begins with an investigation of the relation between mental ability and schooling attainment. Drawing on a large number of samples that provide data from the 1920s into the 1960s, Paul Taubman and Terence Wales find that the rapid growth in the proportion of young people attending college has not been associated with any decline in the average ability of those entering college, but rather with an increase in average ability.

The remainder of the papers in Part One are concerned with the determinants of earnings in the market. Jacob Mincer, studying a large sample of white urban males, finds that a significant fraction of the difference in annual full-time earnings can be explained by differences in the distribution of investments in human capital, including both schooling investments and investments represented by learning on the job. Mincer's results suggest that labor force experience, rather than age, is one of the strongest determinants of the earnings profile, and consequently of the distribution of earnings. Sherwin Rosen, writing about the obsolescence of knowledge, is less occupied with the effects of formal schooling on earnings than with the returns to postschool investments. Using a relatively small sample, Rosen finds that at least part of the observed lifetime differential in earnings between high school and college graduates might be attributed to the greater efficiency with which the latter accumulate knowledge, which in turn leads them to invest a relatively greater amount in postsecondary school training and education.

Several papers examine the role of basic ability and the quantity and quality of formal schooling in determining earnings. Taubman and Wales find that the returns to formal schooling are overestimated if ability is not included in the earnings equation. The bias due to the omission of ability seems to be especially serious for those in the highest ability groups. John Hause is also concerned primarily with the relation between measured ability, formal schooling, and earnings. He finds that the coefficient of ability on earnings tends to be a function of the level of formal schooling. In an early attempt to relate future earnings both to the quality and quantity of investments in schooling, Paul Wachtel concludes that the rate of return for undergraduate training tends to be about 10 percent; for graduate training, markedly lower. The part of the return due to differences in number of schooling years shows a much smaller rate of return than the part due to differences in schooling quality. Arleen Leibowitz examines the relationship between labor force participation for married women and education level, and finds that the higher the education level the more likely are younger women without children to be in the labor force. But for women with young children, the amount of labor supplied to the market appears to be independent of education level. For these women, the distribution of time spent on home and child varied by education level, with more highly educated women spending more time on child care.

Part Two examines the impact of differences in educational attainment on

At least part of the observed lifetime differential in earnings between high school and college graduates might be attributed to the greater efficiency with which the latter accumulate knowledge, which in turn leads them to invest a relatively greater amount in postsecondary school training and education.

a wide range of economic and noneconomic behavioral variables. Three of the essays look at the relation between education and consumption (or saving behavior). Robert Michael explores the effect of formal schooling on the efficiency of decisions about consumption and concludes that the effect of higher levels of education on the increased efficiency with which households function may represent one of the most important sources of economic gain from investment in formal education. Lewis Solmon's examination of the relationship between schooling and savings behavior documents a hypothesis that "those with more formal education tend to save more out of a given income than those with less formal education." And Gilbert Ghez, also concerned with the influence of educational attainment on behavior with respect to consumption, focuses on life cycle profiles of income and consumption, and finds that, given the same current earnings, differences in levels of educational attainment are positively associated with differences in consumption.

The final three essays report on the effect of education on such disparate matters as crime, fertility, and a spectrum of other economic, social, and political attitudes. Robert Michael's investigation yields results indicating that when total income, husband's wage rate, and other demographic family characteristics are standardized, the husband's and wife's education level have a significant negative association with the number of children in the family. Isaac Ehrlich, writing on education and crime, bases his study on the assumption that people are motivated to commit property crimes by the same considerations—opportunities and costs—that motivate people to turn to legitimate income-producing endeavors. He examines some data from arrest and crime statistics and finds the empirical evidence to be compatible with this basic assumption. One of the main findings is that the incidence of property crimes is positively related to the extent of the inequality in the distribution of earnings in the community. Since that inequality also is known to be positively related to the inequality in the distribution of schooling and training, Ehrlich posits that perhaps society should move to equalize schooling and training opportunities, provided such adjustments would indeed lead to a more equal distribution of educational attainment and legitimate earnings. Albert Beaton, from data on fairly successful men of above-average IQ and at the prime of their earning careers, analyzes the relation between years of schooling, earnings, and an array of variables—parental education and occupation, perceived attitudes about the effectiveness of various aspects of formal schooling, voting behavior, sociopolitical attitudes, and aptitude test scores. The evidence indicates that for the most part the more able people receive more education than the less able, but

The effect of higher levels of education on the increased efficiency with which households function may represent one of the most important sources of economic gain from investment in formal education.

The evidence indicates that for the most part the more able people receive more education than the less able, but that, in general, aptitude is a less forceful variable than education.

that, in general, aptitude is a less forceful variable than education. The more highly educated receive larger salaries; enjoy their work more; tend to be politically middle-of-the-road; feel that the principal key to their success lay in their own performance, rather than in luck or contacts; consider a college degree very important; and believe that the acquisition of general knowledge in college is more important than preparation for a career.

Although the papers in this volume deal with a wide diversity of subjects, their findings and conclusions sound several recurrent themes:

Investment in formal schooling yields a "profit" both to the individual being educated and to society.

Higher education yields profits independently of favorable family background or high ability.

Education extends the time horizon for individual life decisions and fosters a habit of postponing immediate satisfactions in the interests of future gains.

Higher education contributes decisively to the development of decision-making capabilities, and thus to the personal capacity for problem solving that is crucial for successful survival in a world of rapid change.

(1974)

HIGHER EDUCATION AND THE LABOR MARKET
edited by MARGARET S. GORDON

In the early 1970s, for the first time since the depression of the 1930s, college graduates and holders of advanced academic degrees were encountering difficulties in the job market, and their problems were not expected to disappear completely even after the economy recovered from the recession of 1970–71.

This collection of essays explores some of the more significant aspects of the relations between higher education and the labor market to shed light on the implications of the changes for students and their institutions in the 1970s. The authors focus exclusively on higher education's function in preparing students for the labor market, because, as economists, they feel they are best qualified to explore this area; they are not unappreciative of education's nonpecuniary benefits.

The essays were developed around certain main issues, and the first of these concerns the impact of the job market on enrollment rates. It seems likely that accelerated increases in the demand for college graduates played a role in stimulating increases in college enrollment rates in the 1950s and 1960s—but it is difficult to assess the relative importance of this factor compared with other influences. One major factor in rising enrollment rates was the long-run uptrend in the percentage of the relevant age group graduating from high school, although this contrasted with the remarkable stability of the "college entrance rate" in the first three decades of this century. In accounting for the postwar rise in enrollment rates, it is difficult to assess the relative importance of increased demand for college-educated workers in the job market and the increased availability of relatively low-cost student places. If we ask whether a decline in the rate of increase of demand for college-educated workers is likely to depress the rate of increase in the percentage of the relevant age group enrolling in college, we are in even more serious trouble. Past experience, as reflected in Douglas L. Adkins' essay, "The American Educated Labor Force: An Empirical Look at Theories of Its Formation and Composition," sheds very little light on the question.

There is positive and convincing evidence of the impact of the job market on choices of academic fields.

In contrast, there is positive and convincing evidence of the impact of the job market on choices of academic fields. Richard Freeman's essay, "The Implications of the Changing Labor Market for Members of Minority Groups," presents data on shifts in fields of study chosen by black males, which appear to be clearly related to changes in the job market for black male college graduates. He also finds that college students tend to be better informed about relative job and earning opportunities than has generally been supposed. Walter Fogel and Daniel J. B. Mitchell, in "Higher Education Decision Making and the Labor Market," also present data showing a positive relation, with a lag, between changes in employment in selected occupations employing college graduates and changes in the numbers of degrees awarded by field of study. Adkins, however, presents data on living degree holders by field and concludes from his examination that shifts in relative proportions of degrees awarded between 1950 and 1970 were not particularly responsive to labor market changes. Overall, the data in this volume reveal considerable student responsiveness to changes in job opportunities for college-educated workers, but demonstrate that shifts occur within a framework of rather substantial stability in the overall pattern of student tastes and abilities. Adkins' data also show that sex differences in patterns of choices of fields have tended to follow relatively stable and predictable patterns in the past, although the proportions of women overall in all fields have advanced between 1930 and 1970.

College entrants, therefore, fall into loosely defined pools of potential majors in various groups of related fields. Shifts are more likely to occur within one pool, e.g., from mathematics to statistics, than from pool to pool, e.g., from mathematics to history, and many such shifts may be induced by changes in the relative job opportunities among the specific occupational destinations represented within the pool or by the acquisition of improved information about these relative opportunities.

In recent years there has been an increased tendency to deplore "credentialism"—the imposition by employers of educational requirements that are not clearly indicated by the requirements of particular jobs.

In recent years, undoubtedly as part of the interest in equal employment opportunities for racial minority groups and women, there has been an increased tendency to deplore "credentialism"—the imposition by employers of educational requirements that are not clearly indicated by the requirements of particular jobs. The U.S. Supreme Court, in *Griggs et al. v. Duke Power Company,* held that such practice runs contrary to the provisions of the Civil Rights Act of 1964. Several of these essays concern themselves with the issue of credentialism to a greater or lesser extent. V. Lane Rawlins and Lloyd Ulman, in "The Utilization of College Trained Manpower in the United States," report that their data suggest an excess of educational preparation on the part of many employees in modern society, while Lester C. Thurow, in "Measuring the Economic Benefits of Education," identifies employers as responding to depressed labor market conditions by hiring college graduates for jobs previously held by those less well educated. Rawlins and Ulman identify two further forces in this process—high wage increases resulting from collective bargaining, and "sellers' credentialism," by which those in particular occupations press for increased educational requirements under licensing laws. Adkins, and also Samuel Haber, in "The Professions and Higher Education in America: A Historical View," throw additional light on creeping credentialism, as does David E. Kaun's essay, "The College Dropout and Occupational Choice," in which he demonstrates that men who have completed less than four years of college are not only less likely to hold professional or managerial positions than college graduates, but are also more likely to hold jobs that are less demanding intellectually, involve things rather than people, and involve physical labor and unpleasant physical conditions.

If there are uncertainties and complexities surrounding predictions of the future demand for bachelor's degree holders, there is considerably less uncertainty in predicting a gradual decline in the rate of increase in demand for Ph.D.'s, accompanied by a growing surplus of Ph.D.'s in many areas in the 1970s. Allan Cartter, who contributes "The Academic Labor Market" to this volume, predicts that even on the basis of projections of a relatively low Ph.D. supply, a large and growing surplus is likely to develop, particularly between 1975 and 1985. Despite this, prolonged and widespread unemployment of Ph.D.'s is not anticipated; rather, holders of doctorates will increasingly accept jobs that they would have considered unsuitable in the past.

Into this situation unionism may increasingly be injected, as Joseph W. Garbarino points out in "Creeping Unionism and the Faculty Labor Market." Garbarino distinguishes two types of faculty unionism that have evolved around single and multicampus bargaining units and concludes

Although unionism will reduce favoritism to exceptionally able faculty members, it could also affect faculty quality.

that, although unionism will reduce favoritism to exceptionally able faculty members, it could also affect faculty quality.

Since 1960, the economics of education has been a burgeoning field. Much of the research has been concerned with attempts to measure the rate of return to investment in education. "An Appraisal of the Calculations of Rates of Return to Higher Education," by Richard Eckaus et al., reviews the main lines of criticism of rate-of-return calculations and proceeds to illustrate the flaws in traditional methods of computing rates of return. Thurow also launches an attack on rate-of-return estimates and, indeed, on the traditional economic theory of the operation of the labor market. Thurow's model assumes that "credentialism" is pervasive and that it has important implications for long-run trends in income differentials among education groups.

In the debate over the validity of rate-of-return estimates, radical economists also charge that the educational system of the United States helps to preserve the existing class structure and to develop attitudes favoring the preservation of capitalism. Melvin W. Reder's essay, "Elitism and Opportunity in U.S. Higher Education," concedes that universities are elitist in the "connoisseurial" fashion in which faculty are "selected," but points out that abolition of the academic elite would not terminate elitism, but merely transfer the opinion-forming function to some other group—political functionnaires—as under totalitarianism. Additionally, Reder argues, the public institutions of higher education have enormously increased the avenues to upward mobility by countering unequal access to higher education.

Abolition of the academic elite would not terminate elitism, but merely transfer the opinion-forming function to some other group—political functionnaires—as under totalitarianism.

Whether this trend toward equality of opportunity continues will depend, to a large extent, on the financing of higher education in the 1970s, and in "Financing the Opportunity to Enter the 'Educated Labor Market'" Robert W. Hartman confronts this issue. He explores the results that are likely to emanate from three alternative patterns which might emerge—increasing predominance of state and local government funding, substantially increased federal aid, and increased reliance on private philanthropy. These are realistic possibilities for the 1970s, although the third alternative would provide the least encouragement for increased enrollments and equality of opportunity. In permutating these alternatives, Hartman also analyzes their effects upon patterns of labor force participation, occupational choice, and work effort.

The final essays concern how responsive the institutions are, and ought to be, to labor market changes in determining the "mix" of their academic programs; what the decision-making process involves; and the role of professional schools in their fields.

Walter Fogel and Daniel J. B. Mitchell, in "Higher Education Decision Making and the Labor Market," conclude that changes in the number of degrees granted in professional specialities are responsive to labor market conditions, but only weakly. The controversy surrounding whether professions, especially medicine, apply pressure to restrict the supply of practitioners is considered by Carl M. Stevens in "Medical Schools and the Market for Physicians' Services." Having considered the evidence with respect to the profession of medicine, Stevens takes a moderate stance on the question, concluding that while the historical record does show a lag of social response to manpower events, "it takes two to tango."

The policy implications of all these essays are examined by Dr. Gordon, who in the concluding essay stresses that the volume deals with selected issues and that evidence regarding demand-supply relationships in the job market for college graduates in general in the 1970s is by no means entirely clear. What is clear, however, is that employment in some occupational categories will grow much more rapidly than in others. The dangers attending the current situation include the possibility that schools will interpret the labor market situation as a reason to cut back on programs in certain areas, and the legislators will interpret it as another reason to trim fiscal support to higher education. As Dr. Gordon warns, such activities would only compound the general problems currently facing higher education.

(1974)

THE PH.D. AND THE ACADEMIC LABOR MARKET*
ALLAN M. CARTTER

In this study the demand for Ph.D.'s on the part of academic institutions will be analyzed in some detail. Traditionally, half or more of all the nation's doctorate holders have entered college and university teaching or research, although in recent years serious imbalances have developed between the supply and demand of such highly trained personnel.

The history of this situation in the post-World War II years can be divided into three quite different periods. Up to about 1960, except for the brief period of influx of large numbers of veterans, the labor market situation was reasonably stable. The decade of the 1960s was one of rapid expansion in college enrollments, resulting in a critical shortage of Ph.D's in most areas of study, and inducing a rapid—although lagged—expansion in graduate education programs. Around 1970, the rate of growth in college enrollments diminished, due principally to demographic factors, and surpluses quickly emerged in most disciplines.

* This abstract was prepared by the author before the final manuscript for the full report was completed.

Most educational observers and policy makers had misjudged the future demand for Ph.D.'s and a temporary overexpansion of graduate training facilities resulted. The study analyzes the information and the models used to project future needs from the vantage point of the late 1950s and early 1960s, attempting to learn from those mistakes.

The key elements in estimating future demand are knowledge of the size of future cohorts of potential college attenders, projections of likely attendance rates for each age level, estimates of student-faculty ratios, faculty retirement and mortality rates, and the flow of senior doctorate holders between academic and other forms of employment. History provides some lessons that can be used to improve models based on projections, and several recent studies of labor market behavior for professional and scientific personnel improve our knowledge of how the academic labor market works.

History provides some lessons that can be used to improve models based on projections, and several recent studies of labor market behavior for professional and scientific personnel improve our knowledge of how the academic labor market works.

The study will attempt to analyze how job opportunity and salary information influence students in their choice of careers and what the relative time lags are for market-induced adjustments. It will also review the potential effect of different hiring, retention, and retirement policies on the age structure of college faculties. In a special study of job placement of new Ph.D.'s over the last five years, an attempt will be made to measure the impact of affirmative action programs on the hiring of male and female Ph.D.-holders in institutions ranked by quality grouping.

Several selected disciplines will be used as detailed case studies. Physics presents a particularly interesting example, partly because it has undergone the sharpest readjustment to changing job market conditions, and partly because the efforts of its professional association have provided better data to document the flow of new and older Ph.D.'s into and out of academic employment.

It is evident that the adjustments of the 1970s are only a precursor to an even more difficult decade in the 1980s, when total college enrollments are likely to be contracting.

Drawing on this material, the study projects future needs for Ph.D.'s in academic positions under various conditions and constraints, and contrasts these estimates with likely future supplies of highly educated manpower. It is evident that the adjustments of the 1970s are only a precursor to an even more difficult decade in the 1980s, when total college enrollments are likely to be contracting. A number of institutional and national policies are considered which might help to moderate the continuing imbalances in the academic labor market.

(1975)

THE GREAT AMERICAN DEGREE MACHINE*
DOUGLAS L. ADKINS

Part One of this study describes a large-scale model of academic transition developed by the author and presents the following finely disag-

* This abstract was prepared by the author before the final manuscript for the full report was completed.

gregated estimates which have been constructed as input to it or output from it:

1   The annual academic degree output of United States universities, 1890–1971

2   The American population of academic degree holders each year from 1930 to 1971

3   Transition frequencies for attainment of higher degrees by holders of lower degrees

These series are disaggregated by sex, academic specialty, and degree level. The degree-holder population series is disaggregated by age. Part Two analyzes these estimates with respect to rates of growth, specialty composition, degree structure, sex distribution, and vintage distribution. Part Three critically examines alternative theories of the formation and structure of the population of degree-holding human resources in the light of empirical evidence and in the context of a basic discussion of such concepts as "job" and "skill." It also contains a discussion of the implications of the analysis for educational forecasting and planning.

The basic model of academic transition, presented in Part One, is the following: At any given time we have a list of all the population categories which are relevant to our problem and a count of the individuals in each category. The model then determines the population count for the next period as a weighted sum of all population counts in the present period. The weights can be denoted transition frequencies. Expressed in another way, population changes depend on net inflows from certain populations to the population in question and on net outflows from the population in question to others. If transition frequencies are known, if they are stable, and if their time-paths can be predicted, such a model can be used to predict future population counts. (The issues involved in these conditions are discussed at length in Part Three.)

The empirical model was constructed roughly as follows:

1   Degree conferral data were assembled for three degree levels, 44 academic specialties, and the two sexes, and estimates were constructed of missing data, notably pre-1948 academic specialty data.

2   These data and estimates, when disaggregated into 25 single-year age groups, constituted a subset of the population counts required for the model. For example, the count of the 1965 population of 22-year-old men who had just received their bachelor's degree in economics in 1965 but had received no higher degree was straightforwardly available at this step, but the 1971 count of the same population was not.

3   Estimates of the necessary transition frequencies were constructed

since data were unavailable. A computer-intensive model was used to construct estimates of transition frequencies from three inputs: survey data on the earlier degree specialties of advanced degree recipients, the degree conferral estimates of step 1, and demographic survival tables.

4   These transition frequency estimates were then used to construct estimates of all missing population counts. For example, an estimate was constructed of the 1971 count of those remaining in the 1965 population referred to in step 2.

5   The population count estimates were then aggregated to useful analysis levels; for example, the number of holders of bachelor's degrees in economics in 1971 who had not received a higher degree and whose ages were 31 to 45.

To give an illustration of the estimates produced by this procedure, a few estimates for 1930 are as follows:

■ There were an estimated 3,400 men aged 19 to 70 in the United States who had master's degrees in mathematics and statistics but no higher degree; 29.6 percent of them, it is estimated, were 46 years of age or older.

■ There were an estimated 250 men who received master's degrees in mathematics and statistics from universities in the United States, of whom, it is estimated, 24 percent went on to receive a doctorate a median 4.6 years later.

In Part Two of the study, the estimates constructed in Part One are analyzed at three levels of disaggregation. The following are a few of the findings: In 1971 there were over 12 million persons age 70 or under in the United States who possessed academic degrees conferred by United States institutions of higher education, eight times as many as in 1930. They constituted about 10 percent of the population aged 19 to 70. Of these, a little less than three-fourths had received the bachelor's degree but no higher degree, one-fourth had received a second-level (master's or professional) degree but not a doctorate, and 2.5 percent had received a doctorate degree. Somewhat over 1.1 million new degrees were conferred in 1971.

The population of degree holders grew rapidly throughout the 1930–1970 period. Calculated over the whole period, the annual rate of increase was 5.3 percent, a rate which was more than four times the rate of increase of the adult population. Thus, measured by academic degrees, there was a rapid accumulation of human resources per capita. This was also true in each of the four decades which make up the larger period. The rate of growth of the degree-holder population was 5.5 times larger than that of the adult population during the 1930s, 4.5 times larger during the 1940s, 6.1 times larger during the 1950s, and 3.6 times larger during the 1960s. That the multiple for the 1960s is the smallest of the four decades may be somewhat surprising to those who view the 1960s as uniquely the golden age for higher education.

The sex distribution of the degree-holder population in 1971 was 58 percent men and 42 percent women, a distribution which had moved only halfway to equality from the 64–36 percentage distribution of 1930. The split between the sexes was almost even at the bachelor's attainment level but was male-dominated at higher levels. At the second level, it was 70–30; at the doctorate level, 88–12. The sex distribution for doctorates was basically unchanged since 1930.

The distribution across academic specialties moved steadily in the 1930–1970 period toward administration, education, and psychology, and away from health studies. A sciences-technologies-arts disaggregation, however, remained virtually unchanged. Throughout the period, academic specialization was markedly sex-specific at the bachelor's and second levels and somewhat less so at the doctorate level. At the bachelor's level, 43 percent of men in 1970 had their degrees in engineering or administration, while 61 percent of bachelor's-level women had their degrees in education, arts, or humanities.

Considering 1930 to 1971, the proportion of the degree-holder population at the bachelor's level increased, somewhat surprisingly, from 63 percent in 1930 to 73 percent in 1971, whereas the proportion at the second level correspondingly decreased from 35 percent to 24 percent over the same period of time. It would be more precise to locate this shift in time between 1930 and 1947, when approximately the present proportions were attained, and to identify the shift as a strictly male phenomenon related to the relatively slow growth of the major second-level professions. The increase, in the period, of the proportion of doctorate holders from 1.4 percent to 2.5 percent was also primarily a male phenomenon; the proportion of female degree holders at the Ph.D. level was unchanged over the period.

At the specialty level, the degree structure of the engineering population underwent the most marked deepening among the various specialty populations, especially during the 1960s. In the latter period, the number of second-level and doctorate engineering degree holders grew at annual rates of 8.7 percent and 13.2 percent, respectively, while the number of bachelor's-level engineering degree holders grew at only 2.8 percent annually.

The median age of the population of degree holders—37 years in

1971—stayed relatively constant over the 1930–1971 period, as did the median age of the doctorate population—42 years in 1971. The bachelor's-level population (1971 median age—34 years) aged, however, and the second-level population (1971 median—41 years) became younger. Considering the fine specialty categories, the 1971 median age estimates for doctorate-specialty populations ranged from 36 years for male doctorates in geological-mining engineering to 51 years for female doctorates in administration other than business administration.

Current advancement probabilities for bachelor's-degree recipients, according to the estimates of this study, are that half of the men and more than a third of the women will receive advanced degrees. The probability is greater than 60 percent in 17 of the 38 specialties that are not primarily graduate specialties for men and in 9 such specialties for women.

The time-lapse distributions between degrees are rather broad in most cases. For instance, the estimated median time-lapse between bachelor's and second-level degrees for 1965 bachelor's recipients is 4.1 years for men and 5.1 years for women, respectively. The upper quartiles are 8.0 and 9.0 years for men and women, respectively.

In Part Three, an attempt is made to analyze the persuasiveness and empirical validity of competing theories of how the degree-holding populations described in Part Two came to be formed. In particular, an explanation is needed of the long, rapid, steady expansion of these populations over the last four decades. The recent tightening in the labor market for degree-holding manpower lends some urgency to this need. So do the effects of the prospective, demographically caused decline that will occur in the college-age population in the 1980s. Put in another way, will transition frequencies continue to increase in the 1970s, and subsequently, as much as they have in the past? Or will we see a substantial decrease in transition frequencies in the 1970s, resulting from labor market pressures, to be followed in the 1980s by an increase, a sequence of events which will at least partially offset the demographic cycle?

One set of theories of the formation of degree-holding populations, called here the "technogenic" model, holds that changes in these populations happen because of changes in the demand for the skills they provide to the economy. Changes in the demand for productive services, in turn, result first, from changes in the composition of economic output due to economic growth and changes in consumer preference, and second, from changes in production technique.

The technogenic model can rationalize the expansion of the degree-holding population from 1930 to 1971 as a (lagged) response to skill deficits caused by the expansion in the demand for productive services.

Since the growth rate of the population of degree holders has, throughout the period, exceeded the growth rate of occupations in which they have been employed, the technogenic expectation, at least of the manpower requirements version of the model, is that a well-overdue drop in the wage differential paid to degree holders will sufficiently remove the incentive for college attendance to eventually reestablish an equilibrium population of degree holders. If this scenario doesn't commence in the 1970s, it will decisively reduce the explanatory value of technogenic theory. If it does, the enrollment implications for most specialties are for enrollments to decline in the 1970s, and if equilibrium is reestablished in the decade, to expand again with the economy in the 1980s. In terms of transition frequencies, there would be a decline in the 1970s and perhaps a vigorous increase in the 1980s.

Another set of theories of the formation of degree-holding populations, called here the "sociogenic" model, holds that economic forces do not primarily have their effect on enrollment through student calculations based on relative wages. Rather, along with social, political, cultural, and historical forces, they have indirect effects which can best be described in terms of sociological and anthropological paradigms. The sociogenic model explains the formation of degree-holder populations as primarily the result of the demand for educational services. The educational aspirations of young people that determine this demand are likely to be formed, along with other aspirations and values, as a consequence of the social-class background of their families. Enrollment will then depend, first, on the rate of expansion of the college-going middle class. Second, it will depend on intergenerational educational attainment differences. Since the possession of educational credentials has become a condition in the United States for a person's mobility to a higher occupational, and thus social, status than his or her father enjoyed, one consequence of this mobility ethic is that successive generational cohorts will continuously have higher educational attainment. The limit to this process is not obvious, short of universal possession of the bachelor's degree. Third, increasing enrollment can also be seen to be the result of increasing affluence in which consumption of educational services increases along with the consumption of all but a few inferior goods and services.

Sociogenic expectations as to changes in transition frequencies are for relatively smooth changes. This is, first, because the sociogenic explanation seeks to explain degree flows directly, rather than via an acceleration mechanism attendant on the adjustment of degree-holder populations. Variations in the prime exogenous force are, thereby, not amplified as in the technogenic model. Second, the expectation of most sociogenic theory is that the fundamental economic, social, and political forces, which in the model shape educational aspiration, are themselves not subject to severe fluctuation. Hence, sociogenic models typically extrapolate transition frequency values smoothly. Since the number of high school graduates has now become virtually a demographic variable, fertility, lagged two decades, becomes the major source of variability in the model. A few sociogenic observers see recent events as indicative of a decline in transition frequencies caused by the loss of social legitimacy suffered by American universities as an institution. Such a loss of legitimacy would affect universities' ability to attract the young. The usual sociogenic expectation, however, is to expect college enrollment to follow the demographic cycle and, thereby, to continue to increase in the 1970s, decline in the 1980s, and stabilize in the 1990s.

The sociogenic view is more persuasive than the technogenic view because the historical record, while not inconsistent with either model, requires somewhat Ptolemaic rationalizations from the technogenic model. While the historical record is straightforwardly explained by the sociogenic model, it doesn't support sociogenic theory all that much either, because almost any naïve extrapolation model would explain the long steady growth in American degree-holding populations equally well. Therefore, the author's judgment in favor of the sociogenic model depends on theoretical analysis at a deeper level, at the level of "skill" and "job."

The question at the deeper level, which is discussed at length, is how the most productive potential behaviors come into being. Are they created in programs of higher education, or are the people who possess them the ones who attend such programs? It is concluded that very basic social, educational, and perhaps biological forces are responsible for the formation of the potential behaviors that are most highly valued in the labor market.

These questions can be posed with respect to such a phenomenon as a "shortage" of engineers. In such a shortage situation, what personal characteristics do the employers who hire the bulk of engineers have an unsatisfied demand for? Are engineers in demand primarily technical, that is, do they have the ability to use differential equations to analyze data? Or are they primarily motivational and organizational, that is, do they have the ability to perform assigned tasks in an organized fashion with a minimum of supervision, all the while maintaining a respectful relationship with supervisors and an uncomplaining attitude toward life? It may be that the bulk of people who apply to and are accepted into technical engineering curriculums, and who stay there, have these latter characteristics already. The primary economic function that engineering curriculums would perform, then, with respect to such characteristics would be a screening and certifying function carried out by means of a kind of trial by ordeal. It might be most accurate, therefore, to view the shortage of engineers as primarily a shortage of certain nontechnical potential behaviors.

This analysis has implications for both human-resource planning and educational planning. If, as a factual matter, the most economically valuable traits are the results of potentials formed in early life, human-resource policy becomes primarily a social, political, and early-education matter. Planning in these areas, therefore, becomes more important, and planning higher education to produce required numbers of people with given technical skills becomes less so.

(1974)

QUALITY

PART

From the early days of the republic, Americans have had strong faith in education as the instrument of social change and advancement. As the completion of secondary education has become almost the universal experience of our mature citizens, and as the demands of our society have become increasingly centered on intellectual and professional services and goals, this public charge has fallen heavily upon institutions of higher education. And the expectation is that these demands will be met in a way that bespeaks quality in every way.

Colleges and universities are expected to recruit able students, build the best facilities they can afford, and hire the best people they can find to teach in the classrooms and conduct research in the laboratories and libraries. Failure to do these things is regarded as an inadequate effort to provide quality education, and any discussion of quality has to pay a lot of attention to the problem of financing higher education.

The whole question of obtaining resources for higher education has been repeatedly examined, both in Commission reports and in reports based on Commission-sponsored research. The Commission's report *Quality and Equality* pointed out that growth in size and functions, rising costs, and sources of funds must all be examined to "evaluate the present and potential financial strength of higher education." We concluded in that report that continuing expansion will be expensive, and that spiraling costs make the problem worse. The report estimates that the expenditures of our institutions by 1976–77 will total about $41 billion, and these cost figures do not take into account certain federal costs or certain forms of student aid and student expenditures. The report indicates that federal funding, both for student assistance and aid to institutions, must increase. Our report *Institutional Aid* considers these matters in greater detail and urges (as did our earlier reports on this subject) the development of a federal program to provide grants and loans to students with financial need and cost-of-education supplements to colleges and universities. The latter would be based on the numbers of enrolled students who receive need-related financial aid.

The fiscal responsibility of the individual states for higher education is examined in *The Capitol and the Campus*. The Commission urges that states retain their historical and primary responsibility for the development of American higher education. It also recommends that all states create coordinating agencies to foster excellence in the development of expanding postsecondary education systems, that no state spend less than 0.6 percent of per capita personal income through taxes on higher education, and that all states provide at least 30 places in public and private institutions for every 100 persons in the state between 18 and 21 years old.

The Commission's report *Reform on Campus* discusses educational quality in terms of policies and procedures that directly affect the quality of instruction on a campus. The period ahead can be one of the two most experimental, innovative, and progressive periods in our educational history. To realize this potential, however, we must create a more diverse series of optimal learning environments to meet more precisely the needs of each college-age person. If this can be achieved, every young person will, through one educational means or another, enjoy an equal opportunity to maximize the quality of his or her life.

RESOURCES FOR QUALITY

CHAPTER

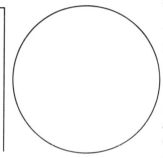

10

The Commission's sponsored research on the fiscal input to quality comes from a variety of sources. Howard Bowen, in *The Finance of Higher Education,* endorses the establishment of national systems of grants and loans to students and proposes a plan for such assistance in his essay for the Commission, but he points out that even with such help, the institutions will still need help in "the finance of their research and service operations and their capital investments."

The subject of student loans is exhaustively examined by Robert Hartman, whose study, *Credit for College,* analyzes both existing and proposed loan programs, including the National Defense Student Loans and the Guaranteed Loan programs of the federal government.

In her second report for the Commission, *Sources of Funds to Colleges and Universities,* June O'Neill compiles detailed statistics on the sources of fund and plant income, by control and by level of institution, for the period 1930–1968. Dr. O'Neill utilizes the assembled data to make some preliminary observations about trends in the way higher education has been financed, with emphasis on the role of tuition.

In *Alternative Methods of Federal Funding for Higher Education,* by Ronald Wolk, the diversity of ways in which higher education has received funds from the federal government over the years is reviewed. Mr. Wolk finds that the funds come from more than 40 agencies and involve massive amounts of money. Wolk indicates that as the amounts increase, new and more efficient ways of channeling the tax dollar into higher education must be found.

William Bowen's monograph, *The Economics of the Major Private Universities,* reviews the financial concerns of institutions of higher education that are vital to the future national development of colleges and universities. Preserving diversity in our system is a priority that has received much attention from the Commission. If diversity is to continue, the major private universities are essential. Financial pressures on this sector of the system continue to intensify, however, as their costs continue to rise. To preserve them it will be necessary to alter public policy toward them.

As the abstracts contained in this part of our summary report indicate, obtaining adequate funding is perhaps the most pressing need that will confront the nation's system of higher education in the remainder of the twentieth century. For without the necessary levels of fiscal support, the maintenance of quality and of all the other major priorities for higher education in the future cannot be realized.

Federal research and development funds expended through universities 1953–1972 (in millions of dollars)

YEAR	TOTAL CURRENT DOLLARS	TOTAL CONSTANT 1958 DOLLARS	NONMEDICAL CONSTANT 1958 DOLLARS
1953	138	157	113
1954	160	178	127
1955	169	184	126
1956	213	225	161
1957	229	235	139
1958	254	254	141
1959	306	297	152
1960	405	383	194
1961	500	465	217
1962	613	562	218
1963	760	685	294
1964	916	810	372
1965	1,073	932	447
1966	1,262	1,067	547
1967	1,409	1,153	581
1968	1,572	1,239	645
1969	1,600	1,201	596
1970	1,658	1,183	632
1971*	1,700	1,147	564
1972*	1,750	1,136	478

* Estimated.

Source: "National Patterns of R & D Resources," NSF 72-300, National Science Foundation, Washington, D.C.; "Resources for Medical Research," Report no. 12, National Institutes of Health, Bethesda, Md. (1968), updated by N.I.H. staff.

THE FINANCE OF HIGHER EDUCATION
HOWARD R. BOWEN

There is much discussion of higher educational finance within government, education, the foundations, and the public press. But the voices heard are not all in harmony—except on the need for action. This paper analyzes the problem and then presents a long-range plan for the finance of higher education. The underlying objectives of the plan are derived from fairly settled national policy:

1   The United States should maintain an excellent system of higher education affording rich opportunities for the personal and vocational development of its young people and giving high priority to the advancement and dissemination of learning.

2   This system should be diversified as to program to meet the needs of various categories of students and various regions; it should be diversified as to control to include both private and public institutions; the

institutions should individually be accorded a maximum of autonomy; and sources of support for higher education should be diversified so that no interest group can dominate higher education.

3   Higher education should be open to all; no person should be deprived by barriers of finance, race, national origin, religion, place of residence, or background, of the opportunity for whatever higher education is within his capacity.

4   Students should have free choice of educational programs and institutions within the limits of their qualifications, and certain programs or certain institutions—whether private or public—should not be set apart for particular socioeconomic classes.

What kind of educational finance will help to attain these objectives? The question breaks down into two subquestions: How should students be financed? and How should institutions be financed? The subject of tuition cuts across both subquestions.

There should be a national system of educational grants available to any student showing need. There would be no scholastic requirement except that the student be enrolled full time in an approved college or university of his choice at any level from the freshman year to the end of graduate or professional study.

For students there should be a national system of educational grants—available to any student showing need. There would be no scholastic requirement except that the student be enrolled full time in an approved college or university of his choice at any level from the freshman year to the end of graduate or professional study. The amount of the individual grant would be set according to need as measured by the cost of a minimal education program and the ability of the parents to contribute and of the student to earn. The purpose would be to provide a financial base for any student, regardless of circumstances, to attend college as long as his abilities permit without his ending up heavily in debt.

This minimal and rigid grant system should be supplemented by a national system of student loans to provide flexibility, to meet individual needs and preferences, and to enlarge opportunity. The loan system would carry with it no means test, and hence would be available to persons of all income classes.

A recent report of the American Council on Education proposed substantial increases in assistance to institutions of higher education. But the principal question the report failed to answer is: By what procedure or formula should broad unrestricted support to institutions be distributed? There are many possible formulas that could be derived for the purpose. The formula below is intended to enable the federal government to contribute year after year toward institutional costs that are rising by reason of the increasing cost of education per student and increasing enrollments. It would operate as follows:

1   The federal government would calculate for a series of past years the

national average cost of instruction per student (FTE) for various classes of students stratified by course of study (i.e., liberal arts, engineering, law, etc.) and by class level (i.e., freshman-sophomore, junior-senior, graduate, etc.).

2   By analysis of these figures and of the plans of a sample of institutions, an estimate of the cost in each category for the coming year would be made.

3   Each institution would estimate the number of students (FTE) it expects in each category in the coming year.

A provisional cost-of-education grant to each institution for each student category would be calculated as some fraction (say one-half) of the estimated increase in cost multiplied by the number of students.

4   A provisional cost-of-education grant to each institution for each student category would be calculated as some fraction (say one-half) of the estimated increase in cost multiplied by the number of students.

5   The provisional cost-of-education and enrollment grants would be paid to the institution in installments during the year.

6   When the year had been completed and the actual costs and enrollments known, the final grant would be determined. Any excess or deficiency in payment as compared with the provisional grant would be adjusted as a reduction or addition to the next year's provisional grant. The system would resemble a pay-as-you-go income tax.

7   The grant for the first year of the plan would be continued into the second and subsequent years of the program, and further additions would be made according to the formula each year. The federal government, then, would gradually assume an increasing role in the finance of educational costs.

Perhaps the most vexing subject in higher educational finance is tuitions. Unfortunately, it gives rise to conflicts between the public and private sectors of higher education. But substantial differences in tuitions between private and public institutions are practically feasible, socially justifiable, and economically necessary.

Substantial differences in tuitions between private and public institutions are practically feasible, socially justifiable, and economically necessary.

The financial plan suggested here has been criticized on the ground that it might encourage an undesirable lowering of admissions standards. Under the plan, any young person could secure funds on the basis of admission to an approved institution, and any approved institution could receive unrestricted grants on the basis of increased enrollments. It is argued that some institutions might be tempted to accept unqualified students for whom cheap and inferior programs would be provided. Also, it is feared that new undergraduate institutions might spring up merely to take advantage of the federal money, or that some existing institutions might be tempted to provide second-rate graduate and professional programs. This criticism, though perhaps plausible, is not, on close inspection, valid.

The plan outlined would provide for diversified support of higher education. The sources of support would include students and their parents, state legislatures, private donors, and the federal government. The share of the federal government would increase over time. But since its contribution would be divided between support of students and support of institutions, and institutional support would be partly in the form of unrestricted grants, the direct power of the federal government over institutions would be held in check. Because of forgone earnings and cash outlays, students would still be the major contributors to the economic cost of higher education.

(1968)

CREDIT FOR COLLEGE: Public Policy for Student Loans
ROBERT W. HARTMAN

For generations, students have been borrowing from banks, individuals, or colleges to finance their higher education, but until recently, the volume of such transactions was small, and there was no significant government involvement in loans to students. Beginning in the late 1950s, however, student borrowing increased and both the state and federal governments entered the picture. In 1958, Congress passed the National Defense Education Act, Title II of which provided for long-term, low-interest loans to students, with direct federal provision of most of the capital. The Higher Education Act of 1965 broadened the federal government's involvement by establishing federal assistance to state loan guarantee agencies and by offering a program of federal loan insurance in states where students did not have access to guaranteed loans.

In the last 10 years, student borrowing under federally supported programs has increased rapidly. Under the National Defense Student Loan program (NDSL), the number of borrowers has more than tripled from the first full-year level of 115,000, and the NDSL annual loan volume increased almost five-fold in the 1960s. In the federal Guaranteed Loan Program's (GLP) first complete fiscal year (1966–67), 330,000 students borrowed about $250 million, and in 1971 over a million students are expected to borrow about $950 million.

Some view the rapid growth of student borrowing as alarming, some view it as encouraging, and how much reliance should be put on student loans has become a major question in discussions of the financing of higher education. Should student loans become a major (or even the sole) mechanism for financing higher education? Or are we already burdening students with too much debt? What should be the role of the federal government in the student loan market? Should it continue existing

programs? Should it facilitate the flow of capital to student loans by establishing a federal lending authority or by providing a secondary market
for student loan paper? Should it increase subsidies to lenders or to borrowers, or should it reduce them?

Different views of the desirable role for student loans reflect, in large
part, the relative importance attached to three basic rationales for government intervention in higher education: (1) student loans are a means
for providing a general subsidy to encourage the growth of higher education; (2) student loans are a means of stimulating enrollment of certain
target groups and particular types of training; (3) government intervention in student loans is a means of compensating for failures of the
private capital market to adequately finance ventures involving high risk.

One possible role for student loans is to support the entire cost of instruction. Another is to finance the cost of all student charges (for
tuition, books, room and board, and so forth). A third is to cover student
charges "net" of family ability to pay. Still another role would be as a
residual item in a financing scheme that makes a minimum amount of
higher education available to everybody through direct grants or low
tuition; loans would be available to cover the additional cost for anyone
who wanted to go beyond the minimum. A final possibility is to continue
student loan programs as they are now.

Some estimate of projected loan volume is required to estimate the
advisability of proposed loan roles and the viability of existing programs.
Although subject to error, estimates in this study indicate a significant
difference between present and proposed loan roles. Shifting from the
present structure to basing loans on student charges net of family ability
to pay would not involve a significant increase in the average loan, but
would more than double the number of students aided. More radical
roles might involve massive changes either in the federal budget or in the
private capital market. With the more radical roles, neither the present
programs nor the nature of the federal commitment could remain unchanged.

Opponents of increasing the role of student loans in higher education
have referred to the "burdensomeness" of large debt accumulations by
young families. There is no consensus on where the line falls between
"acceptable" and "burdensome," but there is general agreement that the
relevant measure of debt oppressiveness is the relation between future
repayments and income. Repayment rates in actual cases under existing loan programs have not been excessive. Comparing the incomes of
recent college graduates with estimates of repayment ceilings under alternative loan roles indicates there is much room for expansion of stu-

There is no consensus on where the line falls between "acceptable" and "burden-some," but there is general agreement that the relevant measure of debt oppres-siveness is the relation between future repayments and income.

dent borrowing without debts becoming oppressive, especially if repayment terms are extended.

Volume of the two major existing loan programs, the NDSL and GLP, has not been limited by the lack of student demand. In the case of the NDSL, inadequate congressional appropriations have been the primary limiting factor. The GLP's volume has been limited by the interplay of federal rules and lenders' reactions to those rules.

Misleading treatment of federal loan programs within the national budget significantly understates the full costs of the GLP relative to the NDSL, because the former is an interest subsidy program while the latter is a "direct loan." The economic difference between the two programs is greatly overstated by the budget's accounting rules. But there are real differences between the programs, and these differences indicate that the subsidy element is larger in the NDSL than in the GLP. Whether for rational reasons, such as limiting subsidies, or irrational ones, such as making the budget appear smaller, it seems likely that heavy reliance on the GLP will continue.

Since the GLP was begun, Congress has amended it several times. Virtually all the changes stemmed from claims of insufficient volume to make loans to all qualified students who want to borrow. As a result of these claims, Congress has progressively liberalized the return to lenders participating in the GLP to allow it to grow. To eliminate the apparent insufficiency and stimulate future growth, Congress has three alternatives: (1) maintain the current cost of loans to students while increasing the return to lenders; (2) encourage the supply of funds by changing nonyield characteristics of loans (for example, their ability to withstand rising interest rates); or (3) remove all subsidies, allowing the loan market to clear itself.

Unless the artificial strictures (imposed by federal rules) that encumbered growth of the GLP in the past are removed, there is little likelihood that it can be relied on to play a major role in loan financing.

Unless the artificial strictures (imposed by federal rules) that encumbered growth of the GLP in the past are removed, there is little likelihood that it can be relied on to play a major role in loan financing. If the barriers are removed, and especially if new lenders are attracted through the development of secondary markets or by other means, there is no reason to believe that financing will not be available for student loans.

Who should and who does benefit from student loans? In attempting to achieve several objectives (stimulate enrollment of low-income students, improve capital market accessibility, provide general federal subsidies for higher education) with too few instruments, the NDSL and GLP resemble other government programs that pass the political test of something-for-everybody. But maximally efficient programs do not yet exist.

A subsidized and targeted loan program can probably play a role in giving special aid to lower-income students. But there is no evidence that the current rate of subsidy in NDSL is optimal. Nor has it been established that, for purposes of equalization, a subsidized loan is preferable to an outright grant. Greater targeting of NDSL funds on low-income students would clearly establish NDSL as an enrollment-equalizing program.

There is reason for the federal government to maintain a program to provide all students with access to capital markets. This can be accomplished easily through guarantees of private loans as provided by the GLP. Since there is no good reason for the federal government to control who gets such loans, the private market approach (as opposed to that of a direct government loan) seems sensible. But such loans should be completely unsubsidized. Under these conditions, a program such as the GLP would be a proper instrument for carrying out a public objective.

General subsidies to higher education provided by the federal government may be warranted. If so, a new instrument of public policy, one that spreads the benefits more or less universally among college students, is necessary. In no way do existing loan programs meet this requirement.

General subsidies to higher education provided by the federal government may be warranted. If so, a new instrument of public policy, one that spreads the benefits more or less universally among college students, is necessary. In no way do existing loan programs meet this requirement, and no loan program is ever likely to be a suitable vehicle for general subsidies. There are alternative means of providing a general subsidy, such as general student grants, institutional grants based on enrollment, and federal support of two years of college.

Most comprehensive studies of higher education finance have included loans for students as one component in their recommendations. Some of the major proposals have dealt with the time-stream of repayments, a National Student Loan Bank, an Educational Opportunity Bank, and cancellation of teacher loans under the NDSL program.

Present federal loan programs allow a repayment term of up to ten years. Lengthening the repayment term under these programs would reduce repayment burdens in early postgraduate years, thereby allowing greater consumption for young college graduates who have borrowed under the programs. A case can be made for lengthened or income-contingent repayments in an unsubsidized program. The case is based on the general failure of capital markets to allow people to enhance their purchasing power when they are young at the expense of consumption in later life. In subsidized loans, the case is weaker: taxpayers should not be asked to pay for enhanced opportunities of college graduates.

Without such changes as lengthened terms and income-contingent repayments in existing programs, there may be reason for establishing a centrally run loan bank. With these changes, such a bank would be essential. If loan repayment rates were contingent upon income, the collecting agency would need access to the borrower's tax reports. It is not likely that such access could (or should) be provided to lenders under either the NDSL or GLP program as they are now administered. Lengthened repayment terms would also make more severe the difficulties of attracting loan funds to the GLP as it presently operates. A longer repayment term would make student loans appear even less liquid to banks, and lenders' collection costs would go up as families moved over the years. Under these circumstances, the financing of a large-scale loan program would have to move beyond the narrow confines of commercial bank finance now occupied by the GLP.

A National Loan Bank could provide the means for attracting new capital into student loans. It could perform the critical functions of origination and collection efficiently under a flexible charter. It could also funnel the subsidy elements in present loan programs—at a saving to the federal budget—with some prospect that new techniques of allotment could further the goals of present subsidies.

The Education Opportunity Bank proposal builds upon the features of the National Loan Bank, and, in addition, attempts to mutualize the risk of investing in higher education. Repayments are based on income, and former students whose incomes are low relative to the amount borrowed are subsidized by those whose incomes are high relative to borrowings. A full-cost Educational Opportunity Bank that attempts to attract a substantial part of the college-going population and provides a modest federal subsidy shifts costs from a poorer group (general taxpayers) to a richer group (the college-educated). Middle-income borrowers, however, will bear a repayment burden greater than that of the most prosperous borrowers. Evaluation of this bank depends in part on the weight attached to the welfare of the groups involved. Since the Educational Opportunity Bank does not require a person to pay off his own loan, such a plan might leave the bank with a preponderance of borrowers who anticipate and realize low earnings. A National Student Loan Bank could provide government subsidies for those with very low earnings and require all others to retire their own loans, thus avoiding the self-selection of those who expect low earnings.

A full-cost Educational Opportunity Bank that attempts to attract a substantial part of the college-going population and provides a modest federal subsidy shifts costs from a poorer group (general taxpayers) to a richer group (the college-educated). Middle-income borrowers, however, will bear a repayment burden greater than that of the most prosperous borrowers.

There appears to be no good reason for retaining the provisions in the NDSL program for canceling the loans of individuals who go into teaching. In a study, the College Entrance Examination Board found no clear-cut evidence that the provisions have contributed to the increase in the number or the improvement in quality of teachers. Also, it appears there is no need to offer young people an incentive to go into teaching. Although shortages may occur in specific subjects and in geographical areas, these are more effectively treated with various provisions under Title V (Education Professions Development) of the Education Act of 1965. Cancellations of loans to teachers are also depriving potential student borrowers of $20 million.

(1971)

SOURCES OF FUNDS TO COLLEGES AND UNIVERSITIES
JUNE A. O'NEILL with the assistance of DANIEL SULLIVAN

Analysis of the financial aspects of American higher education is hampered because relevant data have not always been classified and reported in a consistent manner. In this study an effort was made to remedy that situation and to compile information about sources of funds for colleges and universities between 1930 and 1968, the longest period of time for which reliable data could be assembled. Published data from the U.S. Office of Education were adjusted and missing information was estimated where necessary to provide year-to-year consistency. The results are given in a series of detailed tables that present sources of current fund and plant fund income to colleges and universities, by control and by level of institution. These tables appear as an appendix to the study.

Increasing numbers of colleges and universities came under public control during this period. In the fall of 1970 more than 70 percent of students were enrolled in public institutions; the remainder, with trivial exceptions, were enrolled in private, nonprofit schools. Not surprisingly, user charges (such as tuition and payments for meals and for books from university presses) account for only a portion of all funds. Funds from the government—state and local as well as federal—and funds from private philanthropy, account for the bulk of income to institutions of higher education.

This report utilizes the data assembled to make some preliminary observations about trends in the way higher education has been financed, with emphasis on the role of tuition. First, changes in the tuition charge (both gross and net of student aid) are examined, and it is found that tuition has risen faster, on the average, than the level of prices in the economy, and that tuition in private institutions has risen much faster than tuition in public institutions. Tuition is then compared with instructional cost to see how the contribution of other sources of funds—the implicit subsidy to students—has changed over time.

Surprisingly, despite the shift toward publicly run schools, where tuition covers a smaller portion of the costs, the ratio of tuition to costs in institutions as a whole has not fallen and was roughly the same in 1967–68 as it was in 1929–30.

Surprisingly, despite the shift toward publicly run schools, where tuition covers a smaller portion of costs, the ratio of tuition to costs in institutions as a whole has not fallen and was roughly the same in 1967–68 as it

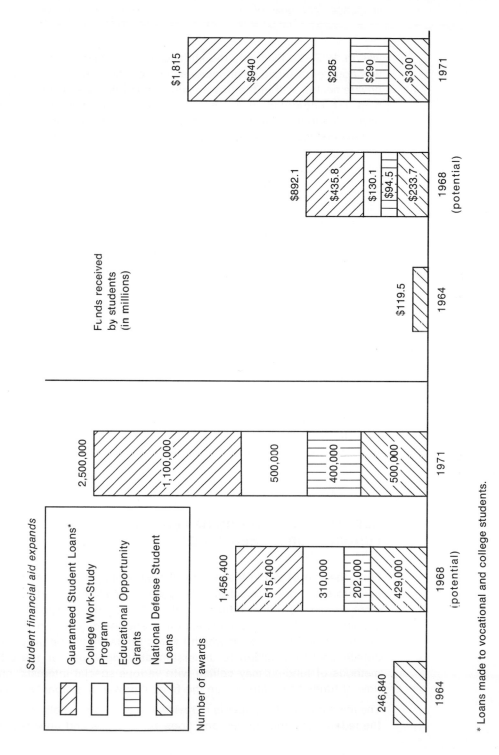

Student financial aid expands

Guaranteed Student Loans*

College Work-Study Program

Educational Opportunity Grants

National Defense Student Loans

Number of awards

246,840

1964

1,456,400

1968 (potential)

515,400

310,000

202,000

429,000

2,500,000

1971

1,100,000

500,000

400,000

500,000

Funds received by students (in millions)

$119.5

1964

$892.1

1968 (potential)

$435.8

$130.1

$94.5

$233.7

$1,815

1971

$940

$285

$290

$300

* Loans made to vocational and college students.

Source: U.S. Dept. of Health, Education, and Welfare, Accomplishments 1963–1968: Problems and Challenges and a Look to the Future. Report to President Lyncon B. Johnson, December 1968, p. 39.

was in 1929–30. Evidently the shift to highly subsidized public schools was counterbalanced by an increase in the ratio of tuition to costs in the private sector. Within the private sector this ratio has become especially high for undergraduates, and in private universities undergraduates paying full tuition may have paid for as much as 83 percent of their costs in 1967–68. With increases in student aid, however, the average student pays much less than full tuition, and the dispersion in subsidies has increased accordingly within the student body.

The second section of the report examines changes over time in the distribution of the various sources of funds that are used by colleges and universities for educational services—a category that unavoidably includes many more activities than student instruction—for example, research. Funds from public sources (state, local, and federal) have become increasingly important to institutions as a whole, both because of the growth of publicly controlled schools and because of the increased reliance of private schools on public funds.

It is suggested that the failure of private philanthropy to keep pace with desired expenditures may have contributed to the rise in tuition relative to instructional expenditures in private colleges and universities, although other factors undoubtedly also influenced that trend. The relatively rapid increase in per student expenditures in private schools appears puzzling in view of this need to increase tuition relative to costs. This may well have resulted, however, from an effort to remain competitive with the expanding public sector by offering a higher quality "product," one that could not readily be obtained in public schools.

(1973)

ALTERNATIVE METHODS OF FEDERAL FUNDING FOR HIGHER EDUCATION
RONALD A. WOLK

From the end of World War II until the launching of the Soviet Sputnik, educators and government officials debated whether the federal government should aid higher education at all. Now, federal support of higher education has become a national policy, and the debate is over the level of support and the ways in which federal funds should be provided. The debate on this question is understandably vigorous, for the different methods of funding may collide with various special interests, and the flow of funds bears directly on the flow of power and monetary benefits.

The main goal of this paper is to review the alternative methods by which the federal government can and does aid colleges and universities. The paper does not present a completely inclusive picture of the nature and level of current federal support to higher education. It is necessarily a summary, for a complete and thorough analysis of present and possible federal programs would require both more time and more space than was available.

In what ways shall federal funds be provided to higher education? There are five major alternative methods of federal funding, and each has its advocates:

Categorical Aid   Funds provided through grants, contracts, or loans in support of specific projects or goals designated by the granting agency.

Aid to Students   Grants or loans directly to students or through institutions to cover all or part of educational expense.

Grants to Institutions   Funds provided to institutions for broad or undesignated purposes.

Tax Relief   Assistance to taxpayers for educational expenses through exemptions, deductions, or credits in the payment of taxes. (Tax relief may also go to institutions and may cover donations as well as expenses.)

Revenue Sharing   The return to the states of certain tax monies collected by the federal government.

The great bulk of direct federal aid is now channeled through the first two of these alternatives. The question at the heart of the debate about the nature of federal support for the future is which of these alternative methods should be used and to what degree. Obviously, future decisions should be based on a careful analysis of the impacts, advantages, and disadvantages of these various methods.

(1968)

THE ECONOMICS OF THE MAJOR PRIVATE UNIVERSITIES
WILLIAM G. BOWEN

Among persons concerned with the affairs of the private universities, there is a pervasive feeling that current sources of financial support are becoming increasingly inadequate in relation to needs. A primary reason why the major universities, public as well as private, need substantial amounts of additional income is that their operating costs have been rising rapidly. The most noticeable feature of the budgets of all institutions of higher education is how fast they have gone up in the years since World War II.

The significance of increases in total educational and general expenditures depends in part on their composition. The phenomenal growth of organized research has, of course, been one of the main forces behind the expansion of university budgets. However, there is a lot of growth in expenditures exclusive of the increase in direct expenditures on organized research.

Why have instructional costs risen at such a rapid rate? It is true that enrollments have increased, but this can only be a partial answer. Instructional costs are affected significantly by the extent to which institutions attempt to cover a wide variety of specialized fields, and one of the noteworthy developments of the last 10 to 15 years has been the broadening of curricular offerings and the establishment of new research programs. Partly in response to purely intellectual developments (the splintering of some fields of knowledge and the development of entirely new specialties) and partly in response to felt national needs, universities have markedly increased their commitments to such relatively costly fields as non-Western studies, biochemistry, and plasma physics. Attempts have also been made to strengthen and bring together those disciplines which have something to contribute to our understanding of the process of economic development and modernization and of the problems associated with the urbanization of our own country, to cite just two areas of interdisciplinary concern. All efforts of this kind—which involve doing something more than just studying traditional subjects in traditional ways—are very expensive.

Universities have also become more conscious of their responsibilities to the communities in which they are located, and of their responsibilities for aiding in the achievement of national goals. Such efforts have been costly in terms of time spent, administrative energy, and unreimbursed costs. Even in the performance of traditional functions within traditional fields, advances in knowledge and in research techniques have made it increasingly expensive for universities to do their jobs.

Still another factor which has caused increases in average instructional cost per student is the changing "mix" of the student body at the typical university. Graduate students, and especially Ph.D. candidates, are much more expensive to educate than undergraduates, and the part of the total student population made up of graduate students has grown greatly. The increased emphasis on graduate education has been accompanied by an increased emphasis on research at many of the major universities, as one would expect in view of the close interrelationship between these activities.

At the root of the cost pressures besetting all educational institutions is the nature of their technology. Over the course of the twentieth century, output per man-hour of labor input (the usual measure of productivity) in the United States has gone up at a remarkably steady rate of approxi-

Over the course of the twentieth century, output per man-hour of labor input (the usual measure of productivity) in the United States has gone up at a remarkably steady rate of approximately 2.5 percent per year. Even in the absence of reliable statistics, it seems safe to assert that educational institutions have not shared fully in this growth in the overall productivity of the economy.

mately 2.5 percent per year. Even in the absence of reliable statistics, it seems safe to assert that educational institutions have not shared fully in this growth in the overall productivity of the economy. And the ability of the universities to keep pace, year after year, with economywide gains in productivity is crucial for their cost position. In every industry in which increases in productivity come more slowly than in the economy as a whole, cost per unit of product must be expected to increase relative to costs in general. There is an important corollary to this fundamental point: the faster the overall pace of technological progress and capital accumulation, the greater will be the increase in the general wage level, and the greater will be the upward pressure on costs in industries in which productivity is more or less stationary.

The task of projecting the course of education expenditures is usually approached in two steps: projecting average cost per student, and projecting future enrollment. The simplest way of projecting average cost per student is to extrapolate the rate of growth which has prevailed in prior years. Following this basic approach, we have determined the implication of recent trends for the amount of money a "typical" major private university might expect to spend for educational and general purposes in 1975–76 compared with what was spent in 1965–66. The results suggest that expenditures over this 10-year period will have nearly tripled, with the absolute amount of money spent rising from a little less than $25 million in 1965–66 to more than $70 million in 1975–76. It must be emphasized that these figures do not include capital expenditures or expenditures for organized research, student aid, or auxiliary activities. It should also be noted that the projection is in current dollars, and includes an implicit allowance of about 2 percent per year for increases in the general price level.

The relative importance of principal sources of income is changing at all private universities. By far the most dramatic change is the sharp increase in the relative importance of government contracts and grants. The item which has declined in relative importance most significantly over the years is endowment income.

The relative importance of principal sources of income is changing at all private universities. By far the most dramatic change is the sharp increase in the relative importance of government contracts and grants. The item which has declined in relative importance most significantly over the years is endowment income.

The increased importance of annual fund raising, and the task of securing and administering government project funds, have added significantly to the workload of faculty members and administrative personnel at all universities. A more fundamental implication of these developments is that the major private universities are now living more dangerously than ever before. The declining relative availability of "hard" sources of income affects the ability of the universities to make long-run commitments, especially in new fields. This problem, which results from the fact that the composition of university income must be considered separately from the level of income, must be borne in mind when considering alternative methods of providing additional funds.

Historically, one of the principal ways in which private universities have met rising costs has been by increasing student fees. Since about 1958, tuition has actually gone up slightly faster than the index of educational costs (a little over 8 percent per annum on the average, compared with an average annual rate of 7.5 percent for the cost index). Will tuition continue to increase at this rate? The answer depends in part—and probably in large part—on the future of student-aid programs. And the question of whether it is going to be possible to continue to increase outlays on student aid at the pace established in recent years depends mainly on the future of foundation and government programs. The ability of the universities to provide increased financial aid to students at both undergraduate and graduate levels will, in turn, affect the rate at which tuition can be increased.

The ability of the universities to provide increased financial aid to students at both undergraduate and graduate levels will, in turn, affect the rate at which tuition can be increased.

Endowment income at all private universities increased at an average annual rate of 6.8 percent per year between 1952 and 1964. The outlook for endowment income is dependent on two considerations: the amount of new endowment secured by the universities, and the rate of return earned on the investment portfolios of the universities.

There has been an extraordinary increase in private gifts and grants since World War II. But several factors suggest that it is very doubtful that the recent rate of increase can be maintained: the unlikelihood that foundations will continue to increase their grants to major private universities at anything like the pace they have set in the last 10 years; recent declining trends in individual giving for all philanthropic purposes; the extent of the competition for money from foundations, corporations, and individuals; the operation of the principle of diminishing returns to fund-raising activities; and the changing composition of the student body at the major private universities, where heretofore alumni have been by far the most important source of private support.

Projecting university income is an extremely hazardous undertaking. The fundamental forces pushing up costs operate in a fairly regular, predictable fashion, but the factors affecting some of the major components of income are much more apt to change in unforeseen ways. Nevertheless, assumptions that we make, when combined, imply that educational and general income received by the mythical "typical" institution from all sources (including present government programs of student aid reflected in gross fee income) will increase from just under $25 million in 1965–66 to between $43 and $51 million in 1975–76—an implicit growth rate of 5.8 to 7.6 percent per year.

The basic inference to be drawn is simply that, in the absence of significant new developments, the economic squeeze already being felt by the major private universities is going to intensify.

When the income and expenditure projections are brought together, the result is a projected deficit of $20–$28 million in 1975–76. In percentage terms, between 28 and 39 percent of educational and general expenditures would not be covered by the traditional sources of income. It must be emphasized that these projections are made on the basis of limited data, crude methods of extrapolation (including a liberal dose of judgment in certain instances), and a number of heroic assumptions. In addition, such significant aspects of university finance as capital expenditures over projected income is probably best viewed in more qualitative terms. The basic inference to be drawn is simply that, in the absence of significant new developments, the economic squeeze already being felt by the major private universities is going to intensify.

There is a clear public interest in maintaining the vitality of the nation's private universities. The special contributions and problems of the private universities must be seen in the light of their role as an essential component of a diverse, complex, diffuse, and yet highly responsive system of higher education, a system whose value to the nation has been amply demonstrated. In this context, private universities appear in proper perspective as a precious set of "assets-in-being" that helps to promote freedom, diversity, and excellence. If their effectiveness is impaired, American higher education as a whole will suffer.

(1968)

STRENGTH-ENING THE INSTITUTIONS

PART 7

It may seem illogical that a higher education system firmly entrenched in the heart of national life could be beset by instability and, in some quarters, acute financial embarrassment. But that is precisely the situation in the 1970s. The reasons are many.

For one thing, the system was for many years elitist in its philosophy. Now, it is changing this orientation drastically to admit more and more students from previously excluded sectors of the population. And the change is proving to be traumatic to some institutions.

In recent years, there has been a growing disaffection with scientific research throughout the country. And some kinds of research—that which has military applications and is classified—are disappearing from campuses. This removal of classified research disengages universities from what many citizens regard as a highly patriotic calling.

The public has been rendered even more suspicious of colleges and universities by virtue of campus disruptions and outbreaks of violence involving large numbers of students. Such occurrences were particularly frequent and alarming in the late 1960s, when the Commission began its work. To a great extent, the unrest on the campuses was simply an early manifestation of public unrest that focused on an unpopular war, unsatisfactory progress in extending civil rights to members of minorities within the population, and concern for the basic values of American life that were being particularly challenged by the nation's youth.

And finally, costs for higher education continued to rise at the same time the public was beginning to feel it had reached a limit in its ability to increase its financial support.

There had developed, in short, a crisis in confidence that had to be overcome by the colleges and universities before legislators, foundations, taxpayers, and private donors could be expected to regain their enthusiasm for higher education. The institutions had to demonstrate that they could operate efficiently, that they could govern themselves without disruption, and that they could come to agreement about their functions and purposes.

Because of the importance of restoring this confidence, several Commission reports were concerned with the subject. *Dissent and Disruption* analyzes problems and issues that arose between 1961 and 1970, when mass protests and confrontations on campuses across the country put a heavy strain on the system as a whole. Part of the study drew upon results of a nationwide survey directed by Martin Trow, which involved over 100,000 students and 60,000 faculty members at over 300 institutions. This massive inquiry revealed that a majority of college and university personnel did not favor violence and disruptive behavior on campuses, and that the majority of respondents are generally satisfied with their institutions, although they felt specific reforms are needed. The Commission recommended that the right to dissent should be protected, although disruption was to be vigorously opposed. It also proposed a Bill of Rights that identifies and protects the rights of all members of the university community—and of the institution itself.

In *Governance of Higher Education* we gave further attention to these problems and made recommendations concerning the participation of faculty members and students in the decision-making processes of the campus, the probable impacts of the organization of faculties into collective bargaining organizations, and the extent to which policies governing tenure for faculty members ought to be modified.

The problem of increasing institutional efficiency is faced in *The More Effective Use of Resources*. The central thrust of this report is that efficiency must be improved to the level where, by 1980, total institutional expenditures can be reduced by nearly $10 billion per year (in 1970 dollars) as compared with the costs which would result if the trend of the 1960s continued. Expenditures should be held to around $41.5 billion as compared to $51 billion per year. Half of this reduction can be achieved by creating shorter time options for students at all degree levels and by reducing the numbers of students who attend college under parental pressures—the reluctant attenders. The other part will demand policy decisions and dramatic action on the part of the individual institutions.

The Purposes and the Performance of Higher Education presents the Commission's findings and conclusions in the difficult matter of determining higher education's goals and functions. We define five broad purposes for American higher education as we move into the twenty-first century. The first is the educational development of individual students, and the provision of an environment for their intellectual and emotional growth. The second is the advancement of human capability in the society at large. The third reflects our interest in lifelong education, and holds that the system should provide learning on an equitable basis to all qualified persons throughout the entire postsecondary age group. The fourth relates to the purpose of pure scholarship, and stresses the importance of the campus as a center for intellectual and artistic endeavors. The final purpose again stresses the service function of higher education, and highlights the role of the institution in evaluating society's ongoing process of self-renewal, but rejects direct political action by institutions of higher education.

The sponsored research activity in this priority area was again substantial, and it is hoped that the results will play a significant role in the struggle of higher education to regain its honored position as a faithful and trusted subsystem of the larger American society.

TOWARD EFFECTIVE GOVERNANCE

CHAPTER 11

Campuses have been called ungovernable anarchies, but the Commission views them as being both governable and worth governing well. James Perkins and his coauthors confirm the complexity of governance in *The University as an Organization,* and establish that universities are too unique to be operated on models provided by such institutions as businesses or government agencies. Suggestions that universities should merely adopt the governance systems of other kinds of institutions are further refuted in *The Multicampus University,* by Eugene Lee and Frank Bowen. In analyzing nine multicampus university systems, Lee and Bowen demonstrate how enormous and unique the problems of governance are in a sector of higher education which enrolls more than 40 percent of all college and university students in the United States.

Studies of the constituent segments of campus society and the ways in which they affect the question of governance were also sponsored by the Commission. In *Leadership and Ambiguity,* James March and Michael Cohen depict the presidency as having emerged from a period of being reactive, parochial, and conventional into a time when the effect of even the most dynamic presidents upon the decision-making process is often illusory.

Current trends in faculty attitudes are explored in an analysis of the politics of American faculty members undertaken by Everett Ladd and Seymour Martin Lipset. The data for the study of political attitudes came from the extensive Commission survey undertaken under the direction of Martin Trow.

The governance and operations of colleges under the unusual strain of ongoing dissent have been given particularly close attention. Students, particularly in dissent, also came under the microscope. In the summer of 1970, Richard Peterson and John Bilorusky surveyed the presidents on 75 percent of the nation's campuses to ascertain the extent of student reaction to the entry of United States armed forces in Cambodia, and to the wounding of nine and the killing of four students at Kent State University. They discovered that 57 percent of the nation's institutions experienced "significant impact," but that on 77 percent of the campuses affected, that impact was "essentially peaceful." A relatively small but hyperactive percentage of students, on a minority of campuses, therefore appears to have been responsible for creating the image of general rebellion that has been impressed upon the mind of the American public.

THE UNIVERSITY AS AN ORGANIZATION
edited by JAMES A. PERKINS

"Why can't a university be like us?" That question almost inevitably arises whenever representatives of other types of organizations first confront the modern American university. The answer provided by this study is that universities constitute "a genus of institution that is unique in its totality and comparable to other organizations only in certain of its many characteristics."

James Perkins stresses that "a new look at university organization is overdue . . . because the university has assumed new functions this century which it has tried to handle . . . within an organizational structure designed essentially for . . . instruction." Evidence as to the inadequacy of this state of affairs is provided by E. D. Duryea, who outlines "three pervasive organizational inadequacies." First, the size and complexity of American universities has resulted in their containing two bureaucracies—faculty and administration—whose interests are divergent. Second, institutional specialization and departmentalization has tended "to push faculty loyalties out from the university," and third, the power base of institutional government is increasingly shifting away from governing boards and presidents and toward the faculty and certain external influences.

A caveat against making any except broad generalizations is voiced by John Millett, who demonstrates the frustrating fact that "diversity is a major characteristic of American higher education . . . [which educators believe] should be preserved." Irwin Sanders, in his discussion of the university as a community, endorses this diversity, but argues that it need not preclude the setting up of a broadbased organizational model, and he suggests that "an organizational model for the university might be the local community," which he finds every bit as diverse and which becomes increasingly appropriate as a model as university autonomy declines.

Barbara B. Burn compares governance at the universities of Freiburg, Paris, Toronto, and Cambridge, and the place of these universities in their respective systems of higher education. In harmony with Perkins, Burn concludes that "as in the United States, the inadequacy of traditional structures and methods has created widened concern for the reshaping of higher education." Delineating the major changes of the last decade, her case studies show that the European experience echoes the American one. She discovers that there has been a general strengthening of central administrations; a decline in professorial power, with middle- and junior-level staff gaining in power; a growing student influence; an emergence of multipartite systems of higher education as "rising costs and enrollments are compelling . . . individual institutions . . . to coordinate with others in the system . . . to apply the most leverage"; and "a broadening of higher education." Both in Europe and North America, it appears that significant first steps were taken in the

Both in Europe and North America, the first significant steps were taken in the 1960s to develop higher education "as a system capable of responsiveness and self-discipline."

1960s to develop higher education "as a system capable of responsiveness and self-discipline."

In the first of several direct comparisons of the university with other organizations, Ralph Besse examines its similarities to business. He concludes that corporation management techniques merit "careful study by university administrations," although such techniques are only applicable to a few of the many functions of the modern university. Stephen K. Bailey compares university organization with a government bureau and emerges with similar warnings. He observes that "the alternatives in university governance are not to make a body or a person supreme. The dilemma is resolved . . . by the development of circularities of responsibility . . . [whereby] . . . mutual dependence becomes clear and there are motivations to seek not power, but consent." He concludes by warning that "the move to enthrone legislatures in university governance can only be viewed with singular foreboding."

The move to enthrone legislatures in university governance can only be viewed with singular foreboding.

Comparing the university with a large foundation, W. McNeil Lowry finds broad superficial similarities, such as a collegial process of operation within both types of organizations striving toward consensus and a comparable influence on both types of organizations by a board of governors. He underscores the fundamental differences, however, by focusing on the interchange between foundations and universities in the development of "concepts and techniques for converting human and material resources to the purposes of social and economic development."

John Corson offers a prescription for university organization by delineating five proposals for reform which "seem to be gaining consensus": (1) The university must be recognized as being made up of groups that are relatively independent of the institution, and of each other, and yet exercise power over the institution. (2) Governance of such a community requires a structure and processes which will facilitate consensus. (3) A communitywide agency is needed as a mechanism through which the president and the board can build essential consensus. (4) The authority of various community segments—president, board, students, faculty—must be defined. (5) A system of accountability must be established.

Following the comparative discussion of organization, the study turns to "Corporate Authority: Trustees and Regents." Lyman Glenny's essay in this part of the work considers the effects of the law on higher education. He concludes that "much of the law has been beneficial" and that, "as never before, law is reshaping the university—forcing new roles, new organizational designs and relationships, and new concerns." This effect can be seen particularly in the dilution of university autonomy and the strengthening of academic freedom. While noting that the long-range effects of the "legalization" of the university are as yet uncertain, it is felt that one logical outcome of the process is clear. Collective bargaining "may be a solution of sorts to the rigidity of the law . . . and the paradigm of a temporary society of scholars linked together for the duration of a negotiated collective bargaining agreement."

Collective bargaining "may be . . . the paradigm of a temporary society of scholars linked together for the duration of a negotiated collective bargaining agreement."

In an examination of the responsibilities of governing boards, James Perkins identifies three mutually conflicting roles. The board is usually expected to act as founder's agent, as the bridge between society and campus, and as the court of last resort for the various internal constituencies of the university. One possible alternative to these conflicts is for the board to become the link between the new entities, the university assembly, and the external coordinating body.

In his essay on trustees and the university community, Samuel Gould echoes some of Perkins' theses. After describing the problems that arise in trustee-community relations, he finds that "these problems can be considerably mitigated . . . when the functions of trustees are thoroughly understood and agreed upon." There is to be a sound relationship between trustees and the rest of the university community; there must be common understanding of university purposes, institutional loyalty, realization by each constituency of its appropriate role, a system of idea-sharing in decision making; and "above all, a full commitment to the protection of university independence." When combined with Morton Rauh's "nuts and bolts" analysis of the internal organization of the board, these essays make clear that "the concept of trusteeship is sound. What remains to be done is to refine the functions of trusteeship until they more nearly match the concept."

In the concluding essay, Perkins redefines the missions and organization of the American university and forecasts certain changes of mission. These will involve the movement of large-scale research off campus, the demise of the residential campus, modification of the public service function of the institution, governance by consensus rather than appointment, and an increase in the importance of systems managers where planning and resource allocation is concerned. He stresses that instruction will remain the university's central mission, around which certain organizational changes will occur; boards of individual institutions will decline in power, and university organizations representative of the various internal constituencies will emerge. He concludes that the presidency will become elective and for a fixed term of years, with the president "becoming, in short, the organization man," with elected administrative officers serving under him.

Instruction will remain the university's central mission, around which certain organizational changes will occur; boards of individual institutions will decline in power, and university organizations representative of the various internal constituencies will emerge.

These developments are presented only as tendencies and with a warning that in most institutions "present arrangements will continue largely intact. The form will remain even as the substance is disappearing." Change will ultimately occur, however, as "the new university must become not only internally accountable to its constituencies but externally accountable to society."

(1973)

THE MULTICAMPUS UNIVERSITY: A Study of Academic Governance
EUGENE C. LEE and FRANK M. BOWEN

Although the governance of several campuses under a single governing board has been an increasingly significant development in American higher education, this is the first detailed examination of the phenomenon. The study examines nine multicampus universities: the Universities of California, Illinois, Missouri, North Carolina, Texas, and Wisconsin, the State and City Universities of New York and the California State University and Colleges System. At the time of the study, each had the following characteristics: responsibility for only a portion of higher education in the state, more than one four-year campus, and a systemwide executive who did *not* have specific responsibility for one of the campuses. These nine institutions enrolled more than 15 percent of all students in public four-year colleges and universities and 25 percent of all graduate students.

Over 250 persons active in the governance of the nine multicampus universities were interviewed. The study is in four sections. The first considers the political and social environment of the multicampus universities and the history of the nine institutions. The second discusses the governing structures—boards, administrators, and faculty and student organizations. The third is concerned with the processes of governance, including academic plans and programs, academic and administrative personnel, budget preparation and administration, admissions, business affairs, and external relations (public, governmental, and alumni). The fourth and final section summarizes the strengths and weaknesses of the multicampus university and looks critically at its future.

In its consideration of the environment of the multicampus universities, the study emphasizes the close relation between state government and the institution:

. . . the state government is inextricably involved in the governance of higher education. In some cases this is explicit . . . although usually . . . [it] . . . is less direct, as in the preparation and administration of the state budget. . . . Most administrators recognize that the legislature is the ultimate coordinator of public higher education . . . constitutions and statutes notwithstanding.

The traditional practices of single institutions are, in many cases, carried into the multicampus contexts. Governing boards make only the necessary adjustments to the additional campuses. Faculty senates seem to be local faculty organizations writ a little larger. Universitywide student organizations are virtually nonexistent.

With respect to the structures of governance, the traditional practices of single institutions are, in many cases, carried into the multicampus contexts. Governing boards make only the necessary adjustments to the additional campuses. Faculty senates seem to be local faculty organizations writ a little larger. Universitywide student organizations are virtually non-existent. A changing mood exists, however, and proposals for specific organizational changes are explored in the study. In contrast to the traditional structures, systemwide administrators and administrative organization of the multicampus universities are unique. With little by way of either guidance or constraint from the past, administrations are at the forefront of developing organizational structures particularly suited to the governance of more than one campus.

The examination of the processes of the multicampus universities covers institutional activity that ranges from planning academic programs to planning buildings, from recruiting a Nobel prize winner at a large salary to the hiring of a stenographer, and from the preparation of a budget for the state to the submission of research project proposals to federal agencies. The study attempts to decide whether these diverse functions contribute to the ability of the multicampus university to maintain diversity among its campuses, encourage cooperation between them, and enforce program specialization. These three difficult tasks are peculiar to governance in the multicampus context, and present opportunities and challenges which distinguish it from the balance of American higher education.

It is in the processes related to academic plans and academic personnel that a major strength of the multicampus university is found.

It is in the processes related to academic plans and academic personnel that a major strength of the multicampus university is found. "Quality control" is a prime concern and is reflected particularly in both the internal but independent "accreditation" of new graduate degree programs and in the recruitment and promotion of faculty. Review procedures in both instances are impressive in their scope.

The emphasis on quality control has two impacts: First, it gives a dimension of excellence to a major achievement of the multicampus universities—the creation of new campuses, the transformation of old ones, and the recruitment of faculty to both. Second, and possibly a weakness, this same emphasis on quality control—with its focus on "scholarly production"—may too often and too uncritically become the dominant value of the system. Accordingly, the full potential for variety and experimentation which a multicampus system affords seems unrealized.

The fourth section summarizes the findings and conclusions of the earlier chapters and explores their implications for the future. The interaction of both the strengths and shortcomings of the multicampus system are described. The clearest weakness is the absence of a stable agreement on the relative authority of the state government, the coordinating agency, and the university over various phases of the governance of higher education. Partly because of this uncertainty, the university systems are frequently unable to develop optimal relationships with and among the campuses. External uncertainty creates internal instability, limiting the capacity of the multicampus university to function as a system.

The clearest weakness is the absence of a stable agreement on the relative authority of the state government, the coordinating agency, and the university over various phases of the governance of higher education.

This uncertainty is often matched by the state government's inadequate delegation of fiscal authority to the university, and red tape often hampers both effective educational administration and budgetary relationships. In no small part, inadequacies in budgetary delegation result from the university's failure to induce confidence in its budgetary ability, and the authors recommend that the multicampus universities develop new concepts of financial reassurement. But, as the study points out, this will be of little value unless state fiscal authorities provide an incentive to the universities to develop more effective budgeting and accept the reality that subjectivity is required in many budget decisions, and that these decisions can more properly be made by responsible university administrators than by state officials.

Of equal importance, the authors say, is the fact that governing boards are not fulfilling their unique role in multicampus universities. A serious need exists for the boards to focus upon systemwide matters. That focus can only be achieved by curtailing the time now spent on details of governance at each campus. But revitalization of board activity cannot be achieved if boards remain structured as they are now. In general, the boards are highly unrepresentative of society, do not possess legitimacy in the minds of students and faculty, and are not sufficiently independent of partisan political currents. The authors propose methods of nomination and selection other than exclusive gubernatorial appointment, which is the dominant mode today.

Within the administration, there is room in almost every multicampus university for an increased delegation of authority to campus executives. At the same time, the system executive himself needs to retain adequate authority. He must be encouraged and expected to act as an educational leader and empowered to do so. Such leadership requires authority and staff. For its part, the faculty must shape its own governing structures so as to have an appropriate impact at the multicampus level. While campus faculty bodies should be jealous of their prerogatives, they must also recognize the necessity and legitimacy of faculty activity at the system level.

To realize its potential, the multicampus university will have to intensify long-range academic planning in new and different ways and pay far more attention to experimental multicampus programs, drawing on the resources of several campuses.

To realize its potential, the multicampus university will have to intensify long-range academic planning in new and different ways and pay far more attention to experimental multicampus programs, drawing on the resources of several campuses. Multiple dimensions of quality in admissions must be accompanied by multiple patterns of recruitment and systems of compensation within the faculty, and the creative containment of these differences among both students and faculty will be one of the most important contributions of the multicampus university in the 1970s.

On balance, the record of the multicampus universities is impressive. However, the decade of the 1970s will mark a greater break with the past than did the 1960s or 1950s.

First, the combination of expanded teaching, research, and public service missions poses the threat of institutional overload, and further enrollment expansion will be accompanied by growing clamor for open-admissions policies and, perhaps paradoxically, for increasingly sophisticated selection procedures.

Increased numbers of students to educate and increased demands for the university to serve the public in other ways will result in greater public involvement in governance, with state and national governments taking the leading role. This situation will, in turn, lead to increased demands for interinstitutional cooperation. In the face of these external pressures, there are equally insistent demands for internal educational reform. An increase in faculty and student activism and a corresponding decline in the current preeminence of "flagship" campuses is foreseen. Second and even third campuses will rival the current "flagship" in importance as administrative lines of authority are more clearly drawn to respond to demands for changes. In the wake of this, presidents and chancellors will see their own roles change so that they may avoid the human equivalent of institutional overload. The issue is larger than the mere survival of the university president. It involves the survival of the university itself.

As stated previously, there is growing concern that institutional overload will confront the American multiversity. One alternative is to disaggregate the functions of teaching, research, and service, much as is done frequently in Europe. The study notes that "the university as we know it was not preordained." However, every advantage to be gained from disaggregation has a price, a disadvantage which could be avoided if the multicampus university could solve the dilemma confronting the multiversity. This might be realized if, in fact as in theory, the multicampus university can develop as a system and become greater than the sum of its parts. It could be that the opportunities for specialization and diversity among campuses and cooperation between them might produce a division of labor which would make the tasks of both the multiversity and the multicampus university possible, if not easier. This proposition will be tested in the near future.

(1971)

LEADERSHIP AND AMBIGUITY: The American College President
MICHAEL D. COHEN and JAMES G. MARCH

In the late 1960s and early 1970s, much of the furor that enveloped the institutions of higher education settled upon the college president. During that period, the role of the American college president changed substantially and much of the traditional power of a person in this office has been eroded. The role, "historically balanced between mediative and authoritative functions, became more primarily mediative." At present, however, a reactive swing seems to be occurring, and presidents appear to be regaining some of the lost ground. But a president can sustain this stronger role only if he understands his position vis-à-vis his own institution and its various constituencies.

This study combines empirical data with speculation to form an interpretive essay. The empirical data were drawn from a 42-college panel, and "41 of the presidents, 39 of their chief academic officers, 36 of their chief business or financial officers, 42 of their secretaries, 28 other college or university officials close to the presidents, and student leaders or editors of student publications at 31 institutions," were interviewed. For the purposes of this study presidents of two-year colleges were excluded.

Several general observations about the presidency are made:

■ The presidency is a reactive job. "Presidents define their role as a responsive one. . . . They allocate their time by a process that is largely controlled by the desires of others."

■ "The presidency is . . . parochial. . . . Presidents are not normally strangers to the institutions that choose them."

■ "Presidents are [typically] academics" and middle-aged, middle class, white males, from a small-town, native born, background. Their values are those of the academic environment in which they have normally spent their working lives.

■ "The presidency is conventional. The president comes to his job through a series of filters that are socially conservative vis-à-vis his major constituents. . . . He allocates his time in response to a series of conventional expectations . . . [and] . . . his activities . . . are constrained within social expectations that he accepts as essentially legitimate." Perhaps stemming from this observation is the fact that the presidency is important to the president. It is the peak of his career, a reward for long service and a tribute to his successful negotiation of the shoals of academe.

"The presidency is an illusion. Decision making in the university [or college] seems to result extensively from a process that decouples problems and choices and makes the president's role more commonly sporadic and symbolic than significant."

■ "The presidency is an illusion. . . . Decision making in the university [or college] seems to result extensively from a process that decouples problems and choices and makes the president's role more commonly sporadic and symbolic than significant."

These major features of the presidents and their role are elaborated and interpreted within a comprehension of the American college and university as an organization. The study places these institutions into a class called "organizational anarchies." The class is defined as any organizational setting that exhibits the following general properties:

■ *Problematic Goals* Apparent operation on a variety of inconsistent and ill-defined preferences.

■ *Unclear Technology* The organization operates on a simple set of trial and error procedures, the residue of learning from the accidents of past experiences, imitation, and inventions born of necessity.

■ *Fluid Participation* Individual participants vary from one time to another. As a result, standard theories of power and choice are inadequate, and the boundaries of the organization appear to be uncertain and changing.

These properties are not unique to institutions of higher education, but they are particularly conspicuous there. The American university is a prototypic organized anarchy. It does not know what it is doing. Its goals are either vague or in dispute. Its technology is familiar but not understood. Its major participants wander in and out of the organization.

While these characteristics conspire to make the institution a very difficult place to describe, to understand, and, particularly, to lead, they do not make it ipso facto a "bad organization," and this study investigates organized anarchies with a view to making the leadership of them easier.

Facing the task of leading such an organization, the president has to deal with four fundamental ambiguities. Because the goals of the organization are unclear, there is an *ambiguity of purpose*. Because the president does not have a clear-cut purpose, he becomes uncertain of the extent of his power and of what he can accomplish, and this constitutes *ambiguity of power* and leads to a parallel, *ambiguity of responsibility.* Further, the president is uncertain as to how he might apply his prior experience to current problems, and this is termed *ambiguity of experience.* College presidents probably have greater confidence in their interpretations of college life—and the general environment—than is warranted. Lastly, there is an *ambiguity of success* because "the ambiguities of purpose, power, and experience conspire to render success and failure equally obscure."

This obscurity of outcome, while it may frustrate the would-be leader, does carry an obverse if somewhat unexpected benefit. It appears that it is probably a mistake for any college president to imagine that what he does in office significantly affects either the long-run position of the institution or his reputation as a president.

It is probably a mistake for any college president to imagine that what he does in office significantly affects either the long-run position of the institution or his reputation as a president.

There are fundamental qualities of the decision-making process in organized anarchies that should be considered when moving to "accomplish" or "lead" within a university setting: "Most issues, most of the time, have low salience for most people," and thus each issue will probably suffer from partial and erratic attention; the total system suffers from inertia; there is constant danger that any decision can easily become "a garbage can" for almost any problem, and thus the processes of choice are frequently subject to overload; the organization has a "weak information base." The study makes certain observations and suggestions for those who seek to influence the system, among them that: No leadership can be exerted without forfeiting large amounts of time and without considerable persistence; many projects should be mounted simultaneously, and opposition to any or all should be both facilitated and countered; and the would-be leader must manage, unobtrusively, to provide "garbage cans" along the decision-making route, and, above all, remember and interpret history and experience.

While this may seem an unusual and unnecessarily cynical approach, it is not so when one remembers that college and university settings are organizationally unusual. In a normal decision-making process, choice is based on three interrelated ideas: the preexistence of purpose, the necessity of consistency, and the primacy of rationality. In an organized anarchy, these ideas are either individually or collectively absent when a decision is needed; to combat this, "we need to develop a way of finding interesting goals, acting before we think, doing things for no good reason."

Further, this study suggests that we need to develop some idea of sensible foolishness that will undermine the superstition of biases erected on purpose, consistency, and rationality. To lead an organized anarchy,

To lead an organized anarchy, such as a university, the leader must escape from the logic of his reason and develop "playfulness"—the deliberate temporary relaxation of rules in order to explore the possibilities of alternative rules. "Playfulness allows experimentation at the same time that it acknowledges reason."

the leader must escape from the logic of his reason and develop "playfulness"—the deliberate temporary relaxation of rules in order to explore the possibilities of alternative rules. "Playfulness allows experimentation at the same time that it acknowledges reason."

Both playfulness and reason are aspects of intelligent choice within the fabric of an organized anarchy, for "a strict insistence on purpose, consistency, and rationality limits our ability to find new purposes." Following from this contention it may well be accurate that "the contribution of a college president may often be measured by his capability for sustaining that creative interaction of foolishness and rationality."

(1974)

THE DIVIDED ACADEMY: Professors and Politics*

EVERETT CARLL LADD, JR. and SEYMOUR MARTIN LIPSET

The need for systematic information about the political orientations of American college and university professors—involving both intramural and national issues—provided a primary objective for initiating the massive national survey (60,028 respondents) of the American professoriate conducted in the spring of 1969 under the sponsorship of the Carnegie Commission on Higher Education. This study draws heavily upon these survey data.

The importance of the academic profession cannot be underestimated; its influence outside of the university has increased as faculty have become more involved in national policy formulations, and as the university has emerged as the great "certifying" institution for a wide range of occupations in postindustrial society. Because this is the case, a study of professorial political orientations appears especially crucial to the larger examination of opinions and attitudes in American society. Faculty are a "strategically placed subgroup" whose orientations are of particular importance as they affect decision making within a primary contemporary institution, the university, and as they influence larger currents of thought in the society.

College and university faculty, together with their student apprentices, have established a reputation as being among the most liberal-left strata in the United States—a reputation challenged by few persons at any place on the political spectrum. This proclivity for politics which is critical of society from liberal and equalitarian value perspectives seemingly

* This abstract was prepared by the authors before the final manuscript for their full report was completed.

manifests itself across virtually the entire range of political activity. John Kenneth Galbraith, for instance, described faculty and students as the fulcrum of the protest politics of the 1960s.

It was the universities—not the trade unions nor the free-lance intellectuals, nor the press, nor the businessmen . . . —which led the opposition to the Vietnam War, which forced the retirement of President Johnson, which are forcing the pace of our present withdrawal [1971] from Vietnam, which are leading the battle against the great corporations on the issue of pollution, and which at the last Congressional elections retired a score or more of the egregious timeservers, military sycophants, and hawks.

Such commentary asserts, in a contemporary context, a very old and well-developed theme—that the intellectual community of which faculty are a part is inherently questioning, critical, inclined toward what Lionel Trilling insightfully described as the "adversary culture."

The intellectual community of which faculty are a part is inherently questioning, critical, inclined toward the "adversary culture."

Our study begins by examining the question of what it is about intellectuality which so frequently leads those associated with this role component to be oppositionists. The view propounded starts from a perception of the position of the intellectual as one whose activities involve the creation of *new* knowledge, *new* ideas, *new* art. He holds reality up to the test of the ideal, the theoretic. This emphasis on critical work and creativity often has led the more original intellectuals to formulate general critiques of society. Thus, Joseph Schumpeter called attention to the fact that the "humanists [of the renaissance] were primarily philologists but . . . they quickly expanded into the realm of manners, politics, religion, and philosophy . . . from criticism of a text to criticism of a society. . . ."

Understanding the critical orientation of intellectuals also requires attention to the creation of a new role in response to the massive social changes of the last two and a half centuries. A set of social and economic transformations began in the seventeenth and eighteenth centuries in Western Europe, the various dimensions of which have received different names: *industrial,* if the view is of economic life; *scientific and technological,* if attention is drawn to the explosion of knowledge; and *egalitarian,* if the focus is on participation or involvement in the making of decisions for the system, the overturning of societies based upon the aristocratic principle. These egalitarian-industrial-technological changes can be properly described as a revolution; and from its beginning in seventeenth-century Europe, this revolution has progressed through a number of stages and has become global. From this perspective, the most important feature of this massive revolutionary surge is that major change became a constant: all manner of social and political institutions were forced into a process of continuing adaptation. The need grew for a category of people who could explain, chart, and direct the flow of societal response. Carl Becker nicely described the emergence of this new social role:

Until recently the chief function of the sophisticated, the priests and scribes, has been to stabilize custom and validate social authority by perpetuating the tradition and interpreting it in a manner conformable to the understanding of common man. During the last 300 years . . . there has emerged a new class of learned men, successors to the priests and scribes, whose function is to increase rather than to preserve knowledge, to undermine rather than to stabilize custom and social authority.

That the pressure "to undermine rather than to stabilize custom and social authority" is compatible with a conservative or right-wing position as well as with a liberal or radical stance, has been amply demonstrated. Still, this study concludes, the record seems to validate the generalization that throughout the twentieth century the political weight of American academics and other intellectuals has been committed to the progressive, liberal, or leftist side. This bias reflects in considerable measure the weakness of a legitimate national conservative tradition in the United States. National identity and national ideology are linked to a value system, stemming from an elaboration of principles enunciated in the Declaration of Independence, which emphasizes egalitarianism and populism. Thus, when American intellectuals point out the gap between reality and the ideal, they define the latter in terms of egalitarian ideas inherent in the American creed.

The study reviews an impressive body of empirical data demonstrating that the politics of American academics, for at least the last half-century, has been disproportionately left-of-center. For example, survey data on faculty, and on the general public, from polls such as those conducted by Gallup and Harris, have shown professors in recent years to be more supportive of Democratic and left third-party presidential candidates than other middle-class occupational groups, the public-at-large, manual workers, or any other identifiable occupational stratum; more opposed to governmental policies in Vietnam, more supportive of measures to promote equitable treatment for blacks, and the like.

The Carnegie data demonstrate conclusively that, in a group whose disproportionate liberalism has been well established, the more successful, high-achieving, and amply rewarded segments display the greatest inclination to support a politics of social criticism from egalitarian and popular value perspectives.

Furthermore, the study indicates, the "top" of academe is more liberal than the "bottom." The Carnegie data demonstrate conclusively that, in a group whose disproportionate liberalism has been well established, the more successful, high-achieving, and amply rewarded segments display the greatest inclination to support a politics of social criticism from egalitarian and popular value perspectives. This appears at first glance a paradox, because of an intellectual readiness to apply a "class theory of politics" to academe. Such a theory—perhaps better described as a set of assumptions—holds that tendencies to criticize society are related to objective deprivation and discrimination; that a politics of change finds its natural supporters among those who suffer from the status quo; that being well rewarded and recognized makes for conservatism, just as being deprived produces liberal and egalitarian perspectives. The application of the class theory of politics to academe carries with it the argument that those who consult for business and government receive large research grants, hold tenured and high-salaried positions at major universities, publish extensively, and dominate the professional activities of their disciplines, have thus been coopted into "the system," have the most to lose from any significant societal or academic change, and hence are the most conservative members of the professoriate.

In fact, however, the survey data examined show just the opposite—that "achievement" in higher education, however measured, has been associated with more liberal-to-left views on a wide array of social and political issues. Illustrative is the finding from analysis of the Carnegie data that, with reference to opposition of the Vietnam War, faculty engaged in research and consulting supported by the federal government were more likely to align themselves against the government's position on crucial issues than colleagues not on the payroll of the "political establishment."

The argument developed suggests that the top of academe is more liberal than the bottom, not because its members are more advantaged in salary, research opportunities, and the various perquisites of academic life, but because as a group their role and orientations are closer to those of the ideal-type intellectual. The fact of greater liberalism among faculty of high attainment and recognition holds because of the essential inapplicability of the "class theory" in explaining dominant characteristics of professorial politics.

The general lines of the argument presented stand as the most satisfying way of accounting for a variety of observed conditions. Why is it that professors at major colleges and universities, with higher salaries, lighter teaching loads, more research opportunities, and the like, consistently show up more liberal in their political views than colleagues at lesser schools? Why are faculty with high levels of scholarly publication more liberal than those who have not published? Why do academics who have attained research grants give more support for left-of-center and critical politics than those who have not received research support? In trying to explain such phenomena, the study has been drawn to a theoretical structure which suggests a relationship between intellectuality and social criticism; a relationship between intellectuality and support for left-of-center politics here in the United States. High-achieving professors stand

High-achieving professors stand to the left of their colleagues of lower attainment, even though they are on the whole better rewarded and of higher status, because they more closely approximate the role and orientations of the ideal-type intellectual.

to the left of their colleagues of lower attainment, even though they are on the whole better rewarded and of higher status, because they more closely approximate the role and orientations of the ideal-type intellectual.

At the same time, major tensions exist between the thrusts of intellectuality on the one hand and objective "class interests" of academics on the other. While it is generally the case that American professors of higher scholarly attainment are more liberal than their less highly achieving brethren, there are instances in which a complex of interests relating to a position of scholarly attainment exerts pressures in the opposing direction. For example, the study finds a generally strong association between a liberal position on national issues and sympathy for unionism in higher education. And there is a high positive correlation between scholarly attainment and support for liberal positions on national issues. However, professors of high academic standing, more liberal in their general political views, show up less supportive of unionism than colleagues of lower attainment. The study concludes that the source of this apparent paradox lies in the intervention of "class interests." Faculty at lesser schools may appear more conservative on national issues, but they have a concrete class interest in unionism which their better compensated, more independent, high status, more "profession-like" colleagues at major institutions do not share.

Professional standing and intellectual attainment constitute one set of factors which contribute importantly to the differentiation of professorial opinion. The study examines others, notably the profound role of academic discipline. Indeed, no other variable differentiates political views among American academics as substantially as their professional field. The discipline differences extend to the entire range of political attitudes. There is a rather neat progression from the most left-of-center to the most conservative, running from the social sciences to the humanities, law, and the fine arts, through the physical and biological sciences, education, and medicine, on to business, engineering, nursing, and home economics, and finally to agriculture, the most conservative. Close to two-thirds of those in the social sciences indicated they approved of "the rise of radical student activism," as compared to two-fifths in the natural sciences, and only one-fifth in agriculture. Richard M. Nixon's 41 percent of the vote among physical and biological scientists in 1968, and 58 percent support among engineers, were markedly greater than his share of the vote in the heavily Democratic social sciences and humanities, where he received only 19 and 22 percent, respectively. Even when basic fields are broken into subgroups as in the case of the social sciences—political science, psychology, economics, etc.—substantial variations exist.

The sharp differences in discipline subcultures exist because the several fields are concerned with very different sorts of subject matter and work, and thereby attract very different sorts of people. There is a selective recruitment of ideological types into the various academic specialties.

The last section of the study, gathering all the fundamental findings together, looks at basic issues of the last decade in university politics. The political agenda of American higher education has shifted profoundly. In the first part of the sixties, higher education was in its "era of growth." The watchword was "more." New institutions were springing up, university budgets increased tremendously, new programs were added, faculty and student populations mushroomed. Then, while growth by no means ceased, higher education entered a new period, "the era of campus confrontation." With the war in Vietnam the most visible precipitating factor, protests and demonstrations (initiating them, resisting them, trying in some measure to cope with them) became the preoccupation of academics. Now, in the 1970s, higher education has entered yet another era, with a new political agenda. "Austerity" in its many forms has come to command as much academic attention now as first growth and then protests did in the decade past. The responses of professors to the shifting panorama of issues over the past decade have contributed to an understanding of why academic battles have been fought out and concluded in the manner they have been, and provide insights into the likely shape of contending alignments in future academic politics.

(1975)

MAY 1970: The Campus Aftermath of Cambodia and Kent State
RICHARD E. PETERSON and JOHN A. BILORUSKY

The protest that broke out on American campuses in early May 1970 was the country's most massive expression of college student discontent. The events preceding the upheaval are almost too well known to require recapitulation and include: The President's unexpected announcement on April 30 that American and South Vietnamese troops were moving against enemy sanctuaries in Cambodia; the killing of four students and the wounding of nine others by National Guardsmen at Kent State University in Ohio on May 4; the killing of two students and the wounding of 12 others by police at Jackson State College in Mississippi on May 14.

For hundreds of thousands of students, faculty, and staff at more than half the nation's institutions of higher education, "business as usual" became unthinkable. It was a mass uprising, embracing many more "moderate" than "radical" students. As a consequence, the protests were overwhelmingly peaceful and legal, though not exclusively so. The reaction was at first largely political, but the Kent State slayings provoked an emotional response and, with the killings at Jackson State, the protest broadened beyond its original focus on the war. Throughout, students experienced exhilaration from doing something personally significant, taking control of events, and "achieving community." All these factors combined on the campuses to make for a period of unparalleled antagonism to the politico-social order and unprecedented renunciation of academic normalcy.

Information about the national campus reaction to Cambodia/Kent/Jackson was gathered through a relatively brief questionnaire sent in July 1970 to all college and university presidents in the country. The presidents were asked whether or not various kinds of activities occurred on their individual campuses and, in addition, nine open-ended questions solicited judgments and interpretations about matters not easily probed by yes/no or multiple choice questions.

The decision to survey presidents alone was prompted by twin desires to carry out the survey while the events were still fresh in the minds of the people involved and to make the resulting information generally available as rapidly as possible. A typical faculty member would probably report greater activity and a typical student would almost certainly do so; from this standpoint, therefore, the picture to be drawn from the data may be somewhat conservative.

"Significant impact" was reported by 57 percent of the nation's colleges and universities to have been felt as a result of Cambodia, Kent, and Jackson. This means that almost 1,350 institutions were in some way stirred by these events, while 43 percent of the total, some 1,200, were reportedly untouched. Students and faculty, on what will henceforth be referred to as the "affected" campuses (57 percent of the sample), expressed their concern and outrage in a great many ways.

The study breaks these down into a variety of categories, the first of which concerns student actions. Forty-four percent of the campuses (77 percent of the affected ones) reported essentially peaceful demonstrations, in which grouping are included such activities as sit-ins, marches, rallies, and guerilla theatre productions, as well as memorial services for those killed at Kent State and Jackson State. Forty percent of the nation's colleges and universities reported that students journeyed off campus to meet with local residents and discuss the issues. Special meetings, seminars, and projects were initiated at 37 percent of the campuses, while some classes were canceled at 25 percent of the institutions reporting. One method chosen to express reaction was the writing of letters to government and administration officials. Letter-writing campaigns were reported at 29 percent of the campuses. Fourteen percent of the presidents reported that groups from their campuses had also gone to Washington personally to express their feelings to national officials. Shutdowns and strikes for one day or longer took place at some 21 percent (536) of the institutions, while violence—demonstrations causing damage to persons or property—occurred at 4 percent of the reporting campuses, with such incidents tapering off significantly after the Kent State killings.

Another feature of the May uprising was the widespread abrogation of normal academic routines, with faculties offering varying measures of support for such action. Across the country 28 percent of the campuses reported that one or more academic courses were modified "to reflect antiwar interests" and 25 percent reported that there were deviations in final examination and grading procedures. Differences in faculty attitudes by subject field and age were also significant, although 49 percent of the presidents of affected colleges believed there had been no "significant impact" on faculty cohesiveness.

Following Cambodia, Kent, Jackson, it was further reported that a variety of problems, not directly related to the war or the campus killings, became of concern to faculty and students on about one-third of the campuses, but the primary thrust of concern across the nation remained concentrated on the main issues. Eighteen percent of the presidents took a personal stand against the events in Cambodia and at Kent State and Jackson State, while, with perhaps more far-reaching possible effects, 4 percent of the institutions took an overt position on one side or the other. Reaction from such off-campus constituencies as alumni, parents, trustees, local citizens, and state legislators varied, largely depending on whether there was violence; as a group, state legislators were least often supportive.

Reaction from such off-campus constituencies as alumni, parents, trustees, local citizens, and state legislators varied, largely depending on whether there was violence; as a group, state legislators were least often supportive.

The study also reveals some interesting data on academic standards, defined as "mastery of a body of knowledge as embodied in a course or course sequence." The events of May 1970 resulted in a decline in academic standards, according to 18 percent of presidents of affected campuses, but the decline appears to have been minimal in that only 9 percent of the total sample prophesied a continuing decline through the remainder of 1970 and 1971. Indeed, 5 percent of those reporting projected a positive effect on the academic standards at their institutions, although 144 institutional heads said they anticipated difficulty in getting the regular academic program started again in the fall of 1970.

Cognizant of the diversity in functions, purposes, and traditions among the institutional subjects of the study, a breakdown was made in terms of this diversity. Large independent and public universities experienced the strongest upheavals, while Catholic and Protestant institutions and two-year colleges saw the least. To explain these phenomena, the study advances the notions of a "critical mass" and a prerequisite level of entrance selectivity. In brief, on perhaps 100 campuses response rapidly escalated into violence, but at many more campuses the response was peaceful, and at 43 percent of all institutions there was no appreciable impact at all.

Asked what they considered the single most significant long-run implication of the events of Spring 1970 for their campuses, the presidents responded in a variety of ways and all but 28 percent prophesied positive outcomes, such as "increased student and staff concern about national issues (15.7 percent), and increased cooperation and mutual trust among students, faculty, and administrators (13.0 percent)." It is stressed, however, that these outcomes were very much the result of each individual president's subjective judgment.

From these data the authors draw certain conclusions. (1) The speed with which hundreds of thousands of people on the campuses proved capable of dropping their usual studies, either completely or to some extent, suggests a degree of academic bankruptcy in American higher education. (2) The speed with which intensive reaction ebbed (by mid-May it was beginning to fade) seems to indicate that American mass student political movements cannot sustain themselves in the absence of new issues or provocations. (3) Trends in educational reform toward more student options and more personalized learning experiences have been accelerated because of the events of May 1970, while at the same time campus opposition to the national government has expanded. (4) Public support and empathy for the university and college in America was eroded, a process which had gradually built up through the 1960s, but accelerated after May 1970. (5) It can happen again, for in the opinion of the presidents, the tinder of discontent on the campuses remains dry, and any future outbreak could have serious results for both campus and society.

It can happen again, for in the opinion of the presidents, the tinder of discontent on the campuses remains dry, and any future outbreak could have serious results for both campus and society.

In the light of these findings the authors recommend that some serious thinking be done. Whatever the structural arrangements may look like and however much they may "alter" the traditional campus "models," a national policy for youth must be in the interests of national reconciliation. And it is imperative that such a policy accommodate all youth—that no segment be written off. A "New Deal" for youth is recommended, as one step toward helping America again become one nation.

A case study is combined with the general survey of college and university presidents as part of this inquiry into the aftermath of Cambodia, Kent State, and Jackson State. It is an in-depth examination of events at the Berkeley campus of the University of California. For several weeks prior to the move into Cambodia, there had been more political activity than usual around the Berkeley campus. The significant campus activism in April concerned the sometimes violent opposition of a few hundred students to ROTC programs on campus. After the President's April 30 announcement, however, protest built quickly, and when news of Kent State reached the campus, over 1,000 students and nonstudents attended a meeting at which they were unsuccessfully urged to "trash" the naval ROTC building. Meanwhile, an ad hoc faculty-student peace committee had commenced planning for a nonviolent, campuswide protest, and on May 6, a campuswide convocation heard the proposal of this group that "this campus is on strike to reconstitute the university as a center for organizing against the war in Southeast Asia." From this moment on the Berkeley protest became known as a "reconstitution." Most students, faculty, and staff were impressed with the convocation—the large numbers of people, the unanimity, the intellectual presentation of the issues and the lack of radical rhetoric and, in the words of one student: "The . . . proposal gave a handle on action. It was a nonviolent yet radical thing . . . in contrast to 'trashing' . . . for once there was a plan for what people could do. . . ." The proposal pledged the time and energy of the university community to stopping the war. It promised organization and cooperation with community antiwar activity while stressing that it did not encourage "destructive actions."

Governor Reagan officially closed all state institutions of higher education even while the convocation was in session, but some campus buildings remained available for the work at hand. One of the most important activities of Berkeley students was canvassing, using hastily written and published leaflets. Other groups on campus wrote letters of protest and disseminated information about the war. Even groups who had not normally been politically active in the past, the athletes and the engineering students, for example, organized and pledged support.

Closed for four days, the university reopened on Monday, May 11, and a mass meeting was held at which it was approved that no regular classes be held for the remainder of the quarter, that all students receive at least a pass grade for all courses, and that no faculty member suffer pecuniary loss from the strike. After this, however, it became increasingly clear that reconstitution activities would be largely determined by individuals acting within a departmental context. An important element in the activity became "flexibility," which Chancellor Heyns outlined as "permitting great flexibility in the organization of courses" in the confidence that "you [the faculty] will discharge your instructional responsibilities fairly, and with proper regard for academic standards." The deans of the schools adopted measures to "provide flexibility for students in adjusting their programs to extraordinary circumstances." Most people thought that the university should be kept open, and though "flexibility" varied from faculty member to faculty member in terms of degree, some classes continued as usual and some did not.

During the first two weeks, interest in reconstitution remained high, but thereafter, interest tailed off among students to the extent that by the end of May only about one-third of the students remained involved.

During the first two weeks, interest in reconstitution remained high, but thereafter, interest tailed off among students to the extent that by the end of May only about one-third of the students remained involved. Despite this, reconstitution seems to have been the beginning of a trend toward greater student involvement in local politics, and in academic reform on the departmental level.

This case study discusses whether reconstitution was in fact a process or merely an event, and concludes that, while it was generally hoped and expected that it would be a process, failures and frustrations took their toll, resulting in alienation and despair or mere apathy, to the extent that, in retrospect, reconstitution (save among a certain few departments) degenerated to the level of an event.

The case study of events at the Berkeley campus of the University of California concludes further that, during reconstitution, two basic strategies were urged by individuals who perceived a need for fundamental social and educational change. Advocates of both courses recognized that the unequal distribution of power in contemporary society supports the status quo, but differed in their suggestions for redistribution of that power. Proponents of "political revolution" argued for wresting power from the ruling class and democratically reapportioning it equally among all people (the mindset of many student radicals), whereas the advocates of "cultural revolution" adhered to a philosophy that the struggle to wrest power from the ruling class would corrupt those seeking to gain power, and suggested instead that individuals must reconstitute their lives in order to change society through personal conduct.

This study supports the "cultural revolution" approach to the problem, both because of its value consistency and its integration of means and ends, and also, perforce, because of its emphasis on people cooperating with one another to find better ways of living and learning. At the same time it is stressed that the Berkeley experience during May 1970 demonstrates that, although this strategy is slower and less dramatic, it may be the only way to an experimental university in an experimental society.

Cambodia/Kent reaction profiles for seven types of colleges and universities based on institutional control and degree level

	TOTAL SAMPLE (N = 1,856)	PUBLIC UNI-VERSITY (N = 114)	PUBLIC 4-YEAR COLLEGE (N = 255)	PUBLIC 2-YEAR COLLEGE (N = 477)	INDEP. UNI-VERSITY (N = 37)	INDEP. 4-YEAR COLLEGE (N = 198)	PROT. INSTI-TUTION (N = 338)	CATHOLIC INSTI-TUTION (N = 227)
Institutional factors								
Regional location								
Pacific states	12.8%	10.5%	9.4%	23.5%	13.5%	9.6%	10.1%	7.1%
Mountain states	4.4	11.4	5.5	6.5	0.0	3.5	2.1	1.8
Northeast	25.2	10.5	23.1	15.9	62.2	43.9	9.8	35.7
Southeast	24.0	27.2	31.0	20.6	10.8	15.7	35.5	15.0
Midwest	33.5	40.4	30.6	33.5	13.5	26.8	42.6	40.5
Enrollment								
Less than 1,000	38.9	0.9	5.1	28.7	0.0	41.9	63.6	61.7
1,000–5,000	40.8	4.4	54.9	51.4	29.7	53.0	34.3	31.3
5,000–12,000	12.5	29.0	31.8	13.8	40.5	4.6	1.8	4.9
More than 12,000	7.4	65.8	7.1	5.5	29.7	0.0	0.3	1.8
Selectivity								
Top 10% of high school class	8.5	11.4	2.8	0.0	54.1	28.3	7.1	6.2
Top 40%	39.6	53.5	53.5	4.8	46.0	50.5	53.6	63.0
Open admissions	50.2	34.2	43.1	95.0	0.0	20.2	37.6	28.6
Perceived impact								
"Significant impact" on campus operations	57.3	91.2	65.9	43.6	97.3	77.3	52.4	55.1
(i.e., percent "affected")	(N = 1,064)	(N = 104)	(N = 168)	(N = 208)	(N = 36)	(N = 153)	(N = 177)	(N = 125)
Student-initiated actions								
Peaceful demonstrations	44.4	76.3	53.7	32.5	89.2	61.6	38.5	41.4
Communication with local area residents	40.3	71.1	45.5	26.6	89.2	61.1	35.2	37.4
Special seminars, workshops, projects, etc.	37.2	67.5	38.0	25.8	81.1	60.1	31.1	33.0
Planning for electioneering	23.1	50.0	24.7	12.4	62.2	40.4	19.5	19.8
Shutdown, one day or longer (all reasons)	20.2	34.2	23.5	16.8	54.1	30.3	11.2	15.4
General student/staff strike, one day or longer	13.6	28.1	12.6	7.8	40.5	26.8	7.4	10.1
Destructive demonstrations	3.9	28.1	4.7	1.1	16.2	3.0	1.2	2.2
Modification of instruction								
Some courses modified to reflect antiwar interests	27.9	53.5	32.6	19.3	54.1	38.9	24.3	25.6
Some faculty-modified grading procedures	23.8	55.3	27.8	12.6	78.4	43.9	13.0	18.9
"Substantial" or "some" departure from normal exam-grading procedures, by academic field:								
Business	6.1	19.5	5.5	2.1	50.0	11.7	1.8	4.4
Education	8.9	31.0	12.6	1.9	52.8	17.3	2.1	7.5
Engineering	4.5	11.5	3.1	1.5	47.2	7.1	0.6	1.3
Fine arts	14.5	38.1	18.8	6.3	66.7	27.4	5.9	10.6
Humanities	20.2	46.9	22.0	13.3	83.3	36.0	9.8	15.9
Life sciences	10.6	26.6	12.2	3.2	69.4	24.4	3.9	6.6
Physical sciences	10.5	25.7	12.2	2.3	66.7	26.4	3.3	7.5
Social sciences	21.3	48.7	23.1	14.7	80.6	37.6	10.1	19.8
Anti-Cambodia incursion positions taken								
By the president, as an individual	17.5	28.1	17.3	8.8	56.8	34.3	15.4	16.3
Institutional stand against the Cambodia invasion	3.9	0.9	6.1	3.3	2.6	4.0	2.9	3.9
Off-campus reactions								
"Mainly critical" reaction to activities on campus in May from:*								
Trustees	17.3	32.7	21.4	18.3	25.0	12.4	7.9	16.0
Alumni	20.1	42.3	22.6	8.2	47.2	20.9	7.3	27.2
Parents	16.9	39.4	17.3	13.9	19.4	15.7	7.9	16.8
Local citizens	30.2	50.0	36.9	32.2	33.3	29.4	20.3	24.0
State legislators	20.6	51.9	33.3	25.5	11.1	15.7	7.3	8.0
Local press	13.1	35.6	15.5	10.1	19.4	13.7	6.2	9.6

	TOTAL SAMPLE (N = 1,856)	PUBLIC UNI- VERSITY (N = 114)	PUBLIC 4-YEAR COLLEGE (N = 255)	PUBLIC 2-YEAR COLLEGE (N = 477)	INDEP. UNI- VERSITY (N = 37)	INDEP. 4-YEAR COLLEGE (N = 198)	PROT. INSTI- TUTION (N = 338)	CATHOLIC INSTI- TUTION (N = 227)
Effect on academic standards								
Perceived "detrimental" impact, on academic standards—spring 1970*	32.1	38.5	34.5	24.0	47.2	43.1	27.7	21.6
"Detrimental" impact—1970–71 academic year*	15.3	18.5	11.9	12.6	25.7	25.0	11.9	12.8
"Beneficial" impact on instructional programs*	23.9	20.4	23.2	22.8	20.0	23.7	27.3	23.2
Student political campaign work								
More than 5% of students engaged in summer political work	11.4	20.2	10.2	4.4	35.1	28.3	10.7	8.8
Campaign recess (e.g., "Princeton Plan")								
Yes	3.1	4.4	2.0	1.1	18.9	7.1	3.6	1.8
Possibly	10.2	8.8	6.7	6.3	29.7	17.7	10.1	14.1

* Percentages are of the "affected colleges."

During reconstitution at Berkeley, the "commitment," in most departments, to a collective process of experimentation, was short-lived, and in others virtually nonexistent. Nonetheless, it was the attempts to create such a process which gave the situation at Berkeley much of its significance. As the study states, "these efforts . . . are a faint light which can guide us on a never-ending journey that is the reconstituting of our world and our lives."

(1971)

FACULTY BARGAINING: Change and Conflict*
JOSEPH GARBARINO

In a fundamental sense at this stage in their development, faculty unionism and collective bargaining do not create problems; they are a response to problems that already exist and a method for dealing with them. The demands that the new faculty union presented to the administration at the City University of New York, after winning official recognition in 1968 as the exclusive bargaining agent, were demands that had been brought up years before by the more informal faculty organization.

This is not to say that over the years an ingenious and aggressive union will not succeed in "raising the consciousness" of its members to an awareness of possibilities that might not have surfaced independently

* This abstract was prepared by the author before the final manuscript for his full report was completed.

and spontaneously. Up to this time, however, and probably for a considerable time to come, it is appropriate to consider collective bargaining as a way of participating more actively in the familiar matters of university governance. Where it has been adopted, it represents a decision by a major part of the union constituency that the existing governance system was not working satisfactorily. A corollary of this view is that where the present governance system is working or can be made to work satisfactorily, unionism is not likely to be adopted as an alternative method of participation in governance. This explains why unions have been least successful in stable institutions with a well-established and a moderately well-functioning system of academic governance.

Faculty unions in the United States are a response to change—change in the size and structure of the institutions themselves and in their relations to state governments and other educational institutions; change in the functions of the institutions that introduce new types of faculty, students, and departmental organization; and change in administrative style and managerial techniques.

The first burst of organization in the United States occurred at widely scattered locations in the mid-sixties and was most visibly manifest in the California state colleges, a loosely organized system of 19 emerging universities with about a quarter of a million students. The specific incidents that caught public attention were tied to the wave of student protest, but surveys of faculty attitudes at the colleges revealed deeper sources of dissatisfaction. A study of some 40 institutions of all types concluded that the root issue was the inadequate faculty role in academic governance. Salaries were rising, positions and promotions were plentiful, and most objective conditions of service were good and improving. As institutions expanded and changed their character, however, they apparently lagged in modifying their internal decision-making systems. At least, the modifications did not meet the expectations of the faculties who tended to set their standards by reference to the governance practices of the major research universities in their own or nearby states.

A study of some 40 institutions of all types concluded that the root issue was the inadequate faculty role in academic governance.

As the boom in higher education faded and problems multiplied in recent years, other issues were added to the basic concern with the distribution of institutional power. The rate of increase in salaries and overall budgets slowed; the growth in enrollments leveled off, leading to changes in program emphasis and a scaling down of plans for expansion; attacks on the tenure system increased; pressure for special consideration for women and ethnic minorities in appointment and promotion grew; and a general surplus of highly trained new graduates appeared with startling rapidity.

The concerns reflected in the new union contracts touch on the whole range of issues, with the emphases in particular universities reflecting their own special problems.

The contracts show an attempt to ensure that the faculty is consulted in the making of academic decisions both at the institutional level and at the departmental level. In general, they appear to aim less at expanding the scope of consultation than in making the process more formal and systematic and increasing the weight given to faculty opinion. Special concern is shown for the methods of evaluating probationary and junior faculty, for procedures of review, for access to personnel files and the right to contest unfavorable evidence on which personnel actions might be based, and timely notification of decisions. One of the major contributions of American unions to industrial relations practice is the use of external review of administrative decisions affecting individuals by an outside third party, a process known as the grievance procedure. Like other unions, faculty unions have made the establishment of grievance procedures the cornerstone of their contracts. University administrators are vigorously resisting the use of professional "neutrals" from outside the university to make academic judgments in personnel matters, but the unions have succeeded in getting more openness and more opportunity to challenge decisions in most contracts. The current situation in the academic labor market is such that most of the grievances processed involve decisions not to reappoint probationary faculty. The understandable concern with job security that this issue reflects unfortunately conflicts directly with the growing concern of administrations about the rising proportion of all faculty holding tenure appointments. The continuing threat to the tenure system is the strongest stimulus to faculty organization looming in the near future.

In the large comprehensive university systems, the question of "parity" between faculty at different academic levels and between faculty and other professional staff has been a major problem.

In the large comprehensive university systems, the question of "parity" between faculty at different types of institutions teaching courses at different academic levels and between faculty and other professional staff has been a major problem. In the City University of New York one of the country's highest salary scales has been extended to include all levels of instruction. This produced increases in salary for each rank in the two-year colleges approximately double those granted the faculty in the senior colleges and the graduate center. The large, complex institutions in the United States have engaged in large-scale research activities since World War II and have also developed a wide range of special programs for special groups. These have been staffed by professionals with similar training to faculty, but these positions have not had the prestige and privileges that have traditionally attached to the faculty role. Large numbers of these "nonteaching professionals" are to be found in the major universities; they make up about 30 percent of the professional staff at SUNY. They have been anxious to achieve as many of the faculty privileges as possible, and they have seen the union movement as a vehicle for achieving their goals. They have been successful in part in winning more security of employment, similar salary scales, and a form of peer evaluation and review in both the City and State University of New York. Their future goals include flexible working schedules and academic year working calendars.

Although there are explanations for the growth of faculty unionism that are specific to individual campuses, and the variety of forms of the phenomenon makes generalizations suspect, it appears that in a fundamental sense faculty unions in the United States are part of the faculty response to the emergence of a system of mass higher education. It is increasingly clear that some form of postsecondary education will be made available to the great bulk of the young adult population and to an increasing proportion of the older population as well. Mass education means a "mass" of students, organized in "mass" institutions and taught by a "mass" of faculty. American institutions of higher education have included heterogeneous programs for a century and have been hospitable to activities that most developed nations would regard as marginally appropriate for universities. As a result, in the United States more of the postsecondary work is provided in the traditional institutions of higher education than it is in countries with a more exclusive definition of university-level intellectual activity. At the moment, well over 600,000 instructional staff are currently teaching in higher education in the tremendous variety of programs in American colleges and universities.

It is in the sectors that grew most rapidly and changed the most during the 1960s that unionism appears to be most firmly established. These are the two-year community colleges, clearly the most rapidly expanding segment for the indefinite future; the emerging universities, most of them converted teachers colleges; and the comprehensive university systems, which evolved in states where the pressures to rationalize the complex set of institutions that grew up in the period of rapid growth have led to the establishment of "supersystems," in which research universities, medical centers, and four-year and two-year colleges are all in a single administrative unit.

In each of these several types of institutions, the traditional methods of faculty government and faculty participation in institutional governance will in some instances prove unequal to the task of the internal administration of faculty affairs. The weaknesses of the traditional mechanisms are that they depend on delegated powers from the administrative agencies, they are staffed by volunteer or part-time faculty serving as officers, they are subject to the constraints of the inadequate budgets provided by the institution at administrative discretion, and they depend on decision by consensus in the ranks of the faculty and persuasion of administrative officers to the faculty viewpoint.

Some institutions will be able to adapt the traditional collegial mechanisms to the new situation of large numbers, diverse interests, and complex institutional structures. In others, new forms of faculty representation and faculty organization will be developed. The most likely new form is unionism of a more or less traditional type. These unions will be much like the unions of other public employees, and the principles they espouse will be essentially those of the civil service. In terms of numbers, most public institutions of higher education have administered faculty affairs for decades in a manner closer to the familiar model of the civil service than to any other. Faculty unionism is part of the general public-employee union movement and at the same time is an attempt to achieve some of the traditional privileges of professionalism, such as professional autonomy, by the methods of collective bargaining. The resulting hybrid is likely to be an interesting version of professional unionism that will combine the tactics and the rhetoric of trade unionism with some of the aspirations and content of professionalism in the style of free professionals. The mix of the two will vary according to the circumstances of individual institutions, but the balance in most will be toward the civil service union end of the spectrum.

Faculty unionism is part of the general public-employee union movement and at the same time is an attempt to achieve some of the traditional privileges of professionalism, such as professional autonomy, by the methods of collective bargaining.

The prestigious private universities are not likely to be affected by the move to unionize. Nor would the dozen or so most prominent of the great public universities, such as Michigan or California, be affected if their faculties are left to decide the issue for themselves. The status of the public research universities is uncertain in those states which follow the trend toward the creation of single administrative systems in the form of comprehensive universities that include higher education at all levels. In these circumstances, the prounion sectors of the faculty from the community colleges in the system, the emerging universities, the research universities themselves, and the nonteaching professionals at all levels may combine to make the decision in favor of unionism for the system as a whole. The fate of these "centers of excellence," as this phrase has been traditionally defined, is already in some jeopardy from a variety of egalitarian pressures in society in general and in higher education in particular, and the faculty unionism movement may well turn out to be one more internal pressure of formidable dimensions toward uniformity. Pressures to equalize salary scales, to equalize workloads, and the other features of the working environment of the system as a whole will make the maintenance of high academic standards in the best of the large public institutions more difficult than it has been in the past.

(1975)

PROFESSORS, UNIONS, AND AMERICAN HIGHER EDUCATION
EVERETT CARLL LADD, JR. and SEYMOUR MARTIN LIPSET

Eras now last only a few years. This fact testifies to the extraordinary scope and extent of social change, and to the rate at which change now occurs. Though cosmic in nature, this theme applies to higher education. Thus, the first part of the 1960s was the "era of growth," the latter part of that decade the "era of confrontation," and the period of the early 1970s the "era of austerity."

During this period of fiscal austerity, loss of public confidence, and growing pessimism, the trade union movement has begun to make notable gains in American higher education. Whereas a decade ago, unionization of college and university professors was not even a ripple on the pond of academic life, now it has become a large splash.

This study emanates from data obtained from the 1969 Carnegie Commission Survey of Faculty and Student Opinion and from a survey conducted by the authors in 1972. It deals with the growth of unionization and collective bargaining in education—their precipitants, the response of professors to them, and their likely consequences.

Unions are new for academics, but faculty members have long been organized into professional associations. The largest of these is the American Association of University Professors, founded in 1915, which currently has about 90,000 members. Having long resisted the notion that it resembled a trade union, this body voted by an overwhelming margin in 1972 "to pursue collective bargaining as a major additional way of realizing [our] goals in higher education."

Founded in 1857, the largest professional organization of teachers is the National Education Association. Although its primary strength exists at the elementary and secondary levels, it has substantial membership among faculty members in institutions of higher education, particularly at institutions, such as teachers colleges and junior colleges, that are closely linked to the lower levels of education. In January 1973, the NEA, now a full-fledged teachers' union, joined with the 525,000-member American Federation of State, County, and Municipal Employees to form the Coalition of American Public Employees (CAPE), for joint organizing,

Faculty attitudes toward collective bargaining and unionism, by professional characteristics and rewards, as percentages of *n*

THE 1969 SURVEY		
	DISAGREE, NO PLACE ON CAMPUS FOR FACULTY COLLECTIVE BARGAINING	AGREE, FACULTY STRIKES CAN BE LEGITIMATE ACTION
All faculty (60,028 respondents)	59	47
Quality of school at which professor teaches*		
A (elite) (*n* = 19,089)	53	49
B (*n* = 25,224)	55	44
C (*n* = 13,110)	60	44
D (lowest tier) (*n* = 2,580)	67	52
Type of institution		
University (*n* = 44,871)	54	46
Four-year college (*n* = 13,020)	61	46
Two-year college (*n* = 2,133)	67	49
Tenure		
Tenured faculty (*n* = 29,853)	54	41
Untenured faculty (*n* = 26,766)	64	53
Received research grants, last 12 months		
Yes [received grant(s)] (*n* = 27,966)	54	49
No (*n* = 29,778)	61	47
Salary		
Over $20,000 (*n* = 6,420)	45	38
$14,000–$20,000 (*n* = 15,567)	52	42
$10,000–$14,000 (*n* = 21,417)	59	47
Under $10,000 (*n* = 15,312)	66	51
Age		
60 years and older (*n* = 4,398)	45	30
50–59 (*n* = 9,408)	53	35
40–49 (*n* = 16,113)	57	44
30–39 (*n* = 20,580)	62	52
Under 30 (*n* = 8,607)	68	60

Changes in the self-conception and activities of AAUP and NEA have been precipitated by recent successes of the American Federation of Teachers (AFT), the oldest teachers' union.

collective bargaining, and political action. Although considerably smaller (30,000 members) than AAUP, the Higher Education Association, as the NEA professional affiliates are collectively termed, promised in 1972 to give priority to organizing higher education.

These changes in the self-conception and activities of AAUP and NEA have been precipitated by recent successes of the American Federation of Teachers (AFT), the oldest teachers' union. Founded in 1915 as an affiliate of the American Federation of Labor, AFT made little progress until the 1960s. It now claims 20,000 faculty members nationally.

THE 1972 SURVEY			
	DO YOU AGREE OR DISAGREE THAT THE RECENT GROWTH OF UNIONIZATION OF COLLEGE AND UNIVERSITY FACULTY IS BENEFICIAL AND SHOULD BE EXTENDED?		
	AGREE	UNCERTAIN; CONFLICTING ASSESSMENTS	DISAGREE
All faculty (n = 471)	43	13	44
Quality of school at which professor teaches†			
Major colleges and universities (n = 193)	39	19	43
Lower tier colleges and universities (n = 278)	45	10	45
Received research grants, last 12 months			
Yes [received grant(s)](n = 241)	36	15	48
No (n = 216)	50	11	39
Age			
Under 35 years (n = 104)	51	14	35
35–49 (n = 227)	46	14	40
50 years and older (n = 139)	32	11	58

* Institutions were ranked on the basis of a three-item Index of Academic Standing including SAT scores required for admission (Selectivity), research expenditures adjusted for the number of students (Research), and total institutional expenditures, also adjusted to a per student basis (Affluence). All colleges and universities were arrayed on this index, with raw scores ranging from 3 (highest standing) to 27 (lowest). Schools in category A had raw scores of 3–9; in B 10–15; in C 16–21; and in D 22–27.

† Because of the smaller n in this study, it has been necessary to compress subcategories more than with the 1969 faculty study.

Despite the rapid growth of unionism, unions remain opposed by a large segment of the professoriate. Michigan State, Fordham, and Manhattan College, for example, all rejected, by faculty vote, union representation in 1972. In view of the magnitude of the issue, the nature of this division in academe deserves attention, as does the relation between faculty attitudes toward union support and other political and educational issues.

Fifty-nine percent of all academics in the 1969 Carnegie Survey gave general endorsement to the principle of collective bargaining, and in 1972 a Ladd and Lipset national survey found professors evenly divided in their assessments of the extraordinary extension of unionism which had occurred in the interval. In examining the characteristics of those who are supportive, two factors stand out. The first relates to aspects of professional standing. There is, as demonstrated by the foregoing table, a strong link between "class interests" of academics and their receptivity to union practices in education. Professors at major schools are known to be much less "employees" than their colleagues in lesser establishments. Data on attitudes toward unionism, by individual attainment, are consistent with the "class interest" hypothesis.

The second factor relates to general political orientation. Of professors scoring in the most liberal quintile on the liberalism-conservatism scale 80 percent concurred that faculty strikes are a legitimate means of collective action, as against 24 percent of those in the most conservative quintile. Further, liberals far outnumber conservatives throughout American academia, and in ascending proportion as the institutions are traversed from minor to major. Holding ideology constant, however, faculty at major institutions are less supportive of unionism than their colleagues at academically weaker institutions, older professors are less supportive than younger, and professors of higher status and remuneration are less supportive than those of lower status and salary.

Liberals far outnumber conservatives throughout American academia, and in ascending proportion as the institutions are traversed from minor to major.

An important tension exists in the relation between ideology and support for unionism on the one hand, and academic status and union sympathies on the other. Faculty of high scholarly standing are more supportive ideologically, but experience a tension between their ideology and their own personal minimal need of unionism. There is an important clash between the interests and values of achieving academics who are involved in a meritocratic reward system, and the normative system of trade unionism. Given the enormous difference in professional status and autonomy characteristic of the several "levels" of academe, the presence of "structural" variations in faculty response to the concept is readily understood. What complicates the development of unionization in higher education, and prevents the matter from being a simple "greater-lesser" relationship, is that academics at the less-prestigious institutions are more conservative, and thus ideologically less receptive to the norms of unionism, than their major-university colleagues.

One background variable which does produce important differences in orientations to unionism is ethnocultural heritage. Jewish faculty demonstrate generally greater support for liberal-left politics than their gentile colleagues. Scholarly discipline is another important factor distinguishing faculty opinion. Social scientists, for example, give more backing to collective bargaining than any other discipline group of faculty.

These and other factors make possible a sketch of the membership of the various unions. Of union members, AAUP adherents show more scholarly output than others. AAUP and AFT are strongest in the social sciences and humanities, while the stronghold of the NEA is schools of education. AFT members are notably younger than other union members, and a higher proportion of AFT members are Jewish. In terms of political ideology, AFT members are furthest to the left, followed by AAUP members and the much more conservative NEA adherents.

As of winter 1972, collective bargaining has remained heavily skewed toward lower-tier schools, especially the junior colleges. Around 70 percent of all formally bargaining institutions are two-year institutions, and only one of these is represented by the AAUP. For the remainder, the NEA leads the AFT about two-to-one, but the AFT has made much headway in state college systems previously represented by the NEA. Most major universities are still not under collective bargaining, with the notable exceptions of the 20-campus City University of New York and the 29-unit State University of New York. Beyond these two, the bulk of four-year schools which negotiate collectively are state institutions, many are former teachers colleges and, again, the AFT and the NEA are dominant. The AAUP represents mostly middle-level universities, including such as Rutgers, Temple, and Wayne State.

Most major universities are still not under collective bargaining, with the notable exceptions of the 20-campus City University of New York and the 29-unit State University of New York.

In spite of the fact that unionism has so far touched only a relatively small segment of academe, examination of such elections as have been held at the Universities of Hawaii, Rhode Island, and Michigan, and SUNY and CUNY, provide a guide as to what is likely to occur as unionization spreads in the years ahead. For one thing, the boundaries for bargaining elections have often been crucial to the outcome. Except for the AAUP, which has always tried to limit a constituency to faculty, the unions have waffled over whether to include nonteaching professionals in the unit. NEA-linked groups in New York wanted them included; the AFT favored including them at CUNY, but sought to exclude them at SUNY.

It is too early to tell what degree of difference unionization will make in university life. Salary parity for jobs in a given category, however, has traditionally been an accompaniment of unionization in other areas. This tendency to try to reduce or eliminate the differential rewarding of "employees" pertains also to job security or tenure. If recruitment and selection procedures are sound, therefore, almost all new faculty members should qualify for tenure.

Governance in academe will also be affected by unionization, for although individually and collectively the faculty will lose power by abdicating it to a bargaining agent, they may also gain power through the activities of that agent. Additionally, the role of students in university governance may be affected, particularly if the prediction comes true that student unions will seek to participate in the bargaining.

In considering the unionization of academe, however, it must be remembered that the academy differs from most other institutions in which unions and related employee groups operate. Such concerns as the tensions between younger untenured faculty and their older tenured colleagues are significant, although these may dwindle in the face of the financial crunch increasingly apparent throughout higher education.

Faced with declining monetary support, faculty may decide that unions are necessary.

This discussion has centered around public rather than private institutions because for a variety of factors the public sector will continue to be the battleground for unionization. State legislative actions regarding finance provide a raison d'être for unions; conditions favorable to unions are also found in multiunit state systems with their extreme heterogeneity in academic standing and interests. In heterogeneous multicampus universities, such as CUNY, SUNY, and Hawaii, the main centers of research and graduate instruction have been much less inclined to favor unionization, particularly its AFT variety, while faculty at the less-prestigious units and nonteaching professionals have been the main protagonists for unionism.

The rapid growth of collective bargaining in higher education during the past half-decade should be seen as the extension of the powerful trends toward equalization and antielitism which have characterized many sectors of American society since the mid-sixties.

From the broadest perspective, the rapid growth of collective bargaining in higher education during the past half-decade should be seen as the extension of the powerful trends toward equalization and antielitism which have characterized many sectors of American society since the mid-sixties. The issues surrounding faculty unionism are far from resolved. Most of higher education is not yet organized, and the more "profession-like" research-oriented sector has thus far resisted unionization. What is clear is that trade unionism will be the focus of major activity and conflict throughout academe over the current decade.

In those cases where various pressures had major school faculty to elect a union as a bargaining agent, the stage will be set for a struggle between junior and senior staff; in statewide systems, the fight will extend to the major center(s) versus the lesser campuses. The mere presence of these conflicts, apart from their resolution, will have profound consequences for the future of American higher education.

(1973)

USE OF RESOURCES

CHAPTER 12

As Earl Cheit discovered in his survey of 41 institutions in 1970, the financial plight of colleges and universities is basically simple to understand: The rate at which the costs of these institutions is rising is faster than the rate of increase in revenues. The situation produced *The New Depression in Higher Education,* which he wrote in 1970 and then reappraised in 1972. Pulling out of their financial difficulties was a critical priority for institutions in the 1970s, partly because their survival was, in some instances, at stake, and partly because public confidence in them depended to a considerable extent on their ability to do so.

The challenge to education was given another dimension in June O'Neill's careful and detailed study of *Resource Use in Higher Education.* She confirmed the generally upward trend of expenditures in higher education during its history, and pointed out that, despite consistent enrollment growth, the costs per student credit hour had not been reduced. Measured on this criterion, at least, productivity of higher education remained almost constant between 1930 and 1967.

The institutional responses to these conditions have been varied, and the Commission's sponsored research has been concerned with certain aspects of it. The collection of essays in *Papers on Efficiency in the Management of Higher Education,* by Alexander Mood and his associates, reports on some of these research efforts. Rashi Fein and Gerald Weber describe patterns of financing a special type of higher learning in *Financing Medical Education.* In *Efficiency in Liberal Education,* Howard Bowen and Gordon Douglass provide a useful and badly needed analysis of the way costs can be altered with the use of different modes of instruction.

Joseph Ben-David, in *The Effectiveness and Effects of Higher Education,* takes a very broad view of the question of effectiveness in order to suggest a conceptual framework for the comparative investigation of the principal uses and effects of higher education in different parts of the world.

THE NEW DEPRESSION IN HIGHER EDUCATION: A Study of Financial Conditions at 41 Colleges and Universities
EARL F. CHEIT

Although some of the elements of the grave financial depression now (1971) confronting American higher education—rising costs, rising demands, rising enrollments—have been present for some time, no one can put an absolute date on its beginning. The new fiscal phenomenon, a declining rate of income growth and in some cases an absolute decline

This cost-income squeeze is new to academic administrators, and its major effect is to force the system of higher education into a period of readjustment.

in income, appeared in the latter half of the 1960s. This cost-income squeeze is new to academic administrators, and its major effect is to force the system of higher education into a period of readjustment.

The decade from 1956 to 1965 will stand as the golden age of college and university development and a period of unusually fast growth in current income in America. Funds flowing from public and private sources enabled an unprecedented growth of enrollment, function, and plans, until sudden fiscal shortages beclouded this vista to the extent that the data indicate that higher educational planning henceforth will be influenced more by financial considerations than by any other single factor. Whereas it has long been established that institutions of higher education expand and assume new activities when their funds increase, and face troubles when that flow is reduced, college and university officials are worried about three new problem areas: their ability to make the needed readjustments on campus; the ability of the schools to cope not only with the new array of economic forces affecting education, but also with new political and public attitudes about education; and their capacity to counter the probability that this financial pressure is not merely part of a general economic recession, but much more complex and potentially more grave.

Because of their lack of experience in confronting these problems, the officials concerned are uncertain, and frequently juggle such questions as: How general is this? Are others in trouble too? Are other schools solving this crisis? Are the reasons for the crisis common to all? This study aimed, therefore, to discover the characteristics of the financial problem facing higher education, how general the problem is among institutions of different types, and how the colleges and universities are responding to these problems—whether with programs, cost reduction, or income production.

The study was conducted between April and September 1970, when there was considerable turmoil on American college and university campuses. The 41 institutions surveyed were selected as an illustrative rather than representative sample of the major types found among 2,729 institutions of higher education in the nation. Six such major types were identified, and examples of each were chosen—the national research university, the leading regional research university, the state and comprehensive college, the liberal arts college, the primarily black college, and the two-year college. While there may be considerable variation in terms of size or quality or aspiration between schools within any given category, each individual category per se presents distinctive institutional characteristics. Within categories, what was sought was wide geographical distribution, as well as both public and private representation and the inclusion of sectarian schools.

The study was undertaken in two stages. In the first stage, basic income and expenditure information about each of the 41 institutions for the decade of the 1960s was gathered; the second stage involved campus visits in every case with extensive interviews, *in situ,* of campus administrators—usually the president and those of his colleagues most closely concerned with fiscal matters.

The essence of the financial problem confronting higher education is that while costs are rising at a constant or slowly growing rate, income is growing at a declining rate.

The essence of the financial problem confronting higher education is that while costs are rising at a constant or slowly growing rate, income is growing at a declining rate. This divergence between growth rates for cost and income began to be visible between 1967 and 1969 when, after a decade of unusual growth, many institutions, unprepared for an economic downturn, found themselves overextended and/or undercapitalized. Some were adding to their responsibilities without long-term financing, and others were still in the expensive process of raising quality standards. Because the cost increases are largely reflected in externally and internally based demands on the schools for research, services, or access, the cost-income problem is much more than a mere consequence of inflation, overextension, and a national economic tightening. This situation is also worsening in that while costs are rising at an average of 8.1 percent per annum, the rate of income growth reported for 1970–71 is markedly smaller than for 1969–70.

On the criteria used in this study, 29 colleges and universities (71 percent) were in, or headed for, financial difficulty while 12 (29 percent) were not. An institution was considered in financial difficulty if, at the time of the study, it was forced because of finances to reduce services regarded as part of its program or to lower quality. Classified as headed for financial trouble were those which, at the time of the study, could not predict that they would continue to meet current program or quality standards much longer, or could not plan support for evolving program growth. The 12 institutions which could meet current quality and program standards and, with a modicum of assurance, plan their desired program growth, were classified as "not in financial trouble."

Because of the "illustrative" rather than "representative" nature of the sample used in this study, the generalization that 71 percent of American institutions of higher education are in financial trouble cannot be made, but other generalizations may be made because all types of institutions are affected.

Institutions heading for financial difficulty are making responses which cluster under a general heading of postponing planned program growth.

Methods of dealing with the crisis vary but can be categorized. Institutions heading for financial difficulty are making responses which cluster under a general heading of postponing planned program growth. In these schools as a group, the courses and programs postponed cover most disciplines and include undergraduate and graduate work. At the time of the campus interviews, limited efforts at cutting academic costs through such methods as leaving staff vacancies empty and cutting marginal academic programs were commonly being employed. Little evidence exists that academic programs other than summer schools are, as yet, being ruthlessly excised.

Schools rated in financial difficulty have, in general, entered more deeply into a more intensive phase of cost cutting, and some have already dropped departments and graduate majors. Changes in structure have only occurred at a minority of schools; in the main, response as yet is only of the belt-tightening variety. For example, student aid, faculty travel allowances, and certain kinds of student services have suffered.

The almost universal response of all categories of schools is to seek more funds, particularly from private sources. More fiscally conscious planning is taking place than ever before. And finally, there is more worrying because the general fiscal picture generates uneasiness and bodes ill for American higher education.

The almost universal response of all categories of schools is to seek more funds, particularly from private sources. More fiscally conscious planning is taking place than ever before. And finally, there is more worrying because the general fiscal picture generates uneasiness and bodes ill for American higher education.

In addition to confronting central questions about the financial status of American higher education, this study provides certain other data which may be of value to institutions interested in surviving the current fiscal crisis. The data reveal that medical schools are not invariably an important factor in precipitating or worsening the impact of the financial crisis, although they may be having a deleterious financial effect at any given institution. The data also suggest that this period of adversity may not be without eventual concomitant benefits. For example, this crisis might eventually permit the removal of "dead wood" either in terms of program or personnel, but the processes for deciding which "wood" is "dead" have not yet been sufficiently fully explored. Additionally, there is a new cost-consciousness which will produce long-term benefits if the campuses survive the crisis. Further findings are that the institutions are working hard to comprehend and survive their financial problems; that the general financial picture confronting American higher education will deteriorate before it gets better; and that the financial crisis will have a "ripple" effect, raising broader issues which will have to be faced.

Before significant improvement may be made, public confidence must be restored in higher education, and three aspects of this large task should be emphasized. First the campuses must show that they are reasonably governable—by which is meant *stable* and not necessarily *placid*. Second, the institutions must reveal an efficiency in their internal operations provided that interest in efficiency and productivity is well motivated. Third, restored confidence will require convincing evidence that the activities of colleges and universities have a unifying set of pur-

Dollar expenditures per student 1967–68

	EXPENDITURE CATEGORY											
CATEGORY OF INSTITUTION	EDUCATIONAL AND GENERAL		INSTRUCTION AND DEPARTMENTAL RESEARCH		LIBRARY		ORGANIZED RESEARCH		STUDENT AID		TOTAL CURRENT FUND	
	STUDY SAMPLE	ALL SCHOOLS	STUDY SAMPLE	ALL SCHOOLS	STUDY SAMPLE	ALL SCHOOLS	STUDY SAMPLE	ALL SCHOOLS	STUDY SAMPLE	ALL SCHOOLS	STUDY SAMPLE	ALL SCHOOLS
Research universities (I and II)												
Public	$3,338	$3,286	$1,297	$1,146	$119	$ 95	$ 859	$ 824	$235	$142	$ 4,165	$4,000
Private	8,440	8,538	1,879	1,890	288	265	4,576	4,073	632	627	10,030	9,964
Other doctoral-granting universities (I and II)												
Public	1,700	2,023	935	821	62	74	45	410	82	85	2,301	2,573
Private	2,349	3,043	1,002	1,076	87	119	435	659	174	301	2,972	3,902
Comprehensive colleges (I and II)												
Public	1,117	1,073	637	601	72	64	22	16	50	51	1,432	1,467
Liberal arts colleges (I)												
Private	2,611	2,426	1,214	1,113	126	127	34	57	336	287	4,048	3,675
Liberal arts colleges (II)												
Private	1,736	1,454	755	651	88	82	21	8	234	146	2,424	2,188
Two-year institutions												
Public	727	739	426	432	39	37	0	0	15	15	918	877

Source: Data from the Carnegie Commission on Higher Education and from individual institutions' financial information. The figures for "study sample" include all 41 institutions, while the figures for "all schools" include about 80 percent of the nation's institutions of higher education. Data from the Rockefeller Institute and California Institute of Technology are excluded from the figures for private institutions in this table.

poses—purposes (it is warned) that the supporting public can comprehend and defer to.

The gap between income and expenditure prospects can be closed only by a conscious, positive effort to restore school finance. As this study demonstrates, recovery cannot and will not come as a by-product of other events and policies. It requires the deliberate application of major financial policies by the schools and the public, directed to the future of higher education.

(1971)

THE NEW DEPRESSION IN HIGHER EDUCATION—TWO YEARS LATER
EARL F. CHEIT

This is a follow-up of a study, published in 1971, of the fiscal situation of 23 private and 18 public colleges and universities. Surveying institutions from six major categories—national research universities, leading regional research universities, comprehensive and state colleges, liberal arts colleges, primarily black colleges, and two-year colleges—the earlier investigation concluded that all were victims, to varying degrees, of a general financial erosion of the traditional sources of support to higher education.

The conclusion of the present study, a report on data from a questionnaire sent to the same institutions two years later, is that the alarming financial downward drift has been slowed enough so that the colleges and universities could be regarded as having achieved a certain degree of stability, fragile but real.

The reality of the relatively balanced equilibrium the institutions are now manifesting (15 seem to have improved financially, 15 are not quite as well off, 11 have held their own) is directly attributable to the objective and pragmatic ways in which the colleges and universities responded to the financial constraints that beset them. The fragility of their situation is related to the extent to which their current stability necessarily rests on factors beyond their control.

The main agent of the successful weathering has been a widespanning process of internal change: in attitudes and awareness, expenditures, managerial practices, organizational relationships, and standards of judgment. While these must be recognized as both admirable and effective, some of the measures taken under stringent circumstances cannot be expected to be continued. The reduction in growth of expenses, for example, has been achieved in large part by holding down increases in faculty salaries and deferring maintenance, inevitably short-term expedients. (The present level of expenditure growth is 0.5 above the rate of inflation, whereas the Carnegie Commission's recommendation of 2.5, although somewhat stark, seems reasonable.) Further, the present financial stasis is also predicated upon assumptions about factors which the institutions can neither predict nor affect—the rate of inflation, the continuance of a recent upturn in private contributions (in 1969–70 voluntary support to higher education had dropped by an estimated $40 million), and at least sustaining support from the state, which in many instances expanded aid when it became apparent that little federal money was likely to be appropriated for higher education.

The consciousness enveloping campuses these days is cost-consciousness.

Overall, the consciousness enveloping campuses these days is cost-consciousness. Faculty, students, and staff members all give evidence of a greater awareness of the role of money in higher education. At meetings, academics are heard from principally about matters of money, and institutions are primarily concerned with defining and serving their own need to support operations (in contrast to earlier concerns about accommodating new students, meeting the nation's needs for research for defense needs, for increased emphasis on languages and science, and responding to urban problems).

As a result of this focusing on fiscal threats and rearrangements, there are lowered expectations, with less building going on, less esoteric programs initiated, and fewer new programs of any kind instituted until they can be proven to be "cost-beneficial." The general climate is also one conducive to change, so that financial troubles, once hidden and viewed as evidence of failure, are now openly discussed and used as an opportunity to demonstrate institutional flexibility and a capability for producing viable solutions without diminishing quality.

Along with the new awareness of costs is the acceptance of the idea of the "managed university" and a proliferation of self-studies, cost analyses, budgetary control programs, management information systems, retrenchment and reallocation stratagems, and priority and planning committees. While acquiring more income is unquestionably a principal goal, attention is increasingly concentrated on cutting and avoiding expenses and on establishing strong, central decision-making structures with the power to set and control targets.

In institutions where planning holds center stage, so do the managers. The role of administrators in colleges and universities has therefore changed. Traditionally at the periphery of operations, where they were expected to make arrangements to implement decisions already made, now the administrators' task is to provide the conditions under which rational operation can take place.

Because institutions of higher education are meeting financial pressure for the most part by substitution and sometimes retraction, changes are being made as a result of choices. And over time such choices come to make a statement about values: questions of money gradually convert to questions of purpose and inevitably challenge the status quo.

Because institutions of higher education are meeting financial pressure for the most part by substitution and sometimes retraction, changes are being made as a result of choices. And over time such choices come to make a statement about values; questions of money gradually convert to questions of purpose and inevitably challenge the status quo. Already there have been changes in views about the best size for classes, the importance of offering a rich academic mix, the superiority of the campus as an environment for learning and teaching, and the value of higher education itself.

What is happening on campus is not inspired by the visions of change educational reformers talk about. No grand design is being followed. No commanding pedagogical ideal informs the main actions being taken. Rather, what we see under way is the painful but undramatic process of adjusting operations and aspirations to relatively poorer financial circumstances. But along with the hard work of teasing out the devices for coping, institutions now have a unique opportunity for evolving and asserting educational values, defining their objectives in terms of efficiency and competitive response to market demand, and developing coherent educational options.

(1973)

RESOURCE USE IN HIGHER EDUCATION: Trends in Output and Inputs, 1930–1967
JUNE O'NEILL

The higher education "industry" has grown faster than most, and this rapid growth has been accompanied by rising public concern about the costs of higher education and the proper role of government in financing these costs. Despite this, however, little firm knowledge exists regarding the magnitude of the costs of higher education and how that may have changed over time.

This state of affairs is largely caused by the difficulties attendant upon devising a satisfactory measure of output for higher education—a measure that distinguishes output from the inputs used in its production. Furthermore, colleges and universities only rarely use accounting systems which provide data on input costs; and expenditures on education are not separated from expenditures on other jointly produced services (for example, research), and costs of the services of the physical plant are generally not included at all.

This study endeavors to surmount these difficulties and to develop some useful knowledge about long-run trends in real resource costs per unit of output in American higher education. The study concentrates on student instruction, the raison d'être of higher education, but points out that student instruction may currently account for only 50 percent of the output of the average school, that this share of the output may have declined over time, and that, at any point in time, it varies widely among various types of schools.

One major finding of the study is that there was no major change in real costs per credit hour over the period 1930–1967. If credit hours are a meaningful measure of the instructional output in higher education, this finding could indicate that, across the "industry" as a whole, there has been no apparent productivity advance. But since changes in credit-hour quality could only be crudely incorporated, it is debatable whether changes in the credit-hour measure developed here truly reflect changes in real output. Furthermore, it is stressed that the underlying data are imperfect and that findings on productivity change must be regarded as tentative.

For the purposes of this research the universe of higher education was confined to those schools, 2,491 in the autumn of 1958, included in the Office of Education surveys and which typically are private and public institutions offering accredited courses in two- and four-year programs. Throughout the study, the data refer to the aggregate United States, including Alaska, Hawaii, and the outlying districts, beginning with 1953–54. For brevity, the year of the spring term is often referred to in the study as the academic year.

The instructional component of the output of colleges and universities is measured in this study by credit hours. The credit hour is the usual transaction unit in higher education and is taken roughly to represent some content of material imparted to students. As a measure, however, it does present disadvantages. It is possible, for example, that over time, qualitative as well as quantitative changes in the credit hour may occur, and the measurement of quality in higher education poses challenges. There is no meaningful system of market prices which can be utilized to differentiate qualitatively among types and kinds of school, tuition cost being so heavily influenced by subsidy that it cannot be relied upon to reflect quality. The best that may be done, therefore, is to substitute cost differences for price differences, even though we do not know how well cost differences reflect quality differences in the setting of a nonprofit system which relies to some extent upon private philanthropy and public subsidy.

Adjusting credit hours for level and subject and also for type of school would provide a quality adjustment similar in spirit to that currently made for most goods, but such an adjustment may be less satisfactory in the case of education. It is certainly possible that instructional quality has changed within a given specification, but measurement, or even specification of all the germane characteristics, is difficult in education, partially because of its service aspects. Education, like medicine, is a treatment, the end results of which are embodied in a person with the result that isolation of the effects of the service is problematic.

Education, like medicine, is a treatment, the end results of which are embodied in a person with the result that isolation of the effects of the service is problematic.

This study made only "very modest" adjustments for the quality of credit hours. Using available cost studies, distinctions are drawn between graduate and undergraduate credits and between lower- versus upper-division undergraduate courses. Separate estimates of outputs and inputs are made for the various types of schools, and by this means costs may be compared across schools and adjustments made for quality due to a change in the mix of schools. Credit hours as measured in this study include most forms of instruction: resident degree and nondegree, extension degree and nondegree during the academic year, and summer degree instruction. The measure is therefore more comprehensive than the norm, which restricts itself to credit-degree students enrolled in the regular session.

Between 1930 and 1967, total expenditures on student instruction increased at an average annual rate of 8.4 percent, and credit hours increased at a rate of 4.8 percent. As a result, the average annual increase in costs per credit hour was about 3.4 percent. This 3.4 percent increase may be viewed as the net outcome of two factors: first, changes in input prices per unit of output, and second, changes in the amount of inputs employed to produce a unit of output. Adjusting for these, the study concludes that the amount of real resources used to produce a credit hour has not significantly changed since 1930. However, there have been fluctuations around the seeming zero trend line, and these appear to correspond to the more pronounced fluctuations in credit hours. The study illustrates this last point dramatically by revealing an inverse relation between inputs per credit hour and credit hours during the period 1930 to the mid-1950s, which was characterized by unusual enrollment fluctuations occasioned by the Depression, World War II, and the postwar G. I. boom. From this it may be gathered that the resources used in education cannot be varied quickly, and further, that expenditures cannot be speedily adapted to sudden changes in enrollment.

Resources used in education cannot be varied quickly, and expenditures cannot be speedily adapted to sudden changes in enrollment.

Another potentially measurable source of output quality change is variation in the mix of schools. This study indicates that, while adjusting for input price changes removes most of the upward trend in unit costs in both public and private institutions, public schools do appear to have attained a higher plateau of inputs per credit hour in the immediate post-World War II period. Private schools, on the other hand, seem to have used more resources per credit hour than public schools over the entire time period, although the gap seems constantly to be narrowing since 1952.

The average cost of a credit hour varies considerably among the different kinds of colleges and universities, but, as a general rule, this study shows that private institutions, whether universities or four- or two-year colleges, expended more, per credit hour, than their public counterparts. Composition of output with respect to graduate and lower-division courses varies with the type of school, but there are indications that schools with a larger graduate component (universities) have high average costs while two-year schools, which are almost exclusively lower-division undergraduate, typically have the lowest cost.

The study further reveals trends in real inputs per unit of output by eliminating price changes, and the situations of the various types of schools are worthy of note. Whereas public four-year colleges and universities demonstrated a small decline in inputs per unit of output, their private counterparts showed small increases, which cannot entirely be accounted for by the relative increase in graduate credits. When it is remembered, however, that during the 1950s, inputs per credit hour were particularly low in all private schools, and particularly high in all public schools throughout the whole period 1930–1967, it is reasonable to conjecture that these situations held for the component schools as well.

It is reassuring to note from the data that alternate indicators of resources used per credit hour show much the same pattern across the different types of schools. The study summarizes some of the available quantitative evidence on the relationship of credit hours (converted into full-time student equivalents) to full-time-equivalent faculty, with other professional staff, and physical space available.

That private schools continue to attract even a shrinking portion of all students is circumstantial evidence of higher quality in private than in public schools, particularly when it is considered that the ratio of tuitions in the two sectors is much greater than the ratio of costs.

Research undertaken in this study scarcely permits of a confrontation with the issue of whether or not the differences in inputs per credit hour among the different schools can be taken to reflect quality differences. Were this study observing a perfect market with a working pricing system, the answer to the question would be affirmative, but in the education industry there are grounds for being less positive. The various types of schools are financed differently and, regrettably, the effects of such considerations as public control on efficiency have received so little professional attention from economists that no definitive answer may be given, although "casual speculation suggests that the quality differences implied by these estimates of inputs per credit hour are probably in the right direction." That private schools continue to attract even a shrinking portion of all students is circumstantial evidence of higher quality in private than in public schools, particularly when it is considered that the ratio of tuitions in the two sectors is much greater than the ratio of costs.

If the observed differences in costs per credit hour do reflect quality, then public two-year institutions would occupy the lowest rung of the higher educational ladder, even after taking account of grade-level differences among the schools. Accordingly, the speedy rise in popularity of the two-year school suggests a shift in the output mix toward lower quality, which would indicate an upward bias in the measure of real instructional output and a corresponding downturn in the measure of real inputs per measure of real output.

To make this additional adjustment in the study, costs per standard lower-division credit (in 1957–1959 dollars) were recomputed for all schools (1964–1967) by taking a weighted average across the six kinds of institutions, using as fixed weights the 1954 distribution of credit hours. As a result of thus holding the mix constant, the decline in output per unit of input due to any decline in quality associated with the expansion of two-year schools is removed. The effects, however, were discovered to be small.

Historically, most American industries have experienced productivity change with a high correlation between rapid growth and rapid productivity change. Against this norm the findings of this study raise intriguing questions. Between 1930 and 1967, instructional inputs and credit hours appear to have increased more or less proportionately. If growth in credit hours is a reliable indicator of real instructional output growth, there is a strong possibility that despite astronomical growth rates, education as an industry has experienced no production change over the period 1930–1967.

Unfortunately, the kind of objective evidence needed to settle the credit hours-as-an-output-measure issue is not available, but the study examines the possible deficiencies in the measure as a guide to "educated speculation." The first deficiency concerns the possibility of output bias. Instructional output might be biased because credit hours have not been correctly counted, or because quality change in the credit hour has not been accurately measured. While every effort was made to ascertain accurately the number of credit hours, the problem here is mechanical, whereas, as regards quality variation, the difficulties of measurement involve conceptual as well as statistical difficulties. Assessing again all the relevant data, the study concludes that any potentially serious sources of bias in the measure of output must lie in failure to account for quality change within a grade level, type of school, and subject. This raises the whole elusive problem of quality measurement, however, and the study demonstrates this to be susceptible to perennial debate. On this point, the study concludes that "it [is] questionable whether these quality changes would be sufficient to bring the estimate of growth in output per unit of total input up to the rate of the economy as a whole; . . . others will undoubtedly disagree. . . ."

A second deficiency concerns inputs, where a bias may have occurred since "student's time" was omitted from the measure which included the sum of operating expenditures and estimated capital costs, each deflated by a relevant factor price index. In addition, two problem areas relevant to the inputs measure used may be identified: The price deflators may be inaccurate and the inputs used to produce instructional services may not have been properly separated from those employed to produce research and other jointly produced output. There are, therefore, a number of biases probably at work in the input measure, although "the net result is unlikely to be any serious upward bias in inputs over time."

The study concludes that there is a strong possibility that productivity change in higher education, even if positive, has not kept pace with productivity change in other economic sectors, and several reasons are offered as to why efficiency in resource use might lag in education. There is a presumption that the lure of profit and the rigors of competition provide powerful incentives for efficiency in a free enterprise economy, where the constant search for lower-cost production methods promotes technological advance, while colleges and universities operate within a strikingly different milieu, where profits are not expected and private contributions are a significant percentage of revenue. Furthermore, it is doubtful that income is as closely tied to cost-saving innovation as, for example, it is in private manufacturing industries.

Another reason offered concerns the notion that cost-saving is merely technologically impeded in higher education. Further, it may be that colleges and universities attract unusually dedicated personnel who, despite minimal personal remuneration, struggle as best they can to organize resources in a cost-effective manner.

For whatever reason, it is clear that this area needs systematic and objective empirical studies which try to compare cost differences and productivity change differences between educational institutions operating under different personal incentive environments, but producing similar outputs. This study holds that clarification of this issue will have important implications for future decisions in the vital area of financing higher education.

(1971)

Total instructional costs per credit hour, in current and constant dollars, public and private colleges and universities, selected years, 1929–30 through 1966–67

ACA-DEMIC YEAR	CURRENT DOLLARS			CONSTANT DOLLARS (1957–59 PRICES)		
	ALL SCHOOLS	PUBLIC	PRIVATE	ALL SCHOOLS	PUBLIC	PRIVATE
1929–30	14.6	13.3	16.0	32.8	29.6	36.1
1931–32	14.1	11.7	17.0	35.0	28.7	42.3
1933–34	14.7	11.9	17.8	37.3	30.1	45.1
1935–36	13.8	11.3	16.7	34.2	27.7	41.6
1937–38	13.8	11.3	16.8	32.6	26.6	39.7
1939–40	13.9	11.5	16.8	32.8	27.2	39.8
1941–42	16.0	13.7	18.8	35.3	30.1	41.4
1943–44*	19.6	16.4	23.3	40.5	33.7	48.1
1945–46	17.3	15.2	19.6	31.5	27.6	35.7
1947–48	18.3	17.1	19.7	26.6	24.8	28.6
1949–50	21.6	20.4	23.1	29.8	28.1	31.8
1951–52	27.6	27.2	28.0	34.1	33.7	34.6
1953–54	32.0	31.2	33.0	37.5	36.6	38.7
1955–56	31.6	30.0	33.7	34.7	33.0	37.0
1957–58	35.7	33.8	38.6	36.3	34.3	39.2
1959–60	38.9	36.7	42.4	37.0	34.8	40.2
1961–62	41.2	37.7	46.9	36.6	33.5	41.7
1963–64	45.0	40.5	53.1	37.6	33.9	44.3
1965–66	47.0	42.0	57.0	35.9	32.2	43.6
1966–67	50.1	45.3	60.4	36.4	32.9	44.0

* The credit hours base for 1944 includes credit hours estimated to have been taken by enrolled military personnel.
Sources: Calculated from total instructional costs in Tables D-1, D-2, D-3, and total credit hours in Table A-10, in *Resource Use in Higher Education.*

PAPERS ON EFFICIENCY IN THE MANAGE-MENT OF HIGHER EDUCATION
ALEXANDER M. MOOD, COLIN BELL, LAWRENCE BOGARD, HELEN BROWNLEE, and JOSEPH MCCLOSKEY

These four reports, which derive from an extensive study of the efficiency of higher education carried out by the University of California's Public Policy Research Organization, examine some of the conventional ways in which institutions of higher education are trying to improve efficiency.

The first paper concerns the extent to which institutions are using self-analysis to improve efficiency. Characteristically, institutions of higher education that have adopted the concepts of scientific management have a management organization that serves the following functions:

■ Critical and continuous self-examination of curriculum and administrative and operational procedures, established goals and objectives, and the institutional environment—called Institutional Research (IR)

■ Establishment of relevant goals and objectives, justification for and allocation of resources, and continuous accountability for resource expenditures—called a Planning, Programming, Budgeting System (PPBS)

■ Development of timely and valid information to achieve the above objectives and enhance the validity of decisions—called a Management Information System (MIS)

A brief institutional management questionnaire sought to determine the extent to which these three constituents of effective management were employed throughout higher education. The presidents of all 2,537 institutions listed in the Education Directory 1968–1969, part 3, were canvassed. Usable responses were received from 1,873 (74 percent) of the schools and of these, 884 were from the 1,037 public schools and 989 were from the 1,500 private schools listed. The study shows that of the schools responding, 24 percent had full-time IR offices, 13 percent had MIS, and 31 percent had PPBS. However, a further important question is: How many schools had more than one of these three systems for effective management? The survey indicates that only 2.8 percent have a full-time IR, MIS, and PPBS; 4.2 percent of the public schools and 1.5 percent of all private schools had all three systems. Size is an important consideration here, and schools with 3,000 students or more (8 percent of the public schools and 8.7 percent of the private schools) had all three programs. IR has been called the "heart" of the trend toward modern management in higher education, and the responses to this survey bear that out. An overwhelming percentage of all responses indicates that IR was done, either in a specific office, or, when needed, by the appropriate administrator. The combined responses to this institutional management questionnaire provide deeper insight into institutional capacity in this area than do the individual responses alone. While IR, MIS, and PPBS may be essential to effective management, this study reveals other significant changes in organizational structure, procedure, or technology being made in over 50 percent of institutions. Twenty-two percent reported a recently added computer, while the second most frequently mentioned change concerned the implementation of long-range plans for the organization of a planning group.

Change and innovation are taking place, although evaluation of the success of such change may not be made for some time.

The study concludes that change and innovation are taking place, although evaluation of the success of such change may not be made for some time. Innovation was reported as about evenly divided among organizational structural change, procedural change, and technological change, with considerable overlap.

The second report considers whether mathematical models can contribute to the quest for efficiency in higher education. Large-scale simulations have been used to study the operation of a university, and operations research techniques have been applied to the prediction of such future institutional characteristics as the student body mix by educational level or the faculty mix by rank. A number of large-scale mathematical models of higher educational institutions have been constructed. They permit administrators to estimate the need for new faculty members, departmental majors, new plants, and so on, using assumptions about student-body growth.

There are shortcomings in the structures of the various models because computational technology is not sufficiently advanced to include economies of scale, and error estimates are not included, but more serious are the problems in the implementation and interpretation of the models. For example, there is a sensitive trade-off between the use of readily available past data, which incorporate irrelevant policies and inefficiencies, and the costly and speculative practice of filling input-output matrixes with administrators' "best estimates." Further, no established model can account for environmental factors external to the institution, and this is a serious weakness; it is known, for example, that such factors as future draft policy and the changing job market will affect future student flows. The study bluntly states that "the variables that might have the greatest effect are outside the models and there is no way to bring them in." With this in mind, the conclusion is drawn that "It is important to design a model of realistic scale that does not exert too much costly energy in making computations at an unreasonable level of accuracy."

"It is important to design a model of realistic scale that does not exert too much costly energy in making computations at an unreasonable level of accuracy."

The third research project took the form of a case study of budget expenditure at the University of California, Los Angeles. The primary object of the analysis was to allocate resources for instruction to lower-division, upper-division, and graduate students, but the analysis also made it possible to study allocations to other activities. Basic assumptions were made concerning course format—lecture, seminar, discussion, laboratory, studio, and research—and course instructors were assigned ranks—professor, associate professor, assistant professor, lecturer, instructor, research associate, or graduate student. These classification devices were obtained from UCLA reports. Data were not available concerning health sciences, so departments in those disciplines were eliminated from the study. Additional information about the allocation of faculty time was gleaned from the results of a survey conducted by the University of California on all its campuses during the 1968–69 school year.

Using these data, the total UCLA budget was analyzed. There were no large surprises. That graduate education and research were both extremely expensive endeavors compared with undergraduate education was already well documented. At UCLA, 12 percent of the total budget ($13.6 million) is expended on the teaching of nearly 20,000 undergraduates, an instructional cost of less than $700 per student. While these students also account for some of the other budgeted costs, the amount is not sufficient to bring per undergraduate costs anywhere near the figure of $1,500 widely quoted by private colleges as a bare minimum for the maintenance of an acceptable undergraduate program.

From this the researchers concluded that UCLA is very efficient in providing undergraduate education and that this efficiency spills over into other areas.

The fourth study involves a survey of private colleges and universities in California to search for innovations in efficiency which might not have appeared in the literature of higher education. It is known that private colleges have been under severe pressure to economize and that some of those in California have been experimenting toward that end for some time.

The survey consisted of personal and/or telephone interviews with a senior administrator at each institution. Institutions granting diplomas or certificates, and not degrees, were omitted from the 57-institution study. The findings are discussed under the headings of Student Admissions, Faculty Concerns, Facilities, Curriculum, Finance, and General Administration.

The concept of taking educational opportunity from the campus to the student has resulted in a plethora of programs at both graduate and undergraduate levels which take place on such varied sites as military bases, high schools, and, in the case of the Golden Gate College M.B.A. program, at headquarters of the Bechtel Corporation all around the world.

A major change in the sources of students confronts many schools in California with the growth in popularity of the two-year college and the concomitantly large number of transfer students now available to four-year colleges and universities. Larger numbers of disadvantaged students, particularly black and Mexican-American, are being admitted, and a few institutions now have programs which enable educationally disadvantaged students to overcome deficiencies in their schooling prior to entering college. Another area of change relating to students lies in the concept of taking educational opportunity from the campus to the student. This has resulted in a plethora of programs at both graduate and undergraduate levels which take place on such varied sites as military bases, high schools, and, in the case of the Golden Gate College M.B.A. program, at headquarters of the Bechtel Corporation all around the world.

Financing problems have provided the most significant possibility for innovating. Not surprisingly, perhaps, innovation in faculty hiring is a negligible factor. Institutions are increasingly debating the cost-benefit of such factors as small classes, low student-faculty ratios, and proliferation of courses.

Curricular change is so plentiful that this study is unable to detail it all.

Generally, however, it appears that requirements for graduation have been relaxed, and that an increased responsibility has been placed on the student by providing more opportunity for off-campus study than was previously available.

In terms of facilities, financial pressure has resulted in the emergence of new concepts. They include Stanford University's use of mobile homes for student housing, and Chapman College's design of an "educational corridor," a cluster of multiuse buildings to be erected on the present athletic field. A new athletic field is to be laid down on top of the buildings.

The financial problems of private higher education are being exacerbated by campus unrest. Particularly affected are private donations and insurance costs. To offset rising costs due to these and other factors, this study demonstrates that private colleges and universities are taking a long, hard look at the economics of the instructional process. Should the current inflation persist, there is no reason to doubt that fairly drastic cost paring will prove necessary in such areas as student-faculty ratios, class size, and the richness of the curriculum.

In the area of general administration the most exciting innovative concept is the "cluster college." It was pioneered in 1925 when Pomona College joined Scripps College to initiate the Claremont University Center and Graduate School. These two institutions have subsequently been joined, for the purposes of general administration, by Claremont Men's College, Harvey Mudd College, and Pitzer College. Each institution retains all the trappings of institutional autonomy. But they have developed and share a common library far richer than any one of the campuses could afford, and common health and business services. The study concludes that the various applications of the cluster concept "aim at strength that comes from larger size while maintaining the feeling of individuality and the sense of community that characterizes smaller colleges."

Despite the success of the "cluster" concept, other attempts at cooperative arrangements have had no visible success among the private colleges and universities of California. Some arrangements are purely fund-raising devices; others do not require the sharing of services in the usual sense. At the purely administrative level, three areas of interest are revealed by this study:

■ California's private institutions are well versed in the use of computers. Roughly half have access to computers, but the variety of computers employed renders active cooperation, particularly in the area of applications programming, impossible.

■ In the area of planning and budgeting, considerable progress has been made. Most institutions now endure the agonies of preparing an annual budget, although few yet maintain budgetary controls or harness budget projections to long-range planning.

A growing number of private colleges and universities are making judicious use of contracted services. In increasing numbers, banks are preparing payrolls, food chains are supervising the feeding of campus communities, and investment counselors are advising regarding endowment.

■ Perhaps to aid in cost control, a growing number of private colleges and universities are making judicious use of contracted services. In increasing numbers, banks are preparing payrolls, food chains are supervising the feeding of the campus communities, and investment counselors are advising regarding endowment. The ultimate question in this domain is whether the president of the institution should be selected for his potential contribution to education or for his capacity to administer a highly complex business operation. If he is selected for his educational competence, this study holds that "he should be relieved of his duties as innkeeper, caterer, landscape gardener, etc. . . [through the] . . . use [of] contracted services." The number of resignations as opposed to retirements among presidents is cited as indication of a need for fundamental innovation in this area.

(1972)

FINANCING MEDICAL EDUCATION: An Analysis of Alternative Policies and Mechanisms
RASHI FEIN and GERALD I. WEBER

This is a critical time for medical schools and for the system of medical education. Increasing demands are being placed on the schools (and on the teaching hospitals which bear a large part of the burden of educating the M.D.). There is pressure for increasing the number of M.D.'s to be educated, for changes in the socioeconomic mix of students admitted to degree candidacy, and for the development of education and training programs for new types of health personnel.

Schools (and teaching hospitals) are being asked to develop new patterns of patient care, with emphasis on expanding services outside the hospitals and on community involvement. Responsibility for planning and regionalizing the delivery of medical services has often been delegated to the medical school, which is now expected to assume a leading role in changing the system of medical care delivery and organization. The pressure on the schools is to change their apparent priorities—from research to service and education—but funding mechanisms do not enable such changes to be made easily, and there is little agreement on whether this shift should be accompanied by a cutback in research. Increased relevance is also being demanded of medical schools, although agreement on what constitutes relevance is lacking. And these pressures and demands for expansion of activity are being voiced at the very time when there is a substantial decline in the growth rate of federal support.

Never, perhaps, has there been so much need and so much opportunity for a rational examination of the total activities of medical schools to replace the existing, crisis-oriented, patchwork-quilt approach of past years.

Never, perhaps, has there been so much need and so much opportunity for a rational examination of the total activities of medical schools to replace the existing, crisis-oriented, patchwork-quilt approach of past years.

The education of a physician—from entrance into medical school until completion of his residency—is a long, complicated, and costly process. During that time society and the student forgo the productive contribution that the student might make if his efforts were not allocated to training. This lost production represents the opportunity cost in medical education. In addition, the student requires the scarce and valuable time of skilled physicians and scientists and expensive equipment. A basic question is how such resources should be allocated to best serve individual patients and the community, medical research, and the education of various kinds of medical specialists.

There is no single model of a medical school. Schools exhibit considerable variation in size, wealth, apparent quality of their students, and the allocation of their efforts among different outputs. In general, however, the schools have interrelated characteristics. On the average, for example, those schools with the largest expenditures per full-time student attract M.D. candidates who have higher scores on the science achievement test. Thirteen percent of the 1950–1959 graduates from the 10 privately controlled medical schools with the largest expenditures per student were full-time medical faculty in 1967, as compared with 4 percent from 11 publicly controlled schools with the least expenditures per full-time student. Only 10 percent of graduates from the private group considered themselves general practitioners, while 30 percent of graduates from the public schools did.

The expenditures of United States medical schools increased at an annual rate of 14.6 percent between 1947 and 1967. When adjusted for inflation, the rate of increase (in constant dollars) was 8 percent a year. The rapid growth in real resources is illustrated by the expansion of full-time faculty from 3,500 in 1951 to 22,000 in 1967.

Most of the increase in expenditures was financed by research grants and other sponsored funds, federally sponsored research accounting for almost 85 percent of the growth. In 1965–66, federal and other research and training grants provided 57 percent of the support for the lowest expenditures-per-student private schools, but 79 percent of support for the highest expenditure private schools.

There is substantial agreement that the increased availability of grants to individual faculty members has limited the ability of medical-school deans to control the distribution of faculty effort and resources among programs. Also, the fact that increased funding has been provided to such a great extent for research and not for other purposes has placed a number of less research-oriented schools in a relatively disadvantageous financial position, even threatening their survival.

The average physician earns considerably more over his working lifetime than the average individual in other graduate fields and a great deal more than the average B.A. recipient. This high income, however, must be considered in conjunction with the costs of training, the long hours of work, and the lack of fringe benefits for the private practitioner. The evidence that there are twice as many medical-school applicants as openings, and that perhaps a third of those not accepted are qualified to attend, suggests the returns are sufficiently attractive. Monetary costs and benefits have a considerable impact on the characteristics of the student and, perhaps, on his behavior after entering practice.

Medical students tend to come from the higher socioeconomic group; in 1967 the majority came from families with incomes of $15,000 or more. About 25 percent of students at public medical schools and 34 percent at private schools received financial assistance in the form of nonrefundable grants—averaging $700 and $975, respectively. These study grants were unevenly distributed among schools. The 10 privately controlled schools with the greatest expenditure per student administered two and one-half times as many total dollars as the 12 private schools with the least expenditure per student.

The authors believe there should be a basic federal subsidy to reflect the public demand for medical education. While it is true that education brings private benefits to the recipient, it also brings social benefits. A public subsidy would also make it possible to alter the socioeconomic characteristics of students who attend medical school, to provide physicians who might be better equipped to deal with the problems of, for example, blacks, Mexican-Americans, and low-income families. Subsidies could be given directly to students or directly to schools; to achieve a change in the socioeconomic distribution of medical students, however, funds supplied directly to the students would be more effective. But to expand enrollments and provide a stable financial base for medical schools, assistance to schools is also required. The authors believe both kinds should be provided. They also suggest that all M.D. candidates have the option of financing their education through long-term loans if they so desire, since there are some students whose family incomes are too high to qualify for direct subsidies but too low to pay medical-school tuitions. Alternatively, there might be a combination of grants and loans through an Educational Opportunity Bank. Students would repay such loans through an increase in federal tax rates applied to their incomes after completion of training.

The federal government should also be responsible for 100 percent of the costs of capital expansion of medical schools and plant improvement.

The federal government should also be responsible for 100 percent of the costs of capital expansion of medical schools and plant improvement.

State governments now provide considerable support for the operating costs of public medical schools, in addition to the capital funds they make available. A few also give some direct financial aid to private medical schools. But the amount of state support varies considerably, both in absolute terms and in relation to population and personal income. The authors hold that states will not adequately support medical education and should not be expected to do more than supplement the basic federal subsidy to schools for M.D. candidates.

(1971)

EFFICIENCY IN LIBERAL EDUCATION: A Study of Comparative Instructional Costs for Different Ways of Organizing Teaching-Learning in a Liberal Arts College
HOWARD R. BOWEN and GORDON K. DOUGLASS

The financial burdens of colleges and universities are still growing. One approach to a solution is to improve operating efficiency. Some observers hold that educational costs per student could be quickly reduced by a quarter or even a half by applying the principles of business management. It is also argued that to raise educational efficiency one needs only to raise the teaching loads of professors. There is, however, another approach which brings gains in cost effectiveness without any sacrifice in standards and possibly with improvement in educational quality.

The study explored the possibility of improving educational quality while reducing its cost. Focusing on undergraduate instruction in a hypothetical small liberal arts college of 1,200 students, six different educationally and economically promising modes of instruction were examined:

Conventional Plan   In which an instructor gives lectures and leads discussions, working with a small group of students who follow a common course outline, read the same books, write related papers, take identical examinations, and meet regularly in a classroom throughout a semester

Ruml Plan   In which large lecture courses are included in the schedule of classes, along with more traditional liberal arts college courses

Programmed Independent Study Plan   In which, unlike usual independent study, a carefully devised independent study program is followed by many students on roughly the same time schedule

Bakan Plan In which a highly compressed, relatively unstructured curriculum is featured, accompanied by extensive use of tutorials

Kieffer Plan In which courses are created so that students, assisted by modern teaching-learning equipment and instructors, can study at their own pace and convenience

Eclectic Plan In which certain features of all the other plans are used

To cost-out the alternative modes of instruction, some technical information is assembled and special accounting techniques are developed, among them assumptions about the "production" characteristics of key instructional inputs; certain methods of determining average unit "prices" of instructional inputs; and a delineation of the "standard curriculum," i.e., the particular profile of disciplines and courses which anchors this study and makes possible meaningful cost comparisons between teaching methods.

Determination of costs begins with the conventional plan. The study tests the sensitivity of its costs per course and per student to changes in faculty teaching loads, numbers of classes, total enrollments, the distribution of faculty ranks, and the disciplinary mix of classes. Each of these influences the costs of instruction in significant ways, and these factors alone could provide an abundant harvest of savings if they were manipulated in appropriate ways. Compared with the conventional plan, the Ruml Plan and the Programmed Independent Study Plan offer the possibility of reduced costs per student. The Bakan Plan, involving tutorials, tends to be rather more expensive. The Kieffer Plan, using mechanized teaching aids, is the least easy to make specific, and the range of possible costs is enormous. But institutions willing to make the necessary adjustments might find the plan entirely feasible within reasonable budget ranges.

These findings lead to the conclusion that liberal arts colleges might cut costs and at the same time improve instruction by simplifying their curricula and adopting a judicious mixture of educational methods.

This analysis shows that independent study in various forms as well as tutorials are economically feasible, and further, that substantial savings might be achieved through Ruml Plan lectures. It also demonstrates that great savings are possible through simplifying the curriculum and thus reducing the number of small classes. These findings lead to the conclusion that liberal arts colleges might cut costs and at the same time improve instruction by simplifying their curricula and adopting a judicious mixture of educational methods which we call an *Eclectic Plan.* Such a plan would include: a few large lecture courses common to all or most students; courses calling for programmed independent study either with or without learning stations and mechanical systems as in the Kieffer Plan; courses with emphasis on tutorials; and conventional classes. The possible combinations of these various plans are almost infinite; moreover, different methods could be used in various phases of any single course.

This is a useful approach to educational efficiency, but it leaves out some important considerations. The conclusions, therefore, are subject to several qualifications. There is more to educational efficiency than minimizing institutional cost per student for a given quality of education and a given number of students. The time and expense of students, the marginal product of educational expenditures, the caliber of the student body, the size of the institution, noninstructional expenditures, and the wealth of the institution must all be considered. These factors, however, in no way detract from the importance of trying to find less costly ways to operate colleges. They simply point out that there are many variables involved in educational efficiency.

(1971)

> There is more to educational efficiency than minimizing institutional cost per student for a given quality of education and a given number of students.

THE EFFECTIVENESS AND THE EFFECTS OF HIGHER EDUCATION*
JOSEPH BEN-DAVID

To compare systems of higher education in different countries, it is essential to be aware of the uses the countries make of their systems. The uses are well known: training of professionals; advancement of scholarship and science through research; development of the intellectual capacities of the students; raising of the general level of culture and social intelligence through advanced study; and promotion of social justice through the provision of a channel of mobility which can be controlled to ensure a socially equitable allocation of people to higher level occupational roles. But little is known about the effects of using higher education for these various purposes. The fact that an institution is used for certain purposes is no evidence that it is an effective means for attaining them. Furthermore, what may be an effective means under certain conditions may not be effective under other conditions.

The purpose of this book is to establish and document a conceptual framework for the comparative investigation of the principal present-day uses and effects of higher education.

The most widespread and most widely accepted function of higher education is training for the professions. An increasing number and range of occupations have become professionalized through the adoption of the requirement of a university diploma as a condition of entrance into them. This is justified by the argument that university education raises the stan-

---

* This abstract was prepared by the author before the final manuscript for his full report was completed.

dards of the professional services. Another advantage of the university training of professionals (particularly important in developing countries) is that it makes possible the implantation and the diffusion of such roles.

It is far from evident that the transfer of the seat of training from practical apprenticeship to formal study raises the standards of professional work.

But there are numerous limitations of the use of higher education for this purpose. It is far from evident that the transfer of the seat of training from practical apprenticeship to formal study raises the standards of professional work. In very few instances is the university capable of turning out practitioners who can actually do the job expected from them without further practical apprenticeship. It is also difficult to know what kinds of "basic" studies are directly or indirectly relevant to different kinds of professional practice. Finally, there is a basic dilemma in professional training: If it tries to be practically useful, it has to be specific, and graduates will have difficulty transferring to other occupations should either the market or their motivation change in the course of their studies. If, on the other hand, the training is broad, there is a danger that the student will acquire no real competence in anything.

Systems of higher education have dealt in a variety of ways with these problems. Some, like the United States, try to integrate practical training with university study very closely; others, like Britain and Germany, keep the two apart. In some countries (e.g., Italy) there is a general conception of professional training which applies to all the professions; in others (e.g., France) there are different conceptions guiding the training in different fields. There are also great differences in the importance attached to the integration of the training of professionals with research and to the way students are selected for professional studies.

As systems differ from each other in many respects, so do their results. Some produce technically excellent professionals, but may not produce them in sufficient numbers; some may devote major effort to the selection of an elite for the central civil service and for key positions in the economy, while others would consider this incompatible with the "proper" aims of higher education; some may do very well in the training for some of the professions, but rather poorly in the training for others; and finally, there may be differences between societies in the definition of the content and function of certain professional roles.

A relatively new function in the majority of higher educational systems is the education of students who have no clear professional or scholarly aims, but go to the university because of a variety of associated advantages, such as status and general maturation through social contacts and cultural experiences. There are obvious difficulties in devising curricula for this group of students, because of the heterogeneity of their purposes. It is also difficult to provide adequate teachers for this potentially or actually very large clientele.

The main difference, in this respect, between the various systems of higher education is the extent to which they are willing to deal with this problem deliberately and constructively, or insist on dealing with it within the traditional framework of professional or scholarly education, or denying its existence.

Systems which deal with the problem deliberately (the United States and Britain, for example) have ended up with a differentiated system which includes several levels and types of higher education. Those which try to deal with the problem in the traditional framework either force all students into specialized study (Eastern bloc countries), or admit them into ever larger universities where they are supposed to find their own way or drop out (Germany and Italy are examples). The last type seems to have been particularly conducive to unrest and political activism.

The integration of research with the teaching and training functions of the university is one of the perennial problems of higher education. Ideally, such integration should result in an innovative education through theoretically important research.

Institutions of higher education are also supposed to engage in original scientific and scholarly research. The integration of research with the teaching and training functions of the university is one of the perennial problems of higher education. Ideally, such integration should result in an innovative education through theoretically important research—which is the kind recommended for universities. The student who is taught by active researchers, and who participates in research himself, learns something which goes, at least potentially, beyond the existing traditions transmitted in other types of education. He is led to assimilate and discover theories which disclose the logical structure of natural or historical events, and cultural creations. Although something of this is also learned at the lower levels of education, only at the highest level is a student expected to attain a degree of active mastery of theories.

But such a program of innovative education can be carried out without undue difficulty only in the basic scientific disciplines. These fields of study are defined in terms of more or less coherent sets of theoretical approaches which can be handled by a single person.

There are other fields, however, such as the humanities and the social sciences (with the exception of economics), which are defined by substantive cultural or institutional content (e.g., medieval English literature or political science), and professional studies which are defined by practical interest. In all these studies, traditions have to be transmitted, but only a part (and occasionally a small part) of the traditions are amenable to proper theoretical treatment. Chaucer's *Canterbury Tales* cannot be reduced to a formula from which the original can be reproduced, and the differences between American, British, and French democracies can be understood only in a semi-intuitive way based on much reading and observation. And even the best-trained physician will have to rely a great deal on common sense and experience in charting a course of treatment for his patients.

In all these fields it is difficult to decide how to integrate research with teaching and training. Emphasis on the scientific approach may lead to the neglect of important parts of cultural and professional-technical traditions. The result may be impoverishment rather than improvement of the traditions.

Another problem arises from the fact that it is not easy to produce interesting new theories, and that many of those produced turn out to be wrong. This circumstance has different effects on different fields of study. In the basic natural sciences, and in the practical professions related to natural sciences, it simply leads to unpredictable oscillations between stagnation and growth in different fields.

The greatest difficulties arise in the social sciences. In this field it is almost impossible to make experiments and systematically test the validity of new theories; usually, those can be tested only in practice. This predisposes the social scientists to social experimentation with very shaky theories. Apart from the direct damage caused by many of these experiments, they also create a vested interest among social scientists in their experiments which precludes, or at any rate, makes very difficult, the objective evaluation of evidence and the rejection of false theories. This leads to self-destructing cycles in the integration of research with teaching in the social sciences. Discoveries or other favorable conditions which reinforce the motivation to create scientific theories end up in a proliferation of "ideologies" which prefer to falsify empirical evidence, rather than declare themselves false.

Although practically every system of higher education accepts the integration of teaching with research as an ideal, in actual fact they go about it in very different ways. In some countries, such as France and the U.S.S.R., integration consists mainly of a partial overlap between research and teaching personnel. This avoids most of the problems and makes possible the effective transmission of cultural and technical traditions with relatively limited theoretical content, but this occurs at the cost of reduced liveliness of research and fosters academic conservatism and rigidity.

On the other end are British, German, and some of the better American universities, which consider integration of research and teaching a necessary requisite of university study, irrespective of field. Their success in solving the problems noted above depends on their ability to select students and teachers interested in research and capable of doing it, and on the existence of complementary institutions, or institutional arrangements, for the transmission of other cultural and technical traditions. Some of the problems, such as integration of teaching and research in the social sciences without running the risk of making the field into an ideology, have not been treated with complete success anywhere.

Higher education, as education in general, has traditionally been considered a potential channel of social mobility. Lately, as a result of investigations showing that there has been relatively little upward mobility attributable to education, conscious efforts have been made to manipulate higher education so as to turn it into an effective means for the furtherance of social justice.

It seems that a distinction has to be made between different kinds of measures. The least problematic are those designed to remove barriers to both upward and downward educational mobility. These consist of admission purely on the basis of scholarly achievement and the granting of stipends to the needy. These measures are very effective in the initial reduction of inequalities, but in the long run they still leave considerable educational inequalities. There is, at present, no established knowledge about the ways and means to eliminate this residual inequality, and it is also not known what its cost is in terms of individual frustration and social loss. The prevailing assumption, that any differences between the educational attainment of youth from different socioeconomic classes, given equal ability as measured by tests, presents an acute social problem which needs urgent remedy, is questionable. Measured ability is only one of the conditions of education; the other important psychological condition is motivation, which is usually not measured. Also, higher education is not the only channel of mobility, and it is not clear that every person above a certain level of intelligence should be expected and encouraged to go to a college or university.

The effects of measures designed to manipulate higher education in order to use it as a mechanism for the active encouragement of social mobility are much more doubtful. Essentially, these consist of discrimination in favor of groups (blacks, women, etc.) whose educational attainments are lower than desirable by some social criteria. It is conceivable that under certain conditions positive discrimination may be a useful temporary device, especially if it is made sure that those benefiting from it are not unrepresentative of the population whose situation is to be improved, and to the extent that it is combined with other measures (e.g., special coaching) to ensure that those admitted on such a discriminatory basis are able to complete their studies with educational attainments comparable to those of other students.

But such measures are easily abused. Instead of serving the long-term

Lately, as a result of investigations showing that there has been relatively little upward mobility attributable to education, conscious efforts have been made to manipulate higher education so as to turn it into an effective means for the furtherance of social justice.

purpose of improving the situation of a large oppressed group, such discrimination can be used by a subgroup to obtain ascriptive privileges for token representatives of the oppressed group.

Universities have also been used recently for the furtherance of social justice in still another way. Professors in the majority of higher educational systems have certain guildlike privileges which are open to abuse. Where there is abuse, those who suffer from it are the junior academic staff and the students. Attempts at the abolishment of the abuse often take the form of extending the unjust privileges to junior staff and students, thereby transforming an elite privilege of limited social significance into a class privilege with potentially far-reaching political effects.

Finally, an attempt is made to show that the cycles of rapid development of higher education, followed by disappointments and alienation among students and academics and the politicization of the university, are related to the problems analyzed here. Because of the concentration of large numbers of unattached young adults, institutions of higher education can become centers of political activity under conditions of general political tension without any relation to what goes on inside the institutions. But serious unsolved problems within the system of higher education are likely to turn the universities into centers from which political unrest originates.

It is unlikely, however, that the present situation, whereby political activism and ideological indoctrination have become major functions of universities in many countries, is going to lead to the emergence of a new type of higher education. In systems of higher education which have been most successful in creating new and diverse academic structures to cope with the emerging situation, such as those of the United States, Canada, Britain, and some other countries, the trend toward the politicization of higher education seems to have abated. On the other hand, attempts to accept politicization as one of the facts of university life, and to institutionalize it through turning the university into an elective quasi republic, such as was done in France, Germany, Holland, and the Scandinavian countries, have failed to move the system in new directions. Unrest and educational inefficiency have become endemic in the politicized universities, or in the politicized parts of the universities, and there has been a strengthening of alternative nonpolitical institutions of research and advanced training.

(1975)

THE PURPOSES OF HIGHER EDUCATION

CHAPTER

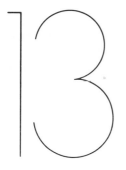

13

The purposes of higher education have evolved and changed substantially in the course of American history, but not since the last half of the nineteenth century, around 1870, have they been comprehensively redirected. We may now be at another point where great redirection is taking place. And the nature of the changes that should be made is subject to extensive debate.

Heinz Eulau and Harold Quinley were requested by the Commission to provide an assessment of the expectations which influential men and women who must assume responsibilities for public higher education hold for colleges and universities. The results, in *State Officials and Higher Education,* give rise to some optimism, for the policy makers, in the nine states surveyed in 1968, retain their faith in higher education despite its recent and current difficulties.

Oscar and Mary Handlin's essay, *The American College and American Culture,* traces the history of one of the oldest of all functions of colleges—the socialization of youth. In the process they remind us, once again, how closely tied to American culture the American college has always been. The essay, coming at a time of widespread social and cultural change, strongly suggests that the time may have come for a conscious reappraisal of the validity of the socialization function, and of what it means in the waning decades of the twentieth century.

STATE OFFICIALS AND HIGHER EDUCATION: A Survey of the Opinions and Expectations of Policy Makers in Nine States
HEINZ EULAU and HAROLD QUINLEY

Legislators' attitudes toward higher education are crucial in a nation where 70 percent of all college and university students attend publicly supported institutions. To learn whether state officials are generally satisfied with higher education and how they appraise its prospects and problems, extensive interviews were conducted in nine states.

States located in the various main geographic regions of the country were chosen. Some have large, complex systems of higher education (California, Texas, Illinois, New York, and Pennsylvania), and some possess less complex systems (Iowa, Kansas, Kentucky, and Louisiana). Legislators and executive officials most intimately connected with higher education, such as chairmen of education and finance committees and floor leaders, were interviewed.

The great contrasts and diversity of regional America—in economic development, social and ethnic stratification, political structure, and popular attitudes—are reflected in the goals which the states set for their colleges and universities, and in the institutions' ability to achieve them.

States with unfavorable political environments, little executive or administrative talent, or small tax bases are likely to find it difficult to achieve many of their educational goals.

States with unfavorable political environments, little executive or administrative talent, or small tax bases are likely to find it difficult to achieve many of their educational goals. A state without some type of centralized coordinating body for higher education may be unable to utilize its resources effectively and efficiently. A state with a politically controlled governing board for higher education may be unable to shield its schools from partisan conflict.

Often of key importance is the idiosyncratic influence of personality. In a number of states surveyed—New York, Texas, and Iowa, for example—an energetic and capable governor was credited with large-scale innovations and improvements in higher education. In at least one other state, a governor had emerged who was trying to reduce the university's budget and influence. Thus individual leadership can be as great a factor in successful higher education as social, economic, or political "givens."

Most officials, it appeared, thought "things" had been going well in their states; each compared his own state's educational system favorably with those in other states. Even so, certain differentiating patterns emerged. Officials from the smaller, less wealthy states seemed more contented with their public colleges and universities—despite the admitted superiority of higher education in the larger, more wealthy states. Paradoxically, while respondents from California and New York recognized their own leadership in higher education, they were generally less optimistic about the situation and saw greater problems in the future. They even suggested that the problems of recent years might outweigh the gains.

Positive appraisals typically were expressed in terms of increased appropriations.

Positive appraisals typically were expressed in terms of increased appropriations. For example, a Texas legislator said: "Well, in the last four years, the state appropriations have doubled. So I would say that we are making very forward steps toward progress." Most Texans seemed to feel that higher education had been doing exceptionally well in the past five years and that, as one respondent put it, Texas "is now in a position to develop a higher educational system second to none in the nation." A colleague said, "The expenditures have gone up some 200 percent in the state of Texas over the last few years. . . . We certainly recognized that education is the solution to many, many problems."

Legislators in Kentucky, Illinois, Iowa, and Kansas generally offered similar comments. Improvements in educational quality, physical facilities, and faculty salaries were cited. A Kansas respondent felt that his state's universities were among the best in the nation and that the junior colleges were quite good.

It was clear that many regarded California and New York as the leaders, and the consensus of New York respondents was that their colleges and universities were rapidly catching up to those in California. They were pleased with the development. A number of California respondents agreed that their state was losing ground to New York. Typical of several remarks: "I think we're number one, but New York is catching up with us. In the next five years we will be number two. . . . At the rate we're going, we will not be able to keep up. We're going to have to be cutting back. Instead of talking about growing in California with population demands, we are talking about backpedaling."

While the majority of state officials were satisfied with their state's progress in higher education, most also felt that serious problems remained unsolved—mainly in financing, planning and coordination, rising enrollments, and student unrest. One pervasive dilemma mentioned by legislators was a lack of relevant information about their colleges and universities—and in many cases, not so much the sheer absence of knowledge as incomplete or inaccurate information.

Paradoxically, these malfunctions of the information system are to some extent built into the legislative process. It is sometimes said that the politician hears with a "third ear," but this ear can be and often is a deceptive organ—hearing what it wants to hear, selecting, screening, distorting, and omitting. It cannot do otherwise; the constraints of the representational process make it so. But the great variety and complexity of the issues, the inexorable pressure of deadlines for action, and the need to respond to political demands regardless of their soundness, make the use of information, even when it is available, extremely difficult.

Most respondents indicated, however, that the public did not demand much information from them on higher education and that the subject had low political salience. One legislator said: "We hear from the voters only about the [secondary] schools; damn near don't hear from anybody about higher education. . . ." The average citizen felt a need to become involved in higher education only when something relevant to him occurred: the inability of his child to get into college, a highly publicized student demonstration, or perhaps a tax increase directly related to education. Although the interviews were conducted prior to the disorders at Columbia University in spring 1968, complaints about student demonstrations reported in the mass media were reaching legislators. In this connection at least, legislators tended to fear the people's voice.

Insofar as matters of control were concerned, most legislators felt that—aside from the built-in controls of the funding process—it would be improper for them to get entangled in decisions on higher education.

A number of California respondents agreed that their state was losing ground to New York.

One pervasive dilemma mentioned by legislators was a lack of relevant information about their colleges and universities—and in many cases, not so much the sheer absence of knowledge as incomplete or inaccurate information.

The average citizen felt a need to become involved in higher education only when something relevant to him occurred: the inability of his child to get into college, a highly publicized student demonstration, or perhaps a tax increase directly related to education.

These they preferred to leave to the relevant executive agencies or to the universities themselves.

The authors found that legislators generally had:

■ A great faith in higher education, evidenced by a tripling of expenditures over the past decade

■ An awareness that parent-constituents want educational opportunities for their children

■ An interstate competitiveness for prestigious colleges and universities as a major factor of progress

■ Strong support for public service activities of colleges and universities

■ A favorable attitude toward long-range planning and centralized coordination to make the best use of resources for education

■ A welcoming approach to federal aid, with a preference that it be spent through state governments

■ Strong support for community colleges

■ A cautious attitude toward state support for private colleges and universities

■ A substantial degree of understanding of student dissent, but a clear preference for dealing with it firmly

(1970)

THE AMERICAN COLLEGE AND AMERICAN CULTURE: Socialization as a Function of Higher Education
OSCAR HANDLIN and MARY F. HANDLIN

The role of socialization as a factor in shaping the actual forms of higher education in the United States has frequently been obscured. Although concerns with religion, professional training, and the possibilities of social mobility have been present through much of the 300-year history of the colleges and universities, other factors also have affected the development of such institutions. Young men—and later women—sought them out for education in the more general sense of adjustment to society. Precisely how the process of socialization operated depended not only on the college but also upon the changing structure of society and the changing conception the individual held of himself. These elements passed through radical alterations.

In the last third of the nineteenth century, for example, the universities changed drastically under the impact of shifts in the social order connected with industrialization. They were influenced too by changes in the kinds of people whose children went to college.

Traditionally, American society lacked the gentry class which, in England, sent its sons to the university and also provided the means of its support. The colonial families with aristocratic pretensions, like the Byrds and Delanceys, were few in number and, if they were interested in higher education, were as likely as not to ship their boys off to the mother country. The American colleges were by no means egalitarian; they gave ample recognition to social distinctions. Family status, along with other factors, influenced the order in class at Harvard and was also deferred to elsewhere. Nevertheless, there never appeared the separation accepted at Oxford and Cambridge between gentlemen and commoners or between earned and pass degrees. The intention may have been present, but the social realities did not permit its implementation.

As one result, university resources remained meager. President Chauncy of Harvard complained in the 1660s of the wealthy who waxed fat yet refused to support learning. A century later, President Witherspoon of Princeton appealed to pulpits throughout the colonies in the effort to extinguish the college debt. There were few generous donors; £550 was so extraordinary a gift that Elihu Yale, who made it, was immortalized in the name of the college which benefited from it. He, like the other great benefactors of these years, was an Englishman rather than a colonial.

In the last analysis, the universities depended for survival on student fees. And to persuade young men and their parents that education was worth payment of the price, the colleges had to assume functions only tangentially related to the purposes stated in their charters. The American universities increasingly edged toward a concept of education which involved training in proper behavior, unrelated to vocational goals. The prerequisite for admission to the bar, for example, was a period of reading and service, not in college but in a lawyer's office.

Liberal education, training in proper manners of action and thought, had a clear—although not always perceived—link with gentlemanly ideals. The connection emerged in the fear expressed by one friend of universities lest learning "become cheap and too common" so that "every man would be for giving his son an education." It was also perceived by a hostile critic, young Benjamin Franklin, who, in *The New England Courant,* accused Harvard of being a refuge of wealthy young men, "where, for want of a suitable Genius, they learn little more than how to carry themselves handsomely, and enter a Room genteely."

No sooner was Harvard established than parents perceived its potential

---

The American colleges were by no means egalitarian; they gave ample recognition to social distinctions. Family status, along with other factors, influenced the order in class at Harvard and was also deferred to elsewhere. Nevertheless, there never appeared the separation accepted at Oxford and Cambridge between gentlemen and commoners or between earned and pass degrees.

The American universities increasingly edged toward a concept of education which involved training in proper behavior, unrelated to vocational goals.

as an asylum for 14- or 15-year-old sons who were idle, disobedient, or too much interested in plantation sports. By 1651, there were complaints against men who presumed "to send their most exorbitant children" to the Cambridge institution. Yet the inclination to do so increased with the passage of time, and discipline sometimes seemed to be the main business of the college.

President Eaton, wrote William Hubbard (class of 1642), was "fitter to have been an officer in the inquisition, or master of an house of correction, than an instructor of Christian youth." Often he had to be! Compulsory attendance at chapel; fixed schedules of daily life; regulations about dress, common meals, and strict oversight of conduct and pastimes were among the methods of inculcating proper habits of behavior.

Again and again, the lads had to be punished for intoxication and carousing, for shooting or stealing turkeys, geese, and other fowl, for the atrocious crime of committing fornication, and for other varieties of abominable lasciviousness. The students were difficult to control for they knew that, in town, the lads and wenches met to drink and dance and were altogether brazen about it. One of them, in 1676–77, had reminded his elders that if there was a war to be fought, "it must be the young men that must do it" and threatened "to burne the towne over their eares" if his personal life were interfered with. Sometimes disobedience flared out into unrestrained riots, the best-known of which was the Harvard food rebellion of 1766.

By 1870 some 500 institutions were awarding bachelor's degrees to aspiring scholars—a total larger than that in all of Europe. Almost as dramatic was the apparent multiplication in the types of institutions. The old colleges became private corporations. These were joined by a variety of newer sectarian institutions and by state universities. Analysis of the connection between the social milieu and the proliferation of colleges shows that the multiplication of these institutions was not simply in response to demand. Growth was rather a reaction to complex impulses and it raised serious questions, then as in the future, about the function of the university.

After the Revolution, a learned magistracy and an informed populace seemed to some citizens more important than ever before. Jefferson envisaged the university as the capstone of a complete educational system which would train each man for a role in society appropriate to his ability. The belief that education advanced the prosperity of society added another dimension to the argument in behalf of colleges. In time, educators would establish a link between economic development and "the intellectual improvement of a people."

Through the centuries, as one activity after another was officially assimilated into the college catalogue and the academic framework, the areas in which undergraduates were left alone to manage matters in their own way, by themselves, narrowed. It became difficult for a young man or woman to conceive of reading a book or playing the cymbals or making a movie without somehow receiving credit for it. By 1960, students, having become totally dependent upon the curriculum, naturally found themselves dissatisfied with it.

It became difficult for a young man or woman to conceive of reading a book or playing the cymbals or making a movie without somehow receiving credit for it. By 1960, students, having become totally dependent upon the curriculum, naturally found themselves dissatisfied with it.

The massive infusion of federal funds into higher education after Sputnik had precedents, although it thereafter operated on a scale larger than before. Enrollments more than doubled between 1960 and 1969, rising to more than 7 million. Education became a growth industry and the information business edged into the province that had formerly been monopolized by the library and the laboratory. Yet at the same time the university was still expected by society to provide a site for socializing an army of young people.

Through all its transformations, the university has also been the home of men for whom learning—the pursuit of truth—was an end in itself.

From generation to generation, however, through all its transformations, the university has also been the home of men for whom learning—the pursuit of truth—was an end in itself and for whom the service of rearing the young was the price paid for the tolerance to pursue their own interests. For the future, a significant question will certainly be the extent to which the obligation of socialization will remain compatible with scholarship.

(1970)

NOTES ABOUT THE AUTHORS

ACKERMAN, JAMES S.

Content and Context: Essays on College Education, contributor, p. 69. James Ackerman is professor of fine arts at Harvard University, having previously been on the faculty of the University of California, Berkeley, and Slade Professor of Fine Arts at Cambridge University. Professor Ackerman holds a doctorate from New York University and an L.H.D. and D.F.A. from Kenyon College and the Maryland Institute, respectively.

ADKINS, DOUGLAS LEE

The Great American Degree Machine, p. 227; *Higher Education and the Labor Market,* contributor, p. 222; *Demand and Supply in U.S. Higher Education,* contributor, p. 50. Douglas Adkins is assistant professor of economics in the graduate school of business administration at New York University. A graduate of the University of California, Berkeley, Professor Adkins is also a 1974 recipient of a doctoral degree from that institution.

ALTBACH, PHILIP G.

Higher Education in Nine Countries: A Comparative Study of College and Universities Abroad, contributor, p. 24; *Academic Transformation: Seventeen Institutions Under Pressure,* contributor, p. 125. Philip Altbach has been on the faculty of the University of Wisconsin, Madison, since 1968 and is currently associate professor of educational policy studies and South Asian studies. Professor Altbach received his Ph.D. from the University of Chicago and has been a Fulbright research professor in India and the recipient of research grants from the Ford Foundation and the United States–Indian Comparative Exchange Program.

ANDERSON, C. ARNOLD

Where Colleges Are and Who Attends: Effects of Accessibility on College Attendance, coauthor, p. 169. Arnold Anderson has been a professor of education and sociology at the University of Chicago since 1958 and director of the university's Comparative Education Center from then until 1972. He received his Ph.D. from the University of Minnesota and has been a member of the faculty at the University of Kentucky, Iowa State University, and Harvard. He has been a recipient of a Fulbright research grant and recently (1973–74) has been a visiting professor of education at the University of Stockholm.

ASHBY, ERIC

Any Person, Any Study: An Essay on Higher Education in the United States, p. 19. Sir Eric Ashby, a member of the Carnegie Commission on Higher Education, is master of Clare College, University of Cambridge, and deputy vice-chancellor of the university. He received his D.Sc. from London University and is a Fellow of the Royal Society of London. He has been president and vice-chancellor of Queen's University of Belfast and head of the Department of Botany at the University of Manchester and the University of Sydney.

ASTIN, ALEXANDER WILLIAM

The Invisible Colleges: A Profile of Small, Private Colleges with Limited Resources, coauthor, p. 88. Currently professor of education at the University of California, Los Angeles, and formerly director of the American Council on Education's Office of Research, Alexander Astin was educated at Gettysburg College and then at the University of Maryland, from which he received a Ph.D. He has been program director and director of research of the National Merit Scholarship Corporation and assistant chief, Psychological Research Unit, of the Veterans Administration Hospital, Baltimore.

AUSSIEKER, BILL

Faculty Bargaining: Change and Conflict, contributor, p. 280. Bill Aussieker is assistant professor in the department of administration at California State College, San Bernardino, and a doctoral candidate at the University of California, Berkeley, where he was a research assistant in the Institute of Business and Economic Research.

BAILEY, STEPHEN KEMP

The University as an Organization, contributor, p. 257. Stephen Bailey is vice-president of the American Council on Education. He has previously served as chairman of the Policy Institute of the Syracuse University Research Corporation and Maxwell Professor of Political Science, of the university's Maxwell Graduate School of Citizenship and Public Affairs. A Rhodes Scholar, he holds a Ph.D. from Harvard University, and among other academic posts, has been William Osborn Professor of Public Affairs and director of the graduate program in the Woodrow Wilson School of Public and International Affairs at Princeton. In addition to holding positions at the state and federal levels, Professor Bailey has been mayor of Middleton, Connecticut and is a past president of the American Society for Public Administration.

BALDERSTON, FREDERICK EMERY

Demand and Supply in U.S. Higher Education, contributor, p. 50. Frederick Balderston is professor of business administration, chairman of the Center for Research in Management Science at the University of California, Berkeley, and part-time academic assistant to the president of the University of California. Holder of a Ph.D. from Princeton University, Professor Balderston has served as vice-president for planning and analysis at the University of California, Berkeley.

BARRO, STEPHEN M.

The Emerging Technology: Instructional Uses of the Computer in Higher Education, contributor, p. 142. Stephen Barro has been senior economist in the resource analysis department of The Rand Corporation since 1964. He holds a Ph.D. from Stanford University.

BEATON, ALBERT EUGENE

Education, Income, and Human Behavior, contributor, p. 219. Albert Beaton, director of the Educational Testing Service's Office of Data Analysis Research and visiting lecturer at Princeton University since 1966, was formerly director of the Statistical Laboratory of Harvard University. Dr. Beaton holds an Ed.D. from Harvard.

BELL, COLIN ELDERKIN

Papers on Efficiency in the Management of Higher Education, coauthor, p. 304. Colin Bell is an assistant professor in the Graduate School of Administration at the University of California, Irvine. He did undergraduate and graduate work in statistics at the University of California, Berkeley, and received a Ph.D. in Administrative Sciences from Yale University.

BEN-DAVID, JOSEPH

American Higher Education: Directions Old and New, p. 9; *The Effectiveness and the Effects of Higher Education,* p. 314. Joseph Ben-David is a professor of sociology at the Hebrew University of Jerusalem, where he also took his M.A. and Ph.D. He has been a Fellow at the Center for Advanced Studies in the Behavioral Sciences, Stanford, California, and a consultant on Science Policy and Higher Education to the OECD, Paris.

BESSE, RALPH MOORE

The University as an Organization, contributor, p. 257. Ralph Besse is a practicing attorney and partner in the firm of Squire, Sanders & Dempsey, Cleveland, and a member of the Carnegie Commission on Higher Education. In addition to having held a number of important posts in industry—among them, president and then chairman of the board of the Cleveland Electric Illuminating Co. and director of American Airlines, Inc., and the Cleveland Trust Co.—he has acted as trustee for several colleges and universities. Mr. Besse has served as chairman of the Cleveland Commission on Higher Education, and as a member of the National Advisory Committee on Junior Colleges, the Ohio Community College Board. He has been vice-president and secretary of the Education Research Council.

BILORUSKY, JOHN ALAN

May 1970: The Campus Aftermath of Cambodia and Kent State, coauthor, p. 273.   John Bilorusky is an assistant professor of urban affairs and a senior research associate at the university's Institute for Research and Training, University of Cincinnati. Professor Bilorusky has been a researcher at the Center for Research and Development in Higher Education at the University of California, Berkeley.

BIRNBAUM, NORMAN

Content and Context: Essays on College Education, contributor, p. 69. Professor of sociology at Amherst College, Norman Birnbaum has held posts at the London School of Economics and Political Science; Nuffield College, Oxford University; the University of Strasbourg; and the New School for Social Research. Professor Birnbaum received his Ph.D. from Harvard University.

BLACKWELL, FREDERICK W.

The Emerging Technology: Instructional Uses of the Computer in Higher Education, contributor, p. 142.   Frederick Blackwell is a member of the research staff of The Rand Corporation. Formerly a member of the technical staff of TRW Systems, he holds a master's degree in mathematics from Stanford University and is currently a doctoral candidate in computer science at the University of Southern California.

BLOLAND, HARLAND GEORGE

American Learned Societies in Transition: The Impact of Dissent and Recession, coauthor, p. 119.   Harland Bloland is an associate professor of higher education at Teachers College, Columbia University. A graduate of the University of Wisconsin, he took a master's degree at the University of Connecticut and a Ph.D. at the University of California, Berkeley, where he was a postgraduate research sociologist at the Center for Research and Development in Higher Education. Professor Bloland has taught educational administration at New York University.

BLOLAND, SUE MARIAN

American Learned Societies in Transition: The Impact of Dissent and Recession, coauthor, p. 119.   Sue Bloland was graduated from Oberlin College and currently is a graduate student in sociology at the New School for Social Research, New York.

BLUMBERG, MARK STUART

Trends and Projections of Physicians in the United States 1967–2002, p. 199.   Dr. Blumberg graduated from Harvard Medical School and is currently Corporate Planning Advisor for the Kaiser Foundation Health Plan. He has been director of Health Planning at the University of California, Berkeley, and director of Health Economics at the Stanford Research Institute.

BOGARD, LAWRENCE MILLER

Papers on Efficiency in the Management of Higher Education, coauthor, p. 304.   Lawrence Bogard is assistant to the Vice-Chancellor for Academic Affairs at the University of California, Irvine. A colonel in the U.S. Air Force until 1967, he was director of Resource Planning for the Air Force Systems Command and has concentrated on the development of management information systems and organization. He has an M.S. in administration from the University of California, Irvine.

BOWEN, FRANK M.

The Multicampus University: A Study of Academic Governance, coauthor, p. 261.   A West Point graduate with a J.D. from the University of Michigan Law School, Frank Bowen is currently completing a doctoral program in higher education at the University of California, Berkeley, where he is also a research specialist at the Center for Research and Development in Higher Education and a specialist with the Institute of Governmental Studies. He has been a practicing attorney in his own law firm and a consultant to the California State Department of Finance.

BOWEN, HOWARD ROTHMANN

Efficiency in Liberal Education: A Study of Comparative Instructional Costs for Different Ways of Organizing Teaching-Learning in a Liberal Arts College, coauthor, p. 312; *The Finance of Higher Education,* p. 238. Chancellor of the Claremont University Center and professor in the Claremont Graduate School since 1969, Howard Bowen has been, successively, dean of the College of Commerce, University of Illinois; president of Grinnell College; and president of the University of Iowa. Chancellor Bowen was graduated from Washington State University and received his Ph.D. from the University of Iowa.

BOWEN, WILLIAM GORDON

The Economics of the Major Private Universities, p. 249.   William Bowen became president of Princeton University in 1972, after having been director of graduate studies in the university's Woodrow Wilson School and provost of the university. President Bowen was graduated from Denison University and received his Ph.D. from Princeton, where he is also professor of Economics and Public Affairs.

BOWLES, FRANK HAMILTON

Between Two Worlds: A Profile of Negro Higher Education, coauthor, p. 75.   Frank Bowles has most recently been visiting professor at Macquarie University, New South Wales, Australia. As project specialist with the Ford Foundation, Professor Bowles was academic vice-president of the Haile Selassie I University in Ethiopia, and among other positions, he has been president of the College Entrance Examination Board and director of university admissions at Columbia University.

BOWMAN, MARY JEAN

Where Colleges Are and Who Attends: Effects of Accessibility on College Attendance, coauthor, p. 169.   Professor in the departments of economics and education at the University of Chicago, Mary Bowman has been, variously, with the U.S. Department of Labor and Agriculture, on the faculty of Iowa State University as teacher and research economist, and a visiting faculty member at the University of California, Berkeley, and the University of Minnesota. Professor Bowman received her Ph.D. from Harvard.

BRADSHAW, TED K.

Teachers and Students: Aspects of American Higher Education, contributor, p. 34. Ted Bradshaw, formerly an instructor at the University of Vermont, is presently with the Institute of Governmental Studies of the University of California, Berkeley, the institution from which he received his Ph.D.

BROWNLEE, HELEN EVE

Papers on Efficiency in the Management of Higher Education, coauthor, p. 304. Helen Brownlee is a graduate trainee in the Australian Government Department of Labour. She has a master's degree from La Trobe University, Melbourne, Australia; her thesis was a sociological study of Americans in Melbourne. Ms. Brownlee was previously a research assistant at the University of California, Irvine, Medical School.

BURN, BARBARA BRADY

Higher Education in Nine Countries: A Comparative Study of Colleges and Universities Abroad, principal author, p. 24; *The University as an Organization,* contributor, p. 357. Barbara Burn is director of the Office of International Programs at the University of Massachusetts, Amherst. Dr. Burn, who holds a Ph.D. from the Fletcher School of Law and Diplomacy, has formerly held such posts as professor of international law and staff political scientist in the Foreign Service Institute, program specialist with the Asia Foundation, and staff associate of the Carnegie Commission.

CARTTER, ALLAN M.

The Ph.D. and the Academic Labor Market, p. 226; *Higher Education and the Labor Market,* contributor, p. 222. Allan Cartter is Professor-in-Residence in the School of Education at the University of California, Los Angeles. Professor Cartter received his Ph.D. from Yale University and has been, variously, dean of the graduate school at Duke University, chancellor of New York University, vice-president of the American Council on Education, and senior research fellow with the Carnegie Commission on Higher Education. He has held numerous professional offices, among them: editor of *The Educational Record,* chairman of the Association of Graduate Schools Committee on International Education, and chairman of the Department of Labor Committee on Scientific and Professional Manpower.

CHEIT, EARL F.

The Useful Arts and the Liberal Tradition, p. 68; *The New Depression in Higher Education: A Study of 41 Colleges and Universities,* p. 291; *The New Depression in Higher Education—Two Years Later,* p. 296. Currently associate director of the Carnegie Council on Policy Studies in Higher Education and professor of business administration and higher education at the University of California, Berkeley, Professor Cheit recently served as program officer in charge of higher education and research at the Ford Foundation and, prior to that time, as executive vice-chancellor at the University of California. He holds two degrees in law and a Ph.D. in economics from the University of Minnesota.

CLARK, BURTON R.

Academic Transformation: Seventeen Institutions Under Pressure, contributor, p. 124. Professor of sociology at Yale University and formerly head of the department, Burton Clark's major publications have dealt with a spectrum of institutions of higher education—from the junior college to the distinctive college. Professor Clark, who holds a Ph.D. from the University of California, Los Angeles, was previously a research sociologist at the Center for Research and Development in Higher Education, Berkeley.

COBLE, JO ANNE

A Degree and What Else?: Correlates and Consequences of a College Education, contributor, p. 216. Jo Anne Coble is a former staff member of the Institute for Social Research at the University of Michigan.

COHEN, MICHAEL DWIGHT

Leadership and Ambiguity: The American College President, coauthor, p. 265. Michael Cohen is an assistant professor of political science at the University of Michigan. His doctorate is from the University of California, Irvine, and he was an NSF-SSRC postdoctoral fellow at Stanford University.

COLEMAN, JAMES SAMUEL

Content and Context: Essays on College Education, contributor, p. 69. James Coleman recently became University Professor in the department of sociology of the University of Chicago, after having been in the department of social relations at Johns Hopkins University from 1959–1973.

Professor Coleman, who received his Ph.D. from Columbia University, has been a fellow at the Center for Advanced Study in the Behavioral Sciences, at Stanford University.

CONWAY, JILL KATHRYN

Academic Transformation: Seventeen Institutions Under Pressure, contributor, p. 124.   Jill Conway, president-elect of Smith College, is currently associate professor of history and vice-president for internal affairs at the University of Toronto. A graduate of the University of Sydney, N.S.W., Australia, Professor Conway holds a Ph.D. from Harvard University and has been appointed to such professional posts as historian member of the committee of the American Academy of Arts and Sciences that analyzed the problems of higher education in industrial societies, member of the editorial board of the *Journal of Social History,* and 1972–73 chairwoman of the CAUT Committee on the Status of Academic Women.

COMSTOCK, GEORGE A.

The Emerging Technology: Instructional Uses of the Computer in Higher Education, contributor, p. 142.   George Comstock is a member of the professional staff of The Rand Corporation. Formerly at the Institute for Communication Research at Stanford University, the institution from which he received his Ph.D., Dr. Comstock has also been assistant professor in the journalism department at New York University and senior research coordinator and science advisor for the U.S. Surgeon General's Scientific Advisory Committee on Television and Social Behavior.

CORSON, JOHN J.

The University as an Organization, contributor, p. 257.   John J. Corson has served as a consultant to such clients as the government of Tanzania, the U.S. Office of Education, the Children's Television Workshop, and the American Council on Education, as well as individual institutions of higher education. As part of extensive experience in industry, education, and government, he has served—among other posts—as chairman of Fry Consultants, Inc., special adviser to John W. Gardner while the latter was Secretary of HEW, director of McKinsey and Company, Inc., and professor of public and international affairs at Princeton. Dr. Corson is currently trustee of Marymount College, the Chicago Medical School, George Mason University, the Salzburg (Austria) Seminar in American Studies, the Institute for Court Management, and the Wolf Trap Foundation.

DALGLISH, THOMAS KILLIN

The University as an Organization, contributor, p. 257. Thomas Dalglish is an associate research specialist at the Center for Research in Management Science, University of California, Berkeley. Formerly assistant attorney general and then special assistant attorney general for the state of Washington, Mr. Dalglish, a graduate of the University of Michigan Law School, has also been assistant to the president of Central Washington State College, a lecturer in political science, and a researcher at the Center for Research and Development in Higher Education, University of California, Berkeley.

DeBAGGIS, AGOSTINO MICHAEL

Education for the Professions of Medicine, Law, Theology, and Social Welfare, coauthor, p. 59. Agostino DeBaggis is associate director for community services of the West-Ros-Park Mental Health Center (Boston State Hospital). A graduate of St. John's Seminary, Brighton, Massachusetts, with a master's degree from Boston College, he was a clergyman from 1968 to 1969.

DeCOSTA, FRANK AUGUSTUS

Between Two Worlds: A Profile of Negro Higher Education, coauthor, p. 75. The late Frank DeCosta was dean of the graduate school at Morgan State College, Baltimore, Maryland, at the time of his death. He had previously been head of the department of education at Alabama State College, dean of the graduate school at South Carolina State College, and statistical officer, Ministry of Education, Kaduna, Northern Nigeria. Professor DeCosta held a doctorate in education from the University of Pennsylvania, and was the recipient of a number of honors, among them: vice-president of the Southern Association of Colleges and Secondary Schools for Negroes and the 1964 Meritorious Honor Award of the United States Agency for International Development.

DOTY, PAUL

Content and Context: Essays on College Education, contributor, p. 69. Paul Doty is Mallinckrodt Professor of Biochemistry at Harvard. Since 1959 he has also worked in arms control and nuclear strategy (President's Scientific Advisory Committee, Consultant to the Arms Control and Disarmament Agency and the National Security Council), in initiating Soviet-American scientific exchanges, in Pugwash Conferences, in international studies of arms control, and in other science advisory roles

(Committee on Science and Public Policy of the National Academy of Science and Advisory Committee on Planning for the National Science Foundation).

DOUGLASS, GORDON KLENE

Efficiency in Liberal Education: A Study of Comparative Instructional Costs for Different Ways of Organizing Teaching-Learning in a Liberal Arts College, coauthor, p. 312. Gordon Douglass is head of the economics department of Pomona College and Elden Smith Professor of Economics at the college and the Claremont Graduate School. Professor Douglass holds a doctorate from the Massachusetts Institute of Technology, and has been chief economist for the Sylvania Electric Products, Inc., manager of its Financial and Operations Analysis, and research director of the Southern California Research Council.

DUNHAM, E. ALDEN

Colleges of the Forgotten Americans: A Profile of State Colleges and Regional Universities, p. 94. An executive associate of the Carnegie Corporation of New York, E. Alden Dunham holds a master's degree from Harvard University and a doctorate from Columbia University. He was an assistant to James B. Conant in his study of the American high school and subsequently was director of admissions at Princeton University.

DUNN, JOHN AINSWORTH, JR.

Academic Transformation: Seventeen Institutions Under Pressure, contributor, p. 124. John Dunn is assistant to the president of Tufts University. A graduate of Wesleyan University with a master's degree in education from Harvard, Mr. Dunn has held various positions in industry, including that of vice-president of Armetac, S.A.C.I. (Argentina).

DURYEA, EDWIN D., JR.

The University as an Organization, contributor, p. 257. Edwin Duryea is professor of higher education at the State University of New York at Buffalo. Among other academic posts, he has been chairman of the program in higher education at Syracuse University and dean of the graduate program at Hofstra University. Professor Duryea, who holds an Ed.D. in higher education from Stanford University, has acted as specialist or consultant to the National Commission on Accrediting (chairman of the advisory committee), to the Dominican Republic and Paraguay, and to the U.S. Office of Education.

ECKAUS, RICHARD S.

Estimating the Returns to Education: A Disaggregated Approach, p. 206; *Higher Education and the Labor Market,* contributor, p. 222. Richard Eckaus is professor of economics at the Massachusetts Institute of Technology, the university from which he received his Ph.D. He has taught at Brandeis University and been a member of the Board of Economic Advisers to the Governor of Massachusetts.

EHRLICH, ISAAC

Education, Income, and Human Behavior, contributor, p. 219. Isaac Ehrlich is associate professor of business economics at the University of Chicago and a research associate of the National Bureau of Economic Research. A graduate of the Hebrew University of Jerusalem, Professor Ehrlich holds a Ph.D. in economics from Columbia University.

EHRLICH, THOMAS

New Directions in Legal Education, coauthor, p. 152. Dean and professor of law at the Stanford Law School, Stanford University, Thomas Ehrlich has been Special Assistant to the Under Secretary of State and Special Assistant to the Legal Adviser in the Department of State. Dean Ehrlich was graduated from the Harvard Law School, where he was on the *Harvard Law Review.*

EL-SAFTY, AHMAD

Higher Education and the Labor Market, contributor, p. 222. An assistant professor of economics at Eastern Michigan University, Ahmad El-Safty graduated from Alexandria University and received his master's at Wayne State University and his Ph.D. at Massachusetts Institute of Technology. Professor El-Safty has also taught at Cairo University and Wayne State and has held various positions in industry.

EULAU, HEINZ

State Officials and Higher Education: A Survey of the Opinions and Expectations of Policy Makers in Nine States, coauthor, p. 321. Heinz Eulau is head of the political science department at Stanford University and past president of the American Political Science Association. Professor Eulau's doctorate is from the University of California, Berkeley, where he also did his undergraduate and master's work.

FAY, MARGARET ALICE

Political Ideologies of Graduate Students: Crystallization, Consistency, and Contextual Effects, coauthor, p. 122. Margaret Fay is currently a doctoral candidate in sociology at the University of California, Berkeley, and holder of a dean's fellowship for graduate studies. She has a B.A. from Cambridge University, England, and a master's degree in East African Studies from Syracuse University.

FEIN, RASHI

Financing Medical Education: An Analysis of Alternative Policies and Mechanisms, coauthor, p. 309. Rashi Fein is professor of the economics of medicine at Harvard University. He holds a doctorate from Johns Hopkins University and has been on the senior staffs of the Economic Studies Division of the Brookings Institution and the Council of Economic Advisers in the Executive Offices of the President (1961–1963).

FELDMAN, SAUL DANIEL

Escape from the Doll's House: Women in Graduate and Professional School Education, p. 173; *Teachers and Students: Aspects of American Higher Education,* contributor, p. 34. Saul Feldman is assistant professor of sociology at Case Western Reserve University. Previously a research sociologist at the Survey Research Center, University of California, Berkeley, Professor Feldman holds a Ph.D. from the University of Washington.

FOGEL, WALTER A.

Higher Education and the Labor Market, contributor, p. 222. Walter Fogel is professor of industrial relations in the graduate school of management of the University of California, Los Angeles, and research economist at the university's Institute of Industrial Relations. Professor Fogel has a Ph.D. from the Massachusetts Institute of Technology.

FREEMAN, RICHARD B.

Black Elite: The Economic Status of Highly Qualified Black Workers in the United States, p. 178; *Higher Education and the Labor Market,* contributor, p. 222. Richard Freeman is an associate professor at Harvard University, the institution from which he holds a doctorate. He was previously on the faculty of the University of Chicago.

FULTON, OLIVER

The American Academics, coauthor, p. 42; *Teachers and Students: Aspects of American Higher Education,* contributor, p. 34. Oliver Fulton is an assistant research sociologist at the Survey Research Center, University of California, Berkeley, and a doctoral candidate in sociology at the university. He is a graduate of Oxford University and a former research fellow at the University of Edinburgh.

GAMSON, ZELDA F.

Academic Transformation: Seventeen Institutions Under Pressure, contributor, p. 124. Zelda Gamson is assistant professor at the Center for the Study of Higher Education at the University of Michigan and a research associate at its Institute for Social Research, of which she was formerly study director. She holds a Ph.D. from Harvard University.

GARBARINO, JOSEPH WILLIAM

Faculty Bargaining: Change and Conflict, p. 280; *Higher Education and the Labor Market,* contributor, p. 222. Joseph Garbarino is professor of business administration and director of the Institute of Business and Economic Research at the University of California, Berkeley. Professor Garbarino received his Ph.D. in economics from Harvard University, and in addition to acting as a labor arbitrator and consultant to various companies, nonprofit corporations, and government agencies, he has been a staff member of the Brookings Institution and a Fulbright lecturer at the University of Glasgow.

GHEZ, GILBERT R.

Education, Income, and Human Behavior, contributor, p. 219. Gilbert Ghez is assistant professor in the department of economics and The College at the University of Chicago. He holds B.A. degrees in law and in economics from the University of Geneva, Switzerland, and a Ph.D. from Columbia University. He has been a research associate of the National Bureau of Economic Research since 1969.

GLAZER, NATHAN

Academic Transformation: Seventeen Institutions Under Pressure, contributor, p. 124. Nathan Glazer is professor of education and social structure at Harvard University. Formerly on the faculty at the University of California, Berkeley, he has been a Guggenheim Foundation Fellow and a fellow at the Center for Advanced Study in the Behavioral Sciences. Professor Glazer received his Ph.D. from Columbia University.

GLENNY, LYMAN A.

The University as an Organization, contributor, p. 257.   Lyman Glenny is professor of higher education and director of the Center for Research and Development in Higher Education at the University of California, Berkeley. He was on the faculties of the University of Iowa and Sacramento State College before becoming associate director and then executive director of the Illinois Board of Higher Education. Professor Glenny holds a Ph.D. from the State University of Iowa.

GODDARD, DAVID ROCKWELL

Academic Transformation: Seventeen Institutions Under Pressure, contributor, p. 124.   David Goddard is provost emeritus and University Professor of Biology at the University of Pennsylvania, where he was also director of the Division of Botany before his appointment as provost. Professor Goddard's Ph.D. is from the University of California.

GORDON, MARGARET S.

Higher Education and the Labor Market, editor, p. 222.   Margaret Gordon edited this volume when she was associate director of the Carnegie Commission on Higher Education and associate director of the Institute of Industrial Relations at the University of California, Berkeley. She is now associate director of the Carnegie Council on Policy Studies in Higher Education. She is a graduate of Bryn Mawr College and holds a doctorate in economics from Radcliffe.

GOULD, SAMUEL B.

The University as an Organization, contributor, p. 257.   Samuel Gould, chancellor emeritus of the State University of New York, is vice-president of the Educational Testing Service and president of the Institute for Educational Development. Mr. Gould attended Oxford University, Cambridge University, and Harvard University and holds a master's degree from New York University. He has held such posts in higher education and television as president of the Educational Broadcasting Company, president of Antioch College, and professor of radio and speech at Boston University.

GRAMBSCH, PAUL VICTOR

Changes in University Organization, 1964–1971, coauthor, p. 114.   Paul Grambsch is professor of management at the University of Minnesota, where he was also dean for ten years. He was previously dean and professor at Tulane University. Professor Grambsch holds a D.B.A. from Indiana University.

GRANT, GERALD

Academic Transformation: Seventeen Institutions Under Pressure, contributor, p. 124.   Gerald Grant is associate professor of sociology and education at Syracuse University. Holder of an Ed.D. from Harvard University, Professor Grant has been an editorial writer, writer on the national staff of the *Washington Post,* and a Nieman Fellow and research fellow in sociology at Harvard.

GREELEY, ANDREW MORAN

From Backwater to Mainstream: A Profile of Catholic Higher Education, p. 78; *Recent Alumni and Higher Education: A Survey of College Graduates,* coauthor, p. 213.   Andrew Greeley is director of the Center for the Study of American Pluralism at the National Opinion Research Center (NORC), University of Chicago. He holds an S.T.L. from St. Mary of the Lake Seminary and a doctorate in sociology from the University of Chicago. Father Greeley has been program director in higher education at NORC and a lecturer in the sociology department at the University of Chicago.

GROSS, EDWARD

Changes in University Organization, 1964–1971, coauthor, p. 114.   Edward Gross is professor of sociology at the University of Washington, Seattle, and has held the same position at the University of Minnesota and Washington State University. A graduate of the University of British Columbia, he holds a Ph.D. from the University of Chicago.

GURIN, ARNOLD

Education for the Professions of Medicine, Law, Theology, and Social Welfare, coauthor, p. 59; *A Degree and What Else?: Correlates and Consequences of a College Education,* contributor, p. 216.   Arnold Gurin is dean of The Florence Heller Graduate School for Advanced Studies in Social Welfare at Brandeis University. He has been a consultant on social work education to the government of Israel and a director of field service for the Council of Jewish Federations and Welfare Funds. Dean Gurin has a Ph.D. in social work and sociology from the University of Michigan.

GURIN, GERALD

A Degree and What Else?: Correlates and Consequences of a College Education, contributor, p. 216. Gerald Gurin is professor of higher education at the University of Michigan, where he received his Ph.D., and program director of the university's Survey Research Center.

HABER, SAMUEL

Higher Education and the Labor Market, contributor, p. 222. Samuel Haber is associate professor of history at the University of California, Berkeley, the institution from which he received his Ph.D. Professor Haber was formerly on the faculty at the University of Delaware.

HANDLIN, MARY F.

The American College and American Culture: Socialization as a Function of Higher Education, coauthor, p. 324. Mary Handlin is a research editor at Harvard University. She graduated from Brooklyn College and has a master's degree from Columbia University.

HANDLIN, OSCAR

The American College and American Culture: Socialization as a Function of Higher Education, coauthor, p. 324. Oscar Handlin is Carl H. Pforzheimer University Professor at Harvard University, where he took his doctorate. Professor Handlin has been Winthrop Professor of History and Charles Warren Professor of American History at Harvard, in addition to having been director of the Center for the Study of the History of Liberty in America and director of the Charles Warren Center for Studies in American History.

HARRIS, SEYMOUR E.

A Statistical Portrait of Higher Education, p. 31. Seymour Harris was Lucius N. Littauer Professor of Political Economy Emeritus, Harvard University, from which he received his Ph.D. and where he held various positions since 1922.

HARTMAN, ROBERT W.

Credit for College: Public Policy for Student Loans, p. 241; *Higher Education and the Labor Market,* contributor, p. 222. Robert Hartman is Senior Fellow at the Brookings Institution. He holds a Ph.D. from Harvard University and has been a Brookings Economic Policy Fellow and assistant professor of economics at Brandeis University.

HAUSE, JOHN C.

Education, Income, and Human Behavior, contributor, p. 219. John Hause is associate professor of economics at the University of Minnesota. Previously a research economist at the Institute for Defense Analysis, he has also been an NBER research fellow. He holds a Ph.D. from the University of Chicago.

HAWKINS, DAVID

Content and Context: Essays on College Education, contributor, p. 69. Professor of philosophy at the University of Colorado since 1949, David Hawkins is also director of the university's Mountain View Center for Environmental Education. Professor Hawkins, who holds a Ph.D. from the University of California, Berkeley, was formerly director of the elementary science study at the Educational Development Center in Newton, Massachusetts, and historian at the Los Alamos Laboratory.

HAWKINS, M. L.

The Emerging Technology: Instructional Uses of the Computer in Higher Education, contributor, p. 142. M. L. Hawkins was a research assistant on the staff of the Rand Corporation.

HECKMAN, DALE M.

Inventory of Current Research on Higher Education, 1968, coauthor, p. 30. Dale Heckman is a consultant on higher education to the Department of Finance, State of California. He received his Ph.D. jointly from the Graduate Theological Seminary in Berkeley and the University of California, Berkeley. He has been dean of the University Chapel at the University of the Pacific and a research associate with the Center for Research and Development in Higher Education, Berkeley, and the Carnegie Commission on Higher Education.

HEISS, ANN M.

An Inventory of Academic Innovation and Reform, p. 117. Ann Heiss is currently an educational consultant. She holds a doctorate from the University of California, Berkeley, where she was most recently a research educator at the Center for Research and Development in Higher Education and a lecturer in the school of education.

HENDERSON, ALGO DONMYER

Academic Transformation: Seventeen Institutions Under Pressure, contributor, p. 124. Algo Henderson, research educator at the Center for Research and Development at the University of California, Berkeley, has held such posts as president of Antioch College, administrator of the New York State college system, and director of the Center for the Study of Higher Education at the University of Michigan, among others. He holds a J.D. from the University of Kansas.

HOCHSCHILD, ARLIE RUSSELL

Women and the Power to Change, coauthor, p. 181. Arlie Hochschild is assistant professor of sociology at the University of California, Berkeley, where she took her Ph.D. A graduate of Swarthmore College with a degree in international relations, Professor Hochschild previously taught at the University of California, Santa Cruz, and has been awarded the Associated Students of the University of California Teaching Award.

HODGKINSON, HAROLD L.

Institutions in Transition: A Study of Change in Higher Education, p. 106. Harold Hodgkinson is a research educator at the Center for Research and Development in Higher Education, University of California, Berkeley. He has been director of the school of education at Simmons College, Boston, dean of Bard College, editor of the *Harvard Educational Review,* and president of the American Association for Higher Education. He has an Ed.D. from Harvard University.

HOFFMAYER, KARL JOSEPH

The Emerging Technology: Instructional Uses of the Computer in Higher Education, contributor, p. 142. Karl Hoffmayer is with The Rand Corporation as operations research specialist. He holds a master's degree in quantitative business analysis from the University of Southern California and has held such positions in industry as adviser on the European staff (in Germany) of the Northrop Corporation and project leader at the Douglas Aircraft Company.

HOLLAND, WADE B.

The Emerging Technology: Instructional Uses of the Computer in Higher Education, contributor, p. 142.   Wade Holland is a self-employed computer consultant, writer, and translator who was formerly with The Rand Corporation both as staff member and consultant. A graduate of Whittier College, Mr. Holland is editor of *Soviet Cybernetics Review,* a professional technical journal.

HOWE, FLORENCE

Women and the Power to Change, editor, p. 181.   A professor of humanities at SUNY/College at Old Westbury, Florence Howe is also director of the Goucher College Poetry Series, member of the board of the Teachers and Writers Collaborative, president of The Feminist Press, and senior project consultant of the Resource Center of Sex Roles in Education, National Foundation for Improvement in Education. Professor Howe's past activities have included teaching in the Mississippi Freedom Schools, teaching and consulting in Roosevelt University's Upward Bound Program, and serving as president of the Modern Language Association.

HUGHES, EVERETT CHERRINGTON

Education for the Professions of Medicine, Law, Theology, and Social Welfare, principal author, p. 59; *Content and Context: Essays on College Education,* contributor, p. 69.   Everett Hughes is visiting professor of sociology at Boston College. He was previously on the faculty at the University of Chicago, the institution from which he received his Ph.D. in sociology and anthropology, and at Brandeis University.

JUSTER, F. THOMAS

Education, Income, and Human Behavior, editor, p. 219.   Thomas Juster is program director for the Survey Research Center, Institute for Social Research at the University of Michigan. He was formerly senior research staff member and a vice-president for research of the National Bureau of Economic Research. He holds a doctorate in economics from Columbia University and previously was an assistant professor at Amherst College and a senior research analyst with the Central Intelligence Agency. Dr. Juster is editor of *Economic Prospects.*

KARWIN, THOMAS JOSEPH

Flying a Learning Center: Design and Costs of an Off-Campus Space for Learning, p. 156. Thomas Karwin is coordinator of instructional services at the University of California, Santa Cruz, and chairman of the President's Advisory Committee for Learning Resources at the university. He holds two degrees in theatre arts and is currently a doctoral candidate in education. Mr. Karwin has been a staff TV-film director at the University of California, Los Angeles.

KAUN, DAVID E.

Higher Education and the Labor Market, contributor, p. 222. David Kaun is professor of economics at the University of California, Santa Cruz. Formerly on the faculty of the University of Pittsburgh and a research associate at the Brookings Institution, Professor Kaun holds a Ph.D. from Stanford University.

KAYSEN, CARL

Content and Context: Essays on College Education, editor, p. 69. Carl Kaysen, a member of the Carnegie Commission on Higher Education, has been director of the Institute for Advanced Study at Princeton since 1966. In addition to having been deputy special assistant for national security affairs to President Kennedy, he formerly held a number of posts at Harvard University, among them: associate dean of the Graduate School of Public Administration and Lucius N. Littauer Professor of Political Economy. He holds a Ph.D. from Harvard University.

KEETON, MORRIS T.

Models and Mavericks: A Profile of Private Liberal Arts Colleges, p. 84. Morris Keeton is vice-president and provost of Antioch College, in addition to being professor of philosophy and religion. He has also been pastor of the college and dean of the faculty. Professor Keeton holds a doctorate from Harvard University and is a past president of the American Association for Higher Education.

KERR, CLARK

Higher Education in Nine Countries: A Comparative Study of Colleges and Universities Abroad, coauthor, p. 24. Clark Kerr was chairman and executive director of the Carnegie Commission on Higher Education, during which time he also was professor in the School of Business Administration and the department of economics of the University of California, Berkeley. He is now chairman and executive director of the Carnegie Council on Policy Studies in Higher Education. He is president emeritus of the University of California and past chancellor and former director of the Institute of Industrial Relations at Berkeley. Dr. Kerr holds a Ph.D. in economics from the University of California, Berkeley, the Alexander Meiklejohn Award for Contributions to Academic Freedom (presented by the American Association of University Professors), and the Clark Kerr Award for Extraordinary and Distinguished Contributions to the Advancement of Higher Education (presented by the Academic Senate, Berkeley Division of the university).

KOONS, LINDA CAROLYN

Academic Transformation: Seventeen Institutions Under Pressure, contributor, p. 124. Linda Koons, assistant ombudsman at the University of Pennsylvania, was previously assistant to the provost. A graduate of the University of Oregon, Ms. Koons was formerly assistant editor of the journal of the Association of Operating Room Nurses.

LADD, EVERETT CARLL, JR.

The Divided Academy, coauthor, p. 268; *Professors, Unions, and American Higher Education,* coauthor, p. 285. Professor of political science and director of the Social Science Data Center at the University of Connecticut, Everett Ladd is also a research fellow at the Center for International Studies at Harvard University and a past Ford Faculty Research Fellow and Guggenheim Fellow. He holds a Ph.D. from Cornell University.

LADD, DWIGHT ROBERT

Change in Educational Policy: Self Studies in Selected Colleges and Universities, p. 109. Dwight Ladd is professor of business administration at the University of New Hampshire. He previously was a member of the faculty of the University of Western Ontario and has taught at the Institute for Social Studies in Den Haag, Holland. Professor Ladd received a D.B.A. from Harvard University.

LEE, CALVIN B. T.

The Invisible Colleges: A Profile of Small, Private Colleges with Limited Resources, coauthor, p. 88. Calvin Lee is chancellor of the University of

Maryland, Baltimore County Campus. He has been executive vice-president, acting president, and dean of the Liberal Arts College at Boston University, assistant director of the Division of College Support, U.S. Office of Education, and staff associate, American Council on Education. Chancellor Lee has a J.S.D. from New York University Law School.

LEE, EUGENE CANFIELD

The Multicampus University: A Study of Academic Governance, coauthor, p. 261.   Eugene Lee is director of the Institute of Governmental Studies and professor of political science at the University of California, Berkeley. He has been executive assistant to the president and vice-president of the university. Dr. Lee has a Ph.D. in political science from the University of California.

LEIBOWITZ, ARLEEN

Education, Income, and Human Behavior, contributor, p. 219.   Arleen Leibowitz is visiting assistant professor of economics at Brown University and a research associate of the National Bureau of Economic Research, where she had been a predoctoral research fellow. Her Ph.D. is from Columbia University.

LESTER, RICHARD ALLEN

Antibias Regulation of Universities: Faculty Problems and Their Solutions, p. 183.   Richard Lester was professor of economics at Princeton University from 1948–1974; he is now emeritus professor and emeritus dean of the faculty. Dr. Lester's Ph.D. in economics is from Princeton.

LEVIEN, ROGER ELI

The Emerging Technology: Instructional Uses of the Computer in Higher Education, principal author, p. 142.   Roger Levien is with the Rand Corporation as deputy vice-president for Washington Domestic Programs and adjunct professor of engineering at the University of California, Los Angeles, where he has taught analysis of public systems for the provision of services such as health care, transportation, public safety, and fire protection. Dr. Levien holds a Ph.D. in applied mathematics from Harvard University and his publications include numerous studies of the uses of computers.

LIPSET, SEYMOUR MARTIN

Education and Politics at Harvard, coauthor, p. 129; *The Divided Academy,* coauthor, p. 268; *Professors, Unions, and American Higher Education,* coauthor, p. 285.   Professor of government and sociology at Harvard University since 1966, Seymour Martin Lipset was previously director of the Institute of International Studies and professor of sociology at the University of California, Berkeley. Professor Lipset received his Ph.D. from Columbia University, where he was subsequently on the faculty in the graduate department of sociology. He has been twice appointed a Fellow at the Center for Advanced Study in the Behavioral Sciences.

LOWRY, W. McNEIL

The University as an Organization, contributor, p. 257.   Vice-president for the humanities and the arts at the Ford Foundation, W. McNeil Lowry was previously vice-president for policy and planning. He has also been an instructor at the University of Illinois, from which he has both a Ph.D. and a Litt.D. He has also served as editor of *Accent* and chief of the Washington Bureau for the Cox newspapers.

MANGELSDORF, PAUL CHRISTOPH, JR.

Academic Transformation: Seventeen Institutions Under Pressure, contributor, p. 124.   Professor of physics at Swarthmore College, Paul Mangelsdorf is also research associate in physical chemistry at the Woods Hole Oceanographic Institution. Professor Mangelsdorf, who received his Ph.D. from Harvard University, has been a Junior Fellow, Society of Fellows, at Harvard and has served on the faculty of the University of Chicago.

MARCH, JAMES G.

Leadership and Ambiguity: The American College President, coauthor, p. 265.   James March is David Jacks Professor of Higher Education, Political Science, Sociology, and Business at Stanford University. He was previously professor of psychology and sociology at the University of California, Irvine, as well as dean of the School of Social Sciences. Professor March received his Ph.D. from Yale University.

MARTIN, WARREN BRYAN

Inventory of Current Research on Higher Education, 1968, coauthor, p. 30.   Warren Martin is vice-president of the Danforth Foundation. He has been provost and professor of history at the California State College, Sonoma, and research educator and coordinator of development at the Center for Research and Development in Higher Education at the University of California, Berkeley. He holds a Ph.D. from Boston University.

MAYHEW, LEWIS B.

Graduate and Professional Education, 1980, p. 112.   Lewis Mayhew is professor of education at Stanford University. He previously held a number of posts, among them: professor at Michigan State University, the institution from which he received his Ph.D., assistant director of the American Council on Education, and director of the North Central Association Study on Liberal Arts Education. Professor Mayhew is a past president of the American Association for Higher Education.

McCLOSKEY, JOSEPH F.

Papers on Efficiency in the Management of Higher Education, coauthor, p. 304.   Joseph McCloskey is general manager of the Heat Engineering & Supply Company in San Gabriel, California. He has been associate professor of history at La Salle College, professor of engineering administration at Case Institute of Technology, and director of research for the Association of Independent California Colleges and Universities. Dr. McCloskey holds a Ph.D. from the University of Pittsburgh and has been coeditor of publications dealing with operations research for management.

McCORMICK, RICHARD P.

Academic Transformation: Seventeen Institutions Under Pressure, contributor, p. 124.   Richard McCormick, professor of history and university historian at Rutgers University, has been a Fulbright lecturer at Cambridge University and a Commonwealth lecturer at the University of London. Professor McCormick received his Ph.D. from the University of Pennsylvania.

MEDSKER, LELAND L.

Breaking the Access Barriers: A Profile of Two-Year Colleges, coauthor, p. 91.   Leland Medsker is director of the Project on Nontraditional Education at the Center for Research and Development in Higher Education at the University of California, Berkeley. He is past director of the center and has also been professor of education at the university, director of Wright Junior College in Chicago, president of Diablo Valley College, and president of both the American Association for Higher Education and the American Association of Community and Junior Colleges. He holds a doctorate from Stanford University.

MEYER, MARSHALL WARNER

Academic Transformation: Seventeen Institutions Under Pressure, contributor, p. 124. Marshall Meyer is associate professor of sociology at the University of California, Riverside. He has been assistant professor of sociology and of industrial and labor relations at Cornell University and a lecturer in the department of social relations at Harvard University. His Ph.D. is from the University of Chicago.

MICHAEL, ROBERT T.

Education, Income, and Human Behavior, contributor, p. 219. Robert Michael is associate professor of economics at Stanford University and on the senior research staff as well as assistant vice-president of the National Bureau of Economic Research. Professor Michael holds a Ph.D. from Columbia University.

MILLER, LEONARD SIDNEY

Demand and Supply in U.S. Higher Education, coauthor, p. 50. Leonard Miller is assistant professor of social welfare at the University of California, Berkeley, the institution from which he received his Ph.D. in economics. Professor Miller has been a fellow at the Center of Economic Research in Athens, Greece, and has been on the faculty of the department of economics at the State University of New York at Stony Brook.

MILLETT, JOHN DAVID

The University as an Organization, contributor, p. 257. John Millett is vice-president of the Academy for Educational Development. Formerly chancellor of the Ohio board of regents and president of Miami University, Ohio, Dr. Millett also was a professor at Columbia University, the institution from which he received his Ph.D.

MINCER, JACOB

Education, Income, and Human Behavior, contributor, p. 219. Jacob Mincer is professor of economics at Columbia University and on the senior research staff of the National Bureau of Economic Research. Professor Mincer received his Ph.D. from Columbia.

MITCHELL, DANIEL J. B.

Higher Education and the Labor Market, contributor, p. 222. Daniel Mitchell is associate professor in the graduate school of management at the University of California, Los Angeles. Professor Mitchell, who received his Ph.D. from the Massachusetts Institute of Technology, was recently on leave from UCLA to act as chief economist of the U.S. Pay Board.

MOOD, ALEXANDER McFARLANE

The Future of Higher Education: Some Speculations and Suggestions, p. 145; *Papers on Efficiency in the Management of Higher Education,* principal author, p. 304. Alexander Mood is professor of administration and director of the Public Policy Research Organization at the University of California, Irvine. He has been assistant U.S. Commissioner of Education, vice-president of the Corporation for Economic and Industrial Research (CEIR), and deputy chief of the mathematics division of The Rand Corporation. Professor Mood received his Ph.D. from Princeton University.

MORRISON, JACK

The Rise of the Arts on the American Campus, p. 57. Jack Morrison is associate director of the Arts in Education Program, JDR 3rd Fund, New York. He has been associate professor of theatre arts at the University of California, Los Angeles, and dean of the College of Fine Arts at Ohio University. He has a doctorate from the University of Southern California.

MOSMANN, CHARLES

The Emerging Technology: Instructional Uses of the Computer in Higher Education, contributor, p. 142. Charles Mosmann is director of computer planning at the University of California, Irvine. Dr. Mosmann, who holds a Ph.D. from Columbia University, was formerly with the System Development Corporation, study director for the Institute for Educational Development, and project director for EDUCOM.

NAGAI, MICHIO

An Owl Before Darkness?, p. 16. Formerly editorial writer for the Asahi Shimbun Press and a lecturer in higher education at Tokyo University, Michio Nagai received both his M.A. and Ph.D. from Ohio State University. In 1973 he served as director of the East-West Communication Institute of the University of Hawaii. Mr. Nagai is currently minister of education in Japan.

NASH, GEORGE
The University and the City: Eight Cases of Involvement, principal author, p. 202. George Nash is professor of sociology at Montclair State College, New Jersey, director of the Drug Abuse Treatment Information Project, and consultant to the Teacher Corps of the U.S. Office of Education. He has been an associate in the Bureau of Social Science Research and a project director in the Bureau of Applied Social Research at Columbia University. Professor Nash has a Ph.D. from Columbia University.

NORMAN, VICTOR DANIELSEN
Higher Education and the Labor Market, contributor, p. 222. Victor Norman is an assistant professor at the Norwegian School of Economics and Business Administration in Bergen, Norway. A graduate of Yale University, Professor Norman holds a Ph.D. from the Massachusetts Institute of Technology.

OETTINGER, ANTHONY G.
Content and Context: Essays on College Education, contributor, p. 69. Professor of linguistics and Gordon McKay Professor of Applied Mathematics at Harvard University, from which he received his Ph.D., Anthony Oettinger is also chairman of the National Academy of Science's Computer Science and Engineering Board and consultant to the Office of Science and Technology, Executive Office of the President of the United States.

O'NEILL, JUNE AVIS
Sources of Funds to Colleges and Universities, p. 246; *Resource Use in Higher Education: Trends in Output and Inputs, 1930–67,* p. 298. June O'Neill is senior staff economist on the Council of Economic Advisers. She has been an instructor in economics at Temple University and a research associate at the Brookings Institution. Dr. O'Neill was graduated from Sarah Lawrence College and holds a Ph.D. in economics from Columbia University.

ORLANS, HAROLD
The Nonprofit Research Institute: Its Origin, Operation, Problems, and Prospects, p. 196. Harold Orlans is senior research associate of the National Academy of Public Administration Foundation. He previously has been senior fellow at the Brookings Institution, director of studies for the

White House Conference on Children and Youth, and section chief at the National Science Foundation. He has a doctorate from Yale University.

PACE, C. ROBERT

Education and Evangelism: A Profile of Protestant Colleges, p. 81; *The Demise of Diversity?: A Comparative Profile of Eight Types of Institutions,* p. 98. C. Robert Pace is professor of higher education in the Graduate School of Education at the University of California, Los Angeles. He has been head of the psychology department and director of the Psychological Research Center at Syracuse University. Professor Pace received his Ph.D. from the University of Minnesota. His major publications have been concerned with teaching and students in higher education.

PACKER, HERBERT L.

New Directions in Legal Education, coauthor, p. 152. The late Herbert Packer was Jackson Eli Reynolds Professor of Law at Stanford Law School at the time of his death. He had been a practicing attorney admitted to appear before the Supreme Court and a member of the U.S. Attorney General's Committee on Poverty and Federal Criminal Justice before he went to Stanford as an associate professor in 1956. A graduate of Yale Law School, Professor Packer was an authority on criminal law and also the recipient of Stanford's distinguished Lloyd W. Dinkelspeil Award for service to undergraduate education.

PEPPER, STEPHEN LAWRENCE

New Directions in Legal Education, contributor, p. 152. Stephen Pepper, a graduate of the Yale Law School, is an associate of the firm of Holland and Hart in Denver, Colorado.

PERKINS, JAMES A.

Higher Education in Nine Countries: A Comparative Study of Colleges and Universities Abroad, coauthor, p. 24; *The University as an Organization,* editor, p. 257. James Perkins, a member of the Carnegie Commission on Higher Education, is chairman of the board and executive officer of the International Council for Educational Development. He has been president of Cornell University; vice-president of the Carnegie Corporation, the Carnegie Foundation for the Advancement of Teaching, and Swarthmore College, his alma mater; and chairman of the board of the United Negro College Fund and the Educational Testing Service. He holds a doctorate in political science from Princeton University.

PETERSON, RICHARD E.

American College and University Enrollment Trends in 1971, p. 136; *May 1970: The Campus Aftermath of Cambodia and Kent State,* coauthor, p. 273.   Richard Peterson has been a research psychologist at the Educational Testing Service since 1962. He was previously an instructor and counselor at Contra Costa College in California. Dr. Peterson received his Ph.D. from the University of California, Berkeley, and his publications include studies of student protest and institutional goals and a survey of academic communities made for the California legislature.

PRICE, ROBERT E.

The University and the City, contributor, p. 202.   Robert Price is completing his Ph.D. in biblical studies at Duke University. A graduate of the Union Theological Seminary, Mr. Price was formerly a research assistant at the Bureau of Applied Social Research at Columbia University.

QUINLEY, HAROLD EARL

State Officials and Higher Education: A Survey of the Opinions and Expectations of Policy Makers in Nine States, coauthor, p. 321.   Harold Quinley is assistant professor of political science at Brown University. Holder of a Ph.D. from Stanford University, he was previously a postdoctoral fellow at the University of California, Berkeley. Dr. Quinley has published on various aspects of the Protestant clergy.

RADNER, ROY

Demand and Supply in U.S. Higher Education, coauthor, p. 50.   Roy Radner is professor of economics and professor of statistics at the University of California, Berkeley. He was previously on the faculty of the University of Chicago, which granted his Ph.D., and of Yale University. Professor Radner has published on economic theory and organization.

RAUH, MORTON ADLER

The University as an Organization, contributor, p. 257.   Morton Rauh is vice-president emeritus of Antioch College, where he was formerly financial vice-president. A magna cum laude graduate of Harvard University and onetime physicist in the U.S. Navy, Mr. Rauh's major publications have been concerned with the trusteeships of institutions of higher learning and financial aid to students at private colleges.

RAWLINS, V. LANE

Higher Education and the Labor Market, contributor, p. 222. V. Lane Rawlins is associate professor of economics at Washington State University and a member of the Washington State Manpower Planning Council. A graduate of Brigham Young University, Professor Rawlins received his Ph.D. from the University of California, Berkeley.

REDER, MELVIN W.

Higher Education and the Labor Market, contributor, p. 222. Melvin Reder is Distinguished Professor of Economics at the Graduate Center, The City University of New York, having previously held posts at Stanford University, the London School of Economics, and the National Bureau of Economic Research, among others. Professor Reder, who holds a Ph.D. from Columbia University, has also been a Guggenheim Fellow, a fellow at the Center for Advanced Study in Behavioral Sciences, and a Ford Faculty Fellow.

RICH, ADRIENNE

Women and the Power to Change, coauthor, p. 181. Professor of English at The City College, CUNY, Adrienne Rich has taught English, writing, and creative literature at Brandeis University, CCNY, Columbia University, and Swarthmore College, of which she is a graduate. Professor Rich is the author of eight volumes of poetry.

RIESMAN, DAVID

Academic Transformation: Seventeen Institutions Under Pressure, coeditor, p. 129; *Education and Politics at Harvard,* coauthor, p. 124. David Riesman is Henry Ford II Professor of Social Sciences at Harvard University and a member of the Carnegie Commission on Higher Education. He has been professor of social sciences at the University of Chicago, deputy assistant district attorney of New York County, and professor of law at the University of Buffalo. Professor Riesman holds a law degree from Harvard Law School, where he was an editor of the *Harvard Law Review;* he subsequently studied social psychology and psychoanalysis.

ROBINSON, JOHN P.

A Degree and What Else?: Correlates and Consequences of a College Education, contributor, p. 216. John Robinson is study director of the

Survey Research Center at the University of Michigan, the institution from which he received his Ph.D. in the mathematics of social psychology. He has held such posts as research coordinator for the U.S. Surgeon General's Scientific Advisory Committee on Television and Social Behavior and conference chairman of the American Association for Public Opinion Research.

ROCKART, JOHN FRALICK

Computers and the Learning Process in Higher Education, coauthor, p. 159. John Rockart is associate professor of management at the Massachusetts Institute of Technology's Sloan School of Management. A graduate of Princeton University, Professor Rockart received his Ph.D. from M.I.T., where he has held several posts in the Sloan School since 1966. He had earlier been a sales and district medical representative for International Business Machines and an M.I.T. Fellow in Africa.

ROIZEN, JUDY

Teachers and Students: Aspects of American Higher Education, contributor, p. 34. Judy Roizen is a research sociologist at the Survey Research Center at the University of California, Berkeley, and a graduate student in the sociology department.

ROSEN, SHERWIN

Education, Income, and Human Behavior, contributor, p. 219. Sherwin Rosen has been professor of economics at Rochester University since 1964 and senior research staff associate of the National Bureau of Economic Research since 1968. A graduate of Purdue University, Professor Rosen holds a Ph.D. from the University of Chicago.

SANDERS, IRWIN TAYLOR

Bridges to Understanding: International Programs of American Colleges and Universities, coauthor, p. 210; *The University as an Organization,* contributor, p. 257. Irwin Sanders is professor of sociology at Boston University. He has previously been research director of Associations for International Research, vice-president of Education and World Affairs, and associate director of the Ford Foundation. Professor Sanders holds a Ph.D. from Cornell University and has written on peoples and societies throughout the world.

SCHEIN, EDGAR H.

Professional Education: Some New Directions, p. 148. Edgar Schein is professor of organizational psychology and management and chairman of the Organization Studies Group at the Massachusetts Institute of Technology. Among the posts he has held are those of undergraduate planning professor at the institute and chief of the social psychology section of the Neuropsychiatry Division of the Walter Reed Army Institute of Research. Professor Schein's Ph.D. in social psychology was awarded by Harvard University.

SCOTT MORTON, MICHAEL STEWART

Computers and the Learning Process in Higher Education, coauthor, p. 159. Michael Scott Morton is director of the Center for Information Systems Research, Sloan School of Management, Massachusetts Institute of Technology, and associate professor of management. A graduate of Carnegie-Mellon University, Professor Scott Morton holds a D.B.A. from Harvard University, where he held posts as an IBM Fellow at the Computation Center and a research associate in the business school. He is a consultant to a number of organizations, among them The First National Bank of Chicago and ALCOA, and he has been awarded the Salgo-Noren Award for Excellence in Teaching. Dr. Scott Morton's principal fields of interest are management information systems and management planning and control.

SHATTUCK, ROGER

Content and Context: Essays on College Education, contributor, p. 69. Roger Shattuck is currently a freelance writer. He formerly held positions in a variety of fields, among them: film officer with UNESCO, in Paris; assistant trade editor with Harcourt Brace & Co.; instructor in French at Harvard University; professor of English and French and head of the department at the University of Texas. A graduate of Yale University, Mr. Shattuck is a translator and editor and has also published literary criticism and poetry.

SIGMUND, PAUL EUGENE

Academic Transformation: Seventeen Institutions Under Pressure, contributor, p. 124. Paul Sigmund is professor of politics at Princeton University. Formerly an instructor in government and Allston Burr Senior Tutor at Harvard University, Professor Sigmund also received his Ph.D. from Harvard.

SMELSER, NEIL JOSEPH

Content and Context: Essays on College Education, contributor, p. 69; *Academic Transformation: Seventeen Institutions Under Pressure,* contributor, p. 124.   Neil Smelser, University Professor of Sociology at the University of California, Berkeley, was formerly assistant chancellor for educational development of the university and associate director of its Institute of International Studies. Professor Smelser has a Ph.D. from Harvard University and is a graduate of the San Francisco Psychoanalytic Institute.

SNYDER, BENSON R.

Academic Transformation: Seventeen Institutions Under Pressure, contributor, p. 124.   Professor of psychiatry at the Massachusetts Institute of Technology, Benson Snyder was formerly psychiatrist-in-chief and dean for institute relations. Professor Snyder, who is a trustee of the Menninger Foundation and Antioch College, is a graduate of the New York University College of Medicine.

SOLMON, LEWIS CALVIN

Education, Income, and Human Behavior, contributor, p. 219.   Lewis Calvin Solmon is executive officer of the Higher Education Research Institute, Inc., Los Angeles, and associate professor in residence at the University of California, Los Angeles. In addition to having been on the faculty at Purdue University, City University of New York, and Virginia Polytechnic Institute, Dr. Solmon has in the most recent past been staff director of the National Research Council's board on human resources and a research associate of the National Bureau of Economic Research.

SPAETH, JOE L.

Recent Alumni and Higher Education: A Survey of College Graduates, coauthor, p. 213.   Joe Spaeth is associate professor of sociology and research associate professor in the Survey Research Laboratory at the University of Illinois, Urbana-Champaign. He has been a research associate at the Survey Research Center, University of California, Berkeley, and program director in higher education at the National Opinion Research Center. Professor Spaeth holds a Ph.D. from the University of Chicago.

SPURR, STEPHEN HOPKINS

Academic Degree Structures: Innovative Approaches, p. 139. Stephen Spurr was president of the University of Texas at Austin and is currently professor of botany and public affairs at that university. He previously held posts at Harvard University, the University of Minnesota, and the University of Michigan. At the latter he had several appointments, among them: professor of silviculture and natural resources, dean of the School of Graduate Studies, and vice-president of the university. Professor Spurr's doctorate is from Yale University, and his publications include studies and photographs of various aspects of forests.

STADTMAN, VERNE A.

Academic Transformation: Seventeen Institutions Under Pressure, coeditor, p. 124. Verne Stadtman served the Carnegie Commission on Higher Education as editor and associate director. He is now associate director and editor of the Carnegie Council on Policy Studies in Higher Education. He has been managing editor of *California Monthly* and president of the American Alumni Council. He is a trustee and former president of Editorial Projects for Education Inc. A graduate of the University of California, Berkeley, he was the university's *Centennial* editor from 1964 to 1969.

STEINBERG, STEPHEN HAROLD

The Academic Melting Pot: Catholics and Jews in American Higher Education, p. 175; *Teachers and Students: Aspects of American Higher Education,* contributor, p. 34. Stephen Steinberg is assistant professor at the graduate school and university center of the City University of New York. He was formerly a postgraduate research sociologist at the Survey Research Center of the University of California, Berkeley, the institution from which he received his Ph.D.

STEVENS, CARL MANTLE

Higher Education and the Labor Market, contributor, p. 222. Professor of economics at Reed College and senior investigator for the Research Center of the Kaiser Foundation, Portland, Oregon, Professor Stevens has been a visiting professor of economics at Harvard University and an associate at the Harvard Center for Community Health and Medical Care. His major publications include studies of behavior theory and social science and strategy in collective bargaining.

STORR, RICHARD J.

The Beginning of the Future: A Historical Approach to Graduate Education in the Arts and Sciences, p. 64.   Richard Storr is professor of history and humanities at York University, Toronto. He has been on the faculties of Bowdoin College, Howard University, and the University of Chicago. His Ph.D., in American history, is from Harvard University.

STRUMPEL, BURKHARD FRIEDRICH

A Degree and What Else?: Correlates and Consequences of a College Education, contributor, p. 216.   Burkhard Strumpel is program director of the Institute for Social Research at the University of Michigan, and formerly director of the Research Center in Empirical Economics at the University of Cologne. Dr. Strumpel holds a doctorate from the University of Cologne, and his major publications have focused on the relationship between economics and human needs and aspirations.

SULLIVAN, DANIEL JOSEPH

Sources of Funds to Colleges and Universities, contributor, p. 246. Daniel Sullivan is assistant professor of economics at Middlebury College. Formerly a research assistant at the Brookings Institution, Dr. Sullivan has a Ph.D. from Yale University.

TAUBMAN, PAUL JAMES

Mental Ability and Higher Educational Attainment in the 20th Century, coauthor, p. 166; *Higher Education and Earnings,* coauthor, p. 188; *Education, Income, and Human Behavior,* contributor, p. 219.   Paul Taubman is professor of economics at the University of Pennsylvania, the institution from which he received his Ph.D. He is, additionally, a senior research associate of the National Bureau of Economic Research and chairman of the National Academy of Sciences' Panel on the Benefits of Higher Education.

TAYLOR, ELIZABETH KEOGH

A Degree and What Else?: Correlates and Consequences of a College Education, contributor, p. 216.   Elizabeth Keogh Taylor, who holds an M.S.S.A. from Case Western Reserve University, is presently a research associate at the Institute for Social Research at the University of Michigan and a field work instructor at the University of Michigan School of Social Work. Formerly a child welfare worker in California and an organizer for the United Farm Workers Union, also in California, Ms. Taylor recently completed a two-year term on the Washtenaw County, Michigan, Board of Commissioners.

THORNE, BARRIE

Education for the Professions of Medicine, Law, Theology, and Social Welfare, coauthor, p. 59. Barrie Thorne is assistant professor of sociology at Michigan State University. She was graduated from Stanford University with a major in anthropology and has been a research associate at Boston College. Professor Thorne holds a Ph.D. in sociology from Brandeis University.

THUROW, LESTER CARL

Higher Education and the Labor Market, contributor, p. 222. Lester Thurow is professor of economics at the Massachusetts Institute of Technology and formerly a staff member of the Council of Economic Advisers. He holds a Ph.D. from Harvard University and has written on the economics of poverty and discrimination, income distribution, and investment in human capital.

TILLERY, DALE

Breaking the Access Barriers: A Profile of Two-Year Colleges, coauthor, p. 91. Dale Tillery is professor of higher education and director of programs in community college education at the University of California, Berkeley, the institution from which he received his Ph.D. Professor Tillery was director of the SCOPE Project.

TINKER, IRENE

Academic Transformation: Seventeen Institutions Under Pressure, contributor, p. 124. Research fellow at the Bureau of Social Science Research and holder of a SEADAG grant to study urbanization and development in Indonesia, Irene Tinker received her Ph.D. from the London School of Economics and Political Science. She was formerly assistant provost and professor of political science at Federal City College and assistant professor of government at Howard University.

TINTO, VINCENT

Where Colleges Are and Who Attends: Effects of Accessibility on College Attendance, coauthor, p. 169. Vincent Tinto is assistant professor of sociology and education at Teachers College, Columbia University. He has been a research associate of the Carnegie Commission on Higher Education, and he has taught at the Middle East Technical University at Ankara, Turkey. Professor Tinto holds a Ph.D. in education from the University of Chicago.

TOURAINE, ALAIN

The Academic System in American Society, p. 13. Alain Touraine is Directeur d' Etudes at l'Ecole Pratique des Hautes Etudes and Directeur of the Centre d'Etudes des Mouvements Sociaux, Paris. He was previously Directeur of the Departement de Sociologie of the University of Nanterre, and he is past president of the Société Française de Sociologie. Professor Touraine holds an Agrégé d'Histoire and a Docteur des Lettres from the University of Paris.

TROW, MARTIN

Teachers and Students: Aspects of American Higher Education, editor, p. 34; *The American Academics,* coauthor, p. 42.   Martin Trow is professor of sociology in the Graduate School of Public Policy at the University of California, Berkeley. Professor Trow, who holds a Ph.D. from Columbia University, formerly was on the faculty at Hofstra College, the Columbia School of General Studies, and Bennington College.

ULMAN, LLOYD

Higher Education and the Labor Market, contributor, p. 222.   Lloyd Ulman is professor of economics and director of the Institute of Industrial Relations at the University of California, Berkeley. Formerly on the faculty of the University of Minnesota and a senior labor economist for the Council of Economic Advisers, Professor Ulman has also been a Guggenheim Foundation Fellow and a visiting fellow at All Souls' College, Oxford University. He holds a doctorate from Harvard University.

VEYSEY, LAURENCE RUSS

Content and Context: Essays on College Education, contributor, p. 69. Laurence Veysey is professor of history at the University of California, Santa Cruz, where he has been since 1966. He was previously at the University of Wisconsin as assistant professor and at Harvard University as instructor. Professor Veysey received his Ph.D. from the University of California, Berkeley.

WACHTEL, PAUL A.

Education, Income, and Human Behavior, contributor, p. 219. Paul Wachtel is assistant professor of economics at the graduate school of business administration at New York University and a research associate of the National Bureau of Economic Research. Professor Wachtel earned his Ph.D. from the University of Rochester.

WALDORF, DAN

The University and the City: Eight Cases of Involvement, contributor, p. 202. Dan Waldorf, project director for the Alameda Regional Criminal Justice Planning Board, has been chief of the Center for the Study of Drug Abuse and Alcoholism for the Scientific Analysis Corporation and a research associate at the Bureau of Applied Social Research at Columbia University. Mr. Waldorf holds a master's degree from the New School for Social Research.

WALES, TERENCE JOHN

Mental Ability and Higher Educational Attainment in the 20th Century, coauthor, p. 166; *Higher Education and Earnings,* coauthor, p. 188; *Education, Income, and Human Behavior,* contributor, p. 219. Terence Wales is associate professor of economics at the University of British Columbia, where he has also served as acting director of the Social Science Statistics Center. He was previously on the faculty of the University of Pennsylvania and a research associate for the National Bureau of Economic Research. Professor Wales holds a doctorate from the Massachusetts Institute of Technology.

WALLACH, ALETA

Women and the Power to Change, coauthor, p. 181. Aleta Wallach has been an associate of the Los Angeles law firm of Loeb & Loeb and law clerk to an associate justice of the California Court of Appeals. She is a graduate of the school of law of the University of California, Los Angeles and is presently a member of the California bar.

WALSH, JOHN RICHARD

Academic Transformation: Seventeen Institutions Under Pressure, contributor, p. 124. John Walsh is news editor of *Science,* the magazine of the American Association for the Advancement of Science, with which he has been associated since 1963 as reporter and European correspondent. Mr. Walsh, who holds a master's degree from Oxford University, was formerly a reporter for the *Louisville Times* and administrative assistant to a member of the House of Representatives.

WARD, JENNIFER CLAUDETTE

Bridges to Understanding: International Programs of American Colleges and Universities, coauthor, p. 210.   Jennifer Ward is a history instructor in the division of social sciences at Medgar Evers College of the City University of New York. Miss Ward was graduated from Vassar College and has a master's degree from the University of California, Los Angeles.

WEBER, GERALD IRWIN

Financing Medical Education: An Analysis of Alternative Policies and Mechanisms, coauthor, p. 309.   Gerald Weber is acting associate research economist at the Childhood and Government Project at the University of California Law School, Berkeley. He has been a research associate at the Brookings Institution and at the National Academy of Sciences. Professor Weber's Ph.D. in economics was granted by the University of California, Los Angeles.

WEINTRAUB, JEFF ALAN

Political Ideologies of Graduate Students: Crystallization, Consistency, and Contextual Effects, coauthor, p. 122.   Jeff Weintraub is a graduate student in the sociology department at the University of California, Berkeley. He was graduated from Columbia University and holds a master's degree in sociology from the London School of Economics.

WILLIAMS, DAVID PAUL

Education for the Professions of Medicine, Law, Theology, and Social Welfare, coauthor, p. 59.   David Williams is assistant director of the Human Services Development Institute at the University of Maine, Portland-Gorham. He has been assistant professor in the School of Social Work at West Virginia University, director of community organization in a California community development project, and adjunct professor in the School of Social Work at Boston University. Mr. Williams is a doctoral candidate in social welfare at Brandeis University.

WITHEY, STEPHEN BASSETT

A Degree and What Else?: Correlates and Consequences of a College Education, principal author, p. 216.   Stephen Withey is professor of psychology at the University of Michigan and program director of the university's Institute for Social Research. He was formerly staff director of the Carnegie Corporation's national exploratory committee on the assessment of education. Professor Withey received his Ph.D. from the University of Michigan.

WOLFE, ARTHUR COFFMAN

A Degree and What Else?: Correlates and Consequences of a College Education, contributor, p. 216.   Arthur Wolfe is senior research associate in the Highway Safety Research Institute at the University of Michigan, the institution from which he holds a Ph.D. He was formerly study director of the university's Institute for Social Research.

WOLFLE, DAEL

The Home of Science: The Role of the University, p. 194.   Dael Wolfle is professor of public affairs at the University of Washington. He has been executive officer of the American Association for the Advancement of Science, director of the Commission on Human Resources, and executive secretary of the American Psychological Association. Professor Wolfle, who received his Ph.D. from Ohio State University, has also taught at the University of Mississippi and the University of Chicago.

WOLK, RONALD A.

Alternative Methods of Federal Funding for Higher Education, p. 248. Ronald Wolk is vice-president for university relations and development at Brown University. He has served as vice-president of the Johns Hopkins Fund, assistant director of the Carnegie Commission on Higher Education, and special assistant to the chairman of the National Commission on the Causes and Prevention of Violence. Mr. Wolk has a master's degree from Syracuse University.

ZAPOL, NIKKI JANE

Content and Context: Essays on College Education, contributor, p. 69. Nikki Zapol is a research associate in the program on information technologies and public policy at Harvard University. Ms. Zapol, who holds a master's degree in education from Harvard, was formerly on the staff of the Commission on Instructional Technology and a research assistant at the Academy for Educational Development.

ZELAN, JOSEPH

Teachers and Students: Aspects of American Higher Education, contributor, p. 34.   Joseph Zelan is a lecturer in education and director of evaluation and research for the extended academic and public service programs of the University of California, Berkeley. After receiving his Ph.D. from the University of Chicago, Dr. Zelan taught sociology and social welfare at Brandeis University and subsequently was an assistant professor of sociology at the University of California, Davis, and an associate research sociologist at the Survey Research Center at the University of California, Berkeley.

ZINBERG, DOROTHY SHORE

Content and Context: Essays on College Education, contributor, p. 69. Dorothy Zinberg is a lecturer in the department of sociology at Harvard University, the institution from which she received her Ph.D., and a research associate in the university's Program for Science and International Affairs. She has written on women and on attitudes toward the study of science in higher education.

CARNEGIE COMMISSION REPRINTS

Resources for Higher Education: An Economist's View, by Theodore W. Schultz, reprinted from Journal of Political Economy, vol. 76, no. 3, University of Chicago, May–June 1968.*

New Challenges to the College and University, by Clark Kerr, reprinted from Kermit Gordon (ed.), Agenda for the Nation, The Brookings Institution, Washington, D.C., 1968.*

What's Bugging the Students?, by Kenneth Keniston, reprinted from Educational Record, American Council on Education, Washington, D.C., Spring 1970.*

Demand and Supply in U.S. Higher Education: A Progress Report, by Roy Radner and Leonard S. Miller, reprinted from American Economic Review, May 1970.*

Student Protest–An Institutional and National Profile, by Harold Hodgkinson, reprinted from The Record, vol. 71, no. 4, May 1970.*

The Politics of Academia, by Seymour Martin Lipset, reprinted from David C. Nichols (ed.), Perspectives on Campus Tensions: Papers Prepared for the Special Committee on Campus Tensions, American Council on Education, Washington, D.C., September 1970.*

Presidential Discontent, by Clark Kerr, reprinted from David C. Nichols (ed.), Perspectives on Campus Tensions: Papers Prepared for the Special Committee on Campus Tensions, American Council on Education, Washington, D.C., September 1970.*

. . . And What Professors Think: About Student Protest and Manners, Morals, Politics, and Chaos on the Campus, by Seymour Martin Lipset and Everett C. Ladd, Jr., reprinted from Psychology Today, November 1970.*

The Unholy Alliance Against the Campus, by Kenneth Keniston and Michael Lerner, reprinted from New York Times Magazine, November 8, 1970.*

Industrial Relations and University Relations, by Clark Kerr, reprinted from Proceedings of the 21st Annual Winter Meeting of the Industrial Relations Research Association, pp. 15–25.*

* The Commission's stock of this reprint has been exhausted.

Jewish Academics in the United States: Their Achievements, Culture and Politics, by Seymour M. Lipset and Everett C. Ladd, Jr., reprinted from *American Jewish Year Book,* 1971.*

A New Method of Measuring States' Higher Education Burden, by Neil Timm, reprinted from *The Journal of Higher Education,* vol. 42, no. 1, pp. 27–33, January 1971.*

Precarious Professors: New Patterns of Representation, by Joseph W. Garbarino, reprinted from *Industrial Relations,* vol. 10, no. 1, February 1971.*

Regent Watching, by Earl F. Cheit, reprinted from *AGB Reports,* vol. 13, no. 6, pp. 4–13, March 1971.*

The Politics of American Political Scientists, by Everett C. Ladd, Jr., and Seymour M. Lipset, reprinted from *PS,* vol. 4, no. 2, Spring 1971.*

American Social Scientists and the Growth of Campus Political Activism in the 1960s, by Everett C. Ladd, Jr., and Seymour M. Lipset, reprinted from *Social Sciences Information,* vol. 10, no. 2, April 1971.*

Scientific Manpower for 1970–1985, by Allan M. Cartter, reprinted from *Science,* vol. 172, no. 3979, pp. 132–140, April 9, 1971.*

The Divided Professoriate, by Seymour M. Lipset and Everett C. Ladd, Jr., reprinted from *Change,* vol. 3, no. 3, pp. 54–60, May 1971.*

College Generations—From the 1930s to the 1960s, by Seymour M. Lipset and Everett C. Ladd, Jr., reprinted from *The Public Interest,* no. 25, summer 1971.*

International Programs of U.S. Colleges and Universities: Priorities for the Seventies, by James A. Perkins, reprinted by permission of the International Council for Educational Development, Occasional Paper no. 1, July 1971.*

Accelerated Programs of Medical Education, by Mark S. Blumberg, reprinted from *Journal of Medical Education,* vol. 46, no. 8, August 1971.*

More for Less: Higher Education's New Priority, by Virginia B. Smith, reprinted from *Universal Higher Education: Costs and Benefits,* American Council on Education, Washington, D.C., 1971.*

* The Commission's stock of this reprint has been exhausted.

Faculty Unionism: From Theory to Practice, by Joseph W. Garbarino, reprinted from *Industrial Relations,* vol. 11, no. 1, pp. 1–17, February 1972.*

Academia and Politics in America, by Seymour M. Lipset, reprinted from Thomas J. Nossiter (ed.), *Imagination and Precision in the Social Sciences,* pp. 211–289, Faber and Faber, London, 1972.*

Politics of Academic Natural Scientists and Engineers, by Everett C. Ladd, Jr. and Seymour M. Lipset, reprinted from *Science,* vol. 176, no. 4039, pp. 1091–1100, June 9, 1972.

The Intellectual as Critic and Rebel, with Special Reference to the United States and the Soviet Union, by Seymour M. Lipset and Richard B. Dobson, reprinted from *Daedalus,* vol. 101, no. 3, pp. 137–198, Summer 1972.

The Politics of American Sociologists, by Seymour M. Lipset and Everett C. Ladd, Jr., reprinted from *The American Journal of Sociology,* vol. 78, no. 1, July 1972.

The Distribution of Academic Tenure in American Higher Education, by Martin Trow, reprinted from *The Tenure Debate,* Bardwell Smith (ed.), Jossey-Bass, San Francisco, 1972.

The Nature and Origins of the Carnegie Commission on Higher Education, by Alan Pifer, based on a speech delivered to the Pennsylvania Association of Colleges and Universities, Oct. 16, 1972, reprinted by permission of The Carnegie Foundation for the Advancement of Teaching.

Coming of Middle Age in Higher Education, by Earl F. Cheit, address delivered to American Association of State Colleges and Universities and National Association of State Universities and Land-Grant Colleges, Nov. 13, 1972.

Measuring Faculty Unionism: Quantity and Quality, by Bill Aussieker and J. W. Garbarino, reprinted from *Industrial Relations,* vol. 12, no. 2, May 1973.

Problems in the Transition from Elite to Mass Higher Education, by Martin Trow, paper prepared for a conference on mass higher education sponsored by the Organization for Economic Co-operation and Development, June 1973.*

* The Commission's stock of this reprint has been exhausted.

INDEX